FOUND CHRISTIANITIES

FOUND CHRISTIANITIES

Remaking the World of the Second Century CE

M. David Litwa

Institute for Religion and Critical Inquiry
Australian Catholic University, Melbourne

LONDON • NEW YORK • OXFORD • NEW DELHI • SYDNEY

T&T CLARK
Bloomsbury Publishing Plc
50 Bedford Square, London, WC1B 3DP, UK
1385 Broadway, New York, NY 10018, USA
29 Earlsfort Terrace, Dublin 2, Ireland

BLOOMSBURY, T&T CLARK and the T&T Clark logo
are trademarks of Bloomsbury Publishing Plc

First published in Great Britain 2022

Cover design by Holly Capper

Cover image: Sculpture *Brazen Serpent* on Mount Nebo at dusk.
© Peter Schickert / Alamy Stock Photo

A catalogue record for this book is available from the British Library.

Library of Congress Cataloging-in-Publication Data

Names: Litwa, M. David, author.
Title: Found Christianities : remaking the world of the second century CE /
M. David Litwa, Institute for Religion and Critical Inquiry, Australian Catholic University, Melbourne.
Description: London ; New York : T&T Clark, 2022. | Includes bibliographical references and index. |
Summary: "Outlines the huge variety of belief and practices in early Christianities, showing how the many
"lost" early Christianities influenced the development of Christian identity"-- Provided by publisher.
Identifiers: LCCN 2021039207 (print) | LCCN 2021039208 (ebook) | ISBN 9780567703866 (pb) |
ISBN 9780567703873 (hb) | ISBN 9780567703880 (epdf) | ISBN 9780567703897 (epub)
Subjects: LCSH: Church history--Primitive and early church, ca. 30-600. | Identification (Religion)
Classification: LCC BR165 .L74 2022 (print) | LCC BR165 (ebook) | DDC 270.1--dc23
LC record available at https://lccn.loc.gov/2021039207
LC ebook record available at https://lccn.loc.gov/2021039208

ISBN: HB: 978-0-5677-0387-3
         PB   978-0-5677-0386-6
         ePDF: 978-0-5677-0388-0
         ePUB: 978-0-5677-0389-7

Typeset by Trans.form.ed SAS

To find out more about our authors and books visit www.bloomsbury.com
and sign up for our newsletters.

For my students
past, present, and future

Contents

Part Six
Theologians in Later Second-century Rome

Part Seven
Later Theologians in Alexandria

Acknowledgments

Here I gratefully acknowledge the help of many friends and colleagues in the writing of this book: Dylan Burns and Lance Jenott on the Sethians, Tuomas Rasimus on the Ophites, Andy Guffey on Julius Cassianus, Matthew Crawford on Tatian, Michael Kok on Cerinthus, David Jorgensen on Ptolemy, and Outi Lehtipuu on the Introduction. My colleagues and ACURF team members (Kylie Crabbe, Devin White, Ben Edsall, and Stephen Carlson) also read and commented on Chapter 10 (Carpocrates, Epiphanes, and Marcellina). My thanks to all for the suggestions and corrections. All errors are my own.

I also acknowledge that parts of Chapter 3 on Simon of Samaria are developed from my earlier treatment in *Desiring Divinity: Self-deification in Early Jewish and Christian Mythmaking* (New York: Oxford University Press, 2016), 91–118. Some of the language in Chapter 2 (Cerinthus and John) derives from my article "The Father of the Devil (John 8:44): A Christian Exegetical Inspiration for the Evil Creator," *Vigiliae Christianae* 74, no. 5 (2020): 540–65. A section of Chapter 14 (Marcion) is developed in my 2021 article from the *Journal of Theological Studies*, "Did Marcion Call the Creator 'God'?"

Abbreviations

Note: Roman numerals (e.g., II,1) refer to the tractates in the Nag Hammadi Codices (NHC). For NHC, I follow the abbreviations listed in Marvin Meyer, ed., *Nag Hammadi Scriptures: International Edition* (New York: Harper Collins, 2007), 799–802. For abbreviations of biblical texts, I follow the *SBL Handbook of Style*, with some exceptions below.

1 Apol.	Justin Martyr, *1 Apology*
2 Apol.	Justin Martyr, *2 Apology*
AAH	Pseudo-Tertullian, *Against All Heresies*
AH	Irenaeus, *Against Heresies*
ANRW	*Aufstieg und Niedergang der römischen Welt*
BG	Berlin Gnostic Codex
BJ	Josephus, *Bellum Judaicum* or *Jewish War*
Cels.	Origen, *Against Celsus*
CH	*Corpus Hermeticum*
DGWE	*Dictionary of Gnosis and Western Esotericism*, ed. Hanegraaff
Dial.	Justin Martyr, *Dialogue with Trypho*
Exc.	*Excerpts from Theodotus*
Fab.	Theodoret, *Heretical Fables*
HE	Eusebius, *Ecclesiastical History*
HTR	*Harvard Theological Review*
Inst.	Lactantius, *Divine Institutes*
JECS	*Journal of Early Christian Studies*
LXX	Septuagint
MTSR	*Method & Theory in the Study of Religion*
NHC	Nag Hammadi Codices
NHMS	Nag Hammadi and Manichaean Studies
NovT	*Novum Testamentum*
NTS	*New Testament Studies*
Or.	Tatian, *Oration against the Greeks*
OTP	*Old Testament Pseudepigrapha*, 2 vols., ed. James H. Charlesworth
Pan.	Epiphanius, *Panarion*
PG	*Patrologia Graeca*
Pr. Haer.	Tertullian, *Prescription against Heretics*
RAC	*Reallexikon für Antike und Christentum*
SH	*Stobaean Hermetica*

SHA	*Historia Augusta*
Strom.	Clement of Alexandria, *Stromata*
VC	*Vigiliae Christianae*
WUNT	Wissenschaftliche Untersuchungen zum Neuen Testament
ZAC	*Zeitschrift für Antikes Christentum*

Chronological Table

Note: All dates are rough estimates delimiting when the figure or group flourished

Figure	Date
Simon of Samaria	35–70 CE
Menander	60–100 CE
Cerinthus	70–110 CE
Nicolaitans	90–100 CE
Saturninus	90–140 CE
Euphrates and Akembes	120–200 CE
Marcion	120–160 CE
Seed of Seth	130–400 CE
Basilides	130–160 CE
Carpocrates	130–160 CE
Valentinus	130–160 CE
Ptolemy	140–152 CE *or* 180 CE
Julius Cassianus	145–180 CE
Heracleon	150–180 CE
Marcus	150–180 CE
Tatian	150–180 CE
Marcellina	160–180 CE
Apelles	160–195 CE
Noetus	160–195 CE
Philumene	170–195 CE
Prodicus	175–195 CE
Theodotus the Shoemaker	180–200 CE
Florinus	190–200 CE
Justin (author of *Baruch*)	190–220 CE
Naassene preacher	190–220 CE
"Sethians" in *Ref.*	190–220 CE

Introduction

Among students of early Christianity, Tertullian's question, "What indeed has Athens to do with Jerusalem?" is well-known. Yet fewer remember his neighboring opposition, "What have heretics to do with Christians?"[1] The context of the remark shows that Tertullian of Carthage (about 160–220 CE) knew very well that his opponents called themselves Christians, but he considered their practice of self-labeling a mere outward profession, a thin cloak of fleece.[2]

Still, in the very same text in which Tertullian sought to de-Christianize his competitors, he showed that they engaged in Christian practices. They gather together for worship, "listen together, pray together." They welcome others into their congregation. They support a catechumenate (schooling for new Christians). They allow women to teach, perform exorcisms, effect cures, and to baptize. They invite other Christians into their churches, quickly promoting them to offices.[3] No wonder they attracted "the most faithful and wisest and most experienced members of the church."[4] Tertullian aimed to exclude these competitors from the category of "Christian," despite the fact that they worshiped Christ and – in a few notable cases – died for him.[5]

Tertullian was hardly alone in his rhetorical practice of exclusion. Ignatius of Antioch (about 140 CE?) attacked those who "bear the name [of Christ] with wicked deceit."[6] Justin Martyr (about 100–165 CE) wrote that his enemies called themselves Christians, confessing that Jesus, their Lord and Messiah, was crucified.[7] Irenaeus

---

[1] Tertullian, *Pr. Haer.* 7. All translations in this work, unless otherwise noted, are my own.

[2] Tertullian, *Pr. Haer.* 4; *Resurrection* 3.

[3] Tertullian, *Pr. Haer.* 41.

[4] Tertullian, *Pr. Haer.* 3.1.

[5] Eusebius, *HE* 4.15.46; 7.12.1; *Martyrs of Palestine* 10; *Martyrdom of Pionius* 11, 21 in H. Musurillo, *Acts of Christian Martyrs* (Oxford: Clarendon, 1972), 165. See further Anthony Hilhorst, "Christian Martyrs Outside the Catholic Church," in *Heretics and Heresies in the Ancient Church and in Eastern Christianity: Studies in Honour of Adelbert Davids,* ed. Joseph Verheyden and Herman Teule (Leuven: Peeters, 2011), 23–36; Philip L. Tite, "Voluntary Martyrdom and Gnosticism," *JECS* 23, no. 1 (2015): 27–54; Candida R. Moss, "Notions of Orthodoxy in Early Christian Martyrdom Literature," in *The Other Side: Apocryphal Perspectives on Ancient "Orthodoxies,"* ed. Tobias Nicklas et al. (Göttingen: Vandenhoeck & Ruprecht, 2017), 165–76.

[6] Ignatius, *Ephesians* 7.1; cf. *Magnesians* 4.1. On the dating, see Jonathan Lookadoo, "The Date and Authenticity of the Ignatius Letters: An Outline of Recent Discussions," *Currents in Biblical Research* 19, no. 1 (2020): 88–114.

[7] Justin, *Dial.* 35.2, 6.

(about 130–202 CE) wrote that his opponents put forward the name of Christ Jesus and taught under his auspices.[8] "Even today," wrote Epiphanius (about 375 CE), "people call the heresies ... by the common name of 'Christians.'"[9] All these writers, however, intentionally refused to call their opponents "Christians." They preferred other, self-chosen names, such as "Marcians [*sic*]," "Valentinians," "Basilideans," and "Saturninians."[10]

Anti-heresy writers were aware of the fact that if one labeled a Christian group by another name, it destabilized that group's Christian identity.[11] Lactantius (about 250–325 CE), for instance, wrote that by demonic fraud, opposing groups have carelessly "lost the name and the worship of God. For when they are called ... Valentinians, Marcionites ... or by any other name, they have ceased to be Christians, who have lost the name of Christ and assumed human and external names."[12] But who was doing the name calling? In most cases, it was opponents – one of whom, Epiphanius (about 320–403 CE), admitted to making up a name for a group that probably never existed (the "Alogi").[13]

The very fact that some Christians sought to undermine the Christian identity of certain others ironically ended up reinforcing that identity. Anti-heresy writers made their attacks to avoid being grouped together with those whom they considered to be politically dangerous subalterns. By the second century CE, Greek and Roman authors tended to use the general descriptor "Christian" for Christ-believers,[14] whereas Christian insiders used a wide variety of differentiating labels to distinguish their movements from putatively false forms of the faith. This kind of internal self-differentiation had been going on since the days of Paul, who imagined four bickering factions among a small group of Corinthian Christians (1 Cor. 1:12).

What was going on here? In the words of the late scholar of religion J. Z. Smith, "while difference or 'otherness' may be perceived as being either *like-us* or *not-like-us*, it becomes most problematic when it is *too-much-like-us* or when it claims to

[8] Irenaeus, *AH* 1.27.4.
[9] Epiphanius, *Pan.* 29.6.6.
[10] Justin, *Dial.* 35.6.
[11] Ignatius, *Magnesians* 10.1: "For the one called by another name [than Christian] beyond this is not of God."
[12] Lactantius, *Inst.* 4.30.10. The heresiological strategy of relabeling goes back to Justin Martyr, *Dial.* 35.5-6; Hegesippus in Eusebius, *HE* 4.22.5; cf. Clement, *Strom.* 7.17.108.1-2.
[13] The case of the "Alogi" in Epiphanius, *Pan.* 51.3.1-2. See Scott Manor, *Epiphanius' Alogi and the Johannine Controversy: A Reassessment of Early Johannine Opposition to the Johannine Corpus* (Leiden: Brill, 2016). The name "Borborian" may also be Epiphanius's creation (*Pan.* 25), as well as "Nazarene/Nazorean" (*Pan.* 29). See further Petri Luomanen, "Nazarenes" in *A Companion to Second-Century Christian "Heretics"*, ed. Antti Marjanen and Petri Luomanen (Leiden: Brill, 2007), 279–314.
[14] E.g., Lucian, *Peregrinus* 11; Pliny the Younger, *Letters* 10.96.7; Tacitus, *Annals* 15.44; Suetonius, *Nero* 16; Justin Martyr, *1 Apol.* 7.3. See further David G. Horrell, "The Label *Christianos* (1 Pet. 4.16): Suffering, Conflict and the Making of Christianity Identity," in *Becoming Christian: Essays on 1 Peter and the Making of Christian Identity* (London: Bloomsbury, 2013), 164–210.

be us."[15] Disagreements about key issues are often based – not just on the sense of difference – but on the sense of similarity. A group that is too close threatens identity because one's own group becomes insufficiently distinct. In cases where differences are not sufficient to exclude a competing group, they can be discovered, enhanced, or invented.[16] These perceived differences can then harden into stereotypes.[17] Stereotypes are often a feature of heresiography, which can be defined as a systematic and descriptive form of writing that polemically presents insiders as outsiders.

Heresiography is a particular, if fluid, genre; yet heresiological discourse can pervade virtually any kind of literature, including (church) history. One of the very first documents of church history, canonized as the book of Acts, tries to convince its readers that Christianity has an essential core – an apostolic message enshrined in the minds of twelve men who moved out of the holy city of Jerusalem and conquered the world by their mission. Internal enemies – depicted as "savage wolves" (Acts 20:29) – came later, joining the ranks of external enemies ("pagans" and Jews who did not believe in Jesus).

Perhaps the most famous instance of church history was that written by Eusebius of Caesarea (263–339 CE) in the first quarter of the fourth century. Eusebius had many aims, one of which was to define those whom he considered to be Christians – to relate their story, and to disqualify certain competitors as (again Acts 20:29) "savage wolves."[18] Some writers in the modern period supposed that the purity of "the" church was corrupted in the reign of Constantine (died 337 CE), the first Christian emperor of Rome.[19] Eusebius – who praised Constantine to the skies – traced the corruption back to the reign of an earlier emperor, Hadrian (117–138 CE).[20] Yet he had to admit that there were even earlier figures who – wrongly in his opinion – presented themselves as Christians. Menander of Antioch appeared about 80 CE. Cerinthus and the Nicolaitans lived in late first-century Asia Minor. Still earlier was Simon of Samaria

[15] J. Z. Smith, "Differential Equations: On Constructing the Other," in *Relating Religion: Essays on the Study of Religion* (Chicago: University of Chicago Press, 2004), 230–50 at 245.
[16] John Turner, *Rediscovering Social Identity: Key Readings*, ed. Tom Postmes and Nyla R. Branscombe (New York: Psychology Press, 2010), 264.
[17] Henri Tajfel, "Cognitive Aspects of Prejudice," *Journal of Social Issues* 25 (1969): 79–97; Amélie Mummendey and Sabine Otten, "Aversive Discrimination," in *Blackwell Handbook of Social Psychology*, 112–32, esp. 126; Henry Tajfel and J. Turner, *Psychology of Intergroup Relations* (Chicago: Nelson Hall, 1986), 7–24; Dominic Abrams and Michael A. Hogg, *Social Identifications: A Social Psychology of Intergroup Relations and Group Processes* (London: Routledge, 1990), 56–67.
[18] Eusebius, *HE* 1.1.1.
[19] J. Z. Smith, *Drudgery Divine: On the Comparison of Early Christianities and the Religions of Late Antiquity* (Chicago: University of Chicago Press, 1990), 1–35.
[20] Eusebius, *HE* 4.7.1. Cf. 3.26.4: "It was assuredly at the instigation of the devil that the name of Christian was adopted by such sorcerers." "Heretics" could only emerge when the apostles died (3.32.7-8). See further Eusebius, *In Praise of Constantine: A Historical Study and New Translation of Eusebius' Tricenniel Orations*, ed. H. A. Drake (Berkeley: University of California Press, 1978).

about 35 CE.[21] So in spite of Eusebius's thesis that "heresy" was late, derivative, and short-lived, his own history indicates that in some cases it was early, independent, and enduring.[22]

Eusebius set a precedent for the "church history" genre. For him, part of the genre was the story of figures construed as "heretics," the internal others ostracized through the power of relabeling.[23] Eusebius's overarching goal was to portray one single church – his own – united for empire.[24] Eusebian history created a field of knowledge, and defined its subject by exclusion, as in any other field. In this case, however, the exclusionary rhetoric had an ethical edge, for it was not just things, but real people who were denounced and – at least mentally – expelled from ecclesial boundaries.

In the past fifty years, however, these boundaries have been boldly redrawn. The truth claims of insiders have been bracketed and interrogated. As a result, early Christianity has been redescribed as a pluralist movement, featuring several different kinds of Christians, bound together in fairly porous groups. Labeling some of these groups "mainstream" and others "heretical," "marginal" or otherwise "deviant" is generally seen as unhelpful because it reinscribes – often in subtle ways – ancient heresiological categories.[25] Similarly, labeling one group "the majority" or "great" church makes little sense when we have no solid demographic data for the diverse locales in which Christianity took root. In 1934, German historian Walter Bauer argued that in certain areas – for instance the cities of Edessa and Alexandria – a Christianity later labeled "heretical" was in fact the common form during the second century CE.[26]

[21] Eusebius, *HE* 2.13; 3.26-29; 4.22.4-5.

[22] Eusebius, *HE* 2.1.12.

[23] Pierre Bourdieu, *Language and Symbolic Power*, trans. Gino Raymond (Cambridge, MA: Harvard University Press, 1993), 239.

[24] See further Robert M. Grant, *Eusebius as Church Historian* (Oxford: Clarendon, 1980), 84–96; Birger Pearson, "Eusebius and Gnosticism," in *Eusebius, Christianity, and Judaism*, ed. Harold W. Attridge and Gohei Hata (Leiden: Brill, 1992), 291–310; and in the same volume Arthur J. Droge, "The Apologetic Dimensions of the *Ecclesiastical History*," 492–509; Mary Verdoner, *Narrated Reality: The 'Historia Ecclesiastica' of Eusebius of Caesarea* (Frankfurt am Main: Peter Lang, 2011), esp. 140–6; Meike Willung, *Euseb von Cäsarea als Häreseograph* (Berlin: de Gruyter, 2009).

[25] *Pace* Rodney Stark, *Cities of God: The Real Story of How Christianity Became an Urban Movement and Conquered Rome* (New York: Harper One, 2006), 141–82. Stark's "sociology" of "Gnosticism" is an expression of his theology which normativizes a particular brand of Christianity while discounting the rest as "bizarre," unconventional, and "outlandish" (178, 181). See further Karen King, *What Is Gnosticism?* (Cambridge, MA: Harvard University Press, 2003), 5–148. See also King, "Which Early Christianity?" in *The Oxford Handbook of Early Christian Studies*, ed. Susan Ashbrook Harvey and David G. Hunter (Oxford: Oxford University Press, 2008), 66–86; King, "'The Gnostic Myth': How Does its Demise Impact Twenty-first Century Historiography of Christianity's Second Century," in *Christianity in the Second Century: Themes and Developments*, ed. Judith Lieu and James Carleton Paget (Cambridge: Cambridge University Press, 2017), 122–36.

[26] Walter Bauer, *Orthodoxy and Heresy in Earliest Christianity*, ed. Robert A. Kraft and Gerhard Krodel (Minneapolis: Fortress, 1971), 1–60.

Whether Bauer was right or wrong is difficult to verify given the dearth of demographical data.[27]

To be sure, institutional structures that could enforce Christian norms eventually emerged in the third and fourth centuries CE.[28] Some Christians of the third and later centuries looked back on their predecessors, depicting some of them as their spiritual and intellectual "fathers" – whence the study of patristics (from *pater* or "father"). Other figures they portrayed as "heretics" or outsiders. This latter process can be described as "secondary hereticalization." Hereticalization is an inherently religious – not a scholarly – mode of classification. Indeed the labels "heretical" and "(proto-) orthodox" are at root religious. Historically speaking, there is little intellectual gain by labelling figures "orthodox" or "heretical" or by making "orthodoxy" and "heresy" the framework of historical inquiry. When dealing with the second century, moreover, such a procedure is almost always anachronistic.[29]

Take, for example, the figure of Valentinus. This Christian theologian, who died about 160 CE, would probably have been surprised to learn that he was hereticalized about 180 CE.[30] In a famous tale of Tertullian, Valentinus was almost voted into high office in the Roman church.[31] The only reason why he lost was because his competitor was a confessor (arrested, that is, for being a Christian). In his surviving writings, Valentinus does not show any sign of feeling ostracized or transgressive. To our knowledge, he was never expelled from any church communion and never banished anyone himself. To call him a "heretic" or even "unorthodox" would unnecessarily lead the reader to take up the perspective of his (later) enemies. To be fair to the forebearers of Christian faith, then, we must tell early Christian stories differently.

Aim

In this volume, I aim to tell the stories of Christians whom other Christians denied were Christian. It is a history of persons and groups that begins in the first century CE and ends in the late second. It focuses on figures and movements in and around Antioch, Alexandria, Asia Minor, Palestine, and Rome. It seeks to integrate figures formerly de-Christianized into the warp and woof of Christian history. Accordingly, it resists working with a conceptual scheme wherein an abstract "Christianity"

---

[27] The guestimates offered by Rodney Stark (*Cities of God*, 63–85) are no replacement for hard data. Stark admits that most of his data derives from the seriously outdated study of Harnack (ibid., 212). Indeed, most of Stark's knowledge of early Christianity derives from studies now outdated and defunct.

[28] On motives for forming orthodoxy, see G. R. Boys-Stones, *Post-Hellenistic Philosophy: A Study of Its Development from the Stoics to Origen* (Oxford: Oxford University Press, 2001), 154–62.

[29] Alister McGrath's definition of heresy as "an intellectually defective vision of the Christian faith" is a deeply anachronistic and evaluative expression of his own faith and to that extent ahistorical (*Heresy: A History of Defending the Truth* [New York: HarperOne, 2009], 83).

[30] Justin Martyr and Hegesippus hereticalized the *followers* of Valentinus in the 160s CE (*Dial.* 35.6; Eusebius, *HE* 4.22.5).

[31] Tertullian, *Against Valentinians* 4.1.

undergoes a secondary crisis or peril from within – the emergence of internal "others." These "others" were *always* within Christianity, and in many ways they still are.

Not every Christian figure or group can here be discussed. For instance, several early Christian groups who maintained Jewish rites and practices – so-called Jewish Christians – were hereticalized as "Ebionites" (among other designations).[32] Members of the "New Prophecy" (later known as "Montanists") were criticized for their ecstatic prophecy, fasts, and female leadership, though generally not for their false doctrines. (We will have occasion to address the New Prophecy in Chapters 17–18.)

This book focuses on people. Chapters are not devoted to texts (such as the *Gospel of Thomas*) unless those texts are closely connected to a known historical person or group.[33] Not every text or heresiographical report represents a historical group. Several groups (for instance the "Cainites" and the "Doketai") seem to have been entirely constructed by heresiologists, and so can be omitted in this history.

What to Call Them?

Scholars of the past century have wondered what to call the de-Christianized Christians of the second century, and it seems fair to say that no single globalizing term (like "gnostic," "esoteric," or even "alternative") will allow us fully to escape heresiographical rhetoric.[34] These people were "othered" in antiquity by the exclusionary discourse of their opponents, and scholars rightly refuse to reinscribe this discourse since it involves (often implicit) negative value judgments about supposed "winners" and "losers."[35]

Consequently, I will class the figures studied here under the umbrella category of "Christians," which I think is more faithful to their own practices of self-definition. Often it will be necessary to differentiate groups within this broad category. In some

---

[32] Nowadays the label "Jewish Christian" is generally recognized as problematic. Joan E. Taylor, "The Phenomenon of Early Jewish Christianity: Reality or Scholarly Invention?" *VC* 44 (1990): 313–34; Daniel Boyarin, "Rethinking Jewish Christianity: An Argument for Dismantling a Dubious Category (to which is Appended a Correction of my *Border Lines*)," *Jewish Quarterly Review* 99, no. 1 (2009): 7–36; James Carleton Paget, "The Definition of the Term 'Jewish Christian'/'Jewish Christianity' in the History of Research," in Paget, *Jews, Christians and Jewish Christians in Antiquity* (Tübingen: Mohr Siebeck, 2010), 289–324; Matt Jackson-McCabe, *Jewish Christianity The Making of the Christianity–Judaism Divide* (New Haven: Yale University Press, 2020), esp. 166–71.

[33] William Arnal, "Blessed are the Solitary: Textual Practices and the Mirage of the Thomas 'Community,'" in *The One Who Sows Bountifully: Essays in Honor of Stanley K. Stowers*, ed. Caroline Johnson Hodge et al. (Providence: Brown University Press, 2013), 271–81.

[34] For scholars like Darrell L. Bock, even "alternative" has the latent sense of "marginal" (*The Missing Gospels: Unearthing the Truth Behind Alternative Christianities* [Nashville: Thomas Nelson, 2006]).

[35] Brakke, *Gnostics*, 7; Michael A. Williams, "On Ancient 'Gnosticism' as a Problematic Category," in *The Gnostic World*, ed. Gary Trompf (London: Taylor & Francis, 2018), 100–117.

respects, it is better to stick to self-chosen labels like "the Spiritual Seed," or "the Seed of Seth." For the sake of clarity, however, I am not averse to using externally applied labels for groups like "Valentinians" and "Basilideans," though I will often take the opportunity to emphasize that these were "Valentinian" and "Basilidean" Christians.[36]

Given this approach, it is important to define what is meant by Christian. In the second century, Christian identity was still in the process of being invented. This was indeed a challenge, since early Christianity did not have an "essence." Despite the prominence of the term "Christ" in "Christian," few Christians agreed on the identity of Christ (was he God? A god? Human? God-Human? Jewish Messiah? An angel? A prophet? and so on). Thus Christianity cannot be determined by the content of its Christology. In fact, not a single early Christian belief can be considered absolutely stable or homogenous in this period of Christian history. Despite the appearance of incipient creeds, there never was a unique script of Christian belief with self-evident meanings.

Socially speaking, however, there were various persons and groups who were devoted to Christ, who supported symbols, rites, stories, texts, and teachings in honor of Christ and his divine Father.[37] In this book, I am prepared to call these people "Christians." In many cases, they felt no need to claim the Christian name because their practices, assumptions, and contexts made such affirmations unnecessary.[38] Many of them, however, did identify as Christian. One group that we will study, the Naassenes (Chapter 25), claimed to be the only true Christians.[39]

Admittedly, some of the Christians discussed in this book were troubled by the Christian name. The author of the *Testimony of Truth* rebuked those who confessed "'We are Christians,' in word only (but) not with power, while giving themselves over to ignorance alone, to a human death. They do not know where they are going nor who Christ is."[40] The author of *The Second Discourse of Great Seth* complains about being persecuted "by those who suppose they abound with the name of Christ."[41] These authors criticized – implicitly or explicitly – the wrongful application of the Christian name (returning the favor to their Christian opponents). They made these criticisms not because they rejected Christian identity, but because this identity was important to them – thus something worth arguing about.

---

[36] On categorization effects, see Craig McGarty, *Categorization in Social Psychology* (London: Thousand Oaks, 1999), 79–81; Philip Tite, "Categorical Designations and Methodological Reductionism," *MTSR* 13 (2001): 269–92.

[37] See further Theodore Schatzki, K. Knorr-Cetina, and Eike van Savigny, *The Practice Turn in Contemporary Theory* (London: Routledge, 2001); Virginia Burrus, ed., *A People's History of Christianity, Volume 2: Late Ancient Christianity* (Minneapolis: Fortress, 2005), 1, 19.

[38] For Christian self-designations, see Cilliers Breytenbach and Christiane Zimmerman, *Early Christianity in Lycaonia and Adjacent Areas: From Paul to Amphilochus of Iconium* (Leiden: Brill, 2017), 26–8.

[39] *Ref.* 5.9.22; cf. Irenaeus, *Haer.* 1.27.3; 2.28.4; *Adamantius* 808e; Epiphanius, *On Faith* 8.4.

[40] *Test. Truth* (IX,3) 31.24–32.1.

[41] *2 Disc. Seth* (VII,2) 59.23-27.

Some might say that categorizing the figures in this book as Christian is an act of domestication. April D. DeConick, for instance, has called such categorization "taming the shrew."[42] I greatly appreciate DeConick's work and perspective. Nevertheless, I believe that in this case she makes certain assumptions worth bringing out into the light. First of all, categorizing the figures and groups studied here as Christian does not make them "an ancillary development" to "real" Christianity.[43] This viewpoint seems to assume that a certain group (for instance, early catholics) had the power to define "real" Christianity in the first place. Moreover, the fact that the figures studied here were Christian does not make them "innocuous" or remove their power to defy social or theological norms.[44] The very reason why some Christians considered the figures discussed here to be dangerous (deviant, transgressive, and so on) is because they had a claim to Christian identity. DeConick seems to presuppose that if we characterize the figures and groups studied here as Christian, we construct them as (Christian) "heretics." In assuming this, however, DeConick herself makes a serious concession to heresiological discourse – as if heresiologists (still) have the power to define who is a "heretic." The category "heretic," as noted above, however, has no place as a category in academic historiography.

It can be granted that the Christians studied in this book and the forms of Christianity they represented were not validated later and do not survive today – at least as they did in antiquity. But this point is largely irrelevant for historical inquiry. After all, early catholic Christianities in Rome about 180 CE look different than any form of Roman Catholicism surviving today. Whether a movement "survived" or not assumes that it had a stable identity throughout time – and that is highly unlikely for complex entities like Christian groups, given their adaptive and protean qualities.

We must reckon with the phenomenon that all sorts of discourses, ideas, and practices are continually recycled and adapted, such that the influence of so-called lost Christianities can still be felt today.[45] Indeed, what we call "Christianity" is a kind of mass conglomerate of discourses, dispositions, and practices, some of which – one could argue – go back to the Christians studied here. (Those interested in the medieval and modern revivals of "lost" Christianities can now consult a growing literature.[46])

---

[42] April DeConick, "The Countercultural Gnostic: Turning the World Upside Down and Inside Out," *Gnosis* 1 (2016): 7–35 at 12; cf. her *Gnostic New Age* (New York: Columbia University Press, 2016), 6–7. Cf. Roelof van den Broek, *Gnostic Religion in Antiquity* (Cambridge: Cambridge University Press, 2013), 224–6.

[43] DeConick, "Countercultural Gnostic," 10.

[44] DeConick, "Countercultural Gnostic," 11.

[45] Bart Ehrman, *Lost Christianities: The Battles for Scripture and the Faiths We Never Knew* (New York: Oxford University Press, 2003).

[46] Richard Smith, "The Revival of Ancient Gnosis," in *The Allure of Gnosticism: The Gnostic Experience in Jungian Psychology and Contemporary Culture*, ed. Robert Segal (Chicago: Open Court, 1995), 204–10; Dylan Burns, "Seeking Ancient Wisdom in the New Age: New Age and Neo-Gnostic Commentators on the *Gospel of Thomas*," in *Polemical Encounters: Esoteric Discourse and Its Others*, ed. Kocku von Stuckrad and Olav Hammer (Leiden: Brill, 2007), 252–89; Antoine

Social Formations

There has been a tendency among some scholars to study the Christian groups in focus here as (philosophical) "schools," or something analogous to them. This model has proved illuminating in many respects.[47] Ancient philosophical schools engaged in what would today be called religious practices. Platonists, for instance, celebrated the birthday of "the divine Plato" with a banquet and readings. The Platonist schools of Plotinus and Iamblichus (third and fourth centuries CE) could fairly be called religious movements.

The fact that this point needs explaining, however, underscores the basic problem. In modern-day parlance, "philosophical school" does not suggest a religious movement. Therefore, if one depicts the Christian social formations described here in solely scholastic terms, one could give the wrong impression. Several Christian leaders introduced in this book deliberately set up entities that they and their opponents called *ekklēsiai* (religious "assemblies," commonly translated "churches"). These assemblies fulfilled some of the functions of ancient schools, but they were not mere study circles gathered around an inspirational teacher. They were worshiping bodies with rites and liturgies. This point is important to emphasize, since heresiographers call the social formations of their opponents "schools" (*scholē*) in order to define them "as a pagan type of institution or as a deviant faction with illegitimate claims."[48]

If I underscore the ecclesial nature of these early Christian groups, I do not subscribe to the view that they were all highly integrated, cohesive societies with a common creed, a single understanding of ritual, and a unified ethos. When early Christian writers described their groups as "churches," they were promoting an ideal of unity that was rarely achieved. To represent the variety of early Christian social

Faivre, "Le terme et la notion de 'Gnose' dans les courants ésotériques occidentaux modernes," in *Les texts de Nag Hammadi: Histoire des religions et approches contemporaines*, ed. Jean-Pierre Mahé, Paul-Hubert Poirier, and Madeleine Scopello (Paris: AIBL, 2010), 87–112; Trompf, ed., *The Gnostic World*, 409–697; Michael Kaler, "Who Is Us? Thoughts on Nag Hammadi and the Modern Recreation of Gnosticism," in *Nag Hammadi à 70 ans*, ed. Tuomas Rasimus, Eric Crégheur, and Louis Painchaud (Leuven: Peeters, 2019), 31–46; Dylan Burns and Almut-Barbara Renger, ed., *New Antiquities: Transformations of Ancient Religion in the New Age and Beyond.* (London: Equinox, 2018).

[47] See Christoph Markschies, *Gnosis und Christentum* (Berlin: Berlin University Press, 2009), 101–2; Christoff Markschies, *Christian Theology and its Institutions in the Early Roman Empire* (Tübingen: Mohr Siebeck, 2015), 59–90; Winrich Löhr, "Christianity as Philosophy: Problems and Perspectives of an Ancient Intellectual Project," *VC* 64, no. 2 (2010): 160–88; Löhr, "Christian Gnostics and Greek Philosophy in the Second Century," *Early Christianity* 3 (2012): 349–377; Löhr, "Modelling Second-Century Christian Theology: Christian Theology as *philosophia*," in Lieu and Paget, eds., *Christianity in the Second Century*, 151–68.

[48] Einar Thomassen, "Were there Valentinian Schools?" in *Christian Teachers in Second-century Rome*, ed. H. Gregory Snyder (Leiden: Brill, 2020), 32–44 at 33. See also Thomassen, "Gnosis and Philosophy in Competition," in *Philosophia in der Konkurrenz von Schulen, Wissenschaften und Religionen*, ed. Christoph Riedweg (Berlin: de Gruyter, 2017), 61–74.

formations, I will employ an assortment of terms such as "networks," "circles," and "movements."[49] I intend none of these terms to indicate an association which displayed "deep social and mental coherence."[50] The nature of our sources does not allow us to reach beyond the mentality of elite Christian writers who did not always represent the attitudes, interests, and practices of their followers.

At the same time, I would argue for what one might call a minimal group mentality among many groups discussed here. Social Identity Theory indicates that the mere act of social categorizing affects the perception of other perceived groups. If an individual is categorized as part of group "x," they will tend to accentuate the differences between their group and perceived group "y" – even if these groups are loosely bound, recently created, and arbitrarily defined (such as blue-eyed people vs. brown-eyed people). The mere act of categorization can generate intergroup competition and an affective preference for the ingroup.[51] Humans naturally form groups, and group belief and identity are important facets of social life.[52]

Method

In the past, the study of the figures in this book has been artificially isolated from Christian history. The "fathers" (and to a much lesser extent, "mothers") of "the" church have been studied under the category of "church history," while the hereticalized others have been shunted into books on "Gnosis/Gnosticism" or "heretical

---

[49] On the native terminology for groups, see Philip A. Harland, *Dynamics of Identity in the World of the Early Christians* (New York: T&T Clark, 2009), esp. 25–46. See further Harland, *Associations, Synagogues and Congregations* (Minneapolis: Fortress, 2003), 25–54; Dennis E. Smith, "Revisiting Associations and Christ Groups," in *Scribal Practices and Social Structures among Jesus Adherents: Essays in Honour of John S. Kloppenborg*, ed. William E. Arnal et al. (Leuven: Peeters, 2016), 483–94; John S. Kloppenborg, *Christ's Associations: Connecting and Belonging in the Ancient City* (New Haven: Yale University Press, 2020).

[50] Stanley K. Stowers, "The Concept of 'Community' and the History of Early Christianity," *MTSR* 23.3–4 (2011): 238–56 at 238. See also Stowers, "Kinds of Myth, Meals, and Power: Paul and the Corinthians," in *Redescribing Paul and the Corinthians*, ed. Ron Cameron and Merrill P. Miller (Atlanta: Society of Biblical Literature, 2011), 105–49 at 108–10; Judith M. Lieu, "From Us but Not of Us? Moving the Boundaries of the Community," in *Early Christian Communities between Ideal and Reality*, ed. Mark Grundeken and Joseph Verheyden (Tübingen: Mohr Siebeck, 2015), 161–75; Jörg Frey, "From Text to Community: Methodological Problems of Reconstructing Communities Behind Texts," in *Jewish and Christian Communal Identities in the Roman World*, ed. Yair Furstenberg (Leiden: Brill, 2016), 167–84; Sarah E. Rollens, "The Anachronism of 'Early Christian Communities,'" in *Theorizing 'Religion' in Antiquity*, ed. Nickolas P. Roubekas (Sheffield: Equinox: 2019), 307–26; Robyn Faith Walsh, *The Origins of Early Christian Literature: Contextualizing the New Testament with Greco-Roman Literary Culture* (Cambridge: Cambridge University Press, 2021).

[51] Abrams and Hogg, *Social Identifications* 18–21, 43.

[52] Daniel Bar-Tal, *Group Beliefs, A Conception for Analyzing Group Structure, Processes, and Behavior* (New York: Springer, 1990), esp. 63–77.

history" (*Ketzergeschichte*).[53] It is high time to integrate these two subfields in an attempt to weave together a more comprehensive history of ancient Christianities. This history is and can never be a "grand narrative" in the sense of offering a "master idea" that legitimates or authorizes one particular social group or its heirs. What unites the figures discussed are the basic factors of time and space (they all lived in roughly the same period in the confines of the Roman Empire), as well as social identity (they were all – in some ways and in some sense – devotees of Christ).

In this kind of inquiry, it is important to distinguish primary from secondary sources. Primary sources are documents often written by insiders that serve as first-hand testimony regarding the thought, structure, leadership, and practices of a particular movement. Secondary sources comment on or build upon the primary sources, often with the benefit (or detriment) of hindsight. In this case, virtually all the relevant secondary sources are hostile heresiological reports. The primary sources, in turn, consist of rediscovered manuscripts, fragments, and excerpts of the Christians here studied. As a basic rule, I endeavor always – where possible – to begin with the primary sources or at least to use them as a touchstone for judging the accuracy of the heresiological reports.

There is nothing special about this procedure at all; in fact, it would hardly need mention were it not for the fact that it has not often been rigorously pursued. In some cases, that is, heresiological reports still serve as the first port of a call for describing a figure (such as Valentinus or Basilides), even when primary sources are available.[54] In theory, this procedure would not be so damaging if ancient heresiologists had aimed at something like level-headed reporting. Instead, heresiologists were some of the fiercest polemicists in the ancient world, intent on destroying the movements and ideas that they described.

The polemical features of heresiography include: (1) the reduction of complex, nuanced teachings and practices to bare-bones, hostile, and disconnected opinions, (2) the grouping of otherwise unconnected figures into schools of thought characterized by genetic links of succession, (3) the practice of psychologizing and character assassination, (4) the use of false inference and the polemical construction of "historical" details, all resulting in (5) the progressive distortion of reports as they were passed down, recopied, expanded, and contracted through time.

---

[53] The classic study is D. Adolf Hilgenfeld, *Die Ketzergeschichte des Urchristentums* (Leipzig: Fues, 1884). More recent works in the same genre include David Christi-Murray, *A History of Heresy* (Oxford: Oxford University Press, 1989); G. R. Evans, *A Brief History of Heresy* (Oxford: Oxford University Press, 2001); Gerd Lüdemann, *Heretics: The Other Side of Early Christianity* (London: SCM, 1996).
[54] E.g., Riemer Roukema, *Gnosis and Faith in Early Christianity: An Introduction to Gnosticism* (Harrisburg: Trinity Press, 1999); Birger Pearson, *Ancient Gnosticism* (Minneapolis: Fortress 2007).

As a result, virtually nothing heresiologists report can be readily or uncritically accepted. Historians must guard, not just against facilely accepting what heresiologists say, but from adopting the intellectual frameworks of heresiologists – frameworks that have proved surprisingly seductive in scholarship on Christianity. For instance, it is still commonly assumed that the heresiologists speak for "mainstream" churches, and that the movements they attack are late and derivative.

Accordingly, I will endeavor in this work to let the primary sources, whenever available, always serve as the criteria for the secondary sources. We can pursue this course in large part because of the discoveries of ancient texts made over the past 150 years – in particular the discovery of about fifty previously unknown writings near the town of Nag Hammadi, Egypt shortly after the Second World War. These writings are enclosed in a set of thirteen books (called codices) copied, it seems, in the fourth century CE. The books contain a number of early Christian works, most of them previously unknown. The writings were composed from the early second to the early fourth century CE. They were originally written in Greek, but translated into the Egyptian language of the time, called Coptic. They were gathered together by later readers (unfortunately unknown) until they were hidden away in sealed jars. Most of the writings appear in genres familiar to the New Testament: gospels, epistles, and apocalypses. There are also philosophical texts, maxims, prayers, and poetry. Apart from the Dead Sea Scrolls, the discovery of the Nag Hammadi codices was arguably the most important archaeological discovery of the twentieth century.[55] Yet other books recovered from Egypt are, cumulatively speaking, of similar value: the Bruce Codex, the Askew Codex, the Berlin Codex (containing the *Gospel of Mary*), and Codex Tchacos (containing the *Gospel of Judas*), among others.[56]

In some cases, unfortunately, a heresiographical report is still all we have for certain figures (for instance, Cerinthus, Menander, and Noetus). Thus we cannot exclude these reports as data. At the same time, however, such reports are not allowed to provide

---

[55] James M. Robinson, *The Nag Hammadi Story: From the Discovery to the Publication*, 2 vols. (Leiden: Brill, 2014); Brent Nongbri, *God's Library: The Archaeology of the Earliest Christian Manuscripts* (New Haven: Yale University Press, 2020), 108–15. To be sure, Coptic sources from Nag Hammadi and elsewhere have been edited by later copyists, but in my view this does not disqualify their use as primary sources – *pace* Jonathan Cahana-Blum, *Wrestling with Archons: Gnosticism as a Critical Theory of Culture* (Lanham: Lexington Books, 2018), 42–4. See further Stephen Emmel, "The Coptic Gnostic Texts as Witnesses to the Production and Transmission of Gnostic (and Other) Traditions," in *The Gospel of St. Thomas: Genesis-Reception-Theology*, ed. Jörg Frey (Berlin: de Gruyter, 2008), 33–49.

[56] Introductions to these codices can be found in their respective editions: Carl Schmidt, ed., and Violet MacDermot, trans., *The Books of Jeu and the Untitled Text in the Bruce Codex* (Leiden: Brill, 1978); Carl Schmidt, ed., and Violet MacDermot, trans., *Pistis Sophia* (Leiden: Brill, 1978); Christopher Tuckett, *Gospel of Mary* (Oxford: Oxford University Press, 2007), 3–13; Johanna Brankaer, *The Gospel of Judas* (Oxford: Oxford University Press, 2019).

independent proof if a primary source is available.[57] Occasionally secondary sources contradict each other and allow us to judge which report is more accurate. We can also work to detect the tendencies of heresiographers from their works as a whole. Frequently they can be caught distorting information because they have an axe to grind.

In other cases (such as for Valentinus, Ptolemy, Basilides), we have at our disposal fragments and even longer texts that have also been excerpted, sometimes at great length, by heresiologists.[58] These fragments and texts can, with circumspection, also be used as primary sources. Care is needed because we often detect interpolated comments from heresiographers, along with omissions and polemical paraphrasing. As a result, proper sifting is always required. Once the sifting is done, however, the fragments and excerpts have one advantage over the Coptic material in that they remain in their original tongue. Such are the primary sources.

We must also introduce the writers of the secondary sources. Most of these have already been mentioned, and one of them has already been sufficiently introduced (Eusebius). For the others, we can be brief.

Justin Martyr

Justin Martyr was a Christian philosopher from central Palestine (Flavia Neapolis, modern Nablus). Thoroughly educated in Greek learning, he tried out a variety of philosophical schools before settling into Platonism and then into a Platonically disposed form of Christianity. He moved to Rome probably in the 130s or early 140s CE. He composed – or made use of – an anti-heresy catalogue (the *Syntagma*) around 145 CE. About 150 CE, he recommended the *Syntagma* in a lengthy *Apology* addressed to the reigning emperors.[59]

Around the same time, Justin wrote a lost tract against Marcion, a competing Christian in Rome. By about 160 CE, Justin composed a lengthy *Dialogue* between himself as a Christian philosopher and a cultured Jew called Trypho. Between 162 and 167 CE, Justin was arraigned before a Roman judge on the charge of being a Christian. Soon afterward he was beheaded, along with some of his disciples.[60]

---

[57] See further Korinna Zamfir, "Elusive Opponents in the Pastoral Epistles," in *Shadowy Characters: and Fragmentary Evidence: The Search for Early Christian Groups and Movements*, ed. Joseph Verheyden, Tobias Nicklas, and Elisabeth Hernitscheck (Tübingen: Mohr Siebeck, 2017), 27–48.

[58] See further M. David Litwa, ed., *Refutation of All Heresies Translated with an Introduction and Notes* (Atlanta: SBL, 2016), li–lii.

[59] For the *Syntagma*, see further Geoffrey S. Smith, *Guilt by Association: Heresy Catalogues in Early Christianity* (Oxford: Oxford University Press, 2014), 49–82; Matthijs Den Dulk, "Justin Martyr and the Authorship of the Earliest Anti-heretical Treatise," *VC* 72 (2018): 471–83.

[60] See further Dennis Minns and Paul Parvis, eds., *Justin: Philosopher and Martyr: The Apologies* (Oxford: Oxford University Press, 2009), 32–70; Matthijs Den Dulk, *Between Jews and Heretics: Refiguring Justin Martyr's Dialogue with Trypho* (London: Routledge, 2018); David E. Nyström, *The Apology of Justin Martyr: Literary Strategies and the Defence of Christianity* (Tübingen: Mohr Siebeck, 2018).

Irenaeus

Irenaeus was born somewhere in Asia Minor (modern western Turkey), likely the city of Smyrna (modern Izmir). There, as a young man, he encountered Polycarp, an aged Christian leader – later martyred – who impressed upon him a certain stream of early Christian tradition.[61] Perhaps after a sojourn in Rome, Irenaeus ended up working as a presbyter in the city of Lugdunum (modern Lyon). In response to a persecution there, he brought letters of imprisoned martyrs to Rome in 177 CE.[62] When he returned to Lyon, he was voted to replace its bishop who had since perished.

As Irenaeus tried to rebuild his Christian sect, he also began writing against a certain Christian group integrated into Roman and local ecclesial networks – the Valentinians. In an attempt to trace them to already-acknowledged enemies, Irenaeus wrote his five-volume work *Refutation and Overthrow of Knowledge Falsely So-called* – better known as *Against Heresies*. Irenaeus also wrote a summary of his faith (*Demonstration of Apostolic Preaching*) and several letters, of which only fragments survive.[63]

Clement of Alexandria

Clement (about 150–215 CE) was a Christian scholar reportedly born in Athens. He was wealthy and traveled much to secure an excellent education, boasting of teachers from Greece, Palestine, and Egypt.[64] He eventually became a teacher in Alexandria. During a persecution there (202–203 CE) Clement fled, resettling in Palestine and perhaps later in Asia Minor (modern Turkey). While still in Alexandria, he drafted most of his massive work called *Stromata* (*Miscellanies*) *of Gnostic Notes according to the True Philosophy*. This work contains quotes and information about Christian writers in second-century Alexandria – for example Basilides, Valentinus, and Julius Cassianus.

With his access to Alexandrian sources, Clement also composed his *Excerpts from Theodotus*. This work is essentially a notebook of quotes and summaries peppered with Clement's own comments. In the first two sections, Clement mentioned a particular Valentinian Christian, a man by the name of Theodotus, five times. But the *Excerpts* do not all represent Theodotus's thought. Clement referred more often to

---

[61] Irenaeus, *AH* 3.3.4; Eusebius, *HE* 5.20.5-7.
[62] Eusebius, *HE* 5.4.1.
[63] On Irenaeus, see further Paul Foster and Sara Parvis, eds., *Irenaeus: Life, Scripture, and Legacy* (Minneapolis: Fortress, 2012); John Behr, *Irenaeus of Lyon: Identifying Christianity* (Oxford: Oxford University Press, 2013); Giuliano Chiapparini, "Irenaeus and the Gnostic Valentinus: Orthodoxy and Heresy in the Church of Rome around the Middle of the Second Century," *ZAC* 18, no. 1 (2013): 95–119; Päivi Vähäkangas, "'That Ill-formed Little Fox': Valentinians as the Enemy in Irenaeus's *Against Heresies*," in *The Faces of the Other: Religious Rivalry and Ethnic Encounters in the Later Roman World*, ed. Maijastina Kahlos (Turnhout: Brepols, 2011), 83–104.
[64] Clement, *Strom.* 1.1.11.1.

"Valentinians" in general.[65] This text has proved to be a vital source for understanding the thought and practice of Valentinian Christians at the time.[66]

Tertullian

Tertullian was a Christian writer of Carthage in North Africa (modern Tunisia). He had an excellent education in literature and rhetoric. He wrote most of his nearly three dozen works during the reign of the emperor Severus (193–211 CE). Among his anti-heresy writings, a general *Prescription against Heretics* forbids discussing the scriptures with opposing Christians. His treatises on *Resurrection*, the *Flesh of Christ*, and *On the Soul* contain valuable testimonies about other Christian groups in Carthage and elsewhere. A short tract *Against the Valentinians* is complemented by a massive five-volume work called *Against Marcion*.

By this time, Tertullian had joined the New Prophecy, an originally Phrygian Christian movement featuring alternative practices of fasting and ecstatic speech. Tertullian never formally left early catholic networks in Carthage, but he did begin referring to catholics as "soulish," as opposed to "spiritual."[67] In criticism of some early catholics, Tertullian spoke out against the practice of remarriage, unveiled young women in church, and the avoidance of persecution.[68]

The Refutator

The Refutator is a name for an anonymous bishop serving a Greek-speaking assembly in Rome sometime between 200–225 CE. He was a competitor to the emerging catholic hierarchy led by bishops Zephyrinus (ruled 199–217 CE) and

---

[65] The view that Theodotus was a direct contemporary of Valentinus is deduced from the – probably late – title of the work: *Excerpts from Theodotus and from the School Called Eastern in the Times of Valentinus*. The assumption that Theodotus lived in Alexandria is based on the fact that Clement who quoted him was in Alexandria. The notion that the *Excerpts* represent the "Eastern" school of Valentinian thought has been contested by Einar Thomassen, *Spiritual Seed: The Church of the Valentinians* (Leiden: Brill, 2006), 62–72. See also Bentley Layton and David Brakke, eds., *The Gnostic Scriptures Translated with Annotations and Introductions*, 2d ed., Anchor Yale Bible Reference Library (New Haven: Yale University Press, 2021), 501–5.
[66] On Clement, see further Salvatore R. C. Lilla, *Clement of Alexandria: A Study in Christian Platonism and Gnosticism* (Oxford: Clarendon, 1971); Andrew C. Itter, *Esoteric Teaching in the Stromateis of Clement of Alexandria* (Leiden: Brill, 2009). Piotr Ashwin-Siejkowski surveys Clement's opponents (*Clement of Alexandria: A Project of Christian Perfection* [London: T&T Clark, 2008], 109–44), though one must disagree that "Clement's account of his opponents' views is pretty accurate" (141).
[67] Tertullian, *Praxeas* 1.7; *Modesty* 1.10; 21.16; *Resurrection* 22.1.
[68] See further Timothy Barnes, ed., *Tertullian: A Historical and Literary Study*, rev. ed. (Oxford: Clarendon, 2011); David Wright, "Tertullian," in *The Early Christian World*, ed. Philip F. Esler (London: Routledge, 2000), 2:1027–47; Geoffrey D. Dunn, *Tertullian* (London: Routledge, 2004); David E. Wilhite, *Tertullian the African: An Anthropological Reading of Tertullian's Contexts and Identities* (Berlin: de Gruyter, 2007).

Callistus (217–222 CE). The Refutator lambasted both bishops, calling the first stupid and greedy while depicting the second as morally loose and openly heretical. In contrast to these men, the Refutator promoted himself as an intellectual, with access to new sources, and as a rigorist in church discipline.[69]

He advertised two of his works, an updated heresy catalogue (*Syntagma Against Thirty-two Heresies*) and a tract *On the Universe* against Plato. Neither of these works survives complete. The longest of his surviving works, the *Refutation of All Heresies*, is missing two books. The remaining eight books were unexpectedly discovered on Mount Athos in the mid-nineteenth century. It may have been unfinished, or at least unpolished, when the Refutator died. How he died is unknown. He is probably not the Roman martyr called "Hippolytus" who died in 235 CE.[70]

Pseudo-Tertullian

An otherwise unknown author probably working in the mid-third century CE apparently used the Refutator's *Syntagma Against Thirty-two Heresies* to compose his own updated, though abbreviated catalogue. It is called *Against All Heresies*. It may have been translated from a Greek version made in Rome. At any rate, it ended up buried in the works of Tertullian as an appendix to his *Prescription Against Heretics*. Despite its concision, *Against All Heresies* occasionally offers new and useful data.

Origen of Alexandria

Origen (185–254 CE) was a Christian ascetic and theologian born in Alexandria, Egypt. He reportedly castrated himself.[71] The bishop of Alexandria, Demetrius, initially lauded Origen's surgery. But when another bishop ordained Origen without Demetrius's approval, the latter raised a storm of protest. Demetrius claimed that a man with mutilated genitals could not become a priest and that Origen taught the salvation of the devil. This and other doctrinal issues (now muffled in the sources) led to Origen's excommunication by Egyptian and perhaps Roman synods.[72] Origen was suddenly barred from living in Alexandria, the intellectual capital of the eastern Roman empire.[73]

Moving to Caesarea on the coast of modern Israel, Origen became a preacher and resident scholar. Although he led a philosophy seminar there, the bulk of his intellectual labor was focused on sermons and biblical commentaries. His most famous apologetic work, *Against Celsus*, was written against a Platonist who wrote an attack

---

[69] Litwa, ed., *Refutation*, xl–xlii.
[70] See further Emanuele Castelli, "Saggio introduttivo: L'*Elenchos*, ovvero una 'biblioteca' contro le eresie," in *'Ippolito.' Confutazione di tutte le eresie*, ed. Aldo Magris (Brescia: Morcelliana, 2012), 21–56; Litwa, ed., *Refutation*, xxvii–liii.
[71] Eusebius, *HE* 6.8; Jerome, *Epistle* 84.8.
[72] Photius, *Bibliotheca* codex 118 at 93a; Jerome, *Epistle* 33.5.
[73] Origen, *Commentary on John* 6.1.8.

on Christianity about 175 CE.[74] Origen preserves about fifty quotes from Heracleon the Valentinian's *Commentary on John* – the first of its kind – in his own commentary of the same name.

Epiphanius

Epiphanius (about 315–403 CE) was a native of Palestine. In his youth, he learned monastic traditions in Egypt. Zealous for bodily and mental discipline, he founded his own monastery in his hometown at a young age. In 367 CE, he was appointed bishop of Salamis, then capital of Cyprus. Between 374–376 CE, he composed the – at that time – longest known heresy catalogue (comprising eighty different figures or groups). It was called the *Panarion*, or *Medicine Chest*. Into this catalogue, Epiphanius combined his knowledge of written sources, personal experience, and hearsay – which often results in the uneven quality of his reports. Although Epiphanius's pen was dipped in bile (he openly apologized for his scurrilous language), he sometimes offers new information from sources long since lost.[75]

Further Reading

Grant Adamson, "Gnosticism Disputed: Major Debates in the Field," in *Religion: Secret Religion* (London: Macmillan, 2016), 39–54 at 46–7.

Todd S. Berzon, *Classifying Christians: Ethnography, Heresiology, and the Limits of Knowledge in Late Antiquity* (Berkeley: University of California Press, 2016).

Dylan M. Burns, "Gnosticism, Gnostics, and Gnosis," in *The Gnostic World*, ed. Gary Trompf (London: Taylor & Francis, 2018), 9–25.

Ron Cameron, "Alternate Beginnings – Different Ends: Eusebius, Thomas and the Construction of Christian Origins," in *Religious Propaganda and Missionary Competition in the New Testament World: Essays in Honor of Dieter Georgi* (Leiden: Brill, 1994), 501–25.

David W. Jorgensen, "Approaches to Orthodoxy and Heresy in the Study of Early Christianity," *Religion Compass* 11 (2017): 1–14.

Karen King, "The Origins of Gnosticism and the Identity of Christianity," in *Was There a Gnostic Religion?*, ed. Antti Marjanen (Helsinki: Finnish Exegetical Society, 1999), 103–20.

Karen King, "Social and Theological Effects of Heresiological Discourse," in *Heresy and Identity in Late Antiquity*, ed. Eduard Iricinschi and Holger M. Zellentin (Tübingen: Mohr Siebeck, 2008), 28–49.

---

[74] See further Horacio E. Lona, *Die 'wahre Lehre' des Kelsos* (Freiburg: Herder, 2005); Anders Christian Jacobsen, *Christ the Teacher of Salvation: A Study on Origen's Christology and Soteriology* (Münster: Aschendorff, 2015); David Rankin, *From Clement to Origen: The Social and Historical Context of the Church Fathers* (London: Routledge, 2016).

[75] See further Aline Pourkier, *L'hérésiologie chez Épiphane de Salamine* (Paris: Beauchesne, 1992), 29–52; Young Richard Kim, *Epiphanius of Cyprus: Imagining an Orthodox World* (Ann Arbor: University of Michigan, 2015), esp. 17–43; Andrew Jacobs, *Epiphanius of Cyprus: A Cultural Biography of Late Antiquity* (Berkeley: University of California Press, 2016).

Outi Lehtipuu, "Who Has the Right to Be Called a Christian? Deviance and Christian Identity in Tertullian's *On the Prescription of Heretics*," in *Methods, Theories, Imagination: Social Scientific Approaches in Biblical Studies*, ed. David J. Chalcraft, Frauke Uhlenbruch, and Rebecca S. Watson (Sheffield: Sheffield Phoenix Press, 2014), 80–98.

Einar Thomassen, "What is Heresy, and Why Did it Matter?" in *Invention, Rewriting, Usurpation: Discursive Fights over Religious Traditions in Antiquity*, ed. Jörg Ulrich, Anders-Christian Jacobsen, and David Brakke (Frankfurt am Main: Peter Lang, 2012), 191–202.

Setting the Scene:
The World of the Second Century CE

Introduction

Before we begin our history, it will be helpful to set the scene of our historical actors by discussing their political, cultural, and social context during our period. The early Roman Empire was a fascinating time in ancient Mediterranean – and indeed world – history. It was a technicolored tapestry of cultural interaction if there ever was one. Here, unfortunately, we can only attempt to reweave it with the thickest of threads.

Edward Gibbon depicted the second century CE as one in which the human race was "most happy and prosperous."[1] It should be noted at the outset that – however happy and prosperous this era might have been for the elite – it was riven with misery for the majority population. Slaves, day-laborers, women, and disabled peoples were largely deprived of what we think of as basic human rights, nutrition, and health services. In the 160s and 170s CE there was terrible plague along with constant warring along the empire's northern frontier (modern central Europe). If one agrees that the second century was an era of noteworthy cultural and scientific achievement, relative political stability, and religious diversity, this says very little about the happiness and prosperity of the majority population! Our scope, however, must be much broader than the individual.

Political Developments

During the second century, the Roman Empire achieved the height of its strength and the furthest extent of its expansion. The government had long devolved into a monarchy lacking a formal constitution in which only a small minority of the subjects were citizens who could avoid burdensome taxes. The emperor stood at the

---

[1] Edward Gibbon, *The History of the Decline and Fall of the Roman Empire, Volume the First* (London: ElecBook, 1999), 108.

pinnacle of a gigantic bureaucracy of provincial governors, generals, imperial slaves, secretaries, tax-collectors (and so on) who ensured that money and goods flowed into and out of the eternal city, Rome.

To control other cities in the empire, Rome made alliances with local elites (kings, nobleman, members of civic assemblies) to keep the peace and maintain the food supply. The major industry was farming, and most of the wealth was generated by cultivating land. There was no Roman police force. Provinces that were distant and difficult to manage had large armies (legions) permanently stationed in the vicinity. Local rebellions might have temporary success, but when the Romans unleashed the full force of their military machine, few of their enemies were left standing.

Emperors

Here I can only offer a whirlwind political history, focused entirely on the twelve men who claimed imperial power between 96 and 200 CE. The story opens with the emperor Nerva (reigned 96–98 CE), the elderly aristocrat chosen to replace the assassinated and tyrannical emperor Domitian. Nerva was remembered fondly by the Roman elite for restoring their sense of respect as well as their ancient aristocratic privileges. Among many small changes in the administration and the completion of a few building projects, Nerva's most important political act was actually the choice of an accomplished heir in his prime, Marcus Ulpius Trajan.

Trajan (reigned 98–117 CE) was a successful general from the Spanish provinces, a good-natured leader, not enthralled with the trappings of authority. He was the first to expand the empire since Caesar Augustus by carving out the province of Dacia (much of modern Romania) after a double invasion. Late in life, Trajan enjoyed military success in the western section of the Parthian Empire (modern Iraq), but these lands won by the spear were mostly abandoned after his death.

With the help of Trajan's widow, Plotina, Trajan's relative Hadrian (reigned 117–138 CE) inherited the empire. Hadrian was a man of culture, not of campaigns. He firmly policed the empire's boundaries, but focused his efforts investing in its cities. In the course of his constant perambulations, Hadrian founded several cities of his own, including one named for his perished boy lover, Antinous, in Egypt. Fiercely pro-Hellenic, Hadrian clashed with nationalist Jews in Palestine, and ruthlessly suppressed them when they revolted in Egypt and Palestine (115–117, 132–135 CE). Months before his death, Hadrian chose the next three emperors to succeed him.

His immediate successor was Antoninus Pius (reigned 138–161 CE), an unassuming, careful governor in his early fifties. Through his generals, Pius pushed the Roman empire deep into Scotland and had success with client kings in the east. He was known for his restoration of buildings and public munificence. (A temple dedicated to his deified wife was later dedicated to him and still stands in the Forum at Rome.) Pius distinguished circumcision from castration, allowing Jews to circumcise their sons. This emperor carefully and responsibly steered the empire through its longest period of relative peace.

This peace crumbled when the next pick, Marcus Aurelius, took the reins in 161 CE. His junior partner, now invested with full powers, was Lucius Verus, whose first task was to repel Parthian incursions on the eastern frontier. When they were put to flight, Lucius brought back a victorious army, along with a devastating plague. As the death toll within the empire surged, Lucius unexpectedly perished by some sort of aneurism in 169 CE.

Marcus, now sole ruler, was already mobilizing for an all-out offensive in central Europe where native tribes, now accustomed to Roman weapons and maneuvers, were on the move – some of whom had even cut their way into northern Italy. It would take Marcus over a decade before these peoples were again prepared to respect Roman boundaries. In the meantime (175 CE), he had to deal with a rebellion in Syria when one of his top generals, Avidius Cassius, claimed the purple. Cassius was later betrayed and beheaded in Alexandria. Marcus – probably a late victim of the plague – would perish in what is now Vienna before the German wars were concluded.

His son and heir was Commodus (reigned 180–192 CE), who, after closing the German wars, enjoyed the fruits of his father's labor. Nestled back in Rome, Commodus seemed increasingly uninterested in the business of governing. He gave more and more free rein to proxies who abused their power and offended the Roman senate. Conspiracies churned against an ever more paranoid and bloodthirsty emperor. One of the plots finally succeeded: the emperor was poisoned and strangled the day before New Year's, 193 CE.

Already in position to take charge was Pertinax – a Roman of the old guard, though not of noble blood. Although he restored the face of government, Pertinax's strictness was hated by the local Roman militia (the Praetorians). A gang of them successfully stormed the palace and slaughtered Pertinax who thought he could talk them down. He had reigned only eighty-seven days.

The Romans groaned as the Praetorians sold the empire to the highest bidder – a senator named Didius Julianus (spring of 193 CE). But three Roman generals abroad thought they had a better claim – or at least better armies. Niger, a Roman nobleman ruling in Antioch of Syria, was initially the favorite at Rome. Two generals from North Africa vied with him – Albinus in Britain and Severus in eastern Europe. Initially, the two Africans clasped hands in alliance. Severus descended on Rome; Didius was murdered; the offending Praetorians disbanded.

A protracted civil war delivered a surprise defeat to Niger in northern Syria. Within a year, however, war reignited when Albinus realized he was being ousted by Severus's son. A momentous battle near what is now Lyon (France) finally decided the outcome. The dust cleared, and Severus emerged victorious. Carrying his enemy's head back to Rome, he planned an eastern campaign. Enjoying the same success as Trajan eighty years before, this time Severus maintained key winnings, carving out a new province of Mesopotamia (northern Iraq). By the end of the second century, the empire was not only firmly back in one piece, it was larger than it had ever been before.

Cultural Achievements

Although chaos could always break out on the corners of the empire, the center (Italy, Greece, Turkey, and North Africa) enjoyed a renaissance in the fields of literature and oratory. It was the age of the so-called Second Sophistic, when intellectuals of all sorts competed in tight social markets for prestige, wealth, and honor, parading their wisdom for a fee. This wisdom was consummately Greek, constantly appealing to the heritage of the "classical" past, centered on Athens in the fifth century BCE. Even those of "barbarian" (non-Greek) heritage could still do well in this world if they learned the codes and modes of classicizing ("Attic") Greek speech and learning.

Philosophy

Philosophers – who traditionally pitted themselves against the orators ("sophists") – also enjoyed relative prosperity.[2] They were the conscience of the empire, serving as moral exemplars and advisors. It was the new fashion, beginning with Hadrian, for men to sport a philosophic beard.[3] Philosophic education was the highest form of study. Marcus Aurelius established four endowed chairs of philosophy in Athens during the late 170s CE, but independent teachers had long established themselves in big cities throughout the empire.

A notable example was the Stoic Epictetus (about 50–135 CE). Epictetus was a former slave from Phrygia. He was bought in Rome by a secretary of the emperor Nero, but allowed to pursue advanced education. Epictetus was disabled with a maimed leg, apparently due to his master's abuse. He obtained his freedom sometime after 68 CE and taught in the capital until 95 CE, when Domitian banished philosophers from Italy. Epictetus sailed to Nicopolis on the coast of western Greece and set up his own school. There, until his death, he taught high-profile Romans like Arrian, Roman governor and historian. It was Arrian who transcribed Epictetus's discourses in the latter's punchy pedagogical style.

Epictetus preached freedom – a freedom that did not depend at all on one's external circumstances, but on one's internal choices to accept reality and to love it as the expression of divine goodness. Epictetus advocated freedom from all negative emotions (*apatheia*), emotions which he thought were based on faulty judgments. He did not promote the sheer absense of emotion; rather, he encouraged the use of positive emotions like joy, caution, and well-wishing.[4]

Marcus Aurelius admired the discourses of Epictetus, though he never met the man. Despite their vast difference in social standing, both men belonged to the

[2] Lucian, *Runaways* 10–11.
[3] Paul Zanker, *The Mask of Socrates: The Image of the Intellectual in Antiquity* (Berkeley: University of California Press, 1995).
[4] Epictetus, *The Discourses, The Handbook, Fragments*, ed. and trans. Christopher Gill and Robin Hard (London: Everyman, 1995). See further A. A. Long, *Epictetus: A Stoic and Socratic Guide to Life* (Oxford: Oxford University Press, 2002), esp. 7–37, 244–54.

same (Stoic) school of thought. Marcus's main work of philosophy, the *Meditations*, remains famous today. It was written on the war front in central Europe between about 170–180 CE. The work was Marcus's tireless attempt at self-improvement and self-motivation. Burdened with the weight of empire, the emperor had to encourage himself to perform his duties – not only in the freezing winter months, but during all seasons in the midst of plague, war, and a court buzzing with sycophants. Marcus had the noted ability to redirect his internal eye away from the worries and anxieties of the day and toward the stillness of eternity. His philosophy was therapy, and his doctrines were medicines soothing the "diseases" of the passions.[5]

A key representative of the Epicurean school at the time was Diogenes of Oenoanda (in modern southwestern Turkey). This wealthy patron funded a rectangular piazza on whose walls he had carved one of the largest inscriptions of antiquity – originally a hundred meters long with some 25,000 words chiseled into stone. Diogenes believed that people were infected by a plague – not of germs, but of false opinions. In his old age, therefore, Diogenes wanted to exhort his fellow citizens to exemplify the virtues by which he had lived, among them justice and mutual love. Diogenes inscribed his own words, but also those of his master Epicurus, the founder of the school which pursued the higher pleasures of life: friendship, serenity, and the acceptance of death.[6]

Not every philosopher at the time proffered a list of teachings. Some even denied the rationality of belief itself. Such was the belief – or rather hypothesis – of Sextus Empiricus, who thrived, in all likelihood, during the late second century CE. Sextus believed that to every argument another argument could be opposed, and for every reason to believe in something there were equal or better reasons not to believe it. In his *Outlines of Pyrrhonism*, he recommended the suspension of belief, especially regarding the central questions of human life – who we are, where we come from, whether there are gods, whether they care for us, what is the purpose of life, and what, if anything, comes after death.

Despite the warnings of philosophical skepticism and debate among the schools, Platonism was slowly edging toward dominance in the field. The most popular Platonic dialogue was the *Timaeus*, Plato's "likely story" of creation, put in the mouth of an ancient Pythagorean from southern Italy. Plato took over and adapted several ideas attributed to Pythagoras – the famous sage and mathematician of southern Italy. Some of Plato's heirs continued this trend, to such an extent that they formed a Neopythagorean revival in the first century BCE which flourished for the next two centuries.

---

[5] *The Meditations of Marcus Aurelius Antoninus*, trans. A. S. L. Farquharson (Oxford: Oxford University Press, 1990). See further Pierre Hadot, *The Inner Citadel: The Meditations of Marcus Aurelius* (Cambridge, MA: Harvard University Press, 1998).

[6] See further Martin Ferguson Smith, *Diogenes of Oinoanda: The Epicurean Inscription* (Naples: Bibliopolis, 1993); Martin Ferguson Smith, *Supplement to Diogenes of Oinoanda: The Epicurean Inscription* (Naples: Bibliopolis, 2003); Diskin Clay, "The Philosophical Inscription of Diogenes of Oenoanda," *Bulletin of the Classical Studies* 1 (2007): 283–91.

The Platonist Plutarch (about 40–125 CE), for instance, showed interest in Pythagorean numerology and was inclined toward vegetarianism.[7] He studied in Athens and Alexandria before becoming a philosopher, orator, and diplomat. Living in Rome for more than a decade, he rubbed shoulders with several leading lights and won Roman citizenship. As an older man, Plutarch served as priest of Apollo at Delphi.[8] During this time, he perfected the genre of moralizing, comparative biography.

Numenius (thrived around 150 CE) was a Platonist who saw Plato as preserving and clarifying the thought of Pythagoras. Numenius had an interest in confirming Platonic doctrines in "Barbarian" philosophies (Syrian, Egyptian, Jewish, and so on). Following the *Timaeus*, he distinguished the creator from the "primal God," also called "the Good itself," and "Father."[9] Numenius believed in a triad of three deities: the Father and two aspects of the creator – the one who contemplates the Father, and the one divided by his interest in matter. The primal God sowed the seeds of souls, and the creator planted them. The souls' fall into the world was a tragedy, and the point of life is to escape physical existence, rise above this world, and contemplate the Father.[10]

Apuleius (about 125–190 CE) was another leading Platonist of the era. Born in Madauros (in modern-day Algeria), he received the finest education in rhetoric at the provincial capital of Carthage. The young orator then moved to Athens to pursue studies in poetry, music, and geometry. Though once put on trial for being a magician, he represented himself as a philosopher. He grew wealthy as a public speaker in Greece and attained high office in Africa. His novel *Metamorphoses* – the adventures of a man turned into a donkey – evince the comic, playful side of his personality as well as his interest in eastern religions. By 161 CE, Apuleius was back in Carthage where he gave speeches and published philosophical essays such as *On the God of Socrates* and *On Plato and His Teachings*.[11]

---

[7] Plutarch, *E Delphi* 387f.

[8] For Plutarch, see further John Dillon, *The Middle Platonists 80 BCE to AD 220*, 2nd ed. (Ithaca: Cornell University Press, 1996), 185–92; Tomas Hägg, *The Art of Biography in Antiquity* (Cambridge: Cambridge University Press, 2012), 239–81; Frederick E. Brenk, *On Plutarch: Religious Thinker and Biographer* (Leiden: Brill, 2017), 10–24.

[9] Numenius, frag. 12, 16 (des Places).

[10] Numenius, frags. 12-13, 16, 21 (des Places). See further Dillon, *Middle Platonists*, 361–79; John D. Turner, *Sethian Gnosticism and the Platonic Tradition* (Laval: Laval University Press, 2001), 385–9; Richard T. Wallis, "Soul and Nous in Plotinus, Numenius and Gnosticism," in *Neoplatonism and Gnosticism*, ed. Richard T. Wallis and Jay Bregman (Albany: SUNY Press, 1992), 461–82; M. J. Edwards, "Atticizing Moses? Numenius, the Fathers and the Jews," *VC* 44, no. 1 (1990): 64–75; Jan Opsomer, "Demiurges in Early Imperial Platonism," in *Gott und die Götter bei Plutarch: Götterbilder-Gottesbilder-Weltbilder*, ed. Rainer Hirsch-Luipold (Berlin: de Gruyter, 2005), 51–99 at 66–73.

[11] See further Stephen Harrison, ed., *Apuleius: Rhetorical Works* (Oxford: Oxford University Press, 2001), 185–94; Harrison, *Apuleius: A Latin Sophist* (Oxford: Oxford University Press, 2004); Richard Fletcher, *Apuleius's Platonism* (Cambridge: Cambridge University Press, 2014), 111–72; Dillon, *Middle Platonists*, 306–38.

Apuleius's work *On Plato* is a handy introduction to second-century Platonism and is complimented by another *Handbook of Platonism* written by an otherwise unknown man called Alcinous. Both handbooks represent a particular phase of Platonism called "Middle Platonism," whose theological doctrines can here be summarized: a transcendent, bodiless deity – sometimes called "the Good" – abides in eternal peace and self-contemplation far above the heavens. A lower being, the creator, made the heavens and the earth after the model existing in the mind of the Good.[12] This world is the best of all possible worlds governed by mediating deities called "daimones" (who are both good and bad).[13] The soul is naturally immortal. Suffering is necessary to train the soul for virtue. Virtue is the domination of "the passions" – raging emotions like fear, anger, jealousy, and greed.[14] The purest part of the soul is the mind (*nous*), considered to be the true, bodiless self, the element most like God and called to be more divine.[15]

One can see why early Christian intellectuals like Justin Martyr came to favor such a philosophy. Plato's "Good," though technically beyond being and deity, closely conformed to their summodeistic ideal.[16] Some Christians identified the Platonic creator (or "demiurge") with the God who spoke in the book of Genesis. Angels fulfilled the function of daimones. Suffering provided a connection to God.[17] The soul is immortal – by God's grace. Life is a battle against the passions, passions that rage until the soul, envelope of the mind, finds release from the body. These doctrines later became as much Christian as they were Platonic.

Literature, Medicine, Astronomy

The second century was the heyday of the romantic novel with the appearance of works like Xenophon's *Ephesian Tale*, *Leucippe and Clitophon* by Achilles Tatius, and Longus's *Daphnis and Chloe*.[18] The novel had a significant influence on Christian fiction, mostly in the Acts literature which related romantic – or rather

---

[12] Atticus was an exception by identifying the creator with the Good (Dillon, *Middle Platonists*, 254).

[13] See further M. David Litwa, *Posthuman Transformation: Becoming Angels and Demons* (Cambridge: Cambridge University Press, 2021), 9–14.

[14] See further Simo Knuuttila, *Emotions in Ancient and Medieval Philosophy* (Oxford: Oxford University Press, 2010); Francesco Becchi, "The Doctrine of the Passions: Plutarch, Posidonius and Galen," in *Plutarch in the Religious and Philosophical Discourse*, ed. Lautaro Roig Lanzillotta and Israel Munoz Gallarte (Leiden: Brill, 2012), 43–53.

[15] On second-century Platonism, see Alcinous, *Handbook of Platonism*, trans. John Dillon (Oxford: Clarendon, 1993), esp. chs. 10, 12, 15–17, 25–32, 35. See further Dillon, *Middle Platonists*, 267–304.

[16] See further *Monotheism between Pagans and Christians in Late Antiquity*, ed. Stephen Mitchell and Peter van Nuffelen (Leuven: Peeters, 2010).

[17] Judith Perkins, *The Suffering Self: Pain and Narrative Representation in the Early Christian Era* (London: Routledge, 1995).

[18] These novels are translated in B. P. Reardon, *Collected Ancient Greek Novels* (Berkeley: University of California Press, 2008). See further G. Schmeling, ed., *The Novel in the Ancient World*

anti-romantic – tales about apostles travelling into new territory and detaching wives from high-profile husbands.[19]

Lucian, a Syrian from what is now eastern Turkey, wrote mostly in the genre of satire. His works were aimed to burst the proverbial bubble of schmoozing politicians, local religious leaders, and pompous philosophers. Lucian had a keen interest in religious cults, criticized animal sacrifice, and thrilled in pointing out the oddity of local customs. Lucian also showed an interest in Cynic philosophers, lauding one (Demonax) while lambasting another (Peregrinus). Peregrinus had at least a brief stint as a Christian leader and ended his life by throwing himself into a bonfire at the Olympic games (165 CE).[20]

The medical doctor Galen (about 129–217 CE) astonished crowds in Rome by dissections revealing his detailed knowledge of anatomy. He traced the nerves back to the brain and identified this organ as the center of human thought, motion, and feeling. He argued that knowledge was only certain when it stemmed from empirical premises and that only keen observation, not outdated theories, led to right diagnoses.[21]

In Alexandria, Claudius Ptolemy (flourished 125–160 CE) composed his handbook of mathematical astronomy, the *Almagest*. In this work, Ptolemy proved earth's spherical shape and argued for a geocentric cosmos with seven revolving planets. Ptolemy also published his *Tetrabiblos*, which sought to place astrology (the influence of stars and planets on human life) on scientific footing.

Religious Movements

Peoples of the ancient Mediterranean believed that "all things are full of gods" (a quote attributed to the ancient philosopher Thales).[22] These gods wanted to be known and worshiped according to ancient customs. Gods and daimones were not all-powerful. They protected and privileged certain locales where they received praise. Gods could be known by different names in different places. In the great family of Gods, there were central ones (the twelve Olympians led by Zeus) and peripheral daimones (like Pan and Priapus). The central ones were Panhellenic – universally recognizable among Greeks (called "Hellenes") and Hellenized peoples. In many areas outside Greece, local deities were assimilated to the Olympians (as happened early on in Rome where the king god Jupiter was identified with Zeus).

(Leiden: Brill, 2003); Tim Whitmarsh, ed., *The Cambridge Companion to the Greek and Roman Novel* (Cambridge: Cambridge University Press, 2008).

[19] See J. K. Elliott, *The Apocryphal New Testament* (Oxford: Oxford University Press, 1993), 229–590.

[20] On Lucian's biography, see Swain, *Hellenism and Empire*, 298–329; Daniel Richter, "Lives and Afterlives of Lucian of Samosata," *Arion* 13, no. 1 (2005): 75–100.

[21] On Galen, see further Swain, *Hellenism and Empire*, 357–79; J. Rocca, *Galen on the Brain: Anatomical Knowledge and Physiological Speculation in the Second Century AD* (Leiden: Brill, 2003); Susan P. Mattern, *The Prince of Medicine: Galen in the Roman Empire* (Oxford: Oxford University Press, 2013).

[22] Aristotle, *On the Soul* 1.5, 411a7.

Gods were worshiped primarily through sacrifice, from cutting the throats of blood-filled beasts, to the sprinkling of humble seeds of grain on a fire. Larger offerings of cattle were typical of state festivals. Lesser offerings were made at home – like libations (a tipping of the goblet to a god presiding over a banquet). Sacrifices were typically accompanied by formulaic prayers and gestures. In times of need, prayers were often accompanied by vows – promises to perform some action to proclaim the god's glory if events turned out well.

Gods were active and present in the lives of their worshipers through dreams, visions, and oracles. Oracles were big business in antiquity. Artemidorus, a dream interpreter in the vicinity of Ephesus, mentioned "dice-diviners, cheese-diviners, sieve-diviners, figure-readers, palm readers, dish-diviners, and necromancers" all offering their services in the streets of big cities.[23] Richer customers could visit official oracle shrines run by priests in gleaming temples.[24] Dreams and healings were sought in "sleep overs" (incubations) within temple chambers.[25]

Imperial Cult

The imperial cult was one of the few empire-wide forms of worship; it was state run, well-funded, and carefully organized. Cities competed with each other in order to house imperial temples, and one of the greatest privileges of the day was to become the priest of a particular emperor.[26] Thousands would gather at the imperial festivals, games, and spectacles held on the reigning emperor's birthday. The emperor was believed to be a god – though one of the lesser ones – worshiped with distinctive rites and often made a partner with a main god in well-known temples.

Translocal Cults

Although the Romans generally looked askance at cults not under their control, they could not halt their proliferation. The native cults of Egypt in honor of Isis and Serapis spread widely during this period. Converts shaved their heads and abstained from meat in preparation for expensive initiations. The initiations involved the vision of the gods, a newfound sense of privilege, and hope for the afterlife. In the account of Lucius, main character in Apuleius's *Metamorphoses*: "I approached the border of Death, tread the threshold of Proserpina [queen of the Underworld]; I

---

[23] Artemidorus, *Dream Interpretation* 2.69. See the edition of Daniel E. Harris-McCoy, *Oneirocritica: Text Translation, and Commentary* (Oxford: Oxford University Press, 2012).

[24] The province of Asia was famous for two large oracle shrines: Claros (near the city of Colophon) and Didyma (near Miletus).

[25] See Aelius Aristides's *Sacred Tales* translated by Charles A. Behr, *The Complete Works, Volume II* (Leiden: Brill, 1981), 278–353.

[26] Steve Friesen, *Twice Neokoros: Ephesus, Asia, and the Cult of the Flavian Imperial Family* (Leiden: Brill, 1993); Barbara Burrell, *Neokoroi: Greek Cities and Roman Emperors* (Leiden: Brill, 2004), 270–87, 331–42.

travelled through every element; at midnight I saw the sun shimmering in clear light; I approached the gods below and the gods above face to face, and I worshiped them close by."[27]

The cult of Cybele, Mother of the gods, and Attis the Phrygian shepherd had long been established in Rome. Although few men followed the priests of Attis in their ritual of self-castration, people of all kinds gawked at their raucous processions in late March. Cybele was commemorated on the coins of Commodus. At Cybele's Roman festival one year, Commodus narrowly escaped a conspiracy to kill him. He gave the Mother credit for his salvation.[28]

Judaism was perceived as a foreign, but recognized religion, one that had long been transplanted into several Greco-Roman cities. With one terrible exception between 115–117 CE, Jews in the "Diaspora," or wider world beyond Judea, proved to be loyal and productive subjects. They built ornate synagogues in many Mediterranean cities, added to the economic vibrancy of major centers, and became local benefactors. Jewish intellectuals like Philo of Alexandria (about 20 BCE–50 CE) offered a philosophical variant of Judaism featuring an imageless, transcendent God and a clear code of ethics (the Mosaic Law). New translations of this Law were being made as the old, standard translation (called "the Seventy" or "Septuagint") was increasingly abandoned to the Christians. Jews boasted of being older than the Greeks and closer to the wellsprings of wisdom. They succeeded in attracting (some prominent) converts (or proselytes) who could attend synagogue services without undergoing full initiation through circumcision.

Emerging Religious Currents

The cult of Mithras, taken to be a Persian deity related to the sun, gained traction especially among Roman soldiers in the second century. It also provided those of middling social status (freedmen, slaves, shopkeepers) with a new sense of identity. Seven grades of initiation led to the holy office of "father." Communal meals in a "cave" or underground chamber fostered a sense of comradery. The secrets of the cult remain buried because no theological treatises were written (at least they do not survive). Mithraic iconography (most famously the tauroctony, a depiction of Mithras slaying a bull) survives, however, and continues to inspire a rich crop of speculation.[29]

---

[27] The key source here is Apuleius, *Metamorphoses* 11.23. See the commentary in S. J. Harrison et al., *Apuleius Madaurensis Metamorphoses Book XI: The Isis Book* (Leiden: Brill, 2015).

[28] Mattingly and Sydenham, eds., *Roman Imperial Coinage*, vol. 3. (London: Spink, 1923–94).

[29] On Mithras, see Roger Beck, *The Religion of the Mithras Cult in the Roman Empire: Mysteries of the Unconquered Sun* (Oxford: Oxford University Press, 2006); Richard Gordon, "Ritual and Hierarchy in the Mysteries of Mithras," in *The Religious History of the Roman Empire: Pagans, Jews, and Christians*, ed. J. A. North and S. R. F. Price (Oxford: Oxford University Press, 2011), 325–65; Luther H. Martin, *The Mind of Mithraists: Historical and Cognitive Studies in the Roman Cult of Mithras* (London: Bloomsbury, 2015); Olympia Panagiotidou, *The Roman Mithras Cult: A Cognitive Approach* (London: Bloomsbury, 2017).

In Egypt, treatises associated with the god Thoth, or Hermes Thrice Great, began to appear. At one time, these treatises were considered purely literary products of Greek philosophy, spiced up with a few Egyptian characters and local color. Today, Egyptian emphases and inspiration in the literature are more properly observed.[30] References to "pure food,"[31] a ritual embrace,[32] and formal prayers[33] suggest to some scholars both a ritual and community life. Some theorize more boldly about a Hermetic "way" that involved "a sequence of concrete ritual practices, some regular, some occasional, some temporary, others developing as a consequence of the disciple's formation."[34] Under the guidance of a teacher, Hermetic initiates progressed from a dualistic view of the world to a monistic one in which God, often depicted as cosmic mind, was all in all.[35] Hermetic writings continued to be read in fourth-century Egypt, and three of them (two excerpts and a complete treatise, the *Discourse on the Eighth and Ninth*) were found at Nag Hammadi.[36]

For an example of a new religious movement with a known founder we can turn to Alexander of Abonuteichos. Alexander had the skill and audacity to establish a new oracle in Paphlagonia (modern north central Turkey). Alexander was able to convince the locals that the healing god Asclepius had been reborn in the form of a snake. This snake – a large python named Glycon – Alexander wrapped underneath his robes and outfitted with a human-like head poking out from the top. In this fashion, Alexander became the god's spokesman. People sent him sealed slips of paper which Alexander read, resealed, and responded to in poetic verse. The answers convinced a great number of people, including a Roman governor who ended up marrying Alexander's daughter. Other people – Epicureans and Christians especially – scorned the new rites and were debarred from Glycon's sanctuary.

Christianity was the daughter or sister of Judaism, depending on one's point of view. Only in the second century, it seems, did Roman elites begin to take note of it as a separate and threatening "superstition." Christians, although they often claimed antiquity, seemed novel and curious to ancient Romans. Christians worshiped a man

---

[30] Thomas McAllister Scott, "Egyptian Elements in Hermetic Literature" (Ph.D. diss., Harvard Divinity School, 1987); Bull, *Tradition of Hermes*, 33–190, 427–55.

[31] *Prayer of Thanksgiving* VI,7 65.6.

[32] *Disc. 8-9* VI,6, 57.26-27; *Prayer of Thanksgiving* VI,7, 65.4.

[33] For example, *The Prayer of Thanksgiving* VI,7, parallel to *Ascl.* 41.

[34] Van den Kerchove, *Voie*, 374–5. See further S. Giversen, "Hermetic Communities?" in *Rethinking Religion: Studies in the Hellenistic Process*, ed. J. P. Sorensen (Copenhagen: Museum Tusculanum, 1989), 49–54; Gebhard Löhr, *Verherrlichung Gottes durch Philosophie: Der hermetische Traktat II im Rahmen der antiken Philosophie- und Religionsgeschicthe* (Tübingen: Mohr Siebeck, 1997), 385–97.

[35] Bull, *Tradition of Hermes*, 191–243.

[36] See Marvin Meyer, ed., *Nag Hammadi Scriptures: The International Edition* (New York: HarperOne, 2008), 409–36. Introductions to the Coptic Hermetica can be found in ibid., 409–12, 419–21, 425–9; Mahé, *Hermes en Haute-Égypte*, 1:31–51, 137–55, 2:47–144; Hans-Martin Schenke, Hans-Gebhard Bethge and Ursula Ulrike Kaiser, ed., *Nag Hammadi Deutsch: Studienausgabe* (Berlin: de Gruyter, 2007), 359–60, 367–8, 370–1.

executed as a criminal by the Roman state during the reign of a known emperor (Tiberius). They had communal meals in private settings only open to initiates. In time, there arose rumors of terrible crimes – group orgies and baby-killing – all thought to take place in secret.[37] Early Christians – who ate the body and blood of a crucified Judean – had a hard time making themselves understood.

Eventually Christian intellectuals (so-called Apologists) began to write tracts explaining Christian beliefs and practices to outsiders.[38] Despite their efforts, Christian groups continued to be distrusted and occasionally arrested, mostly in reaction to natural disasters and civil disturbances.[39] A budding class of Christian intellectuals worked hard to prove the respectability of Christian thought and morals. The early Christian struggle for the scarce resource of symbolic capital in part explains why some Christians turned on each other. If some forms of Christianity could be depicted as subaltern and bizarre, that would establish the positive distinctiveness of other – supposedly rational and moral – forms of Christianity. In this struggle to attain acceptance and distinctiveness, many Christians were de-Christianized by their own kind. It is their stories and ideas that, in what follows, we are now prepared to relate.

Further Reading

A. R. Birley, "Hadrian to the Antonines," in *Cambridge Ancient History, Volume 11: The High Empire, AD 70–192*, ed. Alan K. Bowman, Peter Garnsey, and Dominic Rathbone (Cambridge: Cambridge University Press, 2000), 132–94.

Mary T. Boatwright, *Hadrian and the Cities of the Roman Empire* (Princeton: Princeton University Press, 2000).

Peter Garnsey and Richard Saller, *The Roman Empire: Economy, Society and Culture*, 2d ed. (London: Bloomsbury, 2014).

Martin Goodman and Jane Sherwood, *The Roman World 44 BC–AD 180* (London: Routledge, 1997), 67–75.

Michael Grant, *The Antonines: The Roman Empire in Transition* (London: Routledge, 1994).

Harry O. Maier, *New Testament Christianity in the Roman World* (Oxford: Oxford University Press, 2018).

Daniel S. Richter and William A. Johnson, eds., *The Oxford Handbook of the Second Sophistic* (Oxford: Oxford University Press, 2017).

Chris Scarre, *Chronicle of the Roman Emperors* (London: Thames & Hudson, 1995).

Simon Swain, *Hellenism and Empire: Language, Classicism and Power in the Greek World AD 50–250* (Oxford: Clarendon, 1996).

Simon Swain, Stephen Harrison, and Jaś Elsner, *Severan Culture* (Cambridge: Cambridge University Press, 2007).

---

[37] Robert M. Grant, "Charges of Immorality against Various Religious Groups in Antiquity," in *Studies in Gnosticism and Hellenistic Religions presented to Gilles Quispel*, ed. M. J. Vermaseren and Roelof van den Broek (Leiden: Brill, 1981), 161–70. See also Jennifer Knust, *Abandoned to Lust: Sexual Slander and Ancient Christianity* (New York: Columbia University Press, 2005).

[38] See further Robert M. Grant, *Greek Apologists of the Second Century* (London: SCM, 1988).

[39] See further Candida R. Moss, *Ancient Christian Martyrdom: Diverse Practices, Theologies, and Traditions* (New Haven: Yale University Press, 2012).

Part One

Early Christian Leaders
and their Movements

Cerinthus and John

Introduction

The aim of this chapter is to introduce Cerinthus, a Christian leader of Asia Minor in the late first and early second centuries CE. In order to contextualize Cerinthus's thought, however, we begin with the gospel that seems to have influenced him the most, the one commonly labeled John. Studying John will give us an opportunity to see how Cerinthus's view of Christ and creation emerged from a reading of gospel literature.

There are, of course, endless studies on the gospel of John, and only a brief introduction can be offered here. The gospel of John is a late first- or early second-century narrative about Jesus purporting to go back to the memories of an otherwise unknown "beloved disciple." If this "beloved disciple" is not a fictional character, he seems to be an idealized one.[1] Readers need not identify him with John, son of Zebedee, one of Jesus's earliest disciples. "John's" gospel was probably written during the reigns of the emperors Nerva or Trajan. The author, who does not identify himself as an apostle, is – in all honesty – unknown, and is not necessarily a single person. There may have been one author in addition to one or several editors who revised and added material to John. The twenty-first chapter of the gospel, for instance, is widely thought of as a later addition, and this may also be the case for the majestically written prologue (John 1:1-18).

The author(s) of John appealed to and sought to undermine certain competing social groups, whether these groups were imagined or real. In the prologue, the gospel takes pains to demote a figure called John the Baptist who, it seems, continued to have a following long after his execution in Judea (Mark 6:17-29). John chapter 4 presents the Samaritans in central Palestine as swiftly accepting Jesus's message – initially through the lips of a single female witness (unnamed). A Roman court official and

---

[1] See further Ismo Dunderberg, *The Beloved Disciple in Conflict? Revisiting the Gospels of John and Thomas* (Oxford & New York: Oxford University Press, 2006); Harold W. Attridge, *Essays on John and Hebrews* (Grand Rapids: Baker Academic, 2012).

a group of "Greeks" also show interest in Jesus's message later in the text (4:46-54; 12:20-26).

If there was a specific audience addressed by the author(s) of John, one suspects that it was varied.[2] It may have included a Samaritan contingent.[3] (At one point, Jesus himself is called a Samaritan, though as an intended insult, John 8:48.) One might also suspect that the Johannine author competed with several baptizing groups who looked to John the Baptist as their model (cf. Acts 19:1-7).[4] Since both Samaritans and the baptizing groups were concentrated in Palestine, it is a reasonable guess to place the Johannine writer somewhere in this region (including Galilee and Syria). The author's knowledge of Palestinian topography supports this view.[5] Naturally, many other potential locations have been proposed, most popularly Ephesus and Alexandria.

Opposition to Local Jews

If the author(s) of John took a swipe at local baptizing groups, their central enemy was a group labeled with the blanket term "the Jews" or "Judeans" (*Ioudaioi*).[6] This

---

[2] Opponents of a Johannine community point out that the term "community" is vague and that the Johannine group was not a "sect" in modern sociological terms. See, e.g., Kåre Sigvald Fuglseth, *Johannine Sectarianism in Perspective: A Sociological, Historical, and Comparative Analysis of the Temple and Social Relationships in the Gospel of John, Philo, and Qumran* (Leiden: Brill, 2005), 67–86; E. W. Klink, *The Sheep of the Fold: The Audience and Origin of the Gospel of John* (Cambridge: Cambridge University Press, 2007); D. A. Lamb, *Text, Context and the Johannine Community: A Sociolinguistic Analysis of the Johannine Writings* (London: Bloomsbury, 2014); R. Hakola, *Reconsidering Johannine Christianity: A Social Identify Approach* (London: Routledge, 2015); Hugo Méndez, "Did the Johannine Community Exist?" *JSNT* 42.3 (2020): 350–74. For reassertions of the community hypothesis, see Maarten J. J. Menken, *Studies in John's Gospel and Epistles: Collected Essays* (Leuven: Peeters, 2015), 57–71; Martinus C. de Boer, "The Story of the Johannine Community and Its Literature," in *The Oxford Handbook of Johannine Studies*, ed. Judith M. Lieu and Martinus C. de Boer (Oxford: Oxford University Press, 2018), 65–80.

[3] On Samaritans and John, see, e.g., H. G. Kippenberg, *Garizim und Synagoge. Traditionsgeschichtliche Untersuchungen zur Samaritanischen Religion der Aramäischen Periode* (Berlin: de Gruyter, 1971), 345–9; Charles H. H. Scobie, "The Origins and Development of Samaritan Christianity," *NTS* 19 (1973): 390–414; James D. Purvis, "The Fourth Gospel and the Samaritans," *NovT* 17 (1975): 161–98; Jarl Fossum, *Name of God and the Angel of the Lord* (Leiden: Brill, 1985), 27–45.

[4] Joel Marcus, *John the Baptist in History and Theology* (Columbia: University of South Carolina Press, 2018), 12–26.

[5] See further Klaus Wengst, *Bedrängte Gemeinde und verherrlichter Christus: Der historische Ort des Johannesevangeliums also Schlüssel zu seiner Interpretation* (Neukirchen-Vluyn: Neukirchener Verlag, 1981), esp. 77–93; Michael Theobald, *Das Evangelium nach Johannes. Kapitel 1–12* (Regensburg: Friedrich Pustet, 2009), 96–8.

[6] Controversy continues on whether to translate Ἰουδαῖος by "Jew" or "Judean" (Shaye Cohen, *The Beginnings of Jewishness: Boundaries, Varieties, Uncertainties* [Berkeley: University of California Press, 1999], 69–106; Steve Mason, "Jews, Judeans, Judaizing, Judaism: Problems of Categorization in Ancient History," *JSJ* 38 [2007]: 457–512; Annette Y. Reed, *Jewish-Christianity and the History of Judaism* [Tübingen: Mohr Siebeck, 2018], 474–88). "Judean" brings out a geopolitical

is an imagined group that, in contrast to the Samaritans, rejected Jesus as a divine being (John 5:10-18; 6:41, 52; 8:40-59). Consequently, the Jesus of the narrative fostered an oppositional relationship to the Judeans and their Law.

The author(s) of John did not outright reject Jewish Law (Torah). They did, however, throw doubt upon it and its reputed author, Moses. The programmatic statement that, "the Law was given through Moses; grace and truth came through Jesus Christ" (John 1:17) implicitly contrasts the Law and truth. The following statement, "No one has ever seen God" (1:18) contradicts the Law's claim that Moses conversed with God "face to face" (Exod. 33:11, 23). Jesus told a man to carry a burden on the Sabbath (5:8), something thought to be prohibited by Mosaic Law.[7] His later statement that "all" who came before him were "thieves and brigands" (10:8) would seem to include Moses and the prophets.[8]

Opposition to Jewish Law easily shifted to opposition towards the Judeans themselves. Judeans are portrayed as casting out of their synagogues anyone who accepted Jesus's divine identity (John 9:22; 12:42; 16:2). The expulsion language may reflect the historical situation in the late first century CE when Jewish followers of Jesus felt the pressure of exclusion from more traditional Jewish networks in Palestine and Syria. Whether or not there *were* expulsions, however, remains an open question.[9]

Ritual Practice

Johannine Christians evidently practiced the rituals later known as baptism and the Eucharist. Unlike John the Baptist, Jesus putatively offered a baptism "in the holy Spirit" (John 1:33). He proffered the Samaritan woman "living water" leaping up unto eternal life (4:10, 14). Jesus's statement that "unless one is born from water and Spirit" assumes that his baptism bestows the Spirit (3:5). Jesus himself was

---

sense and is generally preferred in this study. On John's Ἰουδαῖοι, see R. Hakola, *Identity Matters: John, the Jews and Jewishness* (Leiden: Brill, 2005), 10–15; Adele Reinhartz, *Cast Out of the Covenant: Jews and Anti-Judaism in the Gospel of John* (Lanham: Lexington-Fortress Academic, 2018), 93–108.

[7] Jer. 17:19-27; cf. Neh. 13:15-19; Exod. 21:12-17; Num. 15:32-36; *Jub.* 2:29-30; 50:8; *Damascus Document* 11:7-8; *m. Šabb.* 7.2–9.7 (the thirty-ninth prohibition of labor); 10.5.

[8] Christ's statement that "no one has ascended into heaven" apart from himself (John 3:13), contradicts the reputed ascensions of Enoch and Elijah (Gen. 5:24; 2 Kgs 2:1). See April D. DeConick, *Seek to See Him: Ascent and Vision Mysticism in the Gospel of Thomas* (Leiden: Brill, 1996), 72–3; Hakola, *Identity Matters*, 215–21; William Loader, "Jesus and the Law in John," in *Theology and Christology in the Fourth Gospel: Essays by the Members of the SNTS Johannine Writings Seminar*, ed. G. van Belle, J. G. van der Watt, and P. Maritz (Leuven: Leuven University Press, 2005), 135–54.

[9] See further J. Louis Martyn, *History and Theology of the Fourth Gospel*, 3rd ed. (Louisville: Westminster John Knox, 2003), 46–68; John Kloppenborg, "Disaffiliation in Associations and the ἀποσυναγωγός of John," *HTS Teologiese Studies/Theological Studies* 67, no. 1 (2011): 1–16; Martinus de Boer, "Expulsion from the Synagogue: J. L. Martyn's *History and Theology in the Fourth Gospel* Revisited," *NTS* 66, no. 3 (2020): 367–91.

the source of "living water" (19:34). Jesus is said to have baptized more people than John the Baptist himself – though Jesus's disciples were responsible for this (4:1-2).[10]

John 6 presents a distinctive theory of the Eucharist (or Lord's Supper). The Supper was not just a memorial of Jesus, but an event in which Christians truly ate (literally "chewed") his flesh and blood (6:51-58). That this theory caused offense among Judeans – even Judean followers of Jesus – is indicated by the fact that when Jesus's disciples learned of it, many took umbrage and abandoned him (vv. 60-68).[11]

The Father of the Jews

John's prologue distinguishes between the supreme God and the creator called the Logos (traditionally translated "Word," but "Reason," "Mind," and even "Story" are possible translations). The Logos was a divine being who at some point (we are not told when) became Jesus (1:14). Jesus's divine identity proved to be a powder keg of conflict. In context, there was a dispute about the nature of God more generally. According to John, no one had ever seen, let alone known, God. Only the Logos, the only-born god, had both seen and explained him (John 1:18; 6:46).

> **Sidelight on the Unknown God.** The transcendent, unknown God was a staple doctrine in Middle Platonic theology. It was Plato who declared that the maker and father of this universe was hard to find and impossible to declare (*Timaeus* 28c). He later denied that the supreme being – called the One – could be known or named (*Parmenides* 142a). Cicero wrote that the Father of this world could not be named (*Nat. d.* 1.30). Alcinous called God "ineffable," possessing neither good nor bad attributes, beyond all qualities, attributes, and parts.[12] Apuleius called God "unspoken, unnamed … invisible, unmastered."[13] Many Christian descriptions of God in the second century used similar language for the Christian deity.

[10] See further Marcus, *John the Baptist*, 86–7.
[11] Raymond Brown, *New Testament Essays* (New York: Image Books, 1965), 83–136; Menken, *Studies*, 285–308; Udo Schnelle, *Antidocetic Christology in the Gospel of John: An Investigation of the Place of the Fourth Gospel in the Johannine School*, trans. Linda M. Maloney (Minneapolis: Fortress, 1992), 176–210. References to anointing (e.g., 1 John 2:20) and foot washing (John 13) are too tenuous to infer sacramental practice.
[12] Alcinous, *Handbook* 10.4.
[13] Apuleius, *Plato and his Doctrine* 5. See further Curtis L. Hancock, "Negative Theology in Gnosticism and Neoplatonism," in *Neoplatonism and Gnosticism*, ed. Richard T. Wallis, and Jay Bregman (Albany: SUNY Press, 1992), 167–86; Deirdre Carabine, *The Unknown God: Negative Theology in the Platonic Tradition: Plato to Eriugena* (Leuven: Peeters, 1995), 13–278; Michael A. Williams, "Negative Theologies and Demiurgical Myths in Late Antiquity," in *Gnosticism and Later Platonism: Themes, Figures, and Texts*, ed. Ruth Majercik and John D. Turner (Atlanta: Scholars Press, 2000), 277–302.

John's Jesus claims to have been sent from his Father to do his Father's works (10:36-37). His Judean opponents, by and large, fail to recognize him and despise his "signs" (miracles) – which include the raising of a man four-days dead (11). Jesus accuses them of spiritual blindness (9:41; 12:39-40). Their blindness was naturalized by the cultural practice of genealogizing. The Judeans in the story cannot understand Jesus because, Jesus tells them, they have a different father.

The true "father" of these Judeans is revealed in a heated speech during the Feast of Tabernacles (John 7:2). Jesus begins by declaring himself to be "the light of the world" (8:12), a claim that his opponents take as invalid self-testimony. Jesus invokes his "father" as a second witness, a being whom the Judeans, according to Jesus, do not and have not known (8:19, 55). Similarly in John 5:37, Jesus tells them that they have never heard the voice of his Father nor seen his form.

If Jesus's Father is taken to be the Judean deity (known in modern literature as "Yahweh," or "the Lord"), Jesus asserts that the Judeans do not know their own god. This statement flies in the face of Jewish tradition. In the revelation at Sinai, Yahweh's "back" was seen atop a blazing mountain.[14] Isaiah testified, "I saw the Lord" (6:2), and "the word of the Lord came to me" is a constant refrain.[15] Moses, as already mentioned, conversed with Yahweh face to face (Exod. 33:11, 23). One is gradually led to infer that Jesus's father is a different being than Yahweh. Otherwise it is difficult to explain how the Judeans know their own god and not Jesus's Father.

The Judeans in the story declare that "God" is their father (8:41). Jesus denies this point. He identifies "God" as his Father, and if the Judeans truly loved God, then they would love Jesus as well (8:42). Jesus explicitly remarks that these Jews are not from God (v.47). Jesus is not content to identify his Father with the being the Judeans call "God." Jesus's father is God, and this being is not the father of the Judeans (8:47).

Jesus tells the Judeans that the devil – or the devil's father – is their sire (the Greek of John 8:44 is ambiguous).[16] In this way, Jesus demotes the Judeans from their status as God's children, though Jewish scripture, and the Judeans themselves (John 8:41) vociferously contend the opposite.[17] Evidently, then, Jesus identifies Yahweh, the Judean god, with the devil, or identifies Yahweh as the devil's father. In either interpretation, the Judean deity is not the Father of Jesus Christ.

---

[14] Cf. Exod. 19:16-25; Deut. 4:11-12, 33.

[15] E.g., Mic. 1:1; Ezek. 20:5. For Isaiah's vision, cf. *Ascension of Isaiah* 3:8-9.

[16] ὑμεῖς ἐκ τοῦ πατρὸς τοῦ διαβόλου ἐστὲ. See April D. DeConick, "Why Are the Heavens Closed? The Johannine Revelation of the Father in the Catholic–Gnostic Debate," in *John's Gospel and Intimations of Apocalyptic*, ed. Catrin H. Williams and Christopher Rowland (London: Bloomsbury, 2013), 147–79 at 150, 168; St. R. Llewelyn, A. Robinson, and B. E. Wassell, "Does John 8:44 Imply that the Devil has a Father? Contesting the Pro-Gnostic Reading," *NovT* 60 (2018): 14–23.

[17] Exod. 4:22; Deut. 14:1; Isa. 63:16; Hos. 11:1; Mal. 2:10; *Jub.* 1:24-28; 2:20; 19:29-30. See further Marianne Meye Thompson, *The Promise of the Father: Jesus and God in the New Testament* (Louisville: Westminster John Knox, 2000), 35–55; Hermann Spieckermann, "The 'Father' of the Old Testament and Its History," in *The Divine Father: Religious and Philosophical Concepts of Divine Parenthood in Antiquity*, ed. Felix Albrecht and Reinhard Feldmeier (Leiden: Brill, 2014), 73–84.

Indeed, the Judean deity seems to be imagined as wicked. Jesus says that the Judeans wish to do the desires of their father (8:44). What are these desires? We can only infer them from the analogous desires of the children. The fictional Judeans wish to kill Jesus, albeit in secret. As the narrative climaxes, they plot and scheme how to do so (John 8:40; 18:31; 19:6, 15). The implication is that their father, the Judean "god," also (secretly) wants to murder him. And not only that: Yahweh is also working behind the scenes to destroy Jesus through his children, the Judeans.

In the gospel of John another character, called "the ruler of this world" (John 12:31; 14:30), stands in opposition to Jesus. This figure is typically taken to be the devil. But Yahweh as the world's creator and lord is also a logical candidate. And if Jesus called Yahweh or his father "the devil" in 8:44, we should perhaps not think of the devil as a separate character. Granting for the moment that "the ruler of this world" is the Judean deity, then it is this deity who mounts an attack upon Jesus. "The ruler of the world is coming," Jesus warns (John 14:30). Even though the ruler had no case against Jesus, he crucifies him nonetheless. Yet if Yahweh actually kills Jesus through his human agents, then he is not the true God, but – as Jesus says – a liar and a murderer (8:44). He is a liar because he pretended to be the true God in Jewish scripture and the Judeans believed him (8:54). He is a murderer because he killed the sinless Christ.

From the perspective of the Johannine author(s), the children of Yahweh (the Judeans in the story) persecuted Christians not only because Christians violated divine monarchy (by including Jesus into the Godhead), but also because the Judeans worshiped the *wrong* deity, a devilish being who through his human agents attacked and killed Jesus.[18]

Authorship

Based on this evidence, we can attempt to further clarify who wrote the gospel of John.[19] According to Epiphanius, several early Christians (whom he named "Alogi") said that Johannine literature was authored by a man called Cerinthus.[20] Epiphanius was seconded by Filastrius, a heresiographer who wrote in Italy about 380 CE.[21] Given the nearly complete lack of historical information about the author of John, this is a fascinating, if not necessarily reliable, piece of data.

---

[18] Some of the language in this section ("The Father of the Jews") adapts statements in my article "The Father of the Devil (John 8:44): A Christian Exegetical Inspiration for the Evil Creator," *VC* 74, no. 5 (2020): 540–65.

[19] In the next two subsections, I am heavily dependent on DeConick, *Gnostic New Age*, 155–9, with whom I agree, and politely disagree, on many points.

[20] Epiphanius, *Pan.* 51.3.6; cf. 28.1-2. According to Irenaeus, *AH* 3.11.9, there were people who "reject … the gospel [John]" (*evangelium … repellunt*). Even if Manor is right that Irenaeus, Origen, and Eusebius were Epiphanius's sources (*Alogi* 124, 144, 230), we would still not derive from them the tradition of Cerinthus's authorship of John. See further Francis Watson, *Gospel Writing: A Canonical Perspective* (Grand Rapids: Eerdmans, 2013), 479–93.

[21] Filastrius, *Diverse Heresies* 60.

Epiphanius would not have invented the Cerinthian authorship of John. The idea would have been anathema to him. Where then did Epiphanius receive his information? The gospel-like text called the *Epistle of the Apostles* (about 150 CE) accused Cerinthus of "perverting the words and the object, which is Jesus Christ."[22] The report is intriguing, but we have to wait a thousand years for a Syriac-speaking commentator – Dionysius bar Salibi – to provide any more concrete information.

Bar Salibi wrote that "Gaius," a Roman churchman of the late second century, claimed that Cerinthus wrote the gospel of John. Opposing Gaius was "Hippolytus of Rome," who tried to distinguish the teachings of John from those of Cerinthus.[23] A work of Hippolytus *On Behalf of the Gospel and Revelation of John* is chiseled onto a third-century Christian inscription.[24] Since Hippolytus's work itself is lost, however, it is unclear whether it mentioned either Gaius or Cerinthus.

About 180 CE, Irenaeus claimed that the gospel of John was written *against* Cerinthus.[25] The remark is distinctive. It may have been a maneuver to counter a proposed connection between Cerinthus and John. Cerinthus and John are again linked in a story from Polycarp of Smyrna (died about 155 CE). According to this tale, the "apostle John" caught sight of Cerinthus in an Ephesian bathhouse, whereupon John dashed out, crying that the building might collapse since "the enemy of the truth" lay within.[26] The historicity of this tale is doubtful in the extreme. The story may function as an allegory, a rearguard action attempting to prove the incompatibility of John (the gospel) and Cerinthus.[27]

Given this minefield of datapoints, stretched over a thousand years and only weakly connected by gossamer hypotheses, what can we safely conclude? We cannot securely state that Cerinthus wrote John, or that "John" wrote against Cerinthus. We only know, it seems, that the figure of Cerinthus and the gospel of John were associated by about 150 CE. And if Bar Salibi is right (though his witness is very late), Gaius said that Cerinthus wrote John sometime shortly before 200 CE. The question now is why did this tradition arise?

---

[22] *Epistle of the Apostles* 7 (Coptic) in Elliott, *Apocryphal New Testament*, 560.

[23] "Hippolytus" as reported by Dionysius bar Salibi, *In Apocalypsim, Actus et Epistulas Catholicas*, trans. and ed. I. Sedlacek, 2 vols. (Durbecq: Leuven University Press, 1954), 1–2: *Hippolytus Romanus dixit apparuit vir, nomine Caius, qui asserebat evangelium non esse Iohannus, nec Apocalypsim, sed Cerinthi haeretici ea esse* ("Hippolytus of Rome said: 'There appeared a man by the name of Gaius who repeatedly asserted that the Gospel and Revelation do not belong to John but to Cerinthus the heretic'").

[24] Around 1300, the Syrian writer Ebed-Jesu referred to this work as *Defense of the Apocalypse and Gospel of John the Apostle and Evangelist* (Manor, *Alogi*, 32–3).

[25] Irenaeus, *AH* 3.11.1. Victor of Pettau (d. 304 CE) makes the same charge in *On Revelation* 11.1 in Martine Dulaey, ed., *Victorin de Poetovio* (Paris: Cerf, 1997).

[26] Irenaeus, *AH* 3.3.4. The story is repeated by Eusebius, *HE* 3.28.6. Epiphanius, with the same story, switched Cerinthus with "Ebion" (*Panarion* 30.24). Cf. Theodoret, *Fab.* 2.3.3.

[27] See further Ernst Haenchen, *John*, trans. Robert W. Funk, 2 vols. (Minneapolis: Fortress, 1984), 1:24; R. E. Brown, *Epistles of John* (Garden City: Doubleday, 1982), 767; Simone Pétrement, *A Separate God: The Christian Origins of Gnosticism* (New York: Harper & Row, 1990), 301–3.

Cerinthus

Cerinthus was apparently a well-known Christian leader in the late first and early second centuries CE. He was possibly trained in Egypt, although he worked in Asia Minor (modern Turkey).[28] The *Epistle of the Apostles* calls Cerinthus an "apostle," though a false one. If *The Secret Book of James* (found at Nag Hammadi) was written to "my beloved Cerinthus," or "my son Cerinthus" (the text is damaged), then he was evidently thought to be in the apostolic inner circle, a circle that included James and Peter.[29] James, Peter, and John were the apostolic trio whom the apostle Paul called "pillars" (Gal. 2:9). If the trio had turned into James, Peter, and Cerinthus, this is yet more evidence for associating Cerinthus and John.[30]

What was Cerinthus's theology? Unfortunately, we only have heresiological sources to inform us and so must exercise due caution. According to Irenaeus, Cerinthus claimed that the Father of Jesus was unknown, and that he was a different being than the Judean deity.[31] Although the Judean deity was powerful, he himself was ignorant of the true God. Cerinthus also believed that Jesus was not born of a virgin. Christ, the universal Power, descended upon Jesus at his baptism, made known the unknown Father, and left Jesus at his crucifixion.[32]

When we compare these views with John, there are some significant similarities. First, this gospel – along with the gospel called Mark – does not include the virgin birth – or any sort of birth – of Jesus. This was a deliberate choice, since it seems likely that the Johannine author(s) knew other gospels, such as Matthew and Luke, in which a (virgin) birth is narrated.[33] Furthermore, John the Baptist, according to John, saw the divine Spirit come down and permanently rest upon Jesus at his baptism (John 1:32), whereupon Jesus was announced as Son of God (1:34; cf. Mark 1:10-11).[34]

---

[28] *Ref.* 7.33.1; 10.21.1.

[29] The name "[Cerin]thos" by emendation of *The Secret Book of James* (NHC 1,2) 1.1-2 (Christoph Markschies, "Kerinth: Wer war er und was lehrte er?" *JAC* 41 [1998]: 48–76 at 64–5).

[30] Later tradition makes Cerinthus one of the 72 missionaries sent out by Jesus (*Luke* 10) (Markschies, "Kerinth," 63).

[31] Irenaeus, *AH* 1.26.1; 3.11.1.

[32] Irenaeus, *AH* 1.26.1. For the reliability of this (earliest) report, see Charles E. Hill, "Cerinthus Gnostic or Chiliast? A New Solution to an Old Problem," *JECS* 8, no. 2 (2000): 135–72. Cf. Michael J. Kok, "Classifying Cerinthus's Christology," *Journal of Early Christian History* 9, no. 1 (2019): 30–48.

[33] Dwight Moody Smith, *John among the Gospels: The Relationship in Twentieth-Century Research* (Minneapolis: Fortress, 1992); Michael Labahn and Manfred Lang, "Johannes und die Synoptiker: Positionen und Impulse seit 1990," in *Kontexte des Johannesevangeliums: Das vierte Evangelium in religions- und traditionsgeschichtlicher Perspektive*, ed. Jörg Frey and Udo Schnelle (Tübingen: Mohr Siebeck, 2004), 443–515; Wendy E. S. North, "Points and Stars: John and the Synoptics," in *John, Jesus, and History, Volume 3: Glimpses of Jesus Through the Johannine Lens*, ed. Paul N. Anderson, Felix Just, and Tom Thatcher (Atlanta: SBL, 2016), 119–32.

[34] Francis Watson, "Is John's Christology Adoptionist?" in *The Glory of Christ in the New Testament: Studies in Christology*, ed. L. D. Hurst and N. T. Wright (Oxford: Clarendon, 1987), 113–24; C. H. Talbert, "And the Word Became Flesh': When?" in *Future of Christology: Essays in Honor of*

While hanging on the cross, Jesus "hands over" this Spirit, apparently to his Father (John 19:30).

Even more interesting is the finding that the Johannine Jesus, as we saw, distinguishes between the devilish father of the Judeans and his own Father, whom no one has ever seen (John 1:18; 8:44). If the Judean father is the Judean deity Yahweh – as one would presume from Jewish tradition and the Judeans' own testimony (8:41) – then this being is different from the God revealed in Jesus.

These similarities are intriguing, though certainly no smoking gun for Cerinthus's authorship of John. It is not, however, far-fetched to imagine Cerinthus as a *reader* of John – and the first we know of.[35] After all, if John was written in the vicinity of Palestine, and Cerinthus lived in Asia Minor, then we must allow time for the gospel to have migrated west. The simplest explanation for Cerinthian and Johannine similarity is that John was one of the inspirations for Cerinthian Christian thought – and to it we can probably add the gospel called Mark as well.[36]

On the basis of John, Cerinthus distinguished between the Judean deity and the true, unknown God. Using both Mark and John, we hypothesize, Cerinthus maintained a possessionist Christology in which Jesus was inhabited and transformed by a divine entity (an entity or spirit called Christ) during his ministry. Since both possessionist Christology and the unknown God were also associated with John, and since traditions about the apostle John and Cerinthus came from the same area (around Ephesus), Gaius the Roman presbyter could have inferred that Cerinthus wrote John by about 200 CE.

A Puzzle

There is a further puzzle about Cerinthus that must be addressed here. In addition to the Irenaean portrait of Cerinthus as a "gnostic," later heresiologists (notably Epiphanius) also portrayed Cerinthus as a "Jewish Christian."[37] Since the modern categories of "Gnosticism" and "Jewish Christianity" are generally seen to be in conflict, some interpreters have felt the need to pick which version of Cerinthus they find most plausible. Some opt for Cerinthus the "gnostic,"[38] while others select the "Jewish Christian."[39] There has also been an attempt to fuse the "gnostic" and "Jewish Christian" Cerinthus by making him a precursor of Marcion, who taught two Christs – one of a spiritual kingdom, the other of a material one.[40]

Leander E. Keck (Minneapolis: Fortress, 1993); Troels Engberg-Pedersen, *John and Philosophy: A New Reading of the Fourth Gospel* (Oxford: Oxford University Press, 2017), 68–73, 107.

[35] DeConick, *Gnostic New Age*, 157.

[36] Irenaeus stated that Christians who "separate Jesus and Christ" prefer Mark (*AH* 3.11.7).

[37] Epiphanius, *Pan.* 28.1.3.

[38] E.g., Pétrement, *Separate God*, 300–314; DeConick, *Gnostic New Age*, 159.

[39] E.g., Myllykowski, "Cerinthus," in Marjanen and Luomanen, ed., *Companion*, 213–46; Van den Broek, "Cerinthus," in *DGWE* 252–4.

[40] Hill, "Cerinthus, Gnostic or Chiliast?" 135–72.

What one can say here, I think, is that it is not so much *Cerinthus*, but the modern categories of "gnostic" and "Jewish Christian" that must first be rethought in modern scholarship. Neither category fits Cerinthus, and both have roots in heresiological discourse. For the moment, I would propose that both categories be bracketed so as to let Cerinthus be Cerinthus – an early Christian whose thought has the capacity to surprise us.

This position is not to deny that there are serious distortions in the heresiological portraits of Cerinthus, and that some are more accurate than others. Around 180 CE, Irenaeus probably took his report on Cerinthus from a revised version of Justin Martyr's *Syntagma*. This version of Cerinthus is, I have argued, Cerinthus the reader of John and Mark, who distinguished the creator from the supreme deity and upheld a possessionist christology. By the late fourth century, Cerinthus had become a full-blown "Jewish-Christian" (the heresiological term here is "Ebionite") at the hands of Epiphanius. There is clearly a development – one might say a distortion – and Epiphanius himself, it seems, is mostly to blame.

One can see how, in the history of heresiology, Cerinthus was more and more associated with Judaism – by which I mean *Christian conceptions* of Judaism. Irenaeus had claimed that Cerinthus denied the virgin birth, and he treated him immediately before a separate group of "Ebionites," who also – reportedly – denied the virgin birth.[41] By about 200 CE, Gaius hinted that Cerinthus wrote the book of Revelation (also attributed to a John). This text spoke of a thousand-year reign of Christ on earth (or millennium) with celebratory eating, drinking, and marriage.[42] Eventually Christian intellectuals like Dionysius of Alexandria (mid-third century CE) and Eusebius attacked the idea of a literal millennium because they viewed it as materialistic. Some of this eschatological "materialism" was read back into the portrait of Cerinthus so as to justify the allegorical reading of the millennium. Yet all these developments, it seems, came later – much later than Cerinthus himself.

By the third century, Cerinthus was possibly considered to be the author of Revelation.[43] As in the case of John, we might imagine Cerinthus – not as the author – but as a reader of Revelation. At a minimum, Cerinthus might have combined a belief in the millennium with the belief in a spiritual Christ and a subordinate creator (who was not the Father of Jesus Christ). All of this is possible in the laboratory of Christian ideas. Without any primary (non-heresiological) data, however, it is impossible to make any firm conclusions. Irenaeus's report I think is rightly judged better than that of Epiphanius, but even Irenaeus's report was written two generations after Cerinthus. The point here is not to deny the reality behind any Cerinthian tradition, but to read *all* heresiological sources with due care.

One final comment regarding Cerinthus, which deals with his relation to Simon (thus helping to transition us to the following chapter). Interestingly, the *Epistle of the*

---

[41] Irenaeus, *AH* 3.21.1; 5.1.3.
[42] Eusebius, *HE* 3.28.2.
[43] Eusebius, *HE* 3.28.2-4.

Apostles (about 150 CE) closely associates Cerinthus and Simon. It depicts both men as apostles – albeit false ones – who have gone "through the world."[44] Historically speaking, we can inquire about any connections between their thought. Simon was at least a generation older than Cerinthus, so we cannot expect Simon to have been familiar with John. Nevertheless, both Cerinthus and Simon's followers (Simonians) distinguished the true deity from the creator(s) of this world. Simonians imagined angelic creators and so did Cerinthus, according to Pseudo-Tertullian.[45] In Irenaeus, however, Cerinthus conceived of a single creative "Power."[46] Nothing compels us to believe that Cerinthus was dependent on Simonians for the idea of the distinction between the creator and the supreme deity. This idea was already in John's prologue, where the Logos is the creator distinct from God. The distinction between the creator(s) of this world and the supreme deity was probably not *only* based on John, however, but also on other Jewish traditions of angelic creators.[47]

Conclusion

If Cerinthus was an early Christian leader (perhaps itinerant), did he ever have a coherent group of disciples? It is true that Epiphanius raised the battle cry against "Cerinthians" whom he somehow confused with "Merinthians."[48] In second- and third-century sources, however, there is no solid evidence of a Cerinthian group or group mentality. We might imagine the secessionists in 1 John 2:19 ("they went out from us but were not of us") as Cerinthians,[49] but this is almost certainly wrong. We do not actually know why these secessionists split from the larger group. If they denied that Jesus was the Christ or that Jesus had come in the flesh (1 John 2:22; 4:2), then they would have disagreed with Cerinthus, who united Jesus and Christ (at least from baptism to death) and believed that Jesus – born like any human being – had flesh.[50]

Yet even if Cerinthus was completely idiosyncratic, he likely represents a stream of Johannine interpretation – and one that had a rich reception history. According to this reception, the Judean deity is not identified with the Father of Jesus Christ. This idea did not emerge by "splitting" the Jewish deity into a transcendent unknown God and a lower, hostile being.[51] Cerinthus as a reader of John never needed to

---

[44] *Epistle of the Apostles* 1, 7.
[45] Pseudo-Tertullian, *AAH* 3.2 (here the Judean deity is said to be an angel).
[46] Irenaeus, *AH* 1.26.1.
[47] Philo, *On the Creation* 72-75; *Confusion of Tongues* 171-74; *Tri. Trac.* I,5 112.19–113.1; Justin, *Dial.* 62.3; Josephus, *Against Apion* 2.192; Fossum, *Name*, 192–213.
[48] Epiphanius, *Pan.* 28.1.1; 28.8.1-2. See further Hill, "Gnostic or Chiliast?" 145, 147.
[49] Brown, *Epistles of John*, 65; Markschies, "Kerinth," 66–9.
[50] *Pace* DeConick, *Gnostic New Age*, 155–7. See further Judith Lieu, *I, II, and III John: A Commentary* (Louisville: Westminster John Knox, 2008), 10–14, 23–5, 169–70, 210.
[51] For the split theory, see Birger A. Pearson, "Gnosticism as a Religion," in *Was there a Gnostic Religion?*, ed. Antti Marjanen (Helsinki: Finnish Exegetical Society, 2005), 81–101 at 83. DeConick speaks of a "bifurcation" of the Jewish god into a good father and a malicious lawgiver performed

imagine the Judean deity as a transcendent being, but as a local "power" who had never really seen God (Deut. 32:8; John 1:18). This Johannine and Cerinthian idea of one, unknown Father and a lower creator was an idea common to both John and Cerinthus. Cerinthus said that the creator was ignorant of God; the writers of John's prologue insisted that the lower creator, called Logos, revealed God. Cerinthus did not specifically say that his creator was hostile to God (like the Johannine "ruler of this world"). This would, however, be a step taken by later Christian theologians, some of whom we shall explore.

Further Reading

Charles E. Hill, "Cerinthus Gnostic or Chiliast? A New Solution to an Old Problem," *JECS* 8, no. 2 (2000): 135–72.

Michael J. Kok, "Classifying Cerinthus's Christology," *Journal of Early Christian History* 9, no. 1 (2019): 30–48.

Matti Myllykowski, "Cerinthus," in *Companion to Second-century Christian 'Heretics'*, ed. Antti Marjanen and Petri Luomanen (Leiden: Brill, 2005), 213–46.

Simone Pétrement, *A Separate God: The Christian Origins of Gnosticism* (New York: Harper & Row, 1990), 298–314.

Roelof van den Broek, "Cerinthus," in *DGWE*, ed. Wouter Hanegraaff (Leiden: Brill, 2006), 252–4.

B. G. Wright, "Cerinthus apud Hippolytus: An Inquiry into the Traditions about Cerinthus's Provenance," *Second Century* 4 (1988): 103–15.

by a transitional gnostic Christian – the author of the fourth gospel ("Why," in Williams and Rowland, ed., *John's Gospel*, 178; DeConick, *Gnostic New Age*, 146–7). Irenaeus already accused the Marcionites of "slicing the godhead in two" (*dividens deum in duo, AH* 3.25.3). Cf. Origen's "they slice the godhead" (διακόπτουσι τὴν θεότητα, *On Prayer* 29.12).

3

Simon, Helen, and Simonian Christians

Introduction

The man known as Simon of Samaria is an elusive figure. A close contemporary of Jesus, Simon was born in a town called "Gitta" or "Gitthon" in modern-day Palestine.[1] He became associated with Samaria, a region of central Palestine where there lived a distinct ethnic group, the Samarians, who were viewed as distant yet estranged cousins of the Judeans to the south.[2] We do not know if Simon was once a Samaritan (a practitioner of the dominant religion of Samaria), but we might presume his familiarity with Samaritan traditions. Samaritans had their own version of the Pentateuch (the first five books of Jewish scripture), and their own holy sites – most notably a sacred peak called Gerizim (about seventy-five kilometers due north of Jerusalem).

Irenaeus (in)famously portrayed Simon as the father of Christian heresies.[3] This latter claim so captivated later heresiologists that by the fourth century CE, virtually anything deemed "heretical" stuck to Simon like paper to glue. Irenaeus's claims are exactly the kind of heresiological distortion that must always be questioned. Calling Simon "(the first) heretic" reinforces the heresiological perspective of his enemies and contributes to a legendary depiction of Simon as Christianity's first archenemy. If we wish to understand Simon's actual place in early Christian history, we must wipe the slate clean of heresiological rhetoric and begin our reconstruction afresh.

This approach demands that we cannot begin where Irenaeus does, namely with the polemical portrait of Simon in Acts 8:9-24. Here we find Simon "performing magic" (*mageuōn*, v. 9), despite the fact that he was not said to speak spells, secret names, or use amulets and potions. Still, even in modern scholarship, Simon is tagged

---

[1] Clemens Scholten, "Zum Herkunftsort des Simon Magus," *VC* 69 (2015): 534–41.
[2] See further Ingrid Hjelm, *The Samaritans and Early Judaism: A Literary Analysis* (Sheffield: Sheffield Academic, 2000); Magnar Kartveit, *The Origins of the Samaritans* (Leiden: Brill, 2009); Jan Dusek, *The Samaritans in Historical, Cultural, and Linguistic Perspectives* (Berlin: de Gruyter, 2018).
[3] Irenaeus, *AH* 1.23.2; 1.27.4. In the twentieth century, Simon was a popular test case for pre-Christian Gnosticism. See Stephen Haar, *Simon Magus: The First Gnostic?* (Berlin: de Gruyter, 2003), 22–31.

with the heresiological title "Magus," which roughly denotes "magician." Historically speaking, it is unhelpful to label Simon as a "magus."[4] A magus of the ancient world typically identifies some sort of illicit ritual practitioner.[5] When the term is used by the author of Acts – who is followed by the heresiologists – it means little more than "quack" (Acts 13:8).

If we expect Acts to provide a historical portrait of Simon, we will be disappointed. Scholars have long realized that Acts is an apologetic, selective account that depreciates the role of Simon in early Christianity and deprives him of any authority.[6] The account in Acts distorts the Simonian view of Simon, and says almost nothing about Simon's (apparently wide) influence in Samaria and beyond. Those pursuing history must turn to the primary sources of Simon's followers (the Simonians). Regrettably, all Simonian sources have been lost, with the exception of one long report from a document we will call the *(Great) Declaration Commentary*.[7]

The Great Declaration Commentary

We do not know the author of the *Great Declaration Commentary* (henceforth, the commentator), apart from the fact that he was a devotee of Simon. What we have are relatively long, though selective, quotations from it provided by the Refutator

---

[4] *Pace* Haar, *Simon*, 132–227; Carl B. Smith, *No Longer Jews: The Search for Gnostic Origins* (Peabody: Hendrickson, 2004), 129.

[5] Ayse Tuzlak, "The Magician and the Heretic," in *Magic and Ritual in the Ancient World*, ed. Paul Mirecki and Marvin Meyer (Leiden: Brill, 2002), 416–26; Kimberly B. Stratton, "The Rhetoric of 'Magic' in Early Christian Discourse: Gender, Power and the Construction of "Heresy," in *Mapping Gender in Ancient Religious Discourses*, ed. Todd Penner and Caroline Vander Stichele (Leiden: Brill, 2007), 89–114; Maijastina Kahlos, "The Early Church," in *The Cambridge History of Magic and Witchcraft in the West: From Antiquity to the Present*, ed. David J. Collins (Cambridge: Cambridge University Press, 2015), 148–82; Radcliffe G. Edmonds III, *Drawing Down the Moon: Magic in the Ancient Greco-Roman World* (Princeton: Princeton University Press), 5–15.

[6] Gerd Lüdemann, *The Acts of the Apostles: What Really Happened in the Earliest Days of the Church* (Amherst: Prometheus, 2005), 385–401; Loveday Alexander, "Fact, Fiction and the Genre of Acts," *NTS* 44 (1998): 380–99; Alexander, "The Acts of the Apostles as an Apologetic Text," in *Apologetics in the Roman Empire*, ed. Mark Edwards (Oxford: Oxford University Press, 1999), 15–44; Marianne Palmer Bonz, *The Past as Legacy: Luke–Acts and Ancient Epic* (Minneapolis: Fortress, 2000), 183–9. For a survey of ancient historiography with a view to Acts, see Todd Penner, *In Praise of Christian Origins: Stephen and the Hellenists in Lukan Apologetic Historiography* (London: T&T Clark, 2004), 104–222. In general, see T. P. Wiseman, "Lying Historians: Seven Types of Mendacity," in *Greek and Roman Historiography*, ed. John Marincola (Oxford: Oxford University Press, 2011), 314–36.

[7] On the *Declaration Commentary*, see Josef Frickel, *Die "Apophasis Megale" in Hippolyts Refutatio (VI 9-18): Eine Paraphrase zur Apophasis Simons* (Rome: Pontifical Institute of Oriental Studies, 1968). See further Barbara Aland, "Die Apophasis Megale und die simonianische Gnosis," in *Was ist Gnosis? Studien zum frühen Christentum, zu Marcion und zur kaiserzeitlichen Philosophie* (Tübingen: Mohr Siebeck, 2009), 91–102. Catherine Osborne tried to refute Frickel's theory, but was not, in my view, entirely successful (*Rethinking Early Greek Philosophy: Hippolytus of Rome and the Presocratics* [London: Duckworth, 1987], 214–27).

(about 220 CE).[8] Although not free from the Refutator's occasional insertions, the *Declaration Commentary* is the only document with a claim to representing Simonian thought apart from anti-Simon reports. There were other Simonian texts, apparently, but they are lost.[9] The *Declaration Commentary* is thus the best starting point for our inquiry.

According to the commentator, Simon himself composed the *Great Declaration*, a lost text which the commentator expanded and annotated. Some historians have thought that the complexity and philosophical character of the *Great Declaration* disprove this point.[10] Yet we have no reason to deny that Simon was a complex thinker with a measure of philosophical sophistication. Most of the philosophical interventions, however, seem to be those of the commentator.

The Refutator aimed his criticisms at Simonians and occasionally quoted the *Declaration Commentary* with an opening, "they say."[11] The "they" does not necessarily indicate group authorship, but it does suggest that the work was composed by a later follower (or followers) of Simon. The commentator alludes to the gospel of Matthew (3:10, 12) or Luke (3:9, 17), which were likely not written prior to about 80 CE.[12] By this time, Simon had almost certainly perished.[13]

The heart of the *Declaration Commentary* is an allegorical reading on Genesis 1–3, a kind of treatise later called a *hexameron*.[14] A *hexameron* comments on the six (or seven) days of creation, incorporating contemporaneous scientific and medical lore to create a new vision of the world. The *Commentary* begins by identifying God as an infinite, intellectual fire, a cosmic energy which exists in humans who enshrine divine intellect. In the beginning, God made Heaven and Earth (Gen. 1:1), two entities which "Simon" took to represent divine Powers called Mind and Thought.[15]

Mind is called "the Great Power."[16] There are four other powers, making a total of six, as indicated by the six days of creation. The seventh day symbolizes the seventh Power who is identified with the Spirit hovering over the waters (Gen. 1:2) who is also

---

[8] *Ref.* 6.14-18. See the text and notes in Litwa, ed., *Refutation*, 361–87.

[9] Eusebius refers to a Simonian "written oracle" (λόγιον ἔγγραφον) that would astound its hearers (*HE* 2.13.7).

[10] Karlmann Beyschlag, *Simon Magus und die christliche Gnosis* (Tübingen: Mohr Siebeck, 1974), 218–19.

[11] *Ref.* 6.9.1. Φασί appears in, e.g., *Ref.* 6.15.3, 6.17.2.

[12] *Ref.* 6.9.10.

[13] See further Edwin Yamauchi, *Pre-Christian Gnosticism: A Survey of the Proposed Evidences* (London: Tyndale Press, 1973), 62–4; Haar, *Simon*, 97–9; Pearson, *Ancient Gnosticism*, 32–3.

[14] I owe this insight to Tuomas Rasimus (personal communication). See further Markschies, *Christian Theology*, 256–8.

[15] *Ref.* 6.13.1.

[16] *Ref.* 6.18.3. Both Hans G. Kippenberg (*Garizim und Synagoge*, 346–8) and Fossum (*Name*, 173–91) identified the "Great Power" as a Samaritan title, though Kippenberg took it to refer to God as such while Fossum understood it to refer to a being subordinate to God. The title is probably not specifically Samaritan (Hegesippus in Eusebius, *HE* 2.23.13; Epiphanius, *Pan.* 55.1.1; *Ref.* 7.36).

called Wisdom (Prov. 8:23). Wisdom is the image of God according to whom humans are made. Humans become God's likeness by bearing the fruit of Wisdom (Gen. 1:26).

Despite displaying knowledge of Greek philosophy, poetry, and medicine, the author of the *Declaration Commentary* was primarily a biblical exegete. God as fire, for instance, was inspired by the fifth book of the Pentateuch, where God is called "a consuming fire" (Deut. 4:24; 9:3). Heaven and Earth are treated as living entities on the basis of Isa. 1:2 ("Hear O Heaven, and Listen O Earth"). The author also quotes or alludes to the gospels and Paul (for instance, Matt. 3:10; 1 Cor. 11:32) in creative and integrated ways.[17]

Though familiar with the gospels, the author of the *Declaration Commentary* had evidently not encountered the gospel later attributed to John. For the Simonian author, the term *logos* (the "Word" of John 1:1) refers once to scripture and another time to Moses.[18] For a Simonian to call Moses "the Logos" would be surprising if he or she had knowledge of John. The lack of interaction with John is a hint of an early date, since by the mid-second century, unfamiliarity with John would have been unlikely.[19]

Another indication of an early date for the *Declaration Commentary* is its failure to agree with the earliest anti-Simon reports. The earliest of these reports is Acts, which depicts the pre-Christian Simon venerated as "the Power of God called Great" (8:10). The *Declaration Commentary*, by contrast, identifies the Great Power with the Mind of the Universe, and this divine Mind is never identified with Simon. Probably the author of Acts was trying to align Simon with a tradition of self-deifiers (compare Herod in Acts 12:20-23). Justin Martyr and the Refutator both attacked Simon as a man who deified himself.[20]

The *Declaration Commentary* undermines these reports. Simon did not deify himself. The speaker in the *Commentary* never called himself or Simon "God" or "the Great Power." If the author of Acts knew the distinctive title, "Great Power" from the *Declaration*, then the *Declaration* preceded Acts. The date of Acts is disputed. Typical datings range between 85 and 140 CE.[21] Assuming the author of Acts knew the *Declaration Commentary*, then the *Commentary* was probably written prior to 135 CE.

---

[17] *Ref.* 6.14.6; 6.16.5.

[18] *Ref.* 6.13.1; 6.15.4.

[19] See further Charles E. Hill, *The Johannine Corpus in the Early Church* (Oxford: Oxford University Press, 2004), esp. 224, 230–5.

[20] Justin, *1 Apol.* 1.26.1; *Ref.* 6.14.1; 6.18.1. Logan wrongly claimed that Simon had a "novel claim to be God himself" ("Gnosticism," in *The Early Christian World*, ed. Philip F. Esler, 2 vols. [London: Routledge, 2000], 2:907–28 at 917). See M. David Litwa, *Desiring Divinity: Self-deification in Early Jewish and Christian Mythmaking* (New York: Oxford University Press, 2016), 104–10.

[21] Indications that the author of *Acts* used both Josephus's *Antiquities* and a Pauline letter collection puts *Acts*'s *terminus a quo* about 100 CE (Steve Mason, *Josephus and the New Testament*, 2nd ed. [Peabody: Hendrickson, 2003], 251–96; Richard Pervo, *Dating Acts between the Evangelists and the Apologists* [Santa Rosa: Polebridge, 2006], 333, 343). According to Andrew Gregory, there is no evidence to prove the use of Acts until after 150 CE (*The Reception of Luke and Acts in the Period before Irenaeus: Looking for Luke in the Second Century* [Tübingen: Mohr Siebeck, 2003], 353). Both J. C. O'Neill (*The Theology of Acts in Its Historical Setting*, 2nd ed. [London: SPCK,

Simon in Acts

We can now turn our attention to Acts. Here we need to distinguish what would have been embarrassing and what would have been amenable to the author of Acts in the second century. It is clear that the author of Acts opposed Simon and wished to undercut his authority – especially because Simon was contemporary with the apostles. It served the purpose of the author of Acts to depict Simon as a former magician who became guilty of "simony" – the practice of buying or selling spiritual gifts.

At the same time, Simon is also depicted as a baptized Christian who evidently received the Holy Spirit through the laying on of hands. He was baptized by Philip but apparently received the Spirit through the chief apostles Peter and John. When Simon requested authority to convey the Spirit, Peter accused him of marketing spiritual goods. Instead of stamping off in rage, however, Simon obsequiously repented and asked for prayer (Acts 8:12-24). These data (Simon's conversion and repentance) rub against the tendency of the author of Acts and can, I think, be credited. It was a truth the author of Acts recorded and could not smooth away: Simon was a baptized Christian.[22]

Although Irenaeus denied that Simon became a Christian, his judgment needs to be questioned.[23] Irenaeus did not want Simon (the first "heretic") to be viewed as a Christian. Yet Acts – which Irenaeus knew – admits evidence to the contrary. It portrays what apparently could not be discounted – that Simon believed the gospel and was baptized. The Christian identity of Simon relates to the Christian identity of his heirs. About 150 CE, Justin Martyr wrote that the followers of Simon were called Christians.[24] Origen confirmed that the only people who honored Simon are Christians.[25] In the fourth century CE, Epiphanius did not deny that Simon was a

---

1970], 1–43) and Pervo (*Dating Acts*, 333, 343) prefer a date between 115 and 130 CE. A slightly later date is supported by arguments which contextualize *Luke–Acts* as a response to Marcion (John T. Townsend, "The Date of Luke–Acts," in *Luke–Acts: New Perspectives from the Society of Biblical Literature Seminar*, ed. Charles H. Talbert [New York: Crossroad, 1984], 47–62; Joseph B. Tyson, *Marcion and Luke–Acts: A Defining Struggle* [Columbia: University of South Carolina Press, 2006], 50–120; William O. Walker, "The Portrayal of Aquila and Priscilla in Acts: The Question of Sources," *NTS* 54 [2008]: 479–95).

[22] See further Patrick Fabien, "La conversion de Simon le magicien (Ac 8,4-25)," *Biblica* 91 (2010): 210–40.

[23] Irenaeus, *AH* 1.23.1. The judgment is followed by Pearson, who states: "Simon could hardly have become a Christian, and his message had nothing to do with Christianity" (*Ancient Gnosticism*, 26). Fossum thought it "unthinkable" that Simon converted to Christianity, even if he was baptized (*Name*, 164). Fossum reconstructed Simon as a purely Samaritan Messiah. To arrive at this conclusion, he pulled largely from (1) late Samaritan sources with questionable application to Simon, and (2) from novelistic Christian sources like the *Acts of Peter* and the Pseudoclementines (*Name*, 112–28). DeConick follows Fossum's sources and so falls into similar historiographical errors (*Gnostic New Age*, 98–104).

[24] Justin, *1 Apol.* 26.6.

[25] Origen, *Cels.* 1.57.

Christian, only that his followers "do not believe in Christ's name in a right or lawful way."[26]

Historically speaking, Simon required no validation of his faith from so-called apostles in Jerusalem, let alone the heresiologists. The Mediterranean world was vast, and within many of its cities and towns, Christianity took its own course long before "apostolic" validation even seemed important in Christian memory. If the gospel of John reflects history, Jesus himself had a Samaritan tour before his apostles had any influence in the region. He converted many people in the city of Sychar, a town close to Mount Gerizim (John 4). These Christian converts were not looking for later apostolic validation from Jerusalem, and neither, I believe, was Simon.

Simonians at Rome

In the early second century, there are perhaps memories of Simon's thought preserved in the *Declaration Commentary*. Yet there is no solid evidence of a Simonian Christian *group* until the time of Justin Martyr.[27] Sometime in the 140s CE, Justin had written or obtained a heresy catalogue (the *Syntagma*) attacking Simon and probably Simonian Christians.[28] In his *First Apology* (about 150 CE), Justin claimed that *all* Samarians (*pantes ... Samareis*) and some from other ethnicities worship (*proskunousi*) Simon – not as some subordinate or intermediate deity – but as "the primal God," who is – like Christ – "above every principality, authority, and power."[29]

The claim about "all" Samarians worshiped Simon is arresting, even if Justin was prone to exaggerate.[30] Justin may have meant to designate the majority of Samarians who settled in Rome (Justin's location at the time). This would not necessarily have been a large group of people. They were, however, a noticeable group of Christians in the capital, and people from other ethnicities had joined their ranks.[31]

---

[26] Epiphanius, *Pan.* 21.1.1; 21.2.1; 21.7.2.

[27] The following paragraphs adapt material in my book *Desiring Divinity*, 104–5.

[28] Smith, *Guilt* 49-82.

[29] Justin, *1 Apol.* 26.3; *Dial.* 120.6, cf. Eph. 1:21. Πρῶτος ("first") probably indicates rank or degree. Haar, comparing Philo (*Migr.* 181; *Abr.* 115) and Rev. 1:17; 2:8; 22:13, notes that πρῶτος is "not used as a comparative but stresses preeminence with allusions to pre-existence as well as the primal creation of all things" (*Simon*, 245). See Alcinous, *Handbook* 10; Justin, *Dial.* 3.5.

[30] Cf. Justin's claim that "all" (πάντες) rushed to worship Antinous as a deity (*1 Apol.* 29.4). Bruce Hall doubts that many Samaritans became Simonians, but wrongly follows Epiphanius in thinking of Simonians as solely Gentile ("From John Hyrcanus to Baba Rabbah," in *The Samaritans*, ed. Alan D. Crown [Tübingen: Mohr Siebeck, 1989], 43–50).

[31] Alastair H. B. Logan proposed that Justin Martyr "probably got his information about Simon being worshiped as a god in Rome, statue and all, from Simonians there" ("Magi and Visionaries in Gnosticism," in *Portraits of Spiritual Authority: Religious Power in Early Christianity, Byzantium and the Christian Orient*, ed. Jan Willem Drijvers and John W. Watt [Leiden: Brill, 1999], 27–44 at 32–3), citing *1 Apol.* 26.1-3; 56.2-4; *2 Apol.* 15.1; *Dial.* 120.6. W. van der Horst argues that "Justin does not say that Simon was worshipped by Samaritans-in-Rome" ("Samaritans at Rome?" in *Japhet in the Tents of Shem: Studies on Jewish Hellenism in Antiquity* [Leuven: Peeters,

Justin's claim about Samarians worshiping Simon as "the primal God" is also striking. In Greco-Roman culture, deified humans like Romulus, Heracles, and Jesus typically became subordinate gods ("sons" of God), not the high deity. If Justin was influenced by Acts, Simon as "the primal God" interprets Simon's title "the Great Power" (Acts 8:10).[32] In other words, Simon is the Power in comparison to whom none is greater. (It should be noted, however, that in the *Declaration* "the Great Power" is not the primal God, but the subordinate "Mind.")

One suspects that Justin overstated his point to make Simonian Christians appear ridiculous. The imperial capital had long assimilated foreign deities and deified figures who were subordinate to the Roman high God (Jupiter Optimus Maximus). That a no-name Palestinian from some backwater village in the corner of the empire was worshiped as the high God would have seemed laughable to the Roman elite. This is the knife edge of Justin's point: the Romans wrongly persecute his Christian group for worshiping Jesus as a subordinate god (the "Logos"), but support Simonians when they supposedly worship Simon as the high God.

How did the Romans support Simonian Christians? Justin claimed that Simon himself had a debut at Rome. During his sojourn there, he so impressed the senate and people with his miracles that they honored him with a statue. The statue was erected under the emperor Claudius (reigned 41–55 CE) – the very time when the first Christians appeared in Rome.[33] Justin understood the statue to be a divine honor: Simon "was honored with a statue as are the other gods honored by you" Romans.[34]

Simon's statue could be found, Justin said, on Tiber island with the inscription SIMONI DEO SANCTO: "To Simon, Sacred God."[35] The fact that the statue base was found in 1574, and actually reads SEMONI SANCO DEO FIDIO ("To Semo Sancus, faithful God"), would seem to undermine Justin's report.[36] It did not depict Simon, but a native Italic deity associated with oaths, the sky, and lightning.[37]

2002], 251–60 at 259). The question is whether there were *Simonians* (who might *also* have been from Samaria) in Rome. The Greek Σαμαρεύς does not distinguish between Samarian (inhabitant of Samaria) and Samaritan (member of a religious group).

[32] Justin's dependence on *Acts* is supported by Ernst Haenchen (*The Acts of the Apostles: A Commentary*, trans. Bernard Noble and Gerald Shinn [Oxford: Basil Blackwell, 1971], 8) on the basis of Justin, *1 Apol.* 51.12 (which refers to Jesus's ascension and the apostles receiving power). Andrew Gregory believes that there remains "no clear evidence for Justin having used Acts" ("Among the Apologists? Reading Acts with Justin Martyr," in *Engaging Early Christian History: Reading Acts in the Second Century*, ed. Rubén R. Dupertuis and Todd Penner [Durham: Acumen, 2013], 169–86 at 174).

[33] Justin, *1 Apol.* 26.2; Irenaeus, *AH* 1.23.1.

[34] Justin, *1 Apol.* 56.2.

[35] Justin, *1 Apol.* 26.2.

[36] The inscription can be found in *Inscriptiones Latinae Selectae* 3474. Florent Heintz accuses Justin of deliberate falsification in his report (*Simon "Le magicien": Actes 8, 5-25 et l'accusation de magie contre les prophètes thaumaturges dans l'antiquité* [Paris: Gabalda, 1997], 121). Irenaeus (*AH* 1.23.1), Tertullian (*Apol.* 13.9) and Eusebius (*HE* 2.13) followed Justin.

[37] Varro, *Latin Language*, 5:66; Roger D. Woodard, *Indo-European Sacred Space: Vedic and Roman Cult* (Urbana: University of Illinois Press, 2006), 184–9.

Perhaps, however, we ought to grant Justin the benefit of the doubt. Conceivably, Simonians at Rome could have identified the statue of a god called *Semon* with their founder *Simon* (the ancient pronunciation was close).[38] According to Irenaeus's later report, Simonians worshiped another statue of Simon shaped like Zeus.[39]

> **Sidelight on Zeus.** Zeus, the Roman Jupiter, was widely recognized in the ancient Mediterranean as king of the gods. With long flowing beard, bulging chest, and a thunderous nod, this deity appears in Homer and many other classical poets. Yahweh was occasionally identified as a form of Zeus.[40] Stoic philosophers had come to identify Zeus with the supreme principle, which they thought of as an intelligent form of fire (a point seemingly adapted in the *Declaration Commentary*).

Simon and Zeus were not equivalent, but Zeus represented a primal power which Simon – for Simonian Christians – came to embody.[41] Yet why would Simonians venerate Simon in the form of a preexistent deity? Some reverse engineering is required here, which demands knowledge of the historical context.

There was an ancient custom according to which ancient Greeks and Romans heroized or deified deceased family members by likening them, in word or image, with a particular god or superhuman being. The connection between the deceased and the god was typically made on the basis of shared attributes: a child could be likened to a young god like Cupid; an unmarried girl to the virgin goddess Diana; a warrior to Heracles with his club, and so on. In this practice, the individual human is not necessarily equated with the god, but immortalized by association.[42] In the year 130 CE, for instance, Antinous, Hadrian's boy lover, became Osiris-Antinous (*Oseirantinoos*) – a deathless god. An obelisk honoring him with this name still stands on the Pincio hill in Rome.[43]

---

[38] "Semo" would have undergone itacism, as was normal for this period. On the deliberate re-identification of statues, cf. Eusebius, *HE* 7.18.

[39] Irenaeus, *AH* 1.23.4.

[40] *Letter to Aristeas* 16 (*OTP* 2:13).

[41] *Ref.* 6.20.1-2.

[42] Henning Wrede, *Consecratio in formam deorum: Vergöttlichte Privatpersonen in der römischen Kaiserzeit* (Mainz am Rhein: Philipp von Zabern, 1981); Janet Huskinson, *Roman Children's Sarcophagi: Their Decoration and Its Social Significance* (Oxford: Clarendon, 1996), 30–6, 41–54, 101–7; Jason Mander, *Portraits of Children on Roman Funerary Monuments* (Cambridge: Cambridge University Press, 2013), 55–9.

[43] For rites, festivals, games, and statues for Antinous, see Royston Lambert, *Beloved and God: The Story of Hadrian and Antinous* (Secaucus, NJ: Meadowland, 1984), 184–97; Peter Kuhlmann, *Religion und Erinnerung: Die Religionspolitik Kaiser Hadrians und ihre Rezeption in der antiken Literatur* (Göttingen: Vandenhoeck & Ruprecht, 2002), 197–240. Many cult statues of Antinous, along with a picture of the Pincio obelisk can be found in R. R. R. Smith, *Antinous: Boy Made God* (Oxford: Ashmolean, 2018), 41.

Perhaps Simonian Christians about 140 CE did something similar with Simon. They immortalized him by associating him with a statue of a local deity. This local deity was probably identified with a form of Zeus Pistios (the protector of oaths). If Simon was antecedently associated with the supreme power of Zeus, then Simonian Christians had reason to venerate Simon through the statue.[44] All this, of course, is extrapolation from Justin's report in an attempt to make sense of it. Other historians will have different solutions.

Whatever the truth about the statue, Justin was clearly concerned about a group of Simonian Christians, apparently in Rome, about 150 CE. Speaking to a mixed group of Christians and non-Christians in Rome, Justin aimed to undercut the Simonian claim to be Christian. He considered the Simonian veneration of Simon to be blasphemy. He never seems to have examined why Simonians honored Simon's reputed icon. Justin was in no mood for toleration; he curtly demanded that the emperors tear the statue down.[45]

Although it must remain undecided whether Simon himself came to Rome between 35–55 CE, Simonian Christians were there, by Justin's testimony, about a century later. Was there historical continuity between Simon and these Simonian Christians? It is difficult to say, since the only Simonian document we have is the *Declaration Commentary*. Yet if the author of Acts went out of his way to undermine Simon's ability to convey the Spirit between 100 and 140 CE, we might surmise that his actual target was a Simonian circle active during his own time. This circle may have already been making claims about Simon as "the Great Power," though this would represent a later stage of thought than what we find in the *Declaration Commentary* itself.

If Simonian Christians did begin to venerate Simon about 140 CE, their action is analogous to the veneration of Jesus as a deity among Johannine Christians. The identification of Simon with "the Great Power" or "Mind," offspring of ultimate deity, is similar to the identification of Jesus as Logos, only-born god (John 1:1, 18). Indeed, Mind (*Nous*) and Logos overlap in meaning as abstracts denoting divine Intellect.

Evidently the identification of Jesus with the Logos happened around 90–110 CE (a typical date range for the Johannine gospel, though its prologue could have been later). It is not far-fetched to hypothesize that an analogous identification of Simon with Mind occurred in the wake of the *Declaration Commentary*, and for similar reasons: to highlight a human figure as the center and source of divine revelation. Just as Jesus spoke the divine word, he became the divine Logos; so also, just as "Simon" spoke of Mind the "Great Power," he later became the Great Power or its human manifestation.[46]

---

[44] Gerd Lüdemann, *Untersuchungen zur simonianischen Gnosis* (Göttingen: Vandenhoeck & Ruprecht, 1975), 49–56.
[45] Justin, *1 Apol.* 56.4.
[46] *Ref.* 6.17.1.

Simon, Christ, and the Father

In his *First Apology*, Justin Martyr wanted his audience to think that the Simonians worshiped Simon *as opposed* to Christ.[47] Yet for the Simonians who worshiped Simon, Simon was evidently seen as a *manifestation* of Christ. Indeed, Simonians eventually said that Simon *was* Christ. In short, Simon came as Christ to the Jews in Judea and did all the deeds attributed to Christ in the gospels. His suffering in Judea is mentioned, as well as his promise to rise from the dead.[48]

The manifestation of Christ to the Judeans, for Simonians, was only a lesser revelation. To the people of Samaria (evidently more favored than the Judeans), Simon came as the Father himself – presumably to offer a more profound revelation.[49] Between about 130–170 CE, Simonian Christians began to emphasize Simon's identity with the Father. We know from the *Declaration Commentary* that "Father" is another name for "the Great Power," or Mind.[50]

The notion that Simon was considered Father *and* Son resembles a certain kind of Christian theology later called modalism. In modalism, Father and Son are different manifestations of the same essential and singular deity. They appear at different times and places for different purposes in different forms, but they are the same being. The modalistic theology of the Simonians meshes with later modalism manifested in late second-century Smyrna and Rome (see Chapter 18 below).

Helen

According to the *Declaration Commentary*, Mind becomes Father when he generated the primal Thought.[51] "Thought" in the *Declaration Commentary* was called "the Seventh Power," the creatrix who made the angels and rulers who in turn made this world. The idea that angels were helpers in creation was well-known in Judean tradition.[52] A Simonian twist on this tradition was that the angels, in an attempt to retain the power of their Mother (primal Thought), detained and defiled her by imprisoning her in mortal bodies.[53]

According to the *Declaration Commentary*, humans are made in the image of Thought.[54] As such, they are little "thoughts," or micro-expressions of the divine Mind. Tragically, however, they, too, are lost and defiled in bodies. When Mind came

---

[47] Hegesippus followed a similar tack, arguing that "Simonians" and "Menandrians" put forward "false Christs" (Eusebius, *HE* 4.22.5-6).

[48] Irenaeus, *AH* 1.23.3; *Ref.* 6.19.6.

[49] Irenaeus, *AH* 1.23.1.

[50] *Ref.* 6.19.1-4.

[51] *Ref.* 6.18.5.

[52] Josephus, *Against Apion* 2.192; Philo, *On the Creation* 68-76; cf. Justin, *Dial.* 62.3. See further Fossum, *Name*, 199–204. For Rabbinic texts, see ibid. 204–11. Cf. *Test. Truth* IX,3 113.1.

[53] Irenaeus, *AH* 1.23.2. Tertullian, *On the Soul* 34. See further J. H. Waszink, ed., *Tertulliani de Anima* (Leiden: Brill, 2010), 401–10.

[54] *Ref.* 6.14.5-6; cf. 6.17.1.

to rescue his primal Thought, in effect he came to rescue all human souls who have forgotten their connection to Mind.

The story of Thought separated from her true dwelling was reminiscent of an archetypal figure in antiquity, namely Helen of Troy. According to Homeric lore, a strapping young suitor named Paris lured Helen away from her husband Menelaus and brought her to the city of Troy. When Paris was killed, Helen was given to another man before returning, after a decade of war and bloodshed, to her true husband.

Early readers of Homer saw in Helen the story of the soul. The Nag Hammadi tractate called *Exegesis of the Soul* quotes Homer's *Odyssey* 4.260-61, where Helen says: "[My heart] turned itself from me. It is to my house that I want to return."[55] Helen returns back to her home, symbolic of the soul's return to the Father.[56] Helen herself in this text represents the soul, once virgin and dwelling with the Father. But "when she fell down into a body and entered this life, she fell into the hands of many brigands."[57] Raped and abused, the soul elicits the Father's compassion. She "received the divine from the Father, that she might be renewed and receive the place she was since the beginning."[58]

It seems that some Simonians (between about 150–180 CE) fused the stories of Helen with Thought.[59] Primal Thought, although the creatrix, fell away from the Father and was, as soul, trapped and abused in various bodies. Eventually Thought was born in the very body of Helen of Troy.

This story of Helen was not about Helen alone. All souls, for Simonian Christians, were "Helens," who, enticed from their heavenly homes, have been enslaved by angelic powers. Like the shepherd in Jesus's parable (Luke 15:6), Simon-Christ went in search of "Helen," the lost sheep trapped in all human bodies.[60]

Significantly, "Helen" does not appear in the *Declaration Commentary* (another indication of its early composition). Justin, however, reported that a woman called Helen – not of Troy but of Tyre – joined up with Simon. She, supposedly a redeemed prostitute, became Simon's earthly companion during his ministry. This particular story may have been the literalization of an allegory in which Mind (embodied in Simon) came in search of prostituted Thought (embodied in Helen). The literalization of the story was then taken to be historical. Alternatively, Simon actually did have a companion named Helen who was later assimilated to Helen of Troy and Primal Thought.

---

[55] *Exeg. Soul* II,6 136.35–137.1, quoting Homer, *Odyssey* 4.260-61.
[56] Sasagu Arai argued that *Exeg. Soul* is Simonian in its essential features ("Simonianische Gnosis und die *Exegese über die Seele*," in *Gnosis and Gnosticism: Papers Read at the Seventh International Conference on Patristic Studies*, ed. Martin Krause [Leiden: Brill, 1977], 185–203 at 196–203).
[57] *Exeg. Soul* II,6 127.22-28.
[58] *Exeg. Soul* II,6 134.8-11.
[59] Simonians allegorized Helen of Troy with her torch. In Greek lore, Helen held up a torch in Troy to send light signals to the Greeks, allowing them to rescue her (*Ref.* 6.19.1; Vergil, *Aeneid* 6.518-19). We are not told the meaning of this allegory, but Simonians may have imagined Helen as Thought within humanity sending signals for divine rescue. Epiphanius called Helen's torch "the display of the light from on high" (*Pan.* 21.3.2).
[60] Irenaeus, *AH* 1.23.2.

Whatever the case may have been, the memory of Simon's Helen proved influential. For heresiologists, Helen called up the cultural memory of Jezebel, the archetypal wicked woman of Hebrew scriptures.[61] Simonians, by contrast, put the emphasis on Helen as a pattern of redemption. Some Simonians revered Helen as a teacher and were even called "Helenians."[62]

Simon and the Spirit

In his farewell address in John, Jesus promised to bestow the Holy Spirit, called the Paraclete (16:7). The church father Jerome preserved a reputed saying of Simon in which he declared himself to be the Paraclete.[63] The statement accords with the report of Irenaeus that Simon came to Samaria as Father, to Judea as Son, and to the nations as Spirit.[64] The trinitarian language is Christian, and the theology seems deliberately to oppose the claim in Acts. Not only was Simon capable of *bestowing* the Spirit on his converts, he *was* Spirit, and in this capacity saved the nations of the world.

But how did Simon, by the time of Irenaeus, come to be seen as Spirit? The Refutator preserved a tradition in which Simon, sitting Buddha-like under a plane tree in Samaria, prophesied that, if buried alive, he would rise on the third day. After three days, like the Greek heroes Amphiaraus and Trophonius, Simon disappeared under the earth.[65]

Sidelight on Trophonius and Amphiaraus. Trophonius and Amphiaraus were two ancient Greek heroes. Trophonius built the temple of Apollo at Delphi. Amphiaraus was a sage and warrior of the Peloponnese (southern Greece). At the end of their lives, both figures mysteriously disappeared underground. Cults emerged in which both heroes offered oracles from their lairs in mainland Greece. These cults were still operational and influential in the second century CE.

---

[61] Tuomas Rasimus, "Jezebel in Jewish and Christian Tradition," in *Women and Knowledge in Early Christianity*, ed. Ulla Tervahauta et al. (Leiden: Brill, 2017), 108–32 at 128–31.

[62] Celsus in Origen, *Cels.* 5.62. The presence of "Helenians" who venerated Helen indicates that she was more than "an ancient Eliza Doolittle, testimony to male ego and female gullibility" (*pace* Nicola Denzey Lewis, "Women and Independent Religious Specialists in Second-Century Rome," in Tervahauta et al., eds., *Women and Knowledge*, 21–38 at 29). See further Virginia Burrus, "The Heretical Woman as Symbols in Alexander, Athanasius, Epiphanius, and Jerome," *HTR* 84:3 (1991): 229–48.

[63] Jerome, *Commentary on Matthew* 4.24.5 (*ego sum sermo dei, ego sum speciosus, ego paraclitus, ego omnipotens, ego omnia dei*). Jerome professed to take this quote from a writing attributed to Simon.

[64] Irenaeus, *AH* 1.23.1.

[65] *Ref.* 6.20.3. This tradition, which has Simon die in Samaria, is probably older than the polemical tradition that has him die near Rome (in the *Acts of Peter*). Cf. Pindar, *Nemean Ode* 9.10-29; Ps.-Apollodorus, *Library of Mythology* 3.6.8.

The Refutator claimed that Simon did not rise, to be sure – but if Simon became the Spirit, then perhaps this is how Simonians came to conceive of his resurrection. The resurrected Jesus, in Pauline theology, came as life-giving Spirit (1 Cor. 15:45). If Simon was thought to be Christ, then he may have manifested himself after death in a similar way.

Practices

To Simonian Christians were attributed distinctive practices, some of which have already been discussed (their reputed statue veneration in Rome). Eusebius testified that Simonian Christians practiced baptism (a distinctively Christian rite) in his day.[66] In addition, he reported that they worshiped paintings of Simon and Helen with incense, offerings, and libations.[67] Significantly, he also mentioned their "sobriety" and "purity of life" – evidence of sexual fidelity and their high moral standards.[68] Simonians also practiced exorcism – not uncommon among early Christians in the second century.[69]

The *Declaration Commentary* testifies to a practice of allegory, mostly of the Pentateuch. The *Commentary* also indicates that Simonians read prophetic, Pauline, and gospel literature. In the early second century, they read the Synoptic gospels (Matthew and possibly a form of Luke). By 175 CE, they evidently had their own interpretation of John (Simon as the Paraclete).

Other practices are reported, not all of them reliable. April DeConick attributes to Simonians "sacred sexual practices within a consecrated space they called the Holy of Holies. They considered their ritual sexual intercourse to reenact the blessed union of the Father God and the Mother God."[70] To make this claim, DeConick apparently leaned on Epiphanius, who in his treatment of Simon is largely misleading.[71] Heresiologists used many sexual slanders to defame Simonian Christians. The Refutator, for instance, seems to have assumed that because Simon engaged in sex with a former prostitute, later Simonians followed suit. He used slogans like "the holy united to what is holy will be sanctified" – which may or may not have originally applied to sex.[72] Epiphanius knew or imagined a rite in which Christian "gnostics" collected semen and menses. He duly made Simon, the first "gnostic," the founder of the rite.[73] These accusations have little to no basis in fact. The most we can gather

---

[66] Eusebius, *HE* 2.1.12.
[67] Eusebius, *HE* 2.13.7.
[68] Eusebius, *HE* 2.13.6.
[69] Irenaeus, *AH* 1.23.4.
[70] DeConick, *Gnostic New Age*, 103.
[71] DeConick does not cite her source (*Gnostic New Age* has no notes), but see Epiphanius, *Pan.* 21.2-3; cf. *Ref.* 6.19.5.
[72] *Ref.* 6.19.5.
[73] Epiphanius, *Pan.* 21.4.1-2; cf. *Pan.* 26.

from such reports is that Simonian Christians did not promote celibacy. There is no reason, however, to consider their sexual activity profligate. Eusebius himself gave evidence to the contrary when he spoke of the Simonians's sobriety and purity of life.[74]

Origen remarked that Simonians suppose that eating meat sacrificed to Greco-Roman gods is a matter of indifference.[75] This was another standard heresiological charge flung against several Christian groups. Tertullian, for his part, mentioned a kind of *séance* in which Simonian Christians evoked the souls of the prophets.[76] Such a practice might at least indicate the importance of the Jewish prophetic writings for Simonian Christians (confirmed by the *Declaration Commentary*, which often quotes Isaiah). The *séance*-like practice itself, however, is nowhere else attested and so we should probably withhold judgment about its factuality.

Conclusion

The only people who speak of Simon, Origen of Alexandria observed, are Christians. The reason for this was simple: as a religious group, Simonians only proved a threat to Christians (the very people, incidentally, who preserved almost everything we know about Simonians). Other Christians were threatened by Simonians because some of their practices and beliefs were proximate to their own. Simonians appealed to Jewish scriptures (the Torah and the prophets) but also to gospel parables such as the Lost Sheep. They believed in a heavenly Savior figure who was crucified in Judea. They upheld a Trinitarian concept of God, though they eventually saw the Trinity as the manifestation of a single figure – Simon himself.

This focus on Simon was, it seems, a mid-second century development (after the writing of the *Declaration Commentary*). Whether a Simonian circle existed between Simon's death (around 70 CE?) and Justin's surviving report (about 150 CE) is unknown. The only intervening evidence is the *Declaration Commentary* itself. If we surmise that the author of the *Commentary* addressed a larger group, this group probably existed in Samaria until at least the Bar Kokhba revolt (132 CE), when Simonians from Palestine may have migrated to Rome.

By the time of Irenaeus (180 CE), Simon and his companion Helen were identified with divine entities in preexisting Simonian theology (Mind – the Great Power – and Thought). A story of how Mind came to save imprisoned Thought was allegorized to refer to the redemption of every human soul. Salvation in Simonian Christianity was by the gracious intervention of Simon-Christ, not by human works.[77]

One could argue that in Simonian theology Simon the redeemer came to replace Christ. But replacement language, in my view, is not accurate, since Simonians believed the gospel reports about what Christ did and suffered in Judea. They came

---

[74] Eusebius, *HE* 2.13.6.
[75] Origen, *Cels.* 6.11.
[76] Tertullian, *On the Soul* 57.7.
[77] Irenaeus, *AH* 1.23.3; cf. *Eph* 2:8-9.

to see Christ as a manifestation of Simon, who had revealed himself in a higher way in Samaria (as Father). By this theology, Simonians may have wanted to supersede other Christians, but this strategy did not make them unchristian. (Indeed, a supercessionary impulse is characteristic of Christianity in this period.) The story of Simonian salvation presupposes the structure of salvation as it was expressed in other early Christian texts: a redeemer descends from heaven, dies on a cross, and is present in the world as Spirit.[78]

How long did Simonian Christians last? The Naassene preacher (Chapter 25) used the *Declaration Commentary* in late second-century Egypt. Origen testified that a few Simonians lived in third-century Palestine, though elsewhere he claimed that they had perished.[79] Origen was apparently mistaken, however, since Eusebius, in fourth-century Palestine, indicated that Simonians were still baptizing in his day.[80] There is some evidence that Epiphanius encountered Simonians in late fourth-century Cyprus.[81] What happened to the Simonians in Rome is a mystery. If they were known to Tertullian, then they survived at least until the early third century CE.

If Simonians were never numerically large, Simon himself made a large impact on early Christian memory. He appears as a main character in several novelistic Christian writings, namely the *Acts of Peter* (late second to third century), the Pseudo-Clementine *Homilies*, and *Recognitions*, two fourth-century novels based on a common third-century text.[82] In these novels, Simon is depicted as a charlatan, to be sure. But he was also shown as a successful Christian missionary in both Palestine and Rome. His mission preceded that of Peter, who, hot on Simon's trail, constantly nipped at his heels. It is interesting that Peter's gospel consistently followed the good news of Simon. Peter's message could thus be construed as a polemical response.

These are Christian legends, to be sure. Yet they may hint at a historical point: that what was later deemed Christian "heresy" was not derivative at all, but coeval with – and even prior to – traditions subsequently deemed apostolic. Early Christian historians never actually dismissed the view that Simon was a contemporary of Jesus who had a Christian mission in Palestine and Rome – the latter apparently prior to Paul's. If we could extract Simon from legend, we might even call him one of the most successful of early Christian recruiters whose "primal thought" leavened the imaginations of early Christian theologians for generations.[83]

---

[78] Cf. Herbert Schmid, *Christen und Sethianer: Ein Beitrag zur Diskussion um den religionsgeschichtlichen und den kirchengeschichtlichen Begriff der Gnosis* (Leiden: Brill, 2018), 136.

[79] Origen, *Cels.* 6.11; 1.57.

[80] Eusebius, *HE* 2.1.12.

[81] Ps.-Polybius, *Life of Epiphanius* 59 (*PG* 41.99B).

[82] G. P. Luttikhuizen, "Simon Magus as a Narrative Figure in the *Acts of Peter*," in *Apocryphal Acts of Peter: Miracles and Gnosticism*, ed. Jan N. Bremmer (Leuven: Peeters, 1998), 39–51; Jan Bremmer, *The Pseudo-Clementines* (Leuven: Peeters, 2010); Bernard Pouderon, *La genèse du roman pseudo-Clémentine: Études littéraires et historiques* (Paris: Peeters, 2012); Annette Yoshiko Reed, "Heresiology and the (Jewish-)Christian Novel: Narrativized Polemics in the Pseudo-Clementine *Homilies*," in Iricinschi and Zellentin, ed., *Heresy and Identity*, 273–98.

[83] This conclusion adapts elements of my book, *Desiring Divinity*, 115–18.

Further Reading

Mark Edwards, "Simon Magus, the Bad Samaritan," in *Portraits: Biographical Representations in the Greek and Latin Literature of the Roman Empire*, ed. Mark Edwards and Simon Swain (Oxford: Clarendon, 1997), 69–91.

Alberto Ferreiro, *Simon Magus in Patristic, Medieval and Early Modern Traditions* (Leiden: Brill, 2005), 35–54.

Stephen Haar, *Simon Magus: The First Gnostic?* (Berlin: de Gruyter, 2003).

M. David Litwa, *Desiring Divinity: Self-deification in Ancient Jewish and Christian Mythmaking* (New York: Oxford University Press, 2016), 91–118.

Catherine Osborne, *Rethinking Early Greek Philosophy: Hippolytus of Rome and the Presocratics* (London: Duckworth, 1987), 68–86, 214–27.

Simon Pétrement, *A Separate God: The Christian Origins of Gnosticism*, trans. Carol Harrison (San Francisco: Harper & Row, 1990), 233–46.

Edwin Yamauchi, *Pre-Christian Gnosticism: A Survey of the Proposed Evidences* (London: Tyndale Press, 1973), 62–4.

4

The "Nicolaitans" and Nicolaus

Introduction

About 95 CE, a seer imprisoned on a Greek island condemned a group of Christians, dubbed "Nicolaitans," for what he considered to be idolatry and sexual immorality (Rev. 2:6, 15).[1] These "Nicolaitans" were active or at least influential within the populous cities of Ephesus and Pergamum in Asia Minor (western Turkey). This is what we gather, at least, from two letters sent by this seer "John" to Christian communities in those cities.[2] The seer also wrote a letter to the city of Thyatira in which he condemned a Christian female leader, polemically nicknamed "Jezebel," for the same sins of idolatry and sexual immorality (Rev. 2:20).[3] Such polemic does not mean that this woman was herself a leader of the Nicolaitans.[4] Indeed, it is not safe to infer that Nicolaitans were present in Thyatira at all.[5]

The accusations of idolatry and sexual immorality were vague, blanket indictments that would become routine charges hurled back and forth among Christians.[6] What these accusations actually meant varied with the context. Early Christians disagreed with each other, for instance, about what constituted sexual immorality (*porneia*).

---

[1] Scholars who have written on the Nicolaitans typically take a maximalist or minimalist approach. Adolf von Harnack set a precedent for the maximalists in "The Sect of the Nicolaitans and Nicolaus, Deacon of Jerusalem," *Journal of Religion* 3, no. 4 (1923): 413–22. This approach is still advanced in standard reference works, for instance by Duane F. Watson, "Nicolaitans," in *ABD*, 4:1106–7. In what follows, I pursue a minimalist approach as pioneered by Williams, *Rethinking*, 170–1.

[2] On the Nicolaitans in Revelation, see Elizabeth Schüssler Fiorenza, "Apocalyptic and Gnosis in the Book of Revelation and Paul," *JBL* 92, no. 4 (1973): 565–81 at 567–71; Paul B. Duff, *Who Rides the Beast: Prophetic Rivalry and the Rhetoric of Crisis in the Churches of the Apocalypse* (Oxford: Oxford University Press, 2001), 51–8.

[3] Rasimus, "Jezebel," in Tervahauta et al., eds., *Women and Knowledge*, 108–32 at 113–25.

[4] *Pace* Birger Pearson, "Nicolaitans," in *DGWE*, 867. Tertullian was perhaps the first to claim that "Jezebel" took her teaching from the Nicolaitans (*Modesty* 19.4).

[5] *Pace* Kenneth A. Fox, "The Nicolaitans, Nicolaus, and the Early Church," *Studies of Religion* 23, no. 4 (1994): 485–96 at 486; Paul Trebilco, *The Early Christians in Ephesus from Paul to Ignatius* (Tübingen: Mohr Siebeck, 2004), 308–11; Pearson, *Ancient Gnosticism*, 36.

[6] E.g., *Gos. Judas* 54.24-25. See further Knust, *Abandoned to Lust*, 143–63.

In the larger Greek society, this word typically referred to prostitution, but in biblical usage the meaning was expanded to include a variety of sexual practices linked with unfaithfulness to the Judean deity.[7] Technically, any disapproved sexual practice could be labeled *porneia* and thus classed with practices like adultery, pederasty and prostitution. For one Christian to accuse another of *porneia* pricked a nerve, certainly, even if in reality only small differences in sexual practice were at play.

Porneia in the context of Revelation is likely to be figurative.[8] Following a trope in Jewish scripture (for instance, the prophet Hosea), the seer used *porneia* to refer to idolatry (worshiping other gods beside the Judean deity). The specific act of idolatry condemned by the seer is the act of eating meat sacrificed to Greco-Roman gods. Paul of Tarsus had already dealt with this issue in a letter to the Corinthians (1 Cor. 8 and 10). He concluded that a person with "strong" conscience who knows that cultic statues are "nothing" could eat meat sacrificed to them. At the same time, Greco-Roman divinities were actually demons, and thus one should avoid communion with them (for instance, at temple feasts). Nevertheless, if one is at a dinner party with non-Christian friends, eating the meat served on the table was permitted unless the host made a point of it being offered to the gods.

The seer of Revelation took a stricter stance: any eating of any meat offered to any Greco-Roman god in any setting cut one off from Christ.[9] In effect, the seer disagreed with Paul and other Christians influenced by him. Justin Martyr revealed that there were many self-professing Christians who ate meat previously sacrificed to Greco-Roman deities.[10] Such meat ended up in local markets or was given away for free during festivals. Perhaps some Christians ate the meat as a sign of civic duty and local patriotism.

If the Nicolaitans of Ephesus and Pergamum were little more than Christians condemned for participating in civic feasts, however, it is doubtful whether they ever formed a coherent, self-identifying group. If we assume that Nicolaitans cultivated a group mentality, we would expect them to be mentioned by the Christian leader Ignatius who passed through Asia Minor sometime between 115–140 CE (his dates are contested).[11] Ignatius resembled the seer of Revelation with his non-compromising attitude about sexual ethics.[12] He did not write a letter to the Christians in Pergamum or Thyatira.[13] He did, however, write an epistle to the Ephesians. In this letter Ignatius

---

[7] Dale B. Martin, Jennifer W. Knust, and David Wheeler-Reed, "Can a Man Commit Πορνεία with His Wife?" *JBL* 137, no. 2 (2018): 383–93.

[8] Heikki Räisänen, "The Nicolaitans: Apoc. 2; Acta 6," *ANRW* 26.2 (1995): 1602–44 at 1616–18.

[9] Nikolaus Walter, "Nikolaus, Proselyt aus Antiochien, und die Nikolaiten in Ephesus und Pergamon: Ein Beitrag auch zum Thema: Paulus und Ephesus," *ZNW* 93 (2002): 200–26 at 214.

[10] Justin, *Dial.* 35.1.

[11] See T. D. Barnes, "The Date of Ignatius," *Expository Times* 120, no. 3 (2008): 119–30; Lookadoo, "The Date and Authenticity of the Ignatius Letters."

[12] Note for instance Ignatius's concern for holiness and self-control in Ignatius, *Ephesians* 10:3.

[13] Bauer inferred that Ignatius lacked ideological allies in these two cities (*Orthodoxy and Heresy*, 79–80).

did not mention Nicolaitans; but he did warn against Christians who "bear the name (of Christ) in wicked deceit, while acting in ways unworthy of God."[14] In all his letters, Ignatius was concerned to identify and condemn any practice or idea he considered heterodox. If he knew Nicolaitans, he would have mentioned them.[15] This is an argument from silence, admittedly, but given Ignatian practice, the silence roars. The fact is, the seer of Revelation is thus the *only* author to mention "Nicolaitans" until about 170 CE.

Where did the name "Nicolaitans" come from? The fact that the name is not overtly negative does not mean that it was a self-designation of a coherent group. If it was purely up to the seer of Revelation, however, he would have preferred to call these people by pejorative names like "idolaters" and "Balaamites" (Balaam being an anti-Israelite prophet, Rev. 2:14, Num. 25:1-2; 31:16).[16] If we limit ourselves to the book of Revelation, we do not know where the name came from. It is pure speculation to imagine an Asian founder of the group – a man called "Nicolaus" – who is otherwise unknown.[17]

Nicolaus in the *Syntagma* and Irenaeus

As it happened, a literary figure called Nicolaus made his debut upon the publication of the book of Acts. In Acts, Nicolaus was said to be a proselyte (a convert to Judaism) from Antioch (then capital of the province of Syria). He later became a Christian and was chosen to be part of a team of seven "Hellenist" ministers in Jerusalem, later called deacons (Acts 6:5-6). This is all we know about this Nicolaus, and his historicity remains uncertain.[18] Even if one credited the author of Acts on this score, this author likely wrote two generations after Nicolaus and cited none of his sources by name.[19]

In the mid-second century, the heresy catalogue called the *Syntagma* became available in Rome. Justin Martyr had a copy about 150 CE, but he never mentioned Nicolaitans. Likely, then, Nicolaitans did not appear in the first edition of the *Syntagma*.

---

[14] Ignatius, *Ephesians* 7.1; cf. 9.1; 16.1; 17.1.

[15] Nicolaitans are inserted in the fourth-century expanded recension of Ignatius's letters to the *Trallians* 11.2 and *Philadelphians* 6.6.

[16] For speculative connections between the names "Balaam" and "Nicolaus," see Walter, "Nicolaus," 218-19.

[17] Craig R. Koester, *Revelation: A New Translation with Introduction and Commentary* (New Haven: Yale University Press, 2014), 263.

[18] On the historicity of *Acts*, see the sources cited in Chapter 3, n. 6, along with Jerome Murphy O'Connor, *Paul: A Critical Life* (Oxford: Oxford University Press, 1997), 8-23; Joseph B. Tyson, *Luke, Judaism, and the Scholars: Critical Approaches to Luke–Acts* (Columbia: University of South Carolina Press, 1999); Todd Penner, "Early Christian Heroes and Lukan Narrative: Stephen and the Hellenists in Ancient Historiographical Perspective," in *Rhetoric and Reality in Early Christianities*, ed. Willi Braun (Waterloo: Wilfrid Laurier Press, 2005), 75-97.

[19] On the dating of Acts see Chapter 3, n. 21.

Sometime probably between 165 CE (the approximate year of Justin's death) and 180 CE, an entry on Nicolaitans was added. This explains why Irenaeus, who used the *Syntagma*, reported on the Nicolaitans in his own update of Justin's catalogue.[20]

Whoever added the entry on Nicolaitans likely traced them to the Nicolaus of Acts. Why would this connection have been made? Here we should appreciate the fact that heresiography was also a form of historiography. Heresy writers were motivated to make historical connections to increase the "reality effect" of their discourse.[21] Many of these connections, upon further scrutiny, end up being unreal (as we shall see). Whoever added the Nicolaitan entry, at any rate, wanted to connect the Nicolaitans with the "historical" Nicolaus in Acts. Unfortunately, the Nicolaus in Acts had no connection to Asia Minor (he was Antiochene and ministered in Palestine). Furthermore, by introducing Nicolaus, the editor of the *Syntagma* upset the genealogical connection forged between Simon and all other Christian "heresies." In short, Simon was no longer the sole father of heresy. Nicolaus suddenly became the second father – or stepfather, perhaps.

Irenaeus, who paraphrased the updated *Syntagma* in his *Against Heresies* 1.23-28, seems not to have had any new information to report. He treated Cerinthus in *Against Heresies* 1.26.1 then Nicolaitans in 1.26.3. But when Irenaeus returned to the Nicolaitans (in 3.11.1), he stated his own view that Nicolaitans were a branch of the "gnostics." This claim is confusing, since Irenaeus, following the *Syntagma*, presented *Simon* as the father of the "gnostics." Yet Simon (Acts 8) was – at least narratively – later than Nicolaus (Acts 6).

By presenting the Nicolaitans as a "gnostic" forefather, Irenaeus added a doctrinal component. His globalized "gnostics" were said to distinguish between the creator and the Father of Jesus Christ. They also distinguished "Christ" from Jesus, saying that "Christ" left Jesus and flew back to the "Fullness" (an apparent conflation of Cerinthus with Valentinian terminology).[22]

This is the first time (about 180 CE) that a so-called gnostic doctrine was attributed to the Nicolaitans. Later, following Irenaean precedent, a mishmash of other "gnostic" teachings would be attributed to Nicolaitans from the third to the fifth centuries CE – aeons copulating with aeons, darkness tackling light, along with other outlandish lore we learn mostly from Epiphanius.[23]

[20] Irenaeus, *AH* 1. Cf. Smith, *Guilt*, 139–41.
[21] Nancy F. Partner, "Historicity in an Age of Reality-Fictions," in *A New Philosophy of History*, ed. Frank Ankersmit and Hans Kellner (Chicago: University of Chicago Press, 1995), 21–39; Jonathan Potter, *Representing Reality: Discourse, Rhetoric and Social Construction* (London: Sage, 1996); William Hansen, "Strategies of Authentication in Ancient Popular Literature," in *The Ancient Novel and Beyond*, ed. Stelios Panayotakis, Maaike Zimmerman, and Wytse Keulen (Leiden: Brill, 2003), 301–16.
[22] Irenaeus, *AH* 3.11.1.
[23] See Pseudo-Tertullian, *AAH* 1.6; Epiphanius, *Pan.* 25.2.2–5.1.

Nicolaus After Irenaeus

By the early third century, we see two strategies for dealing with "Nicolaitans." Both strategies link them with the Nicolaus of Acts. The first strategy, represented by the Refutator and Epiphanius, sees Nicolaus himself as both a sexual profligate and the "cause" of the "gnostic" systems.[24] The second strategy, championed by Clement of Alexandria, tried to save Nicolaus from the Nicolaitans. After all, Nicolaus was "apostolic" insofar as he was chosen by the apostles, and was supposedly "full of spirit and wisdom" (Acts 6:3).[25] As a convert to Judaism – according to Acts – he would have learned to abhor sexual immorality long before he became a Christian. It would be awful to imagine, so Clement, that he had fallen from grace and formed a lascivious band of "gnostics." About 200 CE, then, Clement inquired about Nicolaus and recovered what he thought was more authentic tradition.

Clement discovered a saying attributed to Nicolaus that "one must abuse (*parachrāō*) the flesh."[26] In itself, the saying lines up well with Paul's remark, "I beat my body and treat it as a slave" (1 Cor. 9:27). Such ascetic claims were common among early Christians and fully approved by Clement. The trouble, according to Clement, was that certain "Nicolaitans" – a group falsely trying to siphon authority from Nicolaus – interpreted the saying to mean that one must "misuse" (another sense of *parachrāō*) the flesh by leading it into profligate acts (*porneia*). Nicolaus, so Clement, was a "noble" man not involved in *porneia* at all.

From unnamed sources, Clement learned of a story, in fact, which he thought vindicated Nicolaus. According to this tale, Nicolaus was shamed by the apostles because he felt jealous anger toward his wife, who was, reportedly, an attractive woman. To vindicate himself, Nicolaus proceeded to present her before all the apostles, daring any of them who desired her to take her as wife.[27] The assumption may have been than Nicolaus had mastery over his wife's body, and that he offered it to the apostles just as other people offered up their private property (Acts 2:44-45).[28] Clement, for his part, took this story to indicate Nicolaus's self-control. Nicolaus was hardly addicted to sex – he was ready to give away his wife.

Upon reflection, however, the story does not seem to reflect very well upon Nicolaus. Indeed, it was tradition attributed to Jesus that any man who divorces his wife causes her to commit adultery when she marries another man (Matt. 5:32).[29] The Nicolaus of Clement's story was prepared to make his wife an adulteress by offering her to other apostles. (The assumption being that Nicolaus would divorce her – thus

---

[24] *Ref.* 7.36.2-3.
[25] Clement, *Strom.* 2.20.118.5.
[26] Clement, *Strom.* 2.20.118.3.
[27] Clement, *Strom.* 3.4.25.5–3.4.26.3.
[28] Ashwin-Siejkowski, *Clement*, 129.
[29] See further Dale B. Martin, *Sex and the Single Savior: Gender and Sexuality in Biblical Interpretation* (Louisville: Westminster John Knox, 2006), 125–47.

making her available for marriage to another apostle.) In effect, Nicolaus prostituted his wife – who, it should be noted, remains utterly silent in this story with apparently zero control over her own body. This is not an image of a righteous Nicolaus, in effect, but of a jealous husband taking measures that are in tension with Christ's own commands.[30]

How did such a story emerge? We cannot assume that Clement's informants were historically reliable. After all, they probably lived in Alexandria some 160 years after Nicolaus putatively ministered hundreds of miles away in Palestine. What other traditions, besides the book of Acts, did they actually have?

I suspect, if a hypothesis be granted, that the story emerged in the manner of haggadah.[31] An unknown Christian took the saying attributed to Nicolaus ("one must abuse the flesh") and understood "the flesh" to refer to his wife (since husband and wife are "one flesh," Gen. 2:24). The saying was then taken to mean that Nicolaus misused his wife.[32] But why? Because he suspected her of adultery. Clement reported that Nicolaus was "shamed in the presence of the apostles with regard to his jealousy (*zēlotupia*)" – apparently because he suspected his wife of being unfaithful. This reading is based on an episode in the book of Numbers in which a husband suspects his wife of adultery due to his "spirit of jealousy" (Num. 5:14). In the context of this biblical passage, the distinctive word *zēlotupia* is used four times (Num. 5:15, 18, 25, 29 LXX). This chapter on the "test" for adultery was likely recalled by the creator of Clement's story of Nicolaus. The apostles took the role of the priests in testing this woman's fidelity. As a result of the examination, the Nicolaus of Clement's story felt that he could "misuse" his wife – giving her to another man – because he judged her unfaithful and thus able to be divorced.

The story's claim to historicity is thin. Clement wanted to save Nicolaus from the supposed sexual profligacy of the Nicolaitans. He did not realize that the connection between Nicolaus and the Nicolaitans was probably constructed only a generation before him. Ironically, Clement's story raised further questions about Nicolaus's character. A man who abused his wife – (wrongly) suspecting her of adultery and putting her body up as if on auction – was no saint or upstanding deacon of the church.

Nicolaus in Epiphanius

In the late fourth century, Epiphanius had no interest in defending Nicolaus. According to this heresiologist, Nicolaus "ranked among the foremost" Christians until the devil entered him. After trying to restrain himself from having sex with his wife, Epiphanius reported, Nicolaus failed due to lust. Ashamed of his defeat, he ventured to justify it by the outrageous saying – appearing first with

---

[30] Theodoret, in a further attempt to save Nicolaus, tried to argue that Nicolaus was not making up new rules but convicting his opponents (*Fab.* 3.1).

[31] On haggadic interpretation see James Kugel, *In Potiphar's House: The Interpretive Life of Biblical Texts* (Cambridge, MA: Harvard University Press, 1994).

[32] Epiphanius made this point explicit (*Pan.* 25.1.6).

Epiphanius – "Unless one engages in lewdness every day, he cannot have eternal life."[33] Nicolaus duly spawned the Nicolaitans, a licentious group of Christians akin to the "gnostics" – a particular group or set of groups that, according to Epiphanius, feasted on their own semen and menses as if it were the body and blood of Christ.[34]

In relating this tale, Epiphanius had, it seems, no more claim to historicity than Clement. Both the attempt to save Nicolaus's character and to destroy it failed, not least because there were no reliable traditions linking Nicolaus to the Nicolaitans at all.[35] The truth is, we cannot know more about Nicolaus than Acts tells us, and anything more about Nicolaitans than Revelation tells us. To link the two leads straight into the brackish waters of the heresiological imagination, where many ships have foundered.

Conclusion

What, in sum, can we know about the putative Christian group called "Nicolaitans"? Despite the polemic of Revelation, we do not even know if they existed as a group. If they did, we do not know if they recognized themselves as a coherent body of "Nicolaitans." If they were a group, they may have simply identified simply as Christians with a "strong" conscience (in the Pauline sense, Rom. 14–15). Not rigorous enough in their sexual ethics, according to the seer of Revelation, and too closely participating in Greco-Roman civic feasts, they were savaged by his rhetorical scimitar. We have no reliable evidence that "Nicolaitans" linked themselves to the deacon Nicolaus (in Acts 6) or even that they knew of him.[36]

About 170 CE, an editor of the *Syntagma* made the link between the Nicolaitans in Revelation and Nicolaus in Acts. A decade or so later, Irenaeus linked Nicolaitans with "gnostics," his omnibus category for Christian "heretics." In later heresiography, "Nicolaitan" meant little more to the heresiologists than "licentious Christian heretic."[37] The Nicolaitans never had a distinctive doctrine and their sexual ethics were a cesspool of the heresiological imagination. At most, the Nicolaitans were a group of Christians whose lifestyle and attitude toward the larger Greco-Roman culture disagreed with the seer of Revelation. His stinging criticism has ensured that we know of Christians who disagreed on civic and moral matters in late first-century Asia Minor, but of them we know, and must confess that we know, virtually nothing else.[38]

---

[33] Epiphanius, *Pan.* 25.1.5.

[34] Epiphanius, *Pan.* 26.4.7-8.

[35] If Nicolaus really was from Antioch, there would presumably be some connection between him and other Antiochenes like Menander, Ignatius, and Saturninus. Yet Nicolaus disappears from early Christian historiography after Acts 6 – only reappearing when he is connected to Nicolaitans by the heresiologists.

[36] *Pace* Norbert Brox, "Nikolaos und Nicolaiten," *VC* 19, no. 1 (1965): 23–30. Brox's arguments fail because Nicolaitans, if they coveted apostolic validation, would not have appealed to the last of the deacons. Nicolaus was not an apostle, as already pointed out in Ps.-Ignatius, *Trallians* 11.2.

[37] Tertullian, *AM* 1.29.2.

[38] *Pace* Walter, who takes a maximalist and speculative approach. He portrays Nicolaus as a deacon who fled Jerusalem, started a Torah-free mission in his hometown of Antioch, who later

Further Reading

Kenneth A. Fox, "The Nicolaitans, Nicolaus, and the Early Church," *Studies of Religion* 23, no. 4 (1994): 485–96.

Hermut Löhr, "Die 'Lehre der Nikolaiten,' Exegetische und theologische Bemerkungen zu einer neutestamentliche 'Häresie,'" in *Kaum zu Glauben. Von der Häresie und dem Umgang mit ihr. FS Heiner Faulenbach* (Rheinbach: CMZ, 1999), 34–55.

Birger Pearson, "Nicolaitans," in *DGWE*, ed. Wouter Hanegraaff, 867–9.

Heikki Räisänen, "The Nicolaitans: Apoc. 2; Acta 6," *ANRW* 26.2, ed. W. Haase (Berlin: de Gruyter, 1995): 1602–44.

Nikolaus Walter, "Nikolaus, Proselyt aus Antiochien, und die Nikolaiten in Ephesus und Pergamon: Ein Beitrag auch zum Thema: Paulus und Ephesus," *ZNW* 93 (2002): 200–26.

expanded his mission to other cities of Asia Minor, in particular Ephesus. In this view, Nicolaus was a quasi "apostle" who founded a Christianity community in Ephesus, a community that Aquila and Pricilla then Paul joined, but which was later opposed by the seer of Revelation ("Nikolaus," 222–6). Even if we credited Acts *in toto*, Walter reconstructs a story whose plausibility we have no means to judge.

Part Two

Early Syrian Teachers

Menander

Introduction

Sometime in the late first century CE, a Christian teacher by the name of Menander promised the people of Antioch that they would be deathless if dunked in his baptismal waters. To some, at least, it must have seemed the best of initiations, for by these waters, eternal life came immediately without pain, extensive training, or burdensome fees. Menander's baptism promised power over the very beings who made this universe, thus an immediate sense of transcendence in a world where many people were powerless to pay their rents or even purchase their daily bread.

My aim in this chapter is to introduce Menander of Antioch. The treatment is necessarily brief, since all that remains of Menander's life and thought is inscribed in heresiological reports, most of which are barely a paragraph in length. (The Refutator, whether by accident or intent, neglected to report on Menander at all.) To a certain extent, these reports can be weighed and checked against each other. Light can also be thrown on Menander by looking at the context of late first-century Antioch. In the end, however, we must acknowledge how much imaginative construction goes into making Menander return to life on the pages of history.

Life

Like Simon of Samaria, Menander grew up in central Palestine. He lived, however, a generation after Simon in the mid- to late first century CE. We know the name of Menander's hometown, a place called Capparetaea.[1] If Menander had a Semitic name, we do not know it. His Greek name recalled the comic poet of Athens who flourished in the late fourth century BCE. (This poet is quoted in one of Paul's letters [1 Cor. 15:32]: "Let us eat and drink, for tomorrow we die!")

Unfortunately, we know nothing about our Menander's upbringing and education. Justin Martyr, probably reiterating the *Syntagma*, called Menander a Samarian (or

---

[1] Theodoret, excluding some sort of error in transmission, called Menander's hometown "Chabrai" (*Fab.* 1.2.1).

Samaritan).[2] Based on his location, we might infer that Menander was familiar with Samaritan biblical traditions, though a practice of biblical exegesis is lacking in his reports (which represent the mere skeletal remains of his thought). If Menander was once a Samaritan, he at some point became a Christian.

Purportedly, Menander believed that he was sent as an ambassador from "the highest and secret Power."[3] His sense of divine commission is reminiscent of Paul, who claimed authorization by a vision of Christ (1 Cor. 9:1; Gal. 1:11-12). Paul urged that he was sent as an apostle to the Gentiles. Menander was sent as an apostle from the eternal realms above for the salvation of humanity.[4] His sense of his own authority was robust, and his message was aimed at people of every nation.

Menander made a sensible entrepreneurial move by establishing his brand of Christian teaching in the metropolis of Antioch.[5] Antioch was the third largest city in the Roman empire and already known for its Christian population in the 50s and 60s CE. One might even call it the central node of early Christian Gentile networks in the east. In this node, Menander gained many followers.[6] Other Christian leaders in Antioch at the time are bare names that echo in the wind.[7] With Menander, we have at least the outline of an early, if not the earliest, Antiochene Christian theology and ritual practice.

Historical Background

In Antioch of the late first or early second century CE, the followers of Christ were first called "Christians" (Acts 11:26). This labeling practice is significant, because those identified as Christians were evidently seen as separate, or at least distinguishable, from local Jewish groups.

What had led to the separate label? In the 40s CE, Paul had clashed with Peter in Antioch on the issue of requiring Gentile Christians to follow Jewish customs (Gal. 2). Paul seems to have left Antioch in protest – possibly in disgrace – but his way of practicing Christianity eventually became dominant among Gentile Christians. By the time we come to Ignatius in the second century, the practice of "Judaism" was presented as incompatible with Christian salvation.[8]

When anti-Jewish sentiment flared in Antioch, Christians like Menander had all the more reason to disassociate themselves from local Jewish groups. In 67 CE, a Jew by the name of Antiochus rose to speak in the Antiochene assembly. He accused his

---

[2] Justin, *1 Apol.* 26.4 (Σαμαρέα); Irenaeus, *AH* 1.23.5 (*Samarites*); followed by Tertullian, *On the Soul* 50.2.

[3] Tertullian, *On the Soul* 50.2, following Irenaeus, *AH* 1.23.5.

[4] Eusebius, *HE* 3.26.1.

[5] Justin, *1 Apol.* 26.4.

[6] Justin, *1 Apol.* 26.4 (πολλοὺς ἐξαπατῆσαι).

[7] *Acts* 13:1 (Simeon Niger, Lucius of Cyrene, Manaen). The same can be said of "Evodius ... Heron, Cornelius, and Eros" in Eusebius, *HE* 3.22.1; 4.20.1.

[8] Ignatius, *Magnesians* 8.1; 10.3.

own Judean brethren of conniving to burn the whole city to the ground, and produced some Judeans as conspirators.[9] Exploding with rage, the Antiochenes torched several of these "conspirators" on the spot and instituted a loyalty test for the rest of the Judean population in Antioch. Judeans were compelled to offer sacrifice in the Greek manner. Those who refused were slaughtered.[10]

After the catastrophic Jewish war in Judea (70 CE), the Antiochenes twice petitioned the emperor's son Titus to exile the Judeans from Antioch – a population probably ranging between 20,000 and 40,000 people. Titus refused; not out of moral principle, but because the expulsion would cause a refugee crisis. The Judeans had nowhere to go because Titus had just destroyed their homeland. He already had with him a host of Judean captives whom he put to death in costly spectacles throughout the cities of Syria.[11] Titus also began to enforce a Jewish tax as part of a war reparations scheme. This tax put an extra financial burden on Judeans throughout the empire, whether born or converted.[12]

Antiochene Christians thus had financial and political motives to distinguish themselves from Judeans. Pauline Christianity provided a mold to make the distinction possible.[13] Paul had shown how and why Christians were not subject to Jewish Law, which was mediated by angels (Gal. 3:19). This practical stance may have raised theological questions. If Christians were not subject to the Law of the Judean god, were they subject to the Judean god at all?

View of God

Menander answered this question in the negative. He described a type of high deity – a "primal Power" unknown to all (compare John 1:18). This Power did not make the world, but – as in Simonian Christian theology – generated a primal Thought. This primal Thought then gave rise to angels who made the world. Some or all of these angels, however, became evil, evidently by their own choice.[14]

Heresiographers noticed the similarity between this story and the Simonian creation account. Accordingly, they depicted Menander as Simon's disciple and successor.[15]

---

[9] Josephus, *BJ* 7.46-47. Jews had earlier attacked several Syrian cities (2.462-63).

[10] Josephus, *BJ* 7.46-53. See further John M. G. Barclay, *Jews in the Mediterranean Diaspora* (Edinburgh: T. & T. Clark, 1996), 256–8.

[11] Josephus, *BJ* 7.96.

[12] Josephus, *BJ* 7.218; Dio Cassius, *Roman History* 65.7.2. See further Marius Heemstra, *Fiscus Iudaicus and the Parting of the Ways* (Tübingen: Mohr Siebeck, 2010).

[13] On Antioch, see further Wayne Meeks and Robert L. Wilken, *Jews and Christians in Antioch in the First Four Centuries of the Common Era* (Missoula: Scholars Press, 1978); D. S. Wallace-Hadrill, *Christian Antioch: A Study of Early Christian Thought in the East* (Cambridge: Cambridge University Press, 1982), 14–26; Magnus Zetterholm, *The Formation of Christianity in Antioch* (London: Routledge, 2003).

[14] Irenaeus, *AH* 1.23.5, Epiphanius, *Pan.* 22.

[15] Justin, *1 Apol.* 26.4, followed by DeConick, *Gnostic New Age*, 149.

The similarity in their theology seems real enough; their social connection, however, remains uncertain. Quite possibly, Simonian Christianity influenced Menander in Samaria. If so, Menander is evidence for the existence of Simonian Christian thought in the late first century. Assuming this was the case, however, Menander steered his own course. His version of Thought, for instance, is not identified with Helen or said to have become incarnate.

Tertullian is the sole source for the tradition that, according to Menander, the human body is the work of angels.[16] Perhaps we should doubt this report, since there is no evidence of harsh discipline of the body in what became Menander's Christian conventicle. On the other hand, creation by angels was a well-known Jewish tradition. Philo in particular argued that certain "co-workers" (widely thought of as angels or powers) made the human body.[17] There was nothing particularly radical about this idea.

Baptism

What other Christians found radical was that Menander instituted his own version of the Christian water rite. Outside of Judea, baptism was already a distinctively Christian practice. Instead of baptism into Christ, Menander reportedly proclaimed a baptism "in" or "with reference to him(self)." This is how Irenaeus put it.[18] Eusebius may preserve Irenaeus's original Greek which referred to baptism simply "from" or "in the interest of" Menander – a fairly innocuous phrase.[19] Being baptized "into the name of the Lord Jesus" was standard jargon for Christian baptism (Acts 8:16; 19:5) and it meant – among other things – being placed in a relationship of belonging to a deity. Paul denied that he baptized people in his own name (1 Cor. 1:13) since that might indicate competition with Christ. Justin Martyr, whose *Syntagma* was the probable source of Irenaeus, wanted to portray Menander as an arrogant self-deifier.[20]

Unfortunately we have no Menandrian source to use as a touchstone against heresiographical portraits. Even if we give heresiographers the benefit of the doubt, baptism "in" or "with reference to him [Menander]" probably meant little more than being initiated into Menander's Christian circle. Even if Menander used his own name in the baptismal rite, it is unlikely that he made this ritual innovation to renounce his devotion to Christ. Later heresiographers thought that Menander, like Simon, aimed to replace Christ as Savior.[21] But if Menander only presented himself as "sent" by the primal deity, then he envisioned himself as an apostle, not as the Savior himself.

---

[16] Tertullian, *Resurrection* 5.2. Perhaps there is conflation here with Saturninus. Cf. Tertullian, *On the Soul* 23.1.

[17] Philo, *On the Creation* 72-75 with Runia, *On the Creation*, 236–44.

[18] Irenaeus, *AH* 1.23.5 (*in eum baptisma*).

[19] Eusebius, *HE* 3.26.2 (πρὸς αὐτοῦ βαπτίσματος)

[20] Justin Martyr, *1 Apol.* 26.1.

[21] Irenaeus, *AH* 1.23.5, followed by Eusebius, *HE* 3.26.1; Theodoret, *Fab.* 1.1.3.

More secure is the report that those baptized "in Menander" received resurrection life – called "immortal and incorruptible" life. Heresiographers apparently understood this immortal life to mean perpetual physical life. Not only were Menander's followers made deathless (according to Justin Martyr's report), they did not even grow old (a point interestingly added by Irenaeus).[22]

Perhaps Menander did use the common poetic tag "immortal and ageless" to describe his baptized initiates. If he did, he probably used the adjectives as synonyms. Around 150 CE, Justin Martyr wrote that Menandrian Christians were still confessing their deathlessness in Syria (or perhaps Rome, where Justin was writing). They did so even though Menander himself had been physically dead for more than a generation. If we could make an educated guess, Menander's promise of immortal life went no further than the promise of the Johannine Jesus: "Truly I say to you, the one who believes in me has eternal life."[23] The experience of eternality was in both cases a spiritual reality obtained in this life.[24]

Menander would have had to admit that his disciples physically died, because the point of baptism was also to transcend and overcome the world-creating angels. It is likely, that is, that Menander envisioned a postmortem ascent in which he and his followers defeated and surmounted the angelic lords (aka demons) roaming the lower heavens. True life was experienced above the heavens, in the realm of the "eternities," otherwise known as "aeons."[25]

Like the author(s) of John, Menander supported a theory of exclusive salvation (John 14:6). Unless people were baptized in Menander's circle, it was impossible to be saved. This datum comes from Pseudo-Tertullian.[26] If this report is true, perhaps we can detect implicit criticism of Menander in "Peter's" declaration that only in Jesus's name can people be saved (Acts 4:12).

According to Menander, salvation came through knowledge, a knowledge open to all and probably mediated through baptism. This knowledge gave Menandrian Christians power to defeat wicked angels (presumably the same ones who made the world). Perhaps we can detect here implicit criticism of other Christians who worshiped one of these angels as the Judean "god."

Tertullian called those baptized by Menander "apostles."[27] If this is not mere sarcasm, we might imagine Menander sending out missionaries to spread his version of Christianity. Where it spread, if anywhere, we do not know. Menander, unlike Paul, apparently remained in a single city (Antioch), but perhaps some of his disciples went abroad. How they spread his message is also unknown. If Menander wrote any work of Christian literature, it has long since been lost.

---

[22] Justin, *1 Apol.* 26.5; Irenaeus, *AH* 1.23.5 (*non senescentes*).

[23] John 6:47; cf. 5:24; 10:28; 11:25-26; 17:3. A similar point is made by Outi Lehtipuu, *Debates over the Resurrection of the Dead: Constructing Early Christian Identity* (Oxford: Oxford University Press, 2015), 195.

[24] Tertullian, *On the Soul* 50.2 (*statim resurrectionis compotes fiant*); cf. Clement, *Strom.* 3.6.48.1.

[25] Eusebius specifically mentions that Menander descended from the aeons (*HE* 3.26.1-2).

[26] Pseudo-Tertullian, *AAH* 1.3. Lehtipuu, *Debates*, 180–200.

[27] Tertullian, *On the Soul* 50.5.5.

Conclusion

What can we conclude from the clipped and often cantankerous accounts describing Menander of Antioch? First of all, he was not just a single, freewheeling theologian. He had a circle of Christians initiated in a particular rite of baptism. He thought of himself as an apostle sent from heaven, and perhaps viewed some of his baptized followers as apostles as well. Even if he had no social connections to Simon, he might have been influenced by Simonian theology which was spread in Samaria.

Menandrian Christianity was similar in some respects to Simonian thought. Equally significant, however, are features shared with Johannine Christianity: an unknown primal God sends a savior figure who employs a baptismal rite. Salvation is the grant of eternal life; it is universal (meant for all nations) but exclusive, saving only a small group. These overlaps are not enough to draw historical links, but they give an impression of the kinds of Christianity that flourished in late first-century Syria.

Apart from the daring claims that Menander supposedly made about himself, the fact that he maintained a baptismal rite would have signaled his Christian identity to his contemporaries in Antioch. It is this very identity that other Christians like Justin Martyr and Eusebius strove to undercut.[28] Menander had, according to Justin, many followers.[29] Some of them, perhaps, made it to Rome by the mid-second century where Justin felt compelled to warn against them. Hegesippus, an early Christian possibly from Palestine, mentioned a group of "Menandrians" between 174–189 CE, though we do not know where they were.[30] If Menander died some time before Hadrian's reign (117 CE), his Christian movement likely survived him for at least two generations – which was ample time to influence several other Christian thinkers and groups.

Further Reading

W. Foerster, "Die 'ersten Gnostiker' Simon und Menander," in *Le origini dello gnosticismo: Colloquio di Messina 13–18 Aprile 1966* (Leiden: Brill, 1970), 190–6.

Christoph Markschies, "Christian Gnosticism and Judaism in the First Decades of the Second Century," in *Jews and Christians in the First and Second Centuries: The Interbellum 70–132 CE*, ed. Joshua Schwartz and Peter J. Tomson (Leiden: Brill, 2018), 340–54 at 348–9.

Birger Pearson, *Ancient Gnosticism: Traditions and Literature* (Minneapolis: Fortress, 2007), 33–4.

Simone Pétrement, *A Separate God: The Christian Origins of Gnosticism*, trans. Carol Harrison (San Francisco: Harper & Row, 1990), 315–28.

Roelof van den Broek, "Menander," in *DGWE*, ed. Wouter Hanegraaff, 786–7.

Meike Willung, *Euseb von Cäsarea als Häreseograph* (Berlin: de Gruyter, 2009), 99–106.

---

[28] Justin, *1 Apol.* 26.6; Eusebius, *HE* 3.26.4.
[29] Justin, *1 Apol.* 26.4.
[30] Hegesippus in Eusebius, *HE* 4.22.5.

Saturninus

Introduction

If the human mind tends to forget facts and dates, colorful images yet sparkle in the memory. The early Christian theologian Saturninus bestowed two images which help to recall the contours of his thought, namely the spark and the worm. The worm was an image for Adam when he was first created. He could not stand upright, and so he slithered on the ground like a worm. What caused him to stand was a spark sent down from heaven originating with the highest deity. This divine spark entered Adam; and because of it, Adam not only stood upright, he towered – intellectually and spiritually – above his creators.

In what follows, I present the life and thought of Saturninus. I can only be brief, as in the case of Menander, since all that survives of Saturninus comes to us via heresiological reports. Thankfully, these reports are somewhat fuller than they were for Menander. They present a theological storyline, mainly a retelling of Genesis 1–3, and an ethic of abstinence from meat and marriage. These two elements of belief and practice were apparently pivotal for the founding of the Sethian Christian group discussed in the next chapter.

Life

Saturninus (also known as Satorneilos and Satornil) lived and worked in Antioch, the same city as Menander, though a generation later. Eusebius dated Saturninus to the reign of the emperor Hadrian (117–138 CE).[1] In the same context, the church historian said that Saturninus set up a "school" (*didaskaleion*), depicting him more as a philosopher than as a religious leader. Nonetheless, we should not exclude the idea that Saturninus's "school" did double duty as a small, ecclesial formation within a larger network of Christian assemblies in Antioch (among them the networks of Menander and Ignatius, for instance).

---

[1] Eusebius, *HE* 4.6.4; 4.7.3.

Saturninus's theology, like Menander's, assumes rising tensions between at least some Jews and some Christians in Syria. Indeed, it expresses a strongly anti-Judaic stance insofar as it openly sought to discredit the Judean deity. In the previous chapter, we discussed how the Judean community in Antioch was in periodic tension with the larger population, due (largely) to political factors during the first Jewish War (66–73 CE). The mutual suspicion flared up again when another Jewish war broke out in Palestine between the years 132–135 CE.

Sidelight on the Bar Kokhba Revolt. Some said that the revolt started when the emperor Hadrian forbade the Jews to circumcise their sons.[2] More likely, it started when Hadrian decided to make Jerusalem – still in ruins – a Roman colony. The city would be refurbished and given tax benefits to attract new colonists. As a crowning "gift," Hadrian began construction of a temple to Zeus on the site of Yahweh's ancient shrine.

Whereas the Athenians were happy to have Hadrian build for them a temple of Zeus (still partly standing today), many Jews were outraged by the colonization not just of their land, but of their religion. About 132 CE, rumblings of revolt burst into all-out war. A man with messianic ambitions – nicknamed "Son of the Star," or Bar Kokhba, emerged as leader of a small Jewish state.

To defeat him, Hadrian called in a trusted general from Britain, Julius Severus. Severus, realizing he could not counter the guerilla tactics of the Judeans without huge losses, drove them into caves and fortresses to starve them. By 135 CE, Roman armies emerged triumphant, with reportedly over half a million Judeans slain and 985 of their villages razed. As a final blow, Hadrian forbade Jews from entering the city of Jerusalem, renamed "Aelia Capitolina."[3]

In relative proximity to this war, Jews in Syria (including its capital, Antioch) showed "signs of disturbance," gathered together, and gave "evidence of great hostility to the Romans."[4] Though we know of no details, these Jews would have been subject to a backlash from civic authorities and other groups eager to appease Roman power and to maintain the *status quo*.

Antioch was thus a place where Christians had reason – selectively – to distinguish their form of worship from Judaism. They could distinguish themselves not only by modifying or rejecting Judean ritual, but by mounting an attack upon the Judean deity. Johannine Christians had shot the first round: the father of the Jews was not the Father of Jesus Christ, but the devil('s father, John 8:44). Saturninus wheeled out

[2] *SHA Hadrian* 13.10.
[3] Dio Cassius, *Roman History* 69.12.1-3; Eusebius, *HE* 4.6. On the Bar Kokhba revolt, see, e.g., Hanan Eshel, "The Bar Kochba Revolt, 132–35," in *The Cambridge Ancient History, Volume 4*, 105–27; Anthony Everitt, *Hadrian and the Triumph of Rome* (London: Head of Zeus, 2013), ch. XXIII; Peter Schäfer, ed., *The Bar Kokhba War Reconsidered: New Perspectives on the Second Jewish Revolt against Rome* (Tübingen: Mohr Siebeck, 2003).
[4] Dio Cassius, *Roman History* 69.13-14.

bigger artillery: Christ was not the loyal son of the Judean "god"; in fact, he arrived in order to destroy him.[5]

Despite Saturninus's seeming antagonism toward the Judean deity, he was deeply familiar with Judean scriptures and traditions, using them as a springboard for his thought. Due to his knowledge of scripture, we might prefer the view that Saturninus had a Judean or Samaritan background. Nevertheless, by Saturninus's time, Christianity had been established in Antioch for at least two generations (since about 40 CE). It is possible, then, that Saturninus first encountered Judean scriptures and exegetical techniques among self-identifying Christians. If Saturninus was born about 80 CE (when Menander flourished), he could have been raised a Christian from birth.

What we do know is that Saturninus approached Judean scripture with no love or loyalty to the Judean deity. He reportedly considered Jewish scripture, at least in part, to be false intelligence whispered by the devil into the ears of Hebrew prophets. Other parts, he thought, were inspired by the angels who made the world.[6] These angels, if anyone, were qualified to tell the story of creation. Yet their self-serving narrative, even if accurate in parts, required a skeptical eye.

View of God

Like Simon and Menander, Saturninus preached an unknown primal deity, a being familiar from both Platonist philosophy and Christian scripture (Matt. 11:27; John 1:18; 1 Tim. 6:16). That the Jewish deity was different from the Father was known from passages like John 5:37 (the Jews are unfamiliar with the shape and voice of Jesus's Father) and 8:44 (the Jews' father is the devil['s father]).

That the Judean deity was himself an angel is understandable from the language of Jewish scripture. The "angel of Yahweh" who once appeared to Moses in the bush, for instance, seems hardly different from Yahweh himself (Exod. 3–4; compare Gen. 21:17; Judg. 13:9). And since the name of Yahweh was said to reside in his angel (Exod. 23:21), they were taken as functionally identical.[7] The fact that Yahweh gave all the nations to angelic princes – reserving Israel for himself – also hinted at Yahweh's angelic identity (Deut. 32:8 LXX).

According to the Hebrew Bible, Yahweh made the world. But he was not alone. Yahweh's regular use of the "Let us (do such and such)" indicated that he worked with a team (Gen. 1:26; 11:7) – the angelic "co-workers" known to Philo (see the previous chapter).[8] Saturninus believed that Yahweh was one of seven world-creating angels. World-creating angels are familiar from Simon and Menander, who more than likely adapted Jewish traditions. What is distinctive about Saturninus is their

---

[5] Irenaeus, *AH* 1.24.2.
[6] Irenaeus, *AH* 1.24.2.
[7] See further Fossum, *Name*, 257–338.
[8] Philo, *On the Creation* 72-75.

number. To arrive at seven, Saturninus probably adapted the Jewish idea of exactly seven archangels.[9]

That the angels had a special hand in making humanity was known from Gen. 1:26, which Saturninus, according to the reports, cited in his own way. Whereas the Septuagint presents the Judean deity as saying, "Let us make a human in *our* image and likeness," Saturninus had his angels say amongst themselves: "Let us make a human in the image and likeness." That is, Saturninus's version lacked the pronoun "our."[10] For him, then, the angels were not using their *own* image as a model, but the image of a higher Human above.

Like Plato's creator in the *Timaeus*, the creating angels worked from a model. Their blueprint was the luminous image of the divine Human. This being emerged from a reading of Gen. 1:3 (LXX), where the divine declaration "Let there be light!" can also be translated, "Let there be Man!" The Greek word for "man" (*phōs*) has the same letters as the Greek word for light. The accents are different, but in an ancient manuscript, these marks were typically absent. Thus Saturninus, among other ancient interpreters, could see a Light Man shining from Gen. 1:3.[11]

When the creating angels caught sight of the Light Man, they fell in love with his beauty (according to Epiphanius) and decided to reproduce it as best they could.[12] But their creation – which they molded from dust in accordance with Gen. 2:7 – was a pathetic mud man, able only to wriggle on the ground like a worm. (Here we can probably detect a narrative expansion of Ps. 22:6: "I am a worm and no man.")

Catching sight of the worm man, the Light Man had pity on his reflection and sent him the spark of life. This spark was perhaps ignited from a reading of John's prologue, where divine light enlightens every person (1:9), and bestows life (1:4). According to Saturninus, the spark of life allowed the first human to stand upright and to become rational.[13]

Later, some humans lost the spark. These are probably humans stemming from Cain, whose father was not Adam but the devil according to certain Jewish traditions.[14] As a result, two human families emerged: one evil, the other good. This kind of dualism (likely simplified by the heresiographers) was watered by the streams of

[9] *Tob* 12:15; 1 En. 20; 81:5; 87:2; 90:21-22. Other texts cited in Pétrement, *Separate God*, 59–61. See further Christoph Berner, "The Four (or Seven) Archangels in the First Book of Enoch and Early Jewish Writings in the Second Temple Period," in *Angels: The Concept of Celestial Beings*, ed. Friedrich Reiterer (Berlin: de Gruyter, 2006), 395–411.

[10] *Ref.* 7.28.2; Epiphanius, *Pan.* 23.1.7.

[11] See further Elaine Pagels, "Exegesis of Genesis 1 in the Gospels of Thomas and John," *JBL* 118, no. 3 (1999): 477–96, and the potpourri of traditions cited by Fossum, *Name*, 266–91.

[12] Epiphanius, *Pan.* 23.1.6-7.

[13] Cf. the righteous spark in *Paraphrase of Shem* VII,1 31.23-30; 33.30-35; 46.13-15, 17-18. Cf. also *Ap. John* II,1 19,18–20.5; *Nat. Rulers* II,4 87.33–88.15; *Orig. World* II,5 115-116.

[14] James Kugel, *Traditions of the Bible: A Guide to the Bible How it Was at the Start of the Common Era* (Cambridge, MA: Harvard University Press, 1998), 78, 100, 121, 123, 147, 157.

Judean sectarian ideology, which sometimes contrasted the "children of light" and the "children of darkness."[15]

In outline, the rest of Saturninus's story of salvation can be derived from gospel and Pauline literature. Christ comes as Savior, fights off demonic powers, and saves those who believe in him. For Saturninus, one of these demonic powers was the Judean deity, whom Christ came to destroy. Compare John 12:31: "Now the ruler of this world will be driven out."

Some heresiographers accused Saturninus of presenting a phantasmal Christ.[16] But Saturninus did not deny Christ's incarnation. He said that Christ in his divine nature was "unborn and formless." His was apparently an early version of the two-nature theory of incarnation. As a human, Christ came in a physical body, but in his divine nature, he was bodiless and unborn just like his Father.

Ethics

Heresiographers said nothing about Saturninian ritual. This is not an indication that Saturninus renounced ritual practice. Assuming he was a Christian – as seems evident from his theology – he probably performed Christian rites. If his ritual practice significantly differed from that of other Christians, one suspects that heresiographers would have accused him of practicing "magic," one of their most common rhetorical maneuvers.[17]

As it happened, heresiographers found more traction when it came to Saturninus's ethics. According to Irenaeus, Saturninus taught that marriage and procreation were from Satan (a name which could – though we are uncertain – have been meant to designate the Judean deity, cf. Gen. 1:28). If this report is true, it strongly suggests that followers of Saturninus practiced celibacy. Most of Saturninus's followers, Irenaeus added, abstained from meat. The fact that *some* evidently did not abstain indicates that vegetarianism was a recommendation for serious members in Saturninus's circle, though not a strict requirement.[18]

Assuming these reports are valid, we might reconstruct the logic of Saturninus's practices. Perhaps we can infer that because Saturninus viewed the angelic creator as demonic, he resisted his command to "be fruitful and multiply" (Gen. 1:28). The point of life was to release the divine spark, not to transmit it to offspring, rebinding it in the flesh of one's children. When one's own flesh perished, the spark would float up whence it came, and the angelic creators would be robbed of their power over it. The spark would then be reunited with the Light Man, its source.[19]

---

[15] *1QS* 1.9-10; 1 Thess. 5.5.
[16] Epiphanius, *Pan.* 23.1.10.
[17] See Chapter 3 (Simon), n. 5.
[18] Irenaeus, *AH* 1.24.2.
[19] Tertullian, *On the Soul* 23.1.

One would think that the entrance fee for joining Saturninus's circle was too high for the Antiochenes (stereotyped in antiquity as lovers of pleasure). Yet heresiographers, at least, indicated that Saturninus's rigorist ethic proved attractive.[20] They assumed that he formed a group cohesive enough to be called "Saturninians," with the upper level of its membership, at least, abstaining from both meat and marriage.

Conclusion

Saturninian Christians evidently survived their founder. Justin Martyr mentioned "Saturninians," possibly at Rome, about 160 CE, and Hegesippus referred to the same group between 174–189.[21] Indeed, Saturninus continued to be mentioned as a threat in heresy catalogues as far as the fifth century CE, though we do not know exactly how long the Saturninian group survived as a discrete social formation.

Regardless of how long Saturninian Christians lasted, the theological seeds sown by Saturninus bore much fruit. Along with Johannine Christians, Saturninians were among the first to create a strong ideological boundary between their group and competing Jewish (and Christian) circles who worshiped the Jewish deity. Saturninus is the first known Antiochene theologian whose theology derives largely from the exegesis of scriptural texts (with a healthy dose of Jewish tradition). He was determined to revise the book of Genesis. In this revision, Saturninus was the first Christian clearly to identify the Judean god as an angel, one of seven wicked creators. This was a fateful move, proving influential for Marcion as well as the "Seed of Seth," a more shadowy but influential group discussed in the following chapter.

Further Reading

Winrich Löhr, "Christian Gnostics and Greek Philosophy in the Second Century," *Early Christianity* 3 (2012): 349–77 at 373–5.

Christoph Markschies, "Christian Gnosticism and Judaism in the First Decades of the Second Century," in *Jews and Christians in the First and Second Centuries: The Interbellum 70–132 CE*, ed. Joshua Schwartz and Peter J. Tomson (Leiden: Brill, 2018), 349–50.

Birger Pearson, *Ancient Gnosticism: Tradition and Literature* (Minneapolis: Fortress, 2007), 34–5.

Simone Pétrement, *A Separate God: The Christian Origins of Gnosticism*, trans. Carol Harrison (San Francisco: Harper & Row, 1990), 329–35.

Roelof van den Broek, "Satornilus," in *DGWE*, ed. Wouter Hanegraaff, 1037–8.

Meike Willung, *Euseb von Cäsarea als Häreseograph* (Berlin: de Gruyter, 2009), 134–40.

---

[20] Irenaeus, *AH* 1.24.2.
[21] Justin, *Dial.* 35.6; Hegesippus in Eusebius, *HE* 4.22.5.

The Seed of Seth

Introduction

It might seem strange today that a group of early Christians would depict the creator as a lion-faced serpent, a miscarriage expelled from the divine world, a rapist and enemy of the spiritual race – but such is the depiction of several Christian thinkers toward the midpoint of the second century.[1] These thinkers were part of a larger Christian movement that called itself, among other names, "the Seed (that is, offspring) of Seth."[2]

Modern scholars have called this movement "Sethian" or "the Gnostics."[3] Seth, third son of Adam, had preserved God's image (Gen. 5:3) to become the spiritual father of the redeemed.[4] Like Saturninus, Sethians envisioned two human families

---

[1] For the serpent and lion face, see *Ap. John* BG 37.21. For the "lion-faced serpent," see *Ap. John* II,1 10.9. The texts are translated by Karen King, *Secret Revelation of John* (Cambridge, MA: Harvard University Press, 2006), 42–3. See further Howard M. Jackson, *The Lion Becomes Man: The Gnostic Leontomorphic Creator and the Platonic Tradition* (Atlanta: Scholars Press, 1985).

[2] For "seed of (great) Seth," see, e.g., *Ap. John* BG 36.3-4; *Gosp. Eg.* III,2 54.10-11; 60.8. The group also used the self-designation "the Immovable Race," but not exclusively (Michael Williams, *The Immovable Race* [Leiden: Brill, 1985], 206).

[3] In delimiting a sociological group called "the Seed of Seth," I follow the method, though not the terminology, of David Brakke, *The Gnostics* (Cambridge, MA: Harvard University Press, 2010), 29–51. For different views on how to refer to this group, see Michael Williams, "On Ancient Gnosticism as a Problematic Category," in Trompf, ed., *Gnostic World*, 100–117; Mark Edwards, "The Gnostic Myth," in Lieu and Paget, eds., *Christianity in the Second Century*, 137–50; Burns, "Gnosticism, Gnostics, and Gnosis," in Trompf, ed., *Gnostic World*, 9–25.

[4] For Seth, see A. F. J. Klijn, *Seth in Jewish, Christian, and Gnostic Literature.* (Leiden: Brill, 1977); Pearson, *Ancient Gnosticism*, 52–83; Guy Stroumsa, *Another Seed: Studies in Gnostic Mythology* (Leiden: Brill, 1984), 73–6; John D. Turner, "The Gnostic Seth," in *Biblical Figures Outside the Bible*, ed. M. Stone and T. Bergren (Harrisburg: Trinity International Press, 1998), 33–58; Bernard Barc, "Seth et sa race dans la Bible et dans le Livre des secrets de Jean," in *Les Textes de Nag Hammadi: Histoire des religions et approches contemporaines*, ed. Jean-Pierre Mahé, Paul-Hubert Poirier, and Madeleine Scopello (Paris: AIBL, 2010), 155–76; Jens Schröter, "The Figure of Seth in Early Jewish and Christian Writings: Was there a Sethian 'Gnosticism'?" in Nicklas et al., eds., *Other Side*, 135–48.

opposed almost since the beginning of time. One branch of the family tree, the seed of Cain (cf. 1 John 3:12), became wicked and were initially wiped out in the great Flood (Gen. 6–8). Seth's offspring, however, were preserved and existed since ancient times as a small enclave like an ark riding on a sea of turmoil.

The language of "seed," though it sounds genetic, did not describe a predetermined or fixed identity.[5] Seth's "seed" were not necessarily Seth's biological descendants. Members became Seth's children by spiritual rebirth in a rite of baptism, a rite which conveyed "the spirit of life." This spirit of life was a higher, light-like substance analogous to Saturninus's "spark" (Chapter 6). This light-spirit endowed people with spiritual insight.[6]

When Irenaeus summarized the Sethian story of God about 180 CE, he had no names for its creator(s).[7] Typically, if Irenaeus could find names for his opponents, he supplied them. This indicates that his source(s) left no name, and likely this was intentional. The seed of Seth often wrote in the persona of ancient sages.[8] They did so to show that theirs was the most ancient wisdom, far older than that of Moses – older even than creation itself. For present purposes, the author(s) of Irenaeus's story can be called "the Sethian teacher(s)" – since we suspect that there were several minds who put the story together. The story told has been identified with an early version of the *Secret Book of John*, two longer and two shorter versions which have been discovered in the sands of Egypt.[9]

Historical Setting

The Sethian teacher(s) probably had several purposes for writing a story of God, but one of them was to attack what he perceived to be Jewish theology. For most Judeans, Yahweh was the only deity and creator, served by myriads of angels. The Sethian teacher conceded that Yahweh (polemically dubbed "Yaldabaoth") was the creator of this world, served by angels; but Yahweh's idea of himself as the only God was a piece of deluded conceit. The name "Yaldabaoth" emphasized that he was the Judean deity, for he bore four of Yahweh's Hebrew titles (Yao, El, Adonai, Sabaoth)

---

[5] Williams, *Immovable*, 160–85; Denise Kimber Buell, *Why This New Race: Ethnic Reasoning in Early Christianity* (New York: Columbia University Press, 2005), 35–137.

[6] For the background in Pauline theology, see Caroline Johnson Hodge, *If Sons Then Heirs: A Study of Kinship and Ethnicity in the Letters of Paul* (Oxford: Oxford University Press, 2007).

[7] Irenaeus, *AH* 1.29.

[8] On the genre and literary strategies of Gnostic texts, see King, "The *Apocryphon of John*: Genre and Christian Re-making of the World," in *Nag Hammadi Schriften in der Literatur und Theologiegeschichte des frühen Christentums*, ed. Jens Schröter (Tübingen: Mohr Siebeck, 2017), 141–60; Turner, "Genres of Gnostic Literature and the 'Classical Gnostic' School of Thought," in Trompf, ed., *Gnostic World*, 133–46.

[9] *Ap. John* BG 22.17–44.17 corresponds to Irenaeus, *AH* 1.29.1-4. For the Coptic texts of *Ap. John*, see Michael Waldstein and Frederik Wisse, eds., *The Apocryphon of John: Synopsis of Nag Hammadi Codices II,1; III,1; and IV,1 with BG 8502,2* (Leiden: Brill, 1995). For the manuscript tradition, see Turner, *Sethian Gnosticism*, 69–77.

fused into one.[10] The fact that the Sethian teacher called Yaldabaoth "Samael" ("blind god") and "Saklas" ("fool") hints that he spoke, or was otherwise familiar with, a Semitic tongue.

The teacher's hostile revision was a not-so-subtle attack on Yahweh, and by extension, an attack on Judeans who worshiped Yahweh as their Lord. Such an attack was most likely executed in a region where Jews were a perceived threat to fledgling Christian groups. By late 117 CE, the Jews in Egypt had been virtually wiped out by Roman legions who crushed them as reprisal for rebellion.[11]

Sidelight on the Diaspora Revolt. As the Emperor Trajan was at the peak of military success in Mesopotamia (specifically, southern Iraq), the Jews of North Africa revolted (about 115 CE). Taking over several cities of Cyrene (modern Libya), a renegade army marched east toward Alexandria. Repulsed from the city, the army swarmed into central Egypt and was barely restrained by local militia until Trajan sent a top general, Marcius Turbo, with crack troops who proceeded indiscriminately to mow down the Jews in Egypt (116–117 CE). After 117, very few Jews survived in Alexandria and the Egyptian countryside.[12]

We know that there were Christian communities in Alexandria during Hadrian's reign (117–138 CE), because we know the names of their leaders: Basilides, Carpocrates, and Valentinus (Chapters 9–11). On present evidence, these theologians did not openly attack the Judean deity. The Sethian teacher did. One suspects that this teacher probably came from an area where Christians lived in proximity to a large and competing Judean community – which, after 117 CE, could not have been Egypt.

Under pressure from Judeans who claimed both antiquity and truth for their religion, early Christians needed to create strong conceptual boundaries to define themselves in an era of political tension between Romans and Jews. Such boundary-making was tricky because Christians shared – one might say appropriated – many Judean texts and traditions, including the book of Genesis. If a group of Christians could compose their own revision of Genesis in which the Judean deity was unveiled as a demonic imposter, they could show that – regardless of their antiquity – the Mosaic writings were, at best, half-truths.

This revision of Genesis was even more daring than what Saturninus devised. It was written into a text that was eventually framed as a kind of sequel to the gospel

---

[10] Tuomas Rasimus, *Paradise Reconsidered in Gnostic Mythmaking: Rethinking Sethianism in Light of the Ophite Evidence* (Leiden: Brill, 2009), 103–5.

[11] Joseph Mélèze Modrzejewski, *The Jews of Egypt from Ramses II to Emperor Trajan*, trans. Robert Cornman (Edinburgh: T&T Clark, 1995), 198–230; Roger S. Bagnall, *Egypt in Late Antiquity* (Princeton: Princeton University Press, 1993), 276–8.

[12] Eusebius, *HE* 4.2-3; Dio Cassius, *Roman History* 68.32; 69.8; Appian, *Civil Wars* 2.90. See further Miriam Pucci Ben Zeev, *Diaspora Judaism in Turmoil 116–117 CE: Ancient Sources and Modern Insights* (Leuven: Peeters, 2005); William Horbury, *Jewish War Under Trajan and Hadrian* (Cambridge: Cambridge University Press, 2014), 164–277.

of John, namely the *Secret Book of John*. But where exactly? Saturninus is evidence of early Christian hostility to the Judean community. Saturninus also lived in an area with a still powerful Jewish community – Antioch.[13] Sethians may have borrowed directly from Saturninus's version of Gen. 1:26, where the creating angels say "Let us make a human in the image of God and with a likeness" – not "*our* image." The omission of the "our" is also a feature of the shorter version of the *Secret Book of John*, where again exactly seven "authorities" say to each other: "Let us create a human in the image of God and the likeness."[14] The *Gospel of Judas* presents a similar saying: "Let us create a human according to the likeness and according to the image."[15]

On current evidence, neither Johannine nor Saturninian Christians presented the Judean deity's backstory. Sethian teachers filled in the blanks. First of all, Yaldabaoth did not always exist. He was born at a certain moment, and not directly from the true God. There were two theories as regards his origin. In the first, Yaldabaoth was a miscarriage of a figure called Wisdom who was expelled from the higher world. In the second, an angelic "luminary" called him into being to rule the "underworld" (that is, this lower cosmos).[16]

Whatever his source, Yaldabaoth became bloated with arrogance. He created a host of angels to worship him. Having a premonition of higher beings, Yaldabaoth tried to convince these angels that he was the only God. He boasted: "I am God and there is no other!" (cf. Deut. 32:39; Isa. 45:5; 46:2).

In contrast to the creator, the Sethian teacher posited a superior principle called "Monad," described as higher than divinity, illimitable, unsearchable, unnamable, outside of time, ever Good, without needs, fixed in self-contemplation, and resting in an expanse of luminous water (Gen. 1:2).[17] This was a God far different than the creator worshiped by most Judeans. At the same time, this God has striking similarity to the God presented by Philo, educated in Pythagorean thought in the first century CE.

Who, then, were the Sethians who taught this story? They were, like Saturninus, Christians deeply familiar with Jewish scripture. From their description of the ultimate God as "Monad," we sense that we are dealing with persons educated in Platonic philosophy with a (Neo-)Pythagorean color. Indeed, their account of God had a

---

[13] Zetterholm (*Formation*, 37–8) estimated that there were twenty to thirty synagogues in Antioch during the first century CE. See further Alistair H. B. Logan, *Gnostic Truth and Christian Heresy* (Edinburgh: T&T Clark, 1996), 29–32. King (*Secret Revelation*, 9–17) would place the Sethian teacher in Alexandria.

[14] Irenaeus *AH* 1.24.1; BG 48:11-14. "Our" likeness reappears in *Secret Book of John* II,1 15.3.

[15] *Gos. Judas* 52.16-17.

[16] *Gos. Judas* 51.3-15; cf. *Gos. Eg.* III,2 56.22–59.9. See further Tobias Nicklas, "Der Demiurg des Judasevangeliums," in *Judasevangelium und Codex Tchacos*, ed. Enno Edzard Popkes and Gregor Wurst (Tübingen: Mohr Siebeck, 2012), 99–120; Lance Jenott, *Gospel of Judas: Coptic Text, Translation and Historical Interpretation of 'The Betrayer's Gospel'* (Tübingen: Mohr Siebeck, 2011), 94–9.

[17] *Ap. John* BG 22.16–26.14; cf. *Ap. John* II,1 2.26–4.18. Cf. Ruth Majercik, *Chaldean Oracles Text, Translation and Commentary* (Leiden: Brill, 1989), 53, frags. 11-12.

certain resemblance to the thought of Numenius, who worked in Apamea (a Syrian city not far from Antioch). Although the Sethian teachers were not Neopythagorean in the strict sense (devotees of Plato or Pythagoras), they were probably influenced by a Philonic or Numenian metaphysics. Like Numenius, they were probably Syrians who taught disciples interested in deeper questions regarding the nature of deity and the origin of the world.

The Sethian Trinity

Though philosophically informed, the Sethian teachers' metaphysics was a Christian metaphysics. They depicted Christ as the Son of the Father, born from the light of the Father by means of the "Virgin Spirit," and anointed in heaven to become Christ (the "anointed one," also called "Self-born").[18] Christ existed long before Jesus, but we can see how elements of Jesus's story were projected onto Christ. Just as Jesus was born of the Father from a Virgin, so was Christ on high.[19]

The primal Godhead was a family of Father, Mother, and Son.[20] A Mother as member of the Trinity might seem strange now; and to this day we have no sure knowledge why these Christians called her "Barbelo."[21] Her femininity may have emerged from her Spirit nature. The word for "Spirit" was feminine in Semitic languages; and if Christ was born from a Virgin on high, then she was understandably female. Yet Barbelo was a gender bender if there ever was one. She was called "thrice male," "male-female," and "Mother-Father."[22] Likely we can think again of Neopythagorean influence, where the Primal deity, the Monad, gives rise to a female principle, the Indefinite Dyad.[23] In addition, we can compare the theology of Wisdom in Jewish lore. Philo had already called Wisdom "Mother,"[24] and Simonians had dealt extensively with the female principle of the Godhead (the Seventh Power, or Thought). The Mother functioned as the divine super-Intellect – the most limpid reflection of the Invisible Spirit.[25]

Christ the Self-born ruled over four realms named "Luminaries." Inside the luminaries were certain model occupants. The first or highest luminary contained the perfect Human called "Adamas," model of the first human (recall the Light Man from Gen. 1:3). The second luminary contained Adamas's son Seth, a lower manifestation

---

[18] Irenaeus, *AH* 1.29.1; *Ap. John* BG 30.14-15. There is a change in the longer version of *Ap. John*, where it is the primal deity who becomes "virginal Spirit" (II,1 4.26–5.11).

[19] See further Logan, *Gnostic Truth*, 82–9.

[20] *Ap. John* BG 21.20-21.

[21] On Barbelo, see Logan, *Gnostic Truth*, 98–100; Pearson, *Ancient Gnosticism*, 57; Layton and Brakke, eds., *The Gnostic Scriptures*, 15 n. 3.

[22] *Ap. John* II,1 5.7; 12.4; BG 75.11; *Tri. Prot.* XIII,1 45.2-10.

[23] Thomassen, *Spiritual Seed*, 270–95; John D. Turner, "The Virgin that Became Male: Feminine Principles in Platonic and Gnostic Texts," in Tervahauta, ed., *Women and Knowledge*, 291–324.

[24] Prov. 8:22-31; Sir. 24; 1 En. 42; Philo, *Fug.* 108-9; *Ebr.* 30-33; *Leg.* 2.49.

[25] See further Logan, *Gnostic Truth*, 76–82; Turner, *Sethian Gnosticism*, 85–7, 499–577, esp. 541–7, 561–4; Brakke, *Gnostics*, 55.

of Christ, Image of God. The third contained Seth's spiritual children, members of the elect generation. The fourth encompassed repentant souls.[26] These were the levels of salvation to which believers could attain.

Dating the Sethian Teacher(s)

The date of the Sethian teacher(s) is unknown, but certain hints allow a rough estimation. Saturninus probably did not know the Sethian stories of God – otherwise he would have used them himself. If Saturninus was active during the reign of Hadrian (117–138 CE), then the Sethian teacher(s) was/were active somewhat later, likely in the reign of Antoninus Pius (138–161 CE). It would not take long for Sethian theology to end up in Rome – the urban magnet for new religious thought and a center for early Christianity.

Who carried the Sethian stories of God to the capital? It is tempting to identify one of the carriers with Cerdo, a Syrian who was at Rome in the early 140s CE. Cerdo was known for teaching in secret, and secret books said to be full of revelations would have appealed to him.[27] Cerdo may have influenced – or reinforced – Marcion, specifically with regard to the idea that the creator was not the true God, but a wicked imposter (a single but central plank in the Sethian story of creation).

The Growth of the Secret Book

When Irenaeus summarized the Sethian story of God, he omitted or did not possess the continuation of the story preserved in the *Secret Book of John* – a section on sacred history (revising Gen. 3–6), as well as a frame story introducing the apostle John.

The frame story indicates opposition to Judeans, represented in the person of a Pharisee named "Arimanias." The story opens when Arimanias attacks John and his view of Jesus in the Judean temple. Dejected, John significantly turned away from the temple and began praying in a deserted place. As in Revelation 1, the post-ascension Christ appears to John; a dialogue ensues, though Christ dominates the discussion.

By the time this frame story was created (probably between 180 and 220 CE), John must have already been recognized as the apostolic eagle – the apostle of greatest insight who wrote the fourth and latest life of Jesus as a "spiritual gospel."[28] It would be wrong to think that the Johannine frame story "Christianized" the *Secret Book*. The *Secret Book*, even without the apostle John, was already Christian – seeing that Christ was already part of the primal Triad.[29] It would be better to call the updated

---

[26] Turner, *Sethian Gnosticism*, 79–80, 86.
[27] Irenaeus, *AH* 3.4.3.
[28] Clement in Eusebius, *HE* 6.14.7; Irenaeus, *AH* 2.22.5; 3.1.1; 3.3.4; 3.11.1.
[29] Waldstein, "Primal Triad," 174–5; Pleše, *Poetics*, 15–16.

Secret Book "apostolized." It came together in a period, that is, when connection to an apostle was important for judging a work's authority.

The sacred history section of the *Secret Book* fortified the negative depiction of the creator. Its author focused on the Paradise story – needling the points where Yahweh appears weak, arbitrary, and jealous. He offered a revision of Genesis 1–6 – likely building on the thought of Saturninus. (In fact, I surmise that one of the reasons we do not often hear of the continuance of a Saturninian group is that this group was absorbed into the Sethian network.)

Scriptural Texts

The *Secret Book of John* reveals an author (or rather authors) familiar with Christian scriptures. Most obvious are John and Revelation. In addition to adopting the character John, the text is riddled with allusions to John,[30] as well as to Luke[31] and to Matthew.[32] Allusions to Pauline letters (Philippians, Colossians, Ephesians, 1-2 Corinthians, and Romans) are also likely.[33] Evidently these texts were authoritative or at least useful to the Sethian writers. Possibly the *Secret Book* itself became a sacred text.

Besides the *Secret Book*, Sethian Christians composed and used other texts. One of them was called *Three Forms of First Thought*. In this hymnic text, the second member of the Trinity, or Mother, speaks in her own voice about her nature and advents. She made three advents into the world and claimed to be incarnate in everyone. The form of the text best resembles contemporaneous hymns of Isis (called aretalogies) in which the goddess speaks in the first person about her nature and deeds. The Mother, however, is a Christian deity insofar as, in her final advent, she "put on Jesus."[34]

Three Forms of First Thought was evidently inspired by the prologue of John ("In the beginning was the Logos …"). It was in turn the outgrowth of a shorter hymn to the Mother (the Providence Hymn) attached to the end of the *Secret Book of John*.[35]

---

[30] E.g., John 1:18 in BG 26.11-14; John 4:14 in BG 26.15-21; John 1:3 in BG 31.16-18; John 5:19-23 in BG 32,8-12; John 2:20-22 in BG 53.10-17; John 3:4 in BG 69.14-17. See further King, *Secret Revelation*, 235–8; Jean-Daniel Dubois, "La tradition johannique dans l'*Apocryphe de Jean*," *Adamantius* 18 (2012): 108–17.

[31] E.g., Luke 3:22 in BG 34.7-18; Luke 10:25 in BG 66.9-12 (cf. Matt. 19:16).

[32] E.g., Matt. 17:5 in BG 38.6-10; Matt. 18:3-5 in BG 69.14-17.

[33] E.g., Col. 2:20-23 in BG 65.13–66.1; 1 Cor. 13:7 in BG 69.9-12.

[34] *Tri. Prot.* XIII,1 50.12-15.

[35] Michael Waldstein sees *Tri. Prot.* as an outgrowth of the Providence hymn in "The Providence Monologue in the Apocryphon of *John* and the Johannine Prologue," *JECS* 3 (1995): 369–402 at 371. See further B. Barc and L. Painchaud, "La réécriture de l'*Apocryphon de Jean* à la lumière de l'hymn final de la version longue," *Muséon* 112 (1999): 317–33; Paul-Hubert Poirier, "The *Three Forms of First Thought* (NHC XIII,1) and the *Secret Book of John* (NHC II,1 and Par.)," in Corrigan and Rasimus, eds., *Gnosticism, Platonism*, 23–41.

Although some material from *Three Forms* might date back to the 120s CE, the basis for the present text (preserved in the Nag Hammadi codices) probably emerged in the mid-second century.[36]

Another Sethian author wrote a work called *Reality of the Rulers*. It seems to have been inspired by the line in Eph. 6:12, quoted at the text's beginning: "our struggle is not against flesh and blood, but against the authorities of the universe and the spirits of wickedness." In this text alone did the Sethian author reveal his own persona (the individual "I") – yet only in the preface. He related a sacred history based on Genesis 1–6, with a special sidelight on Norea, wise and powerful sister of Seth. Norea is also the focus of a short Nag Hammadi text, the *Thought of Norea*, which records and reflects on one of her prayers.[37]

Yet another attempt to revise *Genesis* was the *Apocalypse of Adam*. This revelatory discourse presents a sacred history from the Flood (Gen. 6–8), to the destruction of Sodom (Gen. 19). The *Apocalypse* was put into the mouth of Adam himself, who spoke to his son Seth 700 years after creation. Angels were said to have preserved the discourse on a high mountain.[38] Older scholars dated the *Apocalypse of Adam* to the late first century on the assumption that the work was not Christian.[39] In recent research, Christian features of the text have been discerned, indicating a date roughly contemporary with other Sethian works (mid- to late second century CE or later).[40]

The most recently discovered Sethian Christian text is the *Gospel of Judas* – a rewriting of Christ's final week on earth.[41] In it, Judas is presented as the most knowledgeable of Jesus's disciples, though he too falls short of salvation. The other disciples, representing Christian leaders in other churches, are savaged as morally corrupt and spiritually deficient. In the *Gospel of Judas*, we see a clear attack not only against the Judean god, but against Christian leaders who claimed authority while not grasping Jesus's deeper teachings.[42]

The final second-century Sethian Christian text we will mention is *The Holy Book of the Great Invisible Spirit* (aka the *Egyptian Gospel*). This text, attributed to "the great

[36] For *Three Forms* and *John*'s prologue see Turner, "Johannine Legacy," and Paul-Hubert Poirier, "The *Trimorphic Protennoia*," in *The Legacy of John: Second-century Reception of the Fourth Gospel*, ed. Tuomas Rasimus (Leiden: Brill, 2010), 93–103.
[37] For Norea, see Birger A. Pearson, *Gnosticism, Judaism, and Egyptian Christianity* (Minneapolis: Fortress, 2006), 83–94; Anne McGuire, "Virginity and Subversion: Norea Against the Powers in the *Hypostasis of the Archons*," in *Images of the Feminine in Gnosticism*, ed. Karen L. King (Philadelphia: Fortress, 1988), 239–58.
[38] *Apoc. Adam* V,5 85.10-11.
[39] George MacRae, *Nag Hammadi Codices V,2-5 and VI,152*; Madeleine Scopello in *Nag Hammadi Scriptures*, ed. Marvin Meyer (New York: HarperOne, 2007), 345.
[40] Cf. Turner, *Sethian Gnosticism*, 165. On *Apoc. Adam* as a Christian text, see G. M. Shellrude, "The Apocalypse of Adam: Evidence for a Christian Gnostic Provenance," in *Gnosis and Gnosticism*, ed. M. Krause (Leiden: Brill, 1981), 82–91; Schmid, *Christen und Sethianer*, 136–41.
[41] Simon Gathercole, "Matthean or Lukan Priority? The Use of the NT Gospels in the *Gospel of Judas*," in Popkes and Wurst, eds., *Judasevangelium*, 291–302.
[42] See further Jenott, *Gospel of Judas*, 37–69.

Seth," is preserved in two forms in Nag Hammadi. It relates a rather different story of God and salvation, with many more characters. Distinctively, the creator emerges from a lower luminary (not Wisdom). Moreover, "the great Seth" in heaven explicitly arrives in the form of Jesus.[43]

The Life of Jesus

Sethian Christians saw Christ in the Old Testament, and specifically in the figure of Seth. Seth, son of Adam, corresponded to "the Great Seth" in the second luminary. This higher Seth was in turn a manifestation of Christ, who three times arrived on earth to guide and save the elect.[44] Seth-Christ saved his seed when Yaldabaoth wiped out the world with the Flood, and again when Yaldabaoth blasted the city of Sodom with fire (Gen. 6, 19). The final advent was Seth's incarnation in Jesus.[45]

Although other saints and angels had a role in redemption, Jesus was the ultimate redeemer. In the hymn closing the longer version of the *Secret Book* (the Providence Hymn), Jesus was said to incarnate not just the heavenly Seth, but the Mother herself. He was truly born "through the virgin that the holy people may be conceived by the holy Spirit" (cf. John 1:13).[46]

In the *Apocalypse of Adam*, the kingdoms of darkness present twelve theories about Christ. Their only reliable intelligence is that Christ "came to the water" – apparently of baptism.[47] Christ was baptized in luminous water with five seals, and he baptized his converts in the same way.[48] Jesus taught "unrepeatable doctrines to all who became children of light."[49] He equipped people "with the armor of the knowledge of truth, with incorruptible, invincible power."[50] He "performed signs and wonders for the salvation of humanity" "to bring contempt upon the powers and their ruler" (note again the similarity with Saturninus).[51]

The powers respond by punishing Christ's flesh.[52] Jesus was crucified – not to appease an angry God – but to defeat evil powers (Col. 2:15).[53] By his crucifixion, Jesus "nailed down" the powers of darkness and "destroyed Death."[54] The Mother

---

[43] Dylan Burns, "Jesus' Reincarnations Revisited in Jewish Christianity, Sethian Gnosticism, and Mani," in *Portraits of Jesus: Studies in Christology*, ed. Susan E. Myers (Tübingen: Mohr Siebeck, 2012), 371–92.

[44] *Gosp. Eg.* III,2 63.4-5.

[45] *Gosp. Eg.* III,2 64.2-3; IV,2 75.16-17.

[46] *Gosp. Eg.* III,2 63.13 See further Jeffrey A. Trumbower, *Born from Above: The Anthropology of the Gospel of John* (Tübingen: Mohr Siebeck, 1992).

[47] *Ap. Adam* V,5 77.18–82.19.

[48] *Ap. John* II,1 31.23-24.

[49] *Tri. Prot.* XIII,1 37.18.

[50] *Gosp. Eg.* III,2 64.7.

[51] *Gosp. Judas* 33.7-9 (trans. Jenott); *Apoc. Adam* 77.2-3.

[52] *Apoc. Adam* V,5 77.16-18.

[53] Jenott, *Gospel of Judas*, 23–30.

[54] *Gosp. Eg.* III,2 63.4–64.4; *Melch.* IX,1 14.9.

who "put on" Jesus bore him from the "cursed wood" and established him in the dwelling places of his Father.[55] These data indicate that Jesus or his spirit ascended immediately from the cross. Another Sethian text, however, mentions his burial and resurrection.[56]

Baptism

Sethian Christians did not just compose sacred stories. They formed groups that practiced a baptismal rite called "the Five Seals." The Providence Hymn in the *Secret Book of John* presents Christ as raising and sealing converts "in luminous water with Five Seals, that death might not prevail" (this recalls the promise of Menander's baptism).[57] The Five Seals themselves are enigmatic. They may refer to five steps in the ritual, five dunks in the water, or five anointings with oil.[58]

In the *Secret Book of John*, Christ was anointed in heaven. One would expect a mirroring of this event on earth. The *Reality of the Rulers* speaks of the "oil of eternal life" with which Christ anointed his people.[59] The fivefold anointing may also be illumined by The *Gospel of Thomas*, which mentions five trees in Paradise. Anointing with five types of oil may have been thought to convey eternal life, for – as *Thomas* put it – "whoever knows them [the trees] will not taste death."[60] Sethian baptism, like Menander's, ensured that its participants also did "not taste death."[61]

Sethian Christian baptism involved the renunciation of the world and sin. Baptized persons stripped their clothes to represent the removal of ignorance.[62] They descended into "living water" which may refer, on the physical plane, to running water.[63] On a higher plane, the living water was identified with Jesus, invoked under a mystical name, "Yesseus Mazareus Yessedekeus" (apparently meaning "Jesus of Nazareth, Jesus the Just").[64] Sethian Christians called their baptism "holy." It was meant for "people who have eternal knowledge (*gnosis*)."[65]

In imitation of Christ's baptism, the Seed of Seth received the name of Christ "in the water."[66] In our sole surviving account of a Sethian baptismal invocation, Jesus ("Yesseus") is the primary person invoked. His is the "glorious name." The person baptized is asked to say: "This great name of yours is upon me, you who lack nothing,

---

[55] *Tri. Prot.* XIII,1 50.12-15.
[56] *Melch.* IX,1 3.6, 10-11.
[57] *Ap. John* II,1 31.20-24.
[58] For the five steps, see *Tri. Prot.* XIII,1 48.15-25.
[59] *Hyp. Arch.* II,4 97.3-4.
[60] *Gosp. Thom.* II,2 19.3-4.
[61] *Gosp. Eg.* III,2 66.8.
[62] *Tri Prot.* XIII,1 49.30-31.
[63] *Gosp. Eg.* III,2 66.11.
[64] Cf. Isa. 11:1. *Gosp. Eg.* III,2 64.10-11.
[65] *Ap. Adam* V,5 85.26.
[66] *Ap. Adam* V,5 83.5-6.

you Self-born one, who are not outside me."[67] Bright with the "armor of light," the baptizand stretched out his or her hands, continued to pray to Jesus as the "god of silence," the "place of rest," the "formless one." The invocation mentioned "the sweet smell of life" which may refer to incense or aromatic oil used in the rite.[68]

Three Forms of First Thought mentions five steps in the ritual: robing, baptizing, enthroning, glorifying, and rapturing. The last three steps, though they might have had earthly symbols, probably refer to what happened in a heavenly ascent. Sethian baptism "surpassed the heavens," changing one's status in heaven as well as on earth.[69] In later Sethian thought, a series of heavenly baptisms made the ideal Sethian into an angel and even a god.[70]

The Seed of Seth recognized the distinctive character of their baptism and attacked the water rite of other Christians. They accused them of defiling "the water of life," conforming it to the will of demons.[71] By contrast, three blessed angels presided over Sethian baptism. Their names were Micheus, Michar, and Mnesinous.[72] The first two names may be alterations of the archangel Michael and the prophet Micah.[73] The meaning of Mnesinous seems to be "the Mind who recalls." He may have had a role in reminding Sethian Christians of their true, spiritual identity. Sethian Christians invoked other names and pronounced celestial sounds to ensure the efficacy of their rites.

Ethics and Ethos

The Providence Hymn refers to an identity-altering experience of an ideal convert who awakens to realize a Christian identity. This ideal convert is said to awake from deep sleep, weep, wipe away tears, and ask about the identity of the revealer who "calls my name" and brings "hope."[74]

The Seed of Seth engaged in what Michael Williams has called "bridge-burning acts" – acts which declare an opposition to and condemnation of conventions in the wider society. A key bridge-burning act, as we saw with Saturninus, was the rejection

---

[67] *Gosp. Eg.* III,2 66.23-24.

[68] *Gosp. Eg.* III,2 67.22.

[69] *Gosp. Eg.* III,2 63.24-25; 65.25.

[70] See further Turner, "Baptismal Vision, Angelification, and Mystical Union in Sethian Literature," in Iricinschi et al., eds, *Beyond the Gnostic Gospels*, 204–16; Litwa, *Posthuman Transformation*, 133–50.

[71] *Ap. Adam* V,5 84.18-19; cf. *Gosp. Judas* 55.26–56.5. See further Stroumsa, *Another Seed*, 103. Jenott (*Gospel of Judas*, 30–2, 101) and Schmid (*Christen*, 379–84) attempt to show how the author of *Gosp. Judas* maintains a positive view of baptism. See further Elaine Pagels, "Baptism in the *Gospel of Judas*: A Preliminary Inquiry," in *The Codex Judas Papers*, ed. April D. DeConick, NHMS 71 (Leiden: Brill, 2009), 353–66.

[72] *Ap. Adam* V,5 84.5-6; cf. *Gosp. Eg.* III,2 64.15-16; *Tri. Prot.* XIII,1 48.19.20.

[73] See further Riemer Roukema, "The Sethian Figures Micheus and Michar and their Relationships to Micah the Morasthite," *Gnosis* 2 (2017): 1–14.

[74] *Ap John* II,1 31.5-10. Here I follow the language of Williams, *Immovable*, 191.

of sexual intercourse. The desire for sex, according to the author of the *Secret Book of John*, was an evil and corrupting impulse implanted by Yaldabaoth as a distraction.[75] The author of the *Secret Book* called his readers to follow the ethical ideal of incorruptibility and passionlessness.[76] Marriage was duly spurned.

The Sethian teacher urged his audience to be pure from all involvement in negative emotions (or passions), to root out all envy, desire, and greed. Even if only the elite of the Sethian community attained this state of moral perfection, the very ideal would have made Sethians distinct from the majority of other associations in the ancient Mediterranean. Presumably, a person who fell radically short of the Sethian ethical ideal would be excluded from the group. The *Secret Book of John* speaks of apostates, which is, incidentally, the only group of humans said to be eternally punished.[77]

Even if some members of the group lapsed, there was a scheme set in place for assuring salvation. The *Secret Book's* mention of people who sin and "repent later" indicates a process of reintegration.[78] Spirit-endowed people led astray by the "false spirit" still attain salvation, though apparently of a lesser quality. People who forget spiritual truth are given another chance by means of reincarnation (a theory supported, as we shall see, by Basilides and Carpocrates). Yet reincarnation was still viewed as a punishment to be avoided.[79]

Conclusion

To sum up, the Seed of Seth were Christians who identified Christ as the self-born Son in a Trinity of Father, Mother, and Son. They had their own scriptural texts, self-designations, and their own version of baptism (compare Menander). Sethian Christians cultivated a group consciousness, though we know little about the structure of their group. They called themselves the "holy seed of Seth," the "generation without a king," and even the "church" of Seth.[80]

The Sethian group probably originated in Syria, adapting key elements of Saturninian theology. Yet Sethian stories and texts quickly spread elsewhere. Sethian Christians read what are today considered Jewish and Christian scriptures (the Septuagint, gospels, and letters of Paul). They also composed scriptures of their own (hymns, apocalypses, sacred histories) with different emphases. One of their scriptures lauded the apostle John, another spoke with the voice of Adam, still another was put in the mouth of the Mother herself. The Sethian *Holy Book* and the *Three Steles of Seth* (third century CE) display extensive liturgical material which suggests an active, worshiping assembly.

---

[75] *Ap. John* II,1 24.28-31.
[76] *Ap. John* II,1 25.23–26.7 with Williams, *Immovable*, 127–9, 139. Cf. Williams, "Demiurgical Myth and Social Implications," in Iricinschi et al., eds., *Beyond the Gnostic Gospels*, 51–2.
[77] *Ap. John* BG 71.1-2; II,1 27.30.
[78] Williams, *Immovable*, 194–6.
[79] *Ap. John* II,1 25.16–27.21.
[80] *Melch.* IX,1 5.19.

Sethian Christians were innovators. Along with the Simonians, they were among the first Christian Trinitarians. They were also among the first, if not the first, to provide a full-scale theory of God, the origin of the world, and of human salvation. They perfected the revisionary reading of Genesis initiated by Saturninus. On the basis of their reading practices, they depicted the fullest and most vivid portrait of the evil creator (Yaldabaoth).

Sethian Christian leaders were educated, philosophically astute, and influential. The followers of Valentinus possibly encountered or influenced Sethian thought in Alexandria and again in Rome. Marcion's notion of an evil creator had a possible Sethian impetus or confirmation. The first recorded attack on Sethian Christians, however, came about 180 CE (with Irenaeus). Their assailants apparently felt no need to expel Sethian Christians because they had always formed separate assemblies.[81]

At least one Sethian author (represented by the *Secret Book*) appealed to the apostle John as a mediator of revelation. Another author (represented by the *Gospel of Judas*) attacked Christians who claimed authority from the twelve apostles. The attack on apostolic churches may have been seen as an attack on the apostles themselves, but it would be too hasty to categorize the Seed of Seth as non-apostolic, as some did maintain a link with John and evidently Judas. The author of the *Gospel of Judas* attacked the apostles as corrupt, but other Sethians apparently accepted apostolic authority.[82] (In terms of the reception of *Judas*, it was preserved in a codex with other "apostolic" writings, namely the *Letter of Peter to Philip* and *James*.)

By the third century, Sethian Christians established themselves in Rome and participated in the philosophy seminars of Plotinus (lauded as the founder of Neoplatonism); yet Sethians probably influenced Plotinus already in Alexandria (in the 230s CE).[83] In the third century, these Christians continued to compose scriptural texts. Several of these, *Three Steles of Seth*, *Marsanes*, *Allogenes*, and *Zostrianos* ended up in the Nag Hammadi codices. By the time of Epiphanius (about 375 CE), Sethian Christian groups seem to have proliferated and fanned out across the eastern Mediterranean (from Egypt to Armenia). Epiphanius attacked "Archontics," "Phibionites," "Stratiotics," and "Sethians," who assimilated Sethian Christian doctrines and took them in new directions. Even if a coherent Sethian movement had perished by his time, the rivulets of Sethian thought enriched the streams of later Christian theologies.[84]

---

[81] *Pace* Turner, *Sethian Gnosticism*, 751.

[82] *Pace* April D. DeConick, "Apostles as Archons: The Fight for Authority and the Emergence of Gnosticism in the Tchacos Codex and Other Early Christian Literature," in *Codex Judas Papers*, 243–88 at 264–8; cf. her *Gnostic New Age*, 304–5.

[83] See further Burns, *Apocalypse*, 32–47; Zeke Mazur, *The Platonizing Sethian Background of Plotinus's Mysticism*, NHMS 98 (Leiden: Brill, 2020).

[84] One indication of the long afterlife of Sethian theology is the Macquarie Papyri, a seventh- or eighth-century codex edited by Malcolm Choat and Iain Gardner, *A Coptic Handbook of Ritual Power (P. Macq. I 1)* (Turnhout: Brepols, 2013).

Further Reading

David Brakke, *The Gnostics* (Cambridge, MA: Harvard University Press, 2010).

Johanna Brankaer, "Revisiting Those Elusive Sethians," in *Shadowy Characters and Fragmentary Evidence: The Search for Early Christian Groups and Movements*, ed. Joseph Verheyden et al. (Tübingen: Mohr Siebeck, 2017), 159–76.

Dylan M. Burns, *Apocalypse of an Alien God: Platonism and the Exile of Sethian Gnosticism* (Philadelphia: University of Pennsylvania Press, 2014).

Austin Busch, "Gnostic Scriptural Interpretation," *ZAC* 21, no. 2 (2017): 243–71.

M. David Litwa, *The Evil Creator: Origins of an Early Christian Idea* (New York: Oxford University Press, 2021).

Alistair H. B. Logan, *The Gnostics: Identifying an Early Christian Cult* (London: T&T Clark, 2006).

Gerhard Luttikhuizen, *Gnostic Revisions of Genesis Stories and Early Jesus Traditions* (Leiden: Brill, 2006).

Tuomas Rasimus, "The Sethians and the Gnostics of Plotinus," in *The Routledge Handbook of Early Christian Philosophy*, ed. Mark Edwards (London: Routledge, 2021), 426–37. Zlatko Pleše, *Poetics of a Gnostic Universe: Narrative Cosmology in the Apocryphon of John* (Leiden: Brill, 2006).

John D. Turner, *Sethian Gnosticism and the Platonic Tradition*. BCNH Études 6 (Leuven: Peeters, 2001).

Michael Williams, "Was There a Gnostic Religion? Strategies for a Clearer Analysis," in *Was There a Gnostic Religion?*, ed. Antti Marjanen (Helsinki: Finnish Exegetical Society, 1999), 5–29.

Michael Williams, "Sethianism," in *Companion to Second-century Christian 'Heretics'*, ed. Antti Marjanen and Petri Luomanen (Leiden: Brill, 2005), 36–50.

Part Three

Early Egyptian Theologians

"Ophite" and Peratic Christians

Introduction

Heresiographers accused some early Christians of worshiping a snake, symbol of the devil. To be sure, a certain bronze snake was associated with Christ on the basis of Jesus's statement in John 3:14-15: "Just as Moses exalted the snake in the desert (Num. 21:6-9), so the Child of the Human must be exalted, so that all who believe in him can have eternal life." Most ancient Christians recognized that in this verse Jesus spoke of himself as the Child of the Human, and thus as analogous to the salvific snake. An early Christian group who developed this interpretation was later called "Ophite" after the Greek *ophis*, or snake. Yet the idea of them worshiping the snake in itself must be challenged as heresiological distortion.

My aim in this chapter is to introduce these "Ophites," mainly by combining information from two heresiological reports (Irenaeus and the Refutator) on two groups with significant ideological and exegetical overlap. Irenaeus referred to the group as "others," by which he meant "other gnostics" (keeping in mind that for Irenaeus, "gnostic" became a global term for "heretic").[1] The Refutator reported on people he called "Peratai," sometimes called "Peratics."[2] Another main source, namely Origen of Alexandria, will be used to discuss Ophite ritual and their picture of the cosmos.[3]

Euphrates and Akembes

In the past, scholars have described the term "Ophite" as (1) designating several "gnostic" sects, (2) a type of mythology, or (3) a set of features among texts.[4] According to Origen, however, Ophites were a distinct Christian group that boasted of a named founder who initiated their teachings. This man was called Euphrates.[5]

---

[1] Irenaeus, *AH* 1.30.1.
[2] *Ref.* 5.12-18.
[3] Origen, *Cels.* 6.26-32.
[4] History of research in Rasimus, *Paradise*, 10–28.
[5] Origen, *Cels.* 6.28. To undermine the Christian identity of Ophites, Origen claimed that they cursed Jesus. This claim has been refuted by Rasimus, *Paradise*, 225–42.

Some have doubted the existence of Euphrates.[6] To be sure, his name denoted a place (the Euphrates River in modern Iraq), a river that was allegorized by both Jews and Christians. Nevertheless, Euphrates is an attested name in antiquity. For instance, a "Euphrates the Persian" speaks from an ancient epigram, begging his friend not to cremate him.[7] Euphrates was also the name of a famous Stoic philosopher who committed suicide toward the beginning of Hadrian's reign (about 120 CE).[8] The Christian Euphrates was a contemporary of his Stoic namesake, though probably somewhat younger.[9]

The Refutator referred to the Christian Euphrates as "Euphrates the Peratic." It is true that *Perat* in Hebrew signifies the Euphrates River, but "peratic" was a well-known adjective signifying "from beyond the Euphrates."[10] The Refutator used "Peratic" as a place name.[11] We might surmise, then, that the Christian Euphrates was from the region of Mesopotamia (modern Iraq), or perhaps Persia (Iran).[12] His use of Light–Dark dualism might suggest Zoroastrian influence; his knowledge of astrology might also signal a Babylonian background. But such ideas had long been assimilated in Greco-Roman culture. (In a reputed letter of Hadrian regarding Alexandria, we read that there was "no Christian presbyter who is not an astrologer."[13]) As we shall see, Euphrates's primary interest lay in Jewish scriptures, scriptures which he allegorized in his own peculiar way.

---

[6] G. Salmon, "Euphrates (1)," in *Dictionary of Christian Biography*, ed. Henry Wace and William C. Piercy (London: John Murray, 1911), 296. Rasimus remarks that "Clement says that the Peratics are named after a place … and not a person, as Origen and Hippolytus say," but neither Origen nor the Refutator actually say that "Peratic" referred to a person. The notion that the River Euphrates was associated with snake imagery is probably incidental. Nor is it clear that Origen, assuming he knew *Ref.* (which is doubtful), could have derived all the "snake heresies" ("Naassenes," "Peratics," "Sethians") from Euphrates. Origen would have known that the Refutator mentioned the Ophites as a separate group linked with the Cainites, and with no named leader (*Ref.* 8.20.3) (Rasimus, *Paradise*, 288).

[7] Dioscorides, epigram xxviii in A. S. F. Gow and D. L. Page, *The Greek Anthology: Hellenistic Epigrams*, 2 vols. (Cambridge: Cambridge University Press, 1965), 1:90.

[8] Michael Frede, "Euphrates of Tyre," *Bulletin of the Institute of Classical Studies* 68 (1997): 1–11.

[9] *Pace* Mark Edwards, I do not find it likely that either Origen or Philostratus identified Euphrates the Peratic with Euphrates the Stoic ("Euphrates, Stoic and Christian Heretic," *Athenaeum* 82 [1994]: 196–200).

[10] Pliny the Elder knew that resin from beyond the Euphrates was called "peratic" (*Natural History* 12.19). "Peratic" frankincense was also exported from a town called Malay on the Red Sea ([Anonymous], *Voyage Round the Red Sea* 8.8; 10.9; 11.6) in L. Casson, *The Periplus Maris Erythraei* (Princeton: Princeton University Press, 1989). The adjective *peratikos* could have simply meant "foreign" (LSJ *s.v.* περατικός).

[11] *Ref.* 4.2.1; 10.10.1. Clement of Alexandria clarified that "Peratic" is a place name, a place he thought sufficiently obvious, requiring no discussion (*Strom.* 7.16.108.2).

[12] Sophronius of Jerusalem (died 638 CE) referred to the Christian Euphrates as "Persian."

[13] *SHA* Quadrigae Tyrannorum 8.2. See further Alessandro Galimberti, "The Pseudo-Hadrianic Epistle in the *Historia Augusta* and Hadrian's Religious Policy," in *Hadrian and the Christians*, ed. Marco Rizzi (Berlin: de Gruyter, 2010), 111–20.

The Refutator claimed that Euphrates had a partner, a man whose name has unfortunately been garbled in the manuscript tradition. We can call him "Akembes," but he also appears as "Kelbes" and "Ademes." He was from the town of Karystos on the southern tip of Euboea, the large island east of the Greek mainland.[14] Together with Akembes, Euphrates created what the Refutator called the "Peratic" sect. Although the Refutator tried to derive the name "Peratic" from the Greek verb *perasai* ("to traverse"),[15] I suggest that "Peratic" was originally named after Euphrates's place of origin, or perhaps after "Euphrates the Peratic" himself.

"Peratic" was the adjective corresponding to the noun *peratēs*. In Greek, *peratēs* meant "wanderer," or "emigrant," and it was apparently in this sense that the Judean ancestor Abram (aka Abraham) was called *peratēs* in Gen. 14:13 (LXX). Those familiar with Hebrew, however, knew that in this passage, the Greek term *peratēs* could more literally be translated "Hebrew."[16] Those in the know, perhaps, would realize that "Peratai" (the plural of *peratēs*) signified "the (true) Hebrews."[17]

If Peratic Christians thought of themselves as the true Hebrews, that would in part explain their interest in Jewish scripture. Unlike the "false" Hebrews (the Judeans who did not believe in Jesus), the "true" Hebrews knew the meaning of Jewish scripture. In short, Peratic Christians claimed the spiritual legacy of Israel. This was a common Christian rhetorical move at the time. (See, for instance, the *Epistle of Barnabas* and Justin's *Dialogue with Trypho*.)

Sometime after 180 CE, the Christian heirs of Euphrates, or a group of them, came to be called "Ophites." This seems a reasonable conclusion, given that our sources – namely Celsus (around 175 CE) and Irenaeus (around 180 CE) – knew about Ophite Christian teaching, but were unfamiliar with the name "Ophite." The followers of Euphrates were called "Ophites," it seems, because of the role that the snake played in their biblical exegesis.[18] The name, originally meant as a slur, was, by the time of Origen (about 250 CE), accepted as a compliment.[19]

What the immediate followers of Euphrates called themselves is unknown, although "Christians" seems a fair guess, especially since Celsus readily took them to be a Christian group. Some seventy years later, Origen zealously endeavored to undermine their Christian identity. Yet his argument only makes sense if they were considered to be Christians in the first place.

---

[14] *Ref.* 4.2.1; 5.13.9; 10.10.1. See Richard J. A. Talbert, ed., *Barrington Atlas of the Greek and Roman World* (Princeton: Princeton University Press, 2000), 58, 3c.

[15] *Ref.* 5.16.1, 5-6; cf. the pun in 5.18.1.

[16] Origen, *Exhortation to Martyrdom* 33; *Commentary on Matthew* 11.5; *Homilies on the Psalms* 27.7; Eusebius, *Preparation for the Gospel* 7.8.21; 11.6.40.

[17] See further Annarita Magri, "Il nome dei Perati," *Orpheus* 28 (2007): 138–61.

[18] Clement, *Strom.* 7.17.108.2.

[19] Origen, *Cels.* 6.28.

Teaching

The exact contours of Euphrates's and Akembes's thought are now impossible to discern. What we have are various reports that probably go back to their teaching in ways no longer traceable.

Perhaps we can start with the Ophite Christian exegesis of John 3:14-15. In these verses, Christ compared himself to the bronze snake that Moses set up in the wilderness (Num. 21:6-9). According to this story, disobedient Israelites wandering in the desert had been bitten by poisonous snakes. When the Israelites wailed in grief, God commanded Moses to make a snake molded from bronze. The Israelites who looked upon the snake were subsequently healed. According to John 3:14, Jesus brought a salvation analogous to the healing given by the snake. Just as the snake was lifted up, Christ would be lifted on the cross, so that all who believe in him would receive eternal life. On the basis of this passage, Ophite Christians – among other readers of John – associated Christ with a salvific snake.[20]

Significantly, Justin Martyr refused to identify the bronze snake of Numbers 21 as a snake. Against the biblical text, Justin considered Moses's "emblem" to be a brazen cross.[21] Why Justin Martyr would read the snake out of the story is unknown. One possible answer is that he was already responding to Ophite exegesis (about 160 CE).

Ophite Christians paid close attention to Jesus's self-identification as "Child of the Human" (John 3:14 and elsewhere). If Jesus was "Child of the Human" then his Father was evidently the "Human." The *Wisdom of Jesus Christ* – a Nag Hammadi text with Ophite features – makes explicit the connection between Christ "the Child of the Human" in the gospels. It also develops the conception of God as the primal Human.[22] By about 175 CE, some Ophite Christians distinguished a Trinity of three Humans: the First Human or Father, the Child of the Human, and Christ.[23]

This version of the Trinity depended on the book of Genesis. First there was the "Adam of light" (Gen. 1:3), as we saw with Saturninus, then the embodied Adam (1:26), and finally Adam's son Seth, model of the Savior (5:3). As it turns out, we can roughly date this schema of three Humans to the first half of the second century, for they appear in the work called *Eugnostus*, a philosophical treatise twice appearing in the Nag Hammadi codices.[24] The treatise was later rewritten as the *Wisdom of Jesus*

---

[20] Pseudo-Tertullian, *AAH* 2.1; *Ref.* 5.16.11. See further Rasimus, *Paradise*, 78–81.

[21] Justin, *1 Apol.* 60.3; cf. *Dial.* 94.2.

[22] *Wisd. Jes. Chr.* III,4 103.21–104.2.

[23] See further Frederick Houk Borsch, *The Christian and Gnostic Son of Man* (London: SCM, 1970), 58–122; Mogens Müller, *The Expression 'Son of Man' and the Development of Christology: A History of Interpretation* (Sheffield: Equinox, 2008), 32–52; Rasimus, *Paradise*, 159–88; Adela Yarbro Collins and John Collins, *King and Messiah as Son of God: Divine, Human and Angelic Messianic Figures in Biblical and Related Literature* (Grand Rapids: Eerdmans, 2008), 75–100, 149–203.

[24] *Eug.* III,3 76.12–82.5. *Eug.* also appears in V,1.

Christ (III,4), with most of its content placed into the mouth of Jesus. Sadly, we do not know who wrote *Eugnostus*, though most scholars locate its original author in Egypt.[25]

The three Humans, together with the Spirit – called the First Woman – were said to make up the first and most holy "Church" on high.[26] This "Church" is also a family, since the Spirit, coupled with the first two Humans, generates Christ (on the model of Eve joined with Adam to produce Seth, Gen. 5:3). The fact that the Spirit was the "First Woman" hints that the originator of this teaching spoke a Semitic language in which the word for "Spirit" was female.[27]

Even though Ophite Christians referred to God and Christ as "the Human" and "the Child of the Human," this ought not to obscure the fact that they also used the (to us) more familiar names "Father" and "Son."[28] In the mid-second century, Ophite Christians drew a diagram in which they referred to the "light of Son and Father." They represented Father and Son deities by two circles, one within the other.[29]

Ophite Christians showed knowledge of Jewish exegetical traditions. They speculated on the role and figure of Wisdom (Prov. 8; Sir 24; Wis. 7; 1 En. 42), whom they depicted as daughter of the Holy Spirit. They developed the tradition of seven archangels (Tob. 12:15; Rev. 1:4, 20; 1 En. 20:5) like Saturninus. Distinctively, they portrayed some of these angels in the beastlike forms of the creatures that surround God's throne (Ezek. 1:10; Rev. 4:7; *1 En.* 40:8-9). They also seem to have known stories about Samael (aka the devil) interacting with Eve in the garden of Eden.[30]

Ophite Christians perceived Jewish scripture and tradition within a Christian framework. They considered themselves to be spiritually more astute than Jewish readers and probably other Christians as well. They showed no love or loyalty to the Judean deity. In fact they, like Saturninus, displayed open hostility to him. Citing John 8:44, they observed that the "ruler and creator of matter," was "a murderer from the beginning."[31]

---

[25] *Eug.* III,3 76.12–82.5. For the dating, see Anne Pasquier, *Eugnoste, Lettre sur le dieu transcendant (NH III,3 et V,1): Commentaire* (Leuven: Peeters, 2010), 205–12. On *Eugnostus* and the "Ophites," see Logan, *Gnostic Truth*, 151, 180; Turner, *Sethian Gnosticism*, 209–10; Rasimus, *Paradise*, 45–9.

[26] Irenaeus, *AH* 1.30.2.

[27] Cf. *Gospel of Philip* II,3 55.23-33.

[28] Peratic Christians referred to the first two members of their Trinity as "Fatherly Greatness" and "the Son" (*Ref.* 5.12.2; 10.10.2).

[29] Origen, *Cels.* 6.31, 38. Rasimus offers nine scholarly drawings of the Ophite diagram (*Paradise* Plates I-IX).

[30] 1 John 3:12 (if ἐκ τοῦ πονηροῦ signifies a filial relation); *Targum Pseudo-Jonathan* (Gen. 4:1); *Protoevangelium of James* 13:1; *Ap. John* 62.3; *Gosp. Phil.* II,3 60.34–61.12; Epiphanius, *Pan.* 40.6.9 (Archontics). See further Klijn, *Seth*, 3–11, 16; Stroumsa, *Another Seed*, 35–70; Kugel, *Traditions*, 78, 100, 121, 123, 147, 157.

[31] *Ref.* 5.16.9; 5.17.7.

Besides anti-creator hostility, we can trace at least three more Saturninian themes in Ophite exegesis. The first is that the original Adam, made by angels, crawled like a worm.[32] Another is the spark image.[33] The divine world above sends a spark into Adam enabling him to stand upright. The idea of a divine element inhabiting the human body is common in this period (it appears in Stoicism, for instance), but the spark image is not. Finally, the idea that there are exactly *seven* creator angels was commonly held by Saturninian and Ophite Christians. It was the Ophites, perhaps, who first gave these seven angels their names, mostly based on Hebrew designations for god:

1. Yaldabaoth
2. Iao
3. Sabaoth
4. Adonaeus
5. Eloaeus
6. Horaeus
7. Astaphaeus

These figures formed the first Hebdomad (or group of seven) which were aligned with the seven planets known at the time. "Iao" is the Greek translation of Yahweh; "Sabaoth" refers to the angelic "hosts"; "Adonaeus" is from the Hebrew *Adonai* ("lord"); "Eloaeus" is likely form *Elohim* ("god[s]"). The derivation of "Horaeus" and "Astaphaeus" are more obscure, but they might have been divine names used by Jews in Egypt. (Horaeus sounds like Horus, son of Osiris; but it could go back to *'Ôr*, the Hebrew word for light.)

Sidelight on an Ophite Gem. Significantly, these same seven names were in ancient times carved into an oval pendant of green jasper. On the other side of the pendant was a lion-headed figure with kilt and staff identified with "Aariel" ("the lion of god," aka Yaldabaoth).[34] Some scholars have speculated that this was an Ophite Christian gem. It may only be "Ophite" in the sense of adapting Ophite imagery. It was probably used to protect its wearer from the malign influence of the planetary rulers, in particular their chief, Yaldabaoth.[35]

---

[32] Irenaeus, *Haer.* 1.30.6 (*scarizante*); Pseudo-Tertullian, *AAH* 2.3; Epiphanius, *Pan.* 37.4.1.

[33] Pseudo-Tertullian, *AAH* 2.3; Epiphanius, *Pan.* 37.4.2.

[34] Campbell Bonner, "An Amulet of the Ophite Gnostics," in *Commemorative Studies in Honor of Theodore Leslie Shear* (Amsterdam: Swets & Zeitlinger, 1975), 43–6, 444 (number 188 in the Bonner collection). See also Bonner, *Studies in Magical Amulets, Chiefly Graeco-Egyptian* (Ann Arbor, University of Michigan, 1950), 135–8, 184, plate IX.

[35] *Orig. World* II,5 100.23-26. See further Jackson, *Lion Becomes Man*, 21–6; Roy Kotansky and Jeffrey Spier, "'The Horned Hunter' on a Lost Gnostic Gem," *HTR* 88, no. 3 (1995): 315–37 at 327–9.

From John 8:44 (the "father of the devil" reading), Ophite Christians knew that the devil had a father, whom they identified with Yaldabaoth. Now the devil, based on a traditional reading of Genesis 3, was in serpentine form (Rev. 12:3). Thus they imagined that Yaldabaoth originally created the devil as a snake.[36]

When Yaldabaoth fathered his seven sons (the six creator angels plus the devil), he wanted to convince them that he was the only deity. Thus he proclaimed to them the following boast: "I am god and there is no other!" Immediately after this declaration, Yaldabaoth was rebuked by Wisdom, who proclaimed the existence of "the Human and the Child of the Human" (Heb. 2:6; Ps. 8:5 LXX). These events led to the making of humanity (Gen. 1:26).[37]

Originally, humanity was made in paradise, a heavenly location. In Paradise, Adam and Eve encountered the serpentine devil. The serpent had become wise (Gen. 3:1) because he was temporarily inhabited by Wisdom. Speaking through the snake, Wisdom convinced Adam and Eve to disobey the creator by eating the fruit of knowledge. Here the snake is hardly an unambiguous symbol of good. It is the Spirit-Mother, not the snake itself, who opens up the way of knowledge to human beings.[38]

As a result of their enlightenment, Adam and Eve rejected their creators and were cast out of Paradise. They lost the spirit bodies they enjoyed in Paradise and assumed fleshly platforms for life on earth. Wisdom reminded the first couple of their true identity by sending them the "fragrance of the sweet light moisture." Adam and Eve were persecuted by the devil and by his six demonic sons (a lower Hebdomad in imitation of the higher one). These demons of the lower Hebdomad had the faces of beasts.[39]

In the course of time, Adam and Eve produced four children. The devil filled their son Cain with enough stupidity and audacity to kill his brother Abel. Eve then bore Seth and Norea, models of the redeemed. Yaldabaoth tried to drown their descendants with a Flood. The plan failed when Wisdom saved Noah and his family (Wis. 10:4). Yaldabaoth then chose Abraham and his descendants (the Judeans) to adore and obey him (Gen. 12:1-3). The Judean prophets later spoke with the voices of Yaldabaoth and the higher Hebdomad.[40]

The Life of Jesus

Wisdom secretly inserted prophecies about Christ into Judean scripture. She convinced Yaldabaoth to impregnate the virgin Mary to produce Jesus. Jesus grew up as a man more righteous and wise than all. At some point, probably at his baptism, Jesus was inhabited by Christ from on high. Christ then worked miracles and gathered disciples. Christ left Jesus immediately before the crucifixion

---

[36] Irenaeus, *AH* 1.30.5.
[37] Irenaeus, *AH* 1.30.6.
[38] Irenaeus, *AH* 1.30.7.
[39] Irenaeus, *AH* 1.30.8-9.
[40] Irenaeus, *AH* 1.30.9-11.

(compare Cerinthus); but he raised Jesus's corpse so that it became a spirit body (like the bodies of Adam and Eve in Paradise).[41]

The resurrected Jesus taught his disciples for eighteen months. To mature disciples, he revealed deeper mysteries. Jesus then ascended to heaven, sat at the right hand of his father (Yaldabaoth). He now gathers redeemed souls without Yaldabaoth's knowledge. The consummation occurs when all the divine light in humans (the individual sparks of the true Human above) is gathered and restored to the incorruptible realm.[42]

This Ophite rewriting of Genesis follows the report of Irenaeus. When we compare other reports, however, we discover tensions. Pseudo-Tertullian, for instance, claimed that for Ophites, Christ did not come in flesh and that there was no resurrection of the flesh.[43] Irenaeus's report contradicts the first point inasmuch as Christ assumed the flesh of Jesus, born of the virgin Mary. According to the Refutator, Christ contained the fullness of divinity in *bodily* form (Col. 1:19; 2:9).[44] Against the denial of fleshly resurrection, Origen said that Ophite Christians spoke of "resurrection of the flesh by the tree" of life.[45] Some scholars, however, think that the phrase means "resurrection *from* the flesh."[46] In this view, supercosmic life transcends fleshly existence.

The Seal

Evidently Ophite Christians formed a group, as is indicated by their practices. They enacted a rite they called the "seal," a common Christian metaphor for baptism. The Ophite seal was a ritual that combined both baptism and anointing, though we know more about the anointing. Ophites called the oil for anointing "white," and it possibly consisted of olive oil.[47] This oil, when consecrated, was said to come from the tree of life. Ophite initiates, speaking in response to a formula, proclaimed the words, "I have been anointed with white ointment from the tree of life."[48] The initiate was called "son" or "youth." The one who administered the oil, dabbing it on the forehead of the baptized in a circular motion, was called "father." The formal designation "father" suggests some kind of priesthood in the Ophite assembly.

Baptism and anointing were rites of initiation, but they also helped at the hour of death. The "father" priests who initiated the rite told the baptized that at the moment of their death seven angels of light stood to their right, and seven angels of wickedness stood to their left. The leader of the wicked angels was the creator, Yaldabaoth.[49]

---

[41] Irenaeus, *AH* 1.30.12-14.

[42] Irenaeus, *AH* 1.30.14.

[43] Pseudo-Tertullian, *AAH* 2.4.

[44] *Ref.* 5.12.4; 10.10.4; cf. 8.13.2; Irenaeus, *AH* 1.3.4; Clement, *Exc.* 31.1.

[45] Origen, *Cels.* 6.34 (ἀνάστασιν σαρκός).

[46] DeConick, *Gnostic New Age*, 209.

[47] Speculation about the trees in paradise, and on the olive tree in particular, can be found in *Orig. World* II,5 110.2–111.8; *Ref.* 5.26.6 (Justin); Ignatius, *Trallians* 11.2; *Smyrnaeans* 1; Justin, *Dial.* 86; Clement, *Pedagogue* 3.25.3; *Strom.* 5.11.72.3.

[48] Origen, *Cels.* 6.27.

[49] Origen, *Cels.* 6.27.

Part of baptismal instruction was learning the names of the wicked angels, who were also planetary rulers pictured as gatekeepers.[50] The soul at the hour of death was thought to rise through the heavens, past the gates of the seven planets. Knowing the names and forms of the seven planetary rulers secured power over them, and ensured that the soul could safely pass through the heavens.

As we know from Irenaeus, there was not just one group of seven angels, but two. Even to get to the moon, one had to pass through the lower Hebdomad (the devil's angels). The first of these angels was the leonine Michael. The second was Suriel in the shape of a bull. The third was Raphael in the form of a giant snake. The fourth, Gabriel, had the shape of an eagle. The fifth, Thauthabaoth, had the face of a bear. Erathaoth, the sixth, had a dog's visage. The seventh, Onoel, employed the head of a donkey.

Once one passed through these angels, one attained the "barrier of evil." Crossing this barrier apparently brought one out of earth's atmosphere (the region below the moon). In the superlunary region, the ascending soul met the rulers of the upper Hebdomad, the planetary rulers. The highest of these was Yaldabaoth. To him the dying were bid to show a symbol, engraved with the mark of life (perhaps a picture of the tree of life). Yaldabaoth, like his angelic counterpart Michael, had the form of a lion, and was said to be in sympathy with the planet Saturn (whose gate he guards).[51]

Short speeches and symbols were recited for the six other planetary rulers.[52] At the end of each speech, the repeated locution "let grace be with me father," is probably addressed to the person officiating the rite. This particular rite is specifically said to be a deathbed one, a kind of Last Rites ritual. We might imagine an antiphonal response, with the "father" speaking the formulas to the rulers and the initiate responding "let grace be with me."[53] The ascent was played out in the mind before one's soul rose from the body at death.

As for the Ophite Eucharist, there is less trustworthy testimony. Pseudo-Tertullian claimed that Ophite Christians used a serpent to bless their bread. Epiphanius wrote that Ophites set up a table with loaves of bread. On this table, they set a basket containing a tame snake. When they open the top of the basket, the snake crawls out and coils around the loaves to consecrate them. The Ophites then consume the bread and were even said to kiss the snake. The use of a tame snake resembles the technique of Alexander of Abonuteichos (Chapter 1). The description of the ritual itself, however, does not inspire belief. Epiphanius admitted that he reported hearsay.[54]

---

[50] Origen, *Cels.* 7.40.

[51] Origen, *Cels.* 6.31.

[52] The only difference from the order of the Hebdomad in Irenaeus's Ophite report is that Astaphaeus is in the fifth, not seventh place. See Rasimus, *Paradise*, 104.

[53] Origen, *Cels.* 6.32. For similar practices in antiquity, see Kurt Rudolph, *Gnosis: Nature and History of Gnosticism* (Edinburgh: T&T Clark, 1984), 171–89; Alan Segal, *Life After Death* (New York: Doubleday, 2004), 204–47.

[54] See further Rasimus, *Paradise*, 213–16.

For Ophite Christians it must be remembered that the snake was also a symbol of the devil.

The Peratic Report

The Refutator wrote a report against certain "Peratai" about 222 CE, a report which contains significant similarities to Ophite reports. First, we encounter the Christ as snake exegesis of John 3:14-15. We also meet a similar exegesis of John 8:44, where the creator is father of the devil.[55] There is in both Peratic and Ophite thought a Trinity of three primal Humans.[56] We also note a strong revisionary reading of the Hebrew scriptures, this time focused on the book of Exodus. There is a Peratic remark on the Eden story as well. Christ the "universal snake" is manifest in the "wise word of Eve."[57] Whatever exactly this phrase means, it hints that Eve's eating from the tree of knowledge was seen as a positive act.[58]

Peratic and Ophite reports also indicate a common interest in astrology. Both the Refutator and Origen indicate that the creator or chief ruler is the planetary ruler of Saturn (most likely identified with Yaldabaoth).[59] Both reports show an interest in learning the true names and features of the planetary rulers. The names, to be sure, are different, in part because the Peratic report makes use of a different source called the "Outlying Officials Dwelling as far as the Aether."[60] This treatise was "lauded" by Peratic Christians, but they probably did not compose it.[61] The basic goal of Peratic and Ophite Christians remained similar: they aimed to break out of this cosmos, transcend the planetary rulers, and attain the realm of light.

From another treatise, Peratic Christians were inspired to identify Christ with the constellation Draco, the astral snake encircling the pole star.[62] To see Christ in the sky, however, Peratic Christians needed the "blessed eyes" opened by their reading of scripture. Christ was Draco, the initiator of time, because Christ was "in the Beginning" (John 1:1). The astrological sign was thought to express a biblical meaning.

---

[55] *Ref.* 5.16.9; 5.17.7; Irenaeus, *AH* 1.30.5.

[56] *Ref.* 5.12.3.

[57] *Ref.* 5.16.8.

[58] Cf. Artemidorus, who informs us that, whenever a serpent appears in a dream saying nothing savage, "it signifies great goods coming directly or indirectly" from gods associated with the serpent (*Dream Interpretation* 2.13).

[59] *Ref.* 5.16.1-3; cf. 5.14.2.

[60] *Ref.* 5.14.

[61] *Pace* DeConick, "From the Bowels," in Bull and Turner, eds., *Mystery and Secrecy*, 6. The panoply of characters in the treatise does not appear anywhere else in Ophite theology.

[62] The report of the Aratus allegorizers can be found in *Ref.* 4.46.2–4.50.2. Peratic Christians interpreted the Aratus allegory in their own way. For them, the constellation Draco signified Christ. For the anonymous Aratus allegorizers, it symbolized the devil. On Aratus, see Douglas A. Kidd, ed., *Aratus: Phaenomena: Introduction, Translation, and Commentary* (Cambridge: Cambridge University Press, 1997).

> **Sidelight on an Ophite Gem.** A rediscovered ancient gem may in fact depict Draco. Carved into black steatite, there is an image of a curled snake surrounded by the Zodiacal signs. On the other side of the amulet, Adam and Eve stand to the right and left of the tree of knowledge which bears another coiled snake. Though Adam and Eve are naked, they stand unashamed (they do not cover their genitals). Symbols of life and knowledge encircle them (signified by Hebrew letters). Scholars have speculated that this third- to fourth-century gem could have been carved by or for Ophite Christians.[63]

Even as we point out these similarities, however, we must take account of differences. Trinitarian thought in the Peratic report focuses on the figures of Father, Son, and matter. The Peratic report does not feature the name of Yaldabaoth or the two Hebdomads. In the Peratic report, moreover, Christ is said to come in the time of Herod, not at some later time in the ministry of Jesus.[64] Such differences should be taken seriously, though they would not be uncommon among Christians who had no defined creed.

In the most recent study of Ophite thought, Tuomas Rasimus has identified four main features of Ophite Christian lore: (1) a positive valuation of the first humans eating from the tree of knowledge, (2) seven named rulers, (3) salvific Wisdom figures manifested in Eve, and (4) three heavenly Human figures. Peratic Christians, in my view, display three out of four of these features: (1) a positive eating from the tree, (2) a salvific or at least valorized Eve figure, and (3) three heavenly Humans. (Seven named rulers is not distinctly Ophite. We see it, for instance, in the Seed of Seth.) Both Peratic and Ophite Christians also appealed to the same founder figure (Euphrates) and had a similar exegesis of John 3:14-15.

Conclusion

The closeness of these similarities indicates that we are dealing with the same porous group(s) of Ophite Christians whom the Refutator called "Peratic." These "Peratic" and "Ophite" Christians worshiped Christ as their redeemer. It is inaccurate to say that they considered the snake in paradise to be the initiator of knowledge.[65] It was Wisdom speaking through the snake who deserves that accolade.[66] It is even more erroneous to claim, with the heresiographers, that Ophite Christians worshiped or venerated the snake as such.[67] Rather, they venerated Wisdom who spoke through

---

[63] Erwin R. Goodenough, "A Jewish-gnostic Amulet of the Roman Period," *Greek Roman and Byzantine Studies* 1 (1958): 71–80; Rasimus, *Paradise*, 220–1.

[64] *Ref.* 5.12.4.

[65] Origen, *Cels.* 6.28. On the snake as the beginning of knowledge, cf. Pseudo-Tertullian, *AAH* 2.1; Epiphanius, *Pan.* 37.3.1.

[66] See further Rasimus, *Paradise*, 64–102.

[67] Clement, *Strom.* 7.17.108.2; Epiphanius, *Pan.* 37.1.2. See further Rasimus, *Paradise*, 211–16.

the snake.[68] They also venerated Christ symbolized by two particular snakes – the bronze snake in Numbers and the constellation Draco.

Ophite Christians considered themselves to be part of an ecclesial formation. They believed in a holy "Church" of primal Humans on high. They also spoke of "emanations of an earthly church."[69] Evidently they considered themselves to be members of this earthly assembly. Perhaps they thought of themselves as a reflection of the Church on high.

Ophites used Jewish and Christian scriptures (in particular, Genesis, Exodus, John, Matthew, and 1 Corinthians). Their Christian reading of scripture may seem revolutionary today, but since there was no normative exegesis of scripture in the second century, I hesitate to call it transgressive.[70]

Based on their baptism-plus-anointing ritual, it is likely that the Ophites were based in Syria or Egypt where such practices are widely attested.[71] Links with Saturninian exegesis suggest Syria. On the other hand, the animal heads of the lower Hebdomad suggest familiarity with (and parody of) Egyptian gods.[72] Origen, who lived in Alexandria and then Palestine, was able to obtain the Ophite diagram for his own use about 250 CE. In the 170s, Celsus had obtained a similar diagram. His location is unknown, though Alexandria is a common guess.[73]

We might then imagine two early Christian intellectuals, Euphrates from Mesopotamia and Akembes from Greece, meeting in Syria or Alexandria between 120–140 CE, and forming an early Christian circle centered on their revisionary readings of Genesis. The theology of this group would influence the Seed of Seth as seen in the *Secret Book of John* (written and revised after 180 CE). It would also influence other works like the *Origin of the World*, *Reality of the Rulers*, *Eugnostus*, and the *Wisdom of Jesus Christ* among the Nag Hammadi codices.

The Ophite network was extant until about 180 CE when Celsus obtained the Ophite diagram and Irenaeus transmitted the Ophite revision of Genesis. Origen conceded that a few Ophite Christians existed in his day.[74] The existence of an Ophite gem carved in the third or fourth century might suggest that these Christians lasted longer. Epiphanius and Theodoret still waged war with Ophites in the late fourth and early fifth centuries CE. If Ophite conventicles had dissolved by that time, their influence was not forgotten.

---

[68] Epiphanius, *Pan.* 37.2.6.

[69] Origen, *Cels.* 6.34.

[70] *Pace* DeConick, *Gnostic New Age*, 256, 263.

[71] Andrew McGowan, *Ancient Christian Worship* (Grand Rapids: Baker, 2016), 135–82.

[72] For further Egyptian connections, see Thomas Gaston, "The Egyptian Background of Gnostic Mythology," *Numen* 62, no. 4 (2015): 389–407 at 395–8.

[73] Henry Chadwick, ed., *Origen: Contra Celsum* (Cambridge: Cambridge University Press, 1953), xxiv–xxix.

[74] Origen, *Cels.* 6.26.

Further Reading

April D. DeConick, "From the Bowels of Hell to Draco: The Mysteries of the Peratics," in *Mystery and Secrecy in the Nag Hammadi Collection and Other Ancient Literature: Ideas and Practices*, ed. Christian H. Bull et al. (Leiden: Brill, 2012), 3–37.

Nicola Denzey, "A New Star on the Horizon: Astral Christologies and Stellar Debates in early Christian Discourse," in *Prayer, Magic, and the Stars in the Ancient and Late Antique World*, ed. Scott Noegel, Joel Walker, and Brannon Wheeler (University Park: Penn State University Press, 2003), 207–21.

Nicola Denzey, "The Ophite Diagram and Other Christian Books of the Dead," in *Essays in Honor of Frederik Wisse, ARC, Journal of the Faculty of Religious Studies* 33 (2005): 89–122.

Fred Ledegang, "The Ophites and the 'Ophite' Diagram in Celsus and Origen," *Journal of Eastern Christian Studies* 60 (2008): 51–83.

Tuomas Rasimus, *Paradise Reconsidered in Gnostic Mythmaking: Rethinking Sethianism in Light of the Ophite Evidence*, NHMS 68 (Leiden: Brill, 2009).

A. Welburn, "Reconstructing the Ophite Diagram," *NovT* 23 (1981): 261–87.

Basilides and Isidore

Introduction

The heresiological reports on Basilides are some of the most wild and conflicting that we possess. According to Irenaeus, for instance, Basilides believed in 365 heavens ruled by powers and principalities over whom was stationed the leader "Abrasax." Basilides supposedly believed that Christ descended through the heavens in disguise under the name of "Calacau." Christ was also not really crucified. Instead, another man – temporarily given the facial features of Christ – was crucified as Christ stood by laughing.[1]

These details are not confirmed by other reports on Basilides independent of Irenaeus. A long report offered by the Refutator provides a strikingly different story about a God, called "nonexistent," giving rise to a "triple Sonship."[2] Eusebius reported anti-Basilidean attacks by Agrippa Castor (perhaps a contemporary of Irenaeus). Clement of Alexandria is the only church father who supplied quotes from Basilides and his son Isidore, quotes which do not confirm or even resemble most points mentioned by Irenaeus and the Refutator. Given the nature of the data, it is methodologically safest to prioritize the Clementine fragments, using them as the criterion by which to judge the later reports.[3]

---

[1] Irenaeus, *AH* 1.24.3-7.

[2] The author of *Ref.* (7.20-27) presents a Basilidean cosmogony that differs in significant respects from what we find in Irenaeus (*AH* 1.24). In Irenaeus, for instance, the Ogdoad refers to a set of mental entities, while in *Ref.* it refers to the eighth heaven. The eighth heaven is apparently the highest heaven in *Ref.*, whereas Irenaeus presents 365 heavens. The seventh and eighth heaven of *Ref.* are governed by two rulers and their sons, who differ from the multiplicity of angelic rulers in Irenaeus. The three "Sonships" and the Holy Spirits of *Ref.* go unmentioned in Irenaeus, as does the idea of salvation through differentiation (φυλοκρίνησις). On the basis of Basilides's "vertiginous levels of ineffability," Edwards vouches for the reliability of the Refutator's report (*Aristotle and Early Christian Thought* [London: Taylor & Francis, 2019], 42–3). He argues that the three Sonships have an exegetical basis in Johannine and Pauline literature (*Catholicity and Heresy in the Early Church* [Farnham: Ashgate, 2009], 20–3).

[3] This is the procedure of Winrich Löhr, *Basilides und seine Schule*, WUNT 83 (Tübingen: Mohr Siebeck, 1996), whose order of testimonies and fragments I follow.

Life

Basilides was a Christian theologian who lived in Alexandria, Egypt. Clement dated him to the reigns of Hadrian and Antoninus (between 117–161 CE).[4] When Basilides died is unknown, but he was apparently younger than Marcion, who perished about 160.[5] Epiphanius observed that Basilides taught in other smaller cities of the Nile Delta.[6] Either this report is based on local tradition, or Epiphanius assumed that Basilides must have taught where there were surviving Basilidean groups in the fourth century.[7] Whether Basilides travelled outside of Egypt is unknown. Attempts to place his origins in Syria, or to grant him a Syrian sojourn, are based in part on an effort to connect his thought to Saturninus, a putative fellow "student" of Menander of Antioch.[8]

This connection to Saturninus is probably based on presumed intellectual overlaps. Such presumptions cannot be allowed to stand, since Basilides's disagreements with Saturninus are manifold. According to surviving evidence, for example, Basilides did not discourage marriage and childbearing; he did not affirm the divine spark within humanity; and he had no story of humanity created in the image of God. Indeed, we have no surviving fragments in which Basilides interpreted Genesis 1–6 at all. Basilides was unfamiliar with exactly seven creating angels and he never discouraged the consumption of meat. It is thus inadvisable to connect Basilides to Saturninus in a kind of intellectual genealogy.

View of God

Perhaps because Basilides in Alexandria was not in competition with Jews (who were decimated during the Diaspora Revolt), he felt little need to demonize the Jewish deity. The Judean god, according to Basilides, was ignorant of the true God above him, but his ignorance ripened into wisdom. Basilides commented on Prov. 1:7 ("the fear of the Lord is the beginning of wisdom"). He took the "Lord" to be the Judean deity. The statement was then given a backstory: "the Lord" (the Judean deity) experienced fear when he heard the voice of the ministering Spirit declaring

---

[4] Clement, *Strom.* 7.17.106.4–107.1 = Löhr, *Basilides*, Testimony 5. In his *Chronicle*, Eusebius had Basilides "sojourn" (*commoratur*) in Alexandria in 132 CE (R. Helm, ed., *Die Chronik des Hieronymus* [Berlin: Akademie, 1956], 201 = Löhr Testimony 12). This does not mean that Basilides only appeared at this date.

[5] Clement, *Strom.* 7.17.106.4–107.1 = Löhr, *Basilides*, Testimony 5.

[6] Epiphanius, *Pan.* 24.1.1 = Löhr, *Basilides*, Testimony 13.

[7] The Refutator said that Basilides studied in "Egypt," not Alexandria specifically (7.27.13).

[8] Irenaeus, *AH* 1.24.1 = Löhr, *Basilides*, Testimony, 4. Epiphanius assumes a Syrian origin for Basilides; Pearson grants him a Syrian sojourn ("Basilides," in Marjanen and Luomanen, eds., *Companion*, 1–31).

the good news about Jesus (evidently at his baptism). The Lord's fear then gave way to wisdom (informed knowledge) about Christ.[9]

The Refutator presented another Basilidean interpretation of Prov. 1:7, both similar and different to the previous. In this case, "the Lord" is the greater of two lords who rule the cosmos. The greater Lord hears the gospel, not from the ministering Spirit, but from his own son who sits enthroned beside him. He learned that he was not the highest god, that he was born, and that the unnamable God and the true Sonship exists above him. This knowledge inspired both fear and the wisdom of repentance.[10]

These reports from Clement and the Refutator may or may not be in tension with a report of Irenaeus that the god of the Judeans "wanted to subject all nations to his own." This was why the rulers of the other nations opposed the god of the Jews, and why the peoples of other nations resisted the nation of the Judean deity.[11] We might read this report in light of the Bar Kokhba revolt (132–135 CE), when the Romans attacked the Judean homeland. We might also frame it in terms of an earlier time, prior to the repentance of the Jewish deity when he learned about Christ. Judea's (or Judah's) wars against other nations are of course a major theme in the Hebrew scriptures.

Ritual

Reportedly, Basilidean Christians celebrated Christ's incarnation in early January. On the night prior to January 6th or 10th (there is discrepancy regarding the exact date), they listened all night to (apparently scriptural) texts.[12] At dawn, they celebrated the moment of incarnation, possibly with song. Basilides was known as a songwriter, and Basilidean Christians delighted in psalms.[13]

Despite celebrating on January 6 (the date of the modern festival of Epiphany), Basilidean Christians did not suppose that this was the season of Jesus's birth. For them, the moment of incarnation was not the arrival of Jesus as a baby, but the descent of the Spirit at his baptism. Christ became incarnate in Jesus at the Jordan river. This was also the understanding, as we saw, of Cerinthus, who was probably an interpreter of Mark and John.[14]

---

[9] Clement, *Strom.* 2.8.36.1 = Löhr Frag. 4. Cf. esp. *Ref.* 7.26.1-2. See further Löhr, *Basilides*, 61–78. In *Ref.* 7.22-27 we find quotations and allusions to other passages of Jewish scripture: Ps. 39:9 LXX = 148:5b; Gen. 1:3; Ps. 132:2; Deut. 32:11; Isa. 40:31; Gen. 1:7-8; Isa. 3:3; Exod. 6:3; Pss. 31:5; 50:5 LXX.

[10] *Ref.* 7.26. Note the technical term φυλοκρινήσεως and cf. σοφίας φυλοκρινητικῆς in Clement, *Strom* 2.8.36.1 = Löhr, *Basilides*, frag. 4.

[11] Irenaeus, *AH* 1.24.4.

[12] Clement, *Strom.* 1.21.145.6–146.4 = Löhr, *Basilides*, frag. 1. See further Thomas J. Talley, *The Origins of the Liturgical Year*, 2nd ed. (Collegeville: Liturgical Press, 1986), 119–29.

[13] Origen, *Enarrations on Job* 21.12 (PG 17 80a) = Löhr, *Basilides*, Testimony 11.

[14] Hans Förster, *Die Anfänge von Weihnachten und Epiphanias: Eine Anfrage an die Entstehungshypothesen* (Tübingen: Mohr Siebeck, 2007), 57–67.

Scriptural Practice

Basilides was, like Philo a century before him, a philosophically minded exegete. He commented on Gen. 23:4, where Abraham confessed to be a migrant and sojourner (cf. Ps. 38:13 LXX). Like the author of 1 Pet. (2:11), Basilides applied this sojourner status to all Christians, whom he called the "elect."[15]

Basilides wrote a twenty-four-book commentary, the *Exegetica*, on "the gospel."[16] The idea of writing a commentary on distinctly Christian scripture was novel at the time (most gospels were barely a generation old, and some were still being written). Which "gospel" Basilides commented on is unclear – it need not have been one of the four familiar today. At least one of the parables upon which Basilides commented – that of the Rich Man and Lazarus – comes from what is now known as Luke (16:19-31).[17] Basilides commented on this parable in book thirteen of his *Exegetica*.

The opening of this book survives and gives us a sense of Basilides's authorial persona: "As we are writing the thirteenth book of our treatise, the saving Logos will provide for us the needed, richly abundant content." Apparently, Basilides considered himself to be something of an inspired exegete. God's Logos (John 1:1), not Basilides's own personal genius, supplied his thought like a bubbling spring. To be sure, Basilides was striking a rhetorical pose. Any number of spiritual entrepreneurs during his time claimed inspiration to increase their authority.[18] The rhetoric worked best, however, when the author was sincere.

Basilides had a peculiar allegorical reading of the Lazarus parable. He believed that it showed the origin of "the nature without root or place which impinges on reality." Since we lack the context of this quote, we can no longer tell exactly what Basilides meant by this rootless and placeless "nature." It might be a description of God (if Basilides did in fact describe God as "non-existent").[19] But God has no origin, so he cannot be the nature whose origin Basilides explained. For Basilides, the rootless nature was probably evil itself, which impinged on reality like rust corrodes iron.[20]

What in the parable of Lazarus might have inspired a discussion of evil? Perhaps it was the comment that Lazarus had during his life received "evils" (Luke 16:25). This raises the question why the poor but righteous man was cursed with evil (Lazarus died a beggar). In short, Basilides might have asked (to put it most simply): why do bad things happen to good people – and then, more fundamentally, why is there evil at all?

---

[15] Clement, *Strom.* 4.26.165.3 = Löhr, *Basilides*, frag. 12.
[16] Agrippa Castor in Eusebius, *HE* 4.7.5-8 = Löhr, *Basilides*, Testimony 1. Basilides's exegetical remarks on "the gospel" need not have entirely fit the ancient or modern commentary genre. Other kinds of explanations and lore were also included.
[17] *Acts of Archelaus* 67.5 = Löhr, *Basilides*, frag. 19.
[18] Heidi Wendt, *At the Temple Gates: The Religion of Freelance Experts in the Roman Empire* (Oxford: Oxford University Press, 2016), entire.
[19] *Ref.* 7.21.1.
[20] Clement, *Strom.* 4.12.88.5 = Löhr, *Basilides*, frag. 9.

Based on these inquiries, Basilides would then have launched into a discussion of the origin of evil, stating various preliminary theories before refuting them with his own view. Regrettably, we do not know that this is what Basilides actually did, because the writer who quoted his fragment on Lazarus skipped – as Clement relates – some 500 lines of text! When he restarted his quote, Basilides was already diving into a discussion of Persian theology.

This theology spoke of a primal mixing of the eternal principles of Darkness and Light. Light gazed into Darkness as if through a mirror, and a reflection of the Light was absorbed into the Darkness. With this absorbed reflection of the Light, Darkness generated this world, which then become evil for lack of Light.

Basilides did not subscribe to this theory. He distanced himself from it by calling it "barbarian" – a term which had the general sense of "foreign." How this foreign theology related to the gospel parable (if it did) we can no longer tell. But if the parable inspired a discussion of evil, then Basilides probably appealed to Persian theology as one among several theories explaining how evil arose. (As we know, Basilides's contemporary Plutarch would do the same.[21])

According to Epiphanius, Basilides denied that evil was a substance. Evil was not part of the primordial world; everything was created good. Evil is the result of human choice. All humans – not just the original humans – have the power either to do good or to evil. Humans bring evil into this world by willing it. Evil itself has "no root."[22]

This is an important testimony, consonant with the Refutator's report in which Basilides preached the idea of creation from nothing (*creatio ex nihilo*, a standard Christian doctrine today).[23] The teaching is also reminiscent of a passage from the *Gospel of Mary*, which we know was read in Egypt. In this gospel, Peter asks Jesus about the sin of the world. Jesus replies that there is no such thing as sin. "Rather you yourselves are what produces sin when you act."[24]

Despite denying the substantiality of evil, Basilides took sin seriously. Every person, including infants, have the potential and perhaps even the propensity to sin.[25] Even to think about committing murder or adultery was as good as committing them (Matt. 5:21-22, 27-28). Moreover, not all sins are forgiven in baptism – only those committed ignorantly or involuntary.[26]

---

[21] Cf. *Ref.* 4.43.3; Plutarch, *Is Os.* 46-47.

[22] Epiphanius, *Pan.* 24.6.1-4. Basilides's affirmation of free choice undermines Clement's attempt to depict Basilides as a determinist who said that people are "by nature" faithful and elect (*Strom.* 5.1.3.3).

[23] *Ref.* 7.21.1.

[24] *Gospel of Mary* 3:3-6 with the comments of Karen King, *The Gospel of Mary of Magdala* (Salem: Polebridge, 2003), 49–57. Possibly, this teaching flows from Basilides's doctrine of creation from nothing – if the report in *Ref.* 7.21.1 is reliable. If God made the world from nothing, then evil and matter are not substantial.

[25] Clement, *Strom.* 4.12.82.1 = Löhr, *Basilides*, frag. 7.

[26] Clement, *Strom.* 4.24.153.3 = Löhr, *Basilides*, frag. 10.

Basilides's Library

Origen claimed that Basilides published a gospel under his own name.[27] This allegation seems incorrect. First of all, none of the gospel materials Basilides dealt with are unique to him. Second, Basilides tried to situate himself in a tradition of apostolic succession running from Peter through Glaucias, whom Basilideans identified as an "interpreter" of Peter who evidently settled in Egypt.[28] (The Glaucias tradition is interesting in part because Eusebius later spread what appears to be a counternarrative: that Peter's "interpreter" was Mark, the earliest gospel writer and first "bishop" of Basilides's city, Alexandria.[29])

The point here is that Basilides did not claim personal authority for his form of Christianity, as we also saw from his preface to *Exegetica* book 13. Possibly, Origen's "gospel according to Basilides" was a text that Basilides edited for use in his own group. If so, Basilides resembled Marcion who also edited a gospel (evidently an early form of Luke) for use in his own churches (see Chapter 14).[30]

Apparently, Basilides also claimed that he had heard secret traditions from Matthias. Matthias, in turn, had received these traditions privately from Jesus himself.[31] This "Matthias" is a mysterious figure. He could be the apostle chosen to replace Judas Iscariot according to Acts 1. But writers of Basilides's time show no confirmed knowledge of Acts. Alternatively, Matthias could be the apostle of Jesus later claimed to be a gospel writer (usually referred to as "Matthew"). In either case, "Matthias" was apostolic, which means that Basilides claimed direct contact with an apostle. There are chronological difficulties here, but no ancient writer seems to have noticed them. Marcion and Valentinus also appealed to the teachings of Matthias (with no claim to direct contact),[32] and writings attributed to Matthias became available in the course of the second century.[33]

Basilides also valued Paul's writings, appealing – as we shall see – to a verse in Romans to support a theory of transmigration.[34] Basilides's son and disciple Isidore discussed Paul's directions about marriage in 1 Corinthians 7.[35] Later Basilideans

---

[27] Origen *Homilies on Luke 1* = Löhr, *Basilides*, Testimony 10.

[28] Clement, *Strom.* 7.106.4–107.1 = Löhr, *Basilides*, Testimony 5. See further Markschies, "Das Evangelium des Basilides," in Markschies and Schröter, eds., *Antike christliche Apokryphen in deutscher Übersetzung*, Vol. 1/1.460-65.

[29] Eusebius, *HE* 3.39.15, partly transmitting Papias.

[30] Winrich Löhr, "Editors and Commentators: Some Observations on the Craft of Second-century Theologians," in *Pascha Nostrum Christus: Essays in Honour of Raniero Cantalamessa*, ed. Pier Franco Beatrice and Bernard Pouderon (Paris: Beauchesne, 2016), 65–84.

[31] *Ref.* 7.20.1 = Löhr, *Basilides*, Testimony 7.

[32] *Strom.* 7.17.108.1 = Löhr, *Basilides*, Testimony 6.

[33] Clement, *Strom.* 2.9.45.4; 3.4.26.3; 4.6.35.2; 7.13.82.1. Origen knew of a gospel according to Matthias (*Homily 1 on Luke* = Löhr, *Basilides*, Testimony 10). The *Book of Thomas the Contender* II,7 138.1–3 also mentions a "Mathaias" (ΜΑΘΑΙΑΣ) who records secret words spoken to Judas Thomas. See further Löhr, *Basilides*, 25–9.

[34] Note also the use of Rom. 8 in *Ref.* 7.25.1.

[35] Clement, *Strom.* 3.1.2.1–3.1.3.1 = Löhr, *Basilides*, frag. 6.

seem also to have used Hebrews (perhaps taken to be Pauline). They defined faith as "the assent of the soul to something which is not sensed, since it is absent. Hope is the expectation of a good possession."[36] Such a definition develops, I hypothesize, the language found in Heb. 11:1: "faith is the substance of things hoped for, the proof of objects not seen."

A second-century critic of Basilides, Agrippa Castor, reported that Basilides made use of other unknown prophetic writings attributed to "Barkabbas" and "Barkoph." Although these are Aramaic-sounding names, the writings themselves – assuming they existed – are unknown. We know that Isidore commented on the writings of the prophet Parchor (perhaps a Persian seer), and knew of a text called the *Prophecy of Ham*, reputed ancestor of the Egyptians.[37]

Initiation and Transmigration

In Basilides's circle there were apparently different levels of initiation. Agrippa Castor said that Basilides prescribed a five-year silence for his disciples. This report, if true, would conform Basilidean to Pythagorean practice. (Apollonius of Tyana, perhaps the most famous Pythagorean of the time, apparently went through such a period of silence in the first century CE.[38])

Another attributed Basilidean doctrine was transmigration. Transmigration means that the soul, which carries the identity of the person, survives physical death and enters into the bodies of other humans (and sometimes animals). The point of transmigration is to train and purify the soul as it experiences the pains and struggles of bodily life. For Basilides, transmigration was a system of moral purgation ordained by God for the salvation of the soul. It was a function of divine providence.

As a doctrine, transmigration was associated with Pythagoras and Empedocles, ancient sages of Italy and Sicily, respectively. Empedocles in particular had taught that a soul at the height of wisdom would no longer be condemned to return to the body. To the people of his hometown, Empedocles called himself an "immortal god" no longer subject to death's blight (that is, reentry into a mortal body).[39]

Although transmigration had Pythagorean roots, Basilides believed it had a biblical basis. In his letter to the Romans (7:9), Paul wrote that he once lived apart from Law.

---

[36] Clement, *Strom.* 2.27.2 = Löhr, *Basilides*, frag. 3. Cf. the Basilidean description in *Strom.* 2.3.10.1–11.2 = Löhr frag. 2: "faith is discovered without demonstration from an intellectual conception" with Clement, *Strom.* 5.1.3.2-3 = Löhr, *Basilides*, frag. 13.

[37] Clement, *Strom.* 6.6.53.2-5 = Löhr, *Basilides*, frag. 15. Isidore was the author of two other works: *Ethics*, and *On the Attached Soul*. Clement himself recommended a Persian prophet called Hystaspes (*Strom.* 1.21.129.3; 6.5.43.1).

[38] Agrippa Castor in Eusebius, *HE* 4.7.

[39] See further Joscelyn Godwin, "Pythagoras and Pythagoreanism," with Jessica Elbert Decker and Matthew Mayock, "Parmenides and Empedocles," in Glenn Alexander Magee, ed., *The Cambridge Handbook of Western Mysticism and Esotericism* (Cambridge: Cambridge University Press, 2016), 13–37; Litwa, *Posthuman Transformation*, 31–44.

Since Paul as a Jew was born under Law, there was technically no time for him to have lived apart from Law. Therefore Paul must have been referring to a previous life different from the one he lived as a Jew under Law.[40]

Later Basilidean Christians also cited Deut. 5:9, where God pays back the disobedient to the third and fourth generation.[41] Basilideans took "generation" (*genea*) in the sense of birth, and referred it to multiple births. In short, God punishes disobedient souls by having them live in different bodies for three to four "generations" (that is, lives) – guaranteeing that they learn their lesson.

Ethics and Martyrdom

Agrippa Castor claimed that Basilides allowed his followers to deny under oath that they were Christian in order to avoid martyrdom.[42] This report is doubtful in light of Basilides's genuine fragments. Basilides considered martyrdom a blessing insofar as it cleansed Christians of former wrongdoing while simultaneously allowing them to promote Christ. It was certainly much better than being executed for a crime. Yet since martyrdom was still punishment for sin, or the propensity to sin, it was not something to be proud of in and of itself, and Basilides did not assume it guaranteed a heavenly crown.[43]

The great moral problem for Basilidean Christians was the passions – uncontrolled emotions that attach themselves like "appendages" to the soul. These appendages were conceived of as "spirits" that disturbed and confused the soul. Some of these spirits were animal in nature, manifesting the traits of a wolf, monkey, lion, and goat. Humans possessed by these spirts have the irrational desires and perform what Basilides considered to be animalic.

Clement spurned this tradition because he thought that it undermined free will. Basilideans made the human body, he quipped, like the Trojan horse – packed not with soldiers but with demons.[44] But Basilidean Christians never thought that demon possession annulled free will. In fact, Isidore loudly complained about those people who did not take responsibility for their actions. The point of ethics, for Isidore, was to become superior to the spirits and the passions by the power of reason.[45]

---

[40] Origen, *Commentary on Romans* 5.1.25 = Löhr, *Basilides*, frag. 18. Cf. Origen, *Comm. Ser. 38 on Matthew* = Löhr, *Basilides*, frag. 17. Pierre Nautin rejected these passages as dependent on Clement's false inferences about Basilides in *Strom.* 4 ("Les fragments de Basilide sur la souffrance et leur interpétation par Clément d'Alexandrie et Origène," in *Mélanges des Histoire des Religions offerts à Henri-Charles Puech* [Paris: University Press of France, 1973], 393–404). Subsequent readers took Rom. 7:9 to refer to the bodiless life of the soul (Methodius, *Resurrection* 1.57-58). See further Löhr, *Basilides*, 212–18.

[41] Clement, *Exc.* 28 = Löhr, *Basilides*, frag. 16.

[42] Agrippa Castor in Eusebius, *HE* 4.7.5-8 = Löhr, *Basilides*, Testimony 1; Origen, *Comm. Ser. 38 on Matthew* = Löhr, *Basilides*, frag. 17.

[43] Clement, *Strom.* 4.12.81-83 = Löhr, *Basilides*, frag. 7.

[44] Clement, *Strom.* 2.20.112.1–114.2 = Löhr, *Basilides*, frag. 5.

[45] Clement, *Strom.* 2.20.112.1–114.2 = Löhr, *Basilides*, frag. 5.

This was a Platonic goal that accords with a famous passage in Plato's *Republic* – also copied in the Nag Hammadi codices (VI,5).[46] Plato envisioned the human person as having three entities within it: a human representing rationality, a lion representing drive, and a many-headed, protean monster representing the passions. The point of life is to weaken and starve the monster within, while feeding and cultivating one's reason.

Basilidean ethics was informed not only by the Platonic, but also by the Stoic tradition. The Stoics presented a mediating category for human action. They said that some acts were good, some bad, while others were indifferent. A modern example of an indifferent action might be washing one's car or growing a beard. These acts are neither morally good nor bad in themselves.

For Basilides, one indifferent act was eating meat sacrificed to Greco-Roman deities.[47] We dealt with this issue already in our chapter on the Nicolaitans. Some Christians, apparently on the basis of Paul (1 Cor. 8, 10), did not see a problem with eating meat sacrificed to gods whom they considered to be nonexistent. Eating – in fact eating anything – was indifferent, "for the kingdom of God is not a matter of food and drink" (Rom. 14:17).

Basilides was not an ascetic. As already noted, he had a son, and so presumably a wife (unfortunately unnamed).[48] Though not ascetic, Basilides hardly advocated a life of luxury. Rather, he preached an ethic of self-sufficiency in which one was called to "desire nothing, love everything, and hate nothing." God – not demons – was in control of the earth and human events. Therefore what happened occurred according to God's will and loving care for the world, or providence. Providence was as much a biblical as a philosophical tenet. Those who denied divine providence were widely considered to be impious. In a telling remark, Basilides himself preferred to say anything rather than deny providence.[49]

View of Christ

The Refutator observed that when it came to Jesus's life, Basilidean Christians adhered to the gospel accounts with no significant variation.[50] Nevertheless, it is important to discuss one claimed deviation already mentioned. According to

---

[46] Plato, *Republic* 588a–589b = NHC VI,5.

[47] Agrippa Castor in Eusebius, *HE* 4.7.5-8 = Löhr, *Basilides*, Testimony 1.

[48] Further advice on marriage was offered by Isidore in Clement, *Strom.* 3.1.2.1–3.1.3.1 = Löhr, *Basilides*, frag. 6.

[49] Clement, *Strom.* 4.11.86.1 = Löhr, *Basilides*, frag. 8; Clement, *Strom.* 4.12.82.2. For Providence in antiquity, see further Gretchen J. Reydams-Schils, *Demiurge and Providence: Stoic and Platonist Readings of Plato's Timaeus* (Turnhout: Brepols, 1999); George Boys-Stones, "Providence and Religion in Middle Platonism," in *Theologies of Ancient Greek Religions*, ed. Esther Eidinow et al. (Cambridge: Cambridge University Press, 2019), 317–38; Dylan Burns, *Did God Care? Providence, Dualism and Will in Later Greek and Early Christian Philosophy* (Leiden: Brill, 2020).

[50] *Ref.* 7.27.8.

Irenaeus, Basilides taught that on Jesus's way to Golgotha there was a double transformation. A man named Simon of Cyrene was commissioned to carry Jesus' cross
(as in Mark 15:22; Matt. 27:32). As Simon carried it, he suddenly assumed the
features of Jesus, and Jesus, in turn, appeared with the visage of Simon. As a result,
the Roman soldiers crucified Simon, while Jesus stood by and ridiculed them.[51]

This tradition resembles a passage in *The Second Treatise of Great Seth* (NHC
VII,2), where Christ explains:

> my death which they think happened, (happened) to them in their error and lack
> of sight. They nailed their man to their death. For their minds did not see me, for
> they were deaf and blind. But in doing these things, they condemn themselves. As
> for me, they saw me; and they punished me. Another person lifted the cross on his
> shoulder, Simon ... But I was rejoicing in the height over all the riches of the rulers
> and the offspring of their error and empty glory, and I laughed at their ignorance.
> (55.30–56.20)

The appearance of Simon (of Cyrene) here is striking.[52] Yet it is important to recognize that "their man" in *The Second Treatise* is probably not Simon, but the fleshly
body of Jesus. The Simon of *The Second Treatise* was not crucified; he merely carried
the cross – as in the gospels (Mark 15:20-21; Matt. 27.31-32; Luke 23:26).

This observation indicates that Irenaeus (or his source) might have distorted
information, such that the Roman soldiers (quite blindly) did not realize that Simon
and Jesus were transformed and that Simon himself (quite surprisingly, if not foolishly) did not loudly complain as he was wrongly nailed down. Even apart from
these irregularities, the Christ who lets an innocent man die in his place – even
enjoying a good laugh – is, to say the least, jarring and out of character for the Jesus
of (proto-)Luke. Add to this the Basilidean tradition from the *Refutation* that Jesus's
body suffered on the cross, and we are led to reject Irenaeus's report as false.[53] It
would thus be incorrect to agree with Irenaeus that Basilides "entirely does without a
crucifixion ... of Jesus."[54] Irenaeus's misleading report is a good reminder that heresiologists, rightly or wrongly, tried to portray their opponents as rejecting the notion
of Christ's salvific death.[55]

---

[51] Irenaeus, *AH* 1.24.4.

[52] Jean-Daniel Dubois, argues that there are many Basilidean passages in the Codex VII of
Nag Hammadi, and he quotes several from *2 Treat. Seth* and *Apoc. Peter* ("The Basilideans," in
Verheyden et al., eds., *Shadowy Characters*, 141–57). Problematically, we can only recognize these
passages as "Basilidean" if we accept in some measure Irenaeus's Basilidean report.

[53] *Ref.* 7.27.10. Pearson also understands Jesus's suffering also from Clement, *Strom.* 4.12.83.1
("Basilides the Gnostic," in Marjanen and Luomanen, eds., *Companion*, 23). I think this is
plausible, even though we must depend on Clement's remark that among the famous figures
whom Basilides discussed was Jesus.

[54] Layton and Brakke, eds., *The Gnostic Scriptures*, 611, in reference to Irenaeus, *AH* 1.24.4.

[55] See further T. Christopher Hoklotubbe, "What Is Docetism?" in *Re-making the World: Christianity and Categories: Essays in Honor of Karen L. King*, ed. Taylor G. Petrey (Tübingen: Mohr
Siebeck, 2019), 49–71 esp. 54–8.

Conclusion

To sum up, Basilides was a scholar who probably led a Christian circle in Alexandria with its own distinctive practices and rites. His scriptures included some Pauline letters (including Hebrews), a gospel resembling Luke, prophetic writings – not just from Hebrew prophets – and possibly writings from "Matthias." He pioneered the Christian scriptural commentary, and was one of the first Christian theologians – along with Euphrates and Valentinus – of Alexandria. Though mostly dependent on Jewish and Christian scriptural traditions, Basilides was not afraid to adapt elements of Pythagorean, Stoic, and Platonic thought and ethics. Basilides wrote hymns, celebrated a distinctively Christian holiday, and so was apparently part of an established Christian assembly in Alexandria, predominantly Gentile.

Basilides had an enduring impact on early Christian thought. His son and successor, Isidore, continued the ministry until, perhaps, the closing decades of the second century.[56] Justin Martyr, writing in Rome, knew of "Basilidean" Christians around 160 CE.[57] Hegesippus reported on the same Basilideans between 174–189 CE.[58] In the early third century, a Basilidean work was available in Rome so that the author of the *Refutation* could quote it extensively. Around this time, the author of the *Testimony of Truth* criticized both Basilides and Isidore. He said that Basilides wrote many things and had other disciples.[59] Later Alexandrian theologians like Clement and Origen – for all their criticisms of Basilides – learned a great deal from their predecessor, and transmitted his teachings in adapted forms.[60] About 375 CE, Epiphanius reported that Basilidean Christianity in Egypt was "in full bloom."[61]

Some Basilidean traditions were eventually scorned, such as the doctrine of transmigration. Other practices and ideas, however, became widely accepted. The writing of scriptural commentaries, the affirmation of divine providence, the educational value of suffering, and the non-substantiality of evil all became enduring themes in later forms of Christianity – including those which survive today.

---

[56] Clement, *Strom.* 6.6.53.2.

[57] Justin, *Dial.* 35.6 = Löhr, *Basilides*, Testimony 2.

[58] Eusebius, *HE* 4.22.4-6 = Löhr, *Basilides*, Testimony 3.

[59] *Test. Truth* IX,3 57.1-14. See further Löhr, *Basilides*, 40–1.

[60] Clement and Isidore were agreed, for instance, that philosophers stole information from the Hebrew prophets (Clement, *Strom.* 6.6.53.2-5 = Löhr, *Basilides*, frag. 15).

[61] Epiphanius, *Pan.* 24.1.4 (εἰς δεῦρο ἀκμάζουσα αὐτοῦ αἵρεσις). In 399 CE, Jerome (*Letter* 75.3 = Löhr, *Basilides*, Testimony 14) claimed that Basilidean Christians pervaded the provinces in Spain from the Pyrenees to the Atlantic (roughly everything from northern Spain to Portugal). Löhr considers the Basilideans here to stand in for "Gnostics" in general (*Basilides*, 39). For the "Gnostic" movement brought to Spain by Marcus of Memphis, see Sulpicius Severus, *Chronicles* 2.46 in *Sulpicius Severus: The Complete Works*, ed. Richard J. Goodrich (New York: Newman, 2015), 174. See further Virginia Burrus, *The Making of a Heretic: Gender, Authority, and the Priscillianist Controversy* (Berkeley: University of California Press, 1995), 126–59.

Further Reading

Jean-Daniel Dubois, "The Gospel of Judas and Basilidian Thought," in *Judasevangelium und Codex Tchacos: Studien zur religionsgeschichtlichen Verortung einer gnostischen Schriftensammlung* (Tübingen: Mohr Siebeck, 2012), 121–32.

Jean-Daniel Dubois, "Basilides and the Basilidians," in *The Gnostic World*, ed. Gary Trompf (London: Taylor & Francis, 2018), 156–61.

Ismo Dunderberg, *Gnostic Morality Revisited* (Tübingen: Mohr Siebeck, 2015), 67–70.

Mark Edwards, *Catholicity and Heresy in the Early Church* (Farnham: Ashgate, 2009), 20–3.

Dieter Georgi, "Das Problem des Martyriums bei Basilides: Vermeiden oder Verbergen?" in Kippenberg and Stroumsa, eds., *Secrecy and Concealment*, 247–64.

James Kelhoffer, "Basilides's Gospel and *Exegetica* (*Treatises*)," *VC* 59 (2005): 115–34.

Bentley Layton, "The Significance of Basilides in Ancient Christian Thought," *Representations* 28 (1989): 135–51.

Winrich Löhr, *Basilides und seine Schule*, WUNT 83 (Tübingen: Mohr Siebeck, 1996).

Gerhard May, *Creatio ex nihilo: The Doctrine of 'Creation out of Nothing' in Early Christian Thought*, trans. A. S. Worrall (London: T&T Clark, 2004), 62–84.

Birger Pearson, "Basilides," in *Companion to Second-century Christian "Heretics"*, ed. Antti Marjanen and Petri Luomanen (Leiden: Brill, 2005), 1–31.

Yves Tissot, "A propos des fragments de Basilide sur le Martyre," *Revue d'Histoire et de Philosophie Religieuses* 76 (1996): 35–50.

Daniele Tripaldi, "'Basilides' and 'the Egyptian Wisdom': Some Remarks on a Peculiar Heresiological Notice (Ps.-Hipp. *Haer.* 7.20-27)," in *Beyond Conflicts: Cultural and Religious Cohabitations in Alexandria and Egypt between the 1ˢᵗ and the 6ᵗʰ Century CE* (Tübingen: Mohr Siebeck, 2017), 87–114.

Carpocrates, Epiphanes, and Marcellina

Introduction

At the age of seventeen, Epiphanes, son of Carpocrates, died of unknown causes. He had made so great an impact on his parents that they literally deified him. The practice of posthumous deification was, at the time (the early second century CE), a practice of aristocratic families with heirs who perished in the flower of their youth.[1] To mention only two famous examples, the Roman orator Cicero sought to deify his daughter Tullia by building her a grand shrine or temple (*fanum*).[2] Cicero was in part motivated because he considered his daughter to be "the best and most learned of all women."[3] Antinous, mentioned in Chapter 1, was the teenage favorite of the emperor Hadrian. When Antinous drowned in the Nile river, he was deified in 130 CE. Shrines, statues, rites, and games in his honor were set up in major cities across the Mediterranean world.[4]

Carpocrates could not afford to memorialize his son in every city. His outlay, however, was still extraordinary. Reportedly, he financed a temple (or shrine) for Epiphanes in a major city (Samē) on the island of Cephalonia (west of mainland Greece). According to Clement, the temple was built of quarried stones. It had altars, precincts, and a mouseion (a place for scholars to gather and study).[5] Carpocrates and his wife Alexandria sponsored a religious festival – a New Moon feast – which attracted local crowds. Before the feast, a priest (perhaps Carpocrates himself) sacrificed to Epiphanes (with plant or animal offerings); he poured drink offerings to

[1] Christopher P. Jones, *New Heroes in Antiquity: From Achilles to Antinoos* (Harvard University Press, 2010), 48–65; Zanker, *Mask*, 276–7.
[2] Cicero, *Letters to Atticus* 12.25.1. See Spencer Cole, *Cicero and the Rise of Deification at Rome* (Cambridge: Cambridge University Press, 2013), 1–6.
[3] Cicero quoted in Lactantius, *Inst.* 1.15.
[4] Pausanias, *Description* 8.9.7-8; 8.10.1; Cassius Dio, *Roman History* 69.11.2-4; *SHA Hadrian* 14.5-7; Hegesippus in Eusebius, *HE* 4.8.2; Justin, *1 Apol.* 29.4; Clement, *Protrepticus* 4.49.1; Tatian, *Oration* 10.2; Origen, *Cels.* 3.36. See further Everitt, *Hadrian and the Triumph of Rome* (London: Head of Zeus, 2013), chap. XXII; Jones, *New Heroes*, 75–83.
[5] Clement, *Strom.* 3.2.5.1-3. See Pierre Boyancé, *Le culte des Muses chez les philosophes grecs* (Paris: Boccard, 1937), 231–327, esp. 291–93.

him (typically milk, wine, or honey), and offered a prayer. The people, or perhaps a choir, sang hymns.[6]

Assuming this report is accurate, what was it that inspired such devotion? For Epiphanes, it was not strength of body that proved the quality of his soul. He did not defeat monsters like Heracles; nor did he bestow upon the human race wine like the god Dionysus or grain like Demeter. The gift of Epiphanes was his wisdom. His strength lay in his mind. To be sure, it was in part familial affection that led Carpocrates and Alexandria to deify their son. But it was also something they saw in Epiphanes – a wisdom that proved Plato's doctrine of transmigrating souls. How else could such profound wisdom come to roost in a body so young? The sheer speed of his learning proved that he had lived a previous life; now, like Empedocles, Pythagoras, and Jesus, he transcended biological life altogether.

Let us rewind our story now to arrive at Epiphanes's father Carpocrates, a man of Alexandria Egypt who thrived during the reigns of Hadrian and Antoninus Pius (117–161 CE).[7] Carpocrates was evidently a younger contemporary of Basilides (Chapter 9). His teachings reveal a man who enjoyed the highest level of education. He showed particular familiarity with the lore of Pythagorean and Platonic philosophy, spiced with Stoic ethics. His massive expenditure on Cephalonia indicates a man of wealth and the good social standing that often accompanied it.

Carpocrates's wife Alexandria was from Cephalonia. This island had social and political connections to Athens, still a center of Greek philosophy at the time.[8] Either in Cephalonia or in Egypt, Carpocrates and Alexandria had their son Epiphanes. Epiphanes was a significant name – epithet of the fifth Ptolemaic king of Egypt (reigned 204–180 BCE) – meaning "Manifestation (of a god)."

The name proved prophetic, for Epiphanes was a prodigy. When he was a boy, his father made sure to teach him all the subjects of a well-rounded education, including mathematics, music, astronomy, and literature. All these subjects were seen as preparatory for philosophy.[9] Typically, philosophical education did not begin until a person's late teens or early twenties. Epiphanes, however, was writing philosophical treatises at – or possibly even before – the age of seventeen. Since the writings of Epiphanes are the only quoted fragments of the Carpocratian movement, our method demands that we begin with them, using them to check, as best we can, other information from heresiological reports.[10]

---

[6] Clement, *Strom.* 3.2.5.2; Epiphanius, *Pan.* 32.3.7.

[7] Eusebius understood Carpocrates to be a contemporary of Basilides during the reign of Hadrian (*HE* 4.7.9). Yet if Carpocrates was involved in sending Marcellina to Rome, he lived at least until the mid-150s CE.

[8] Talbert, *Barrington Atlas* 54, C5. For the island under Athenian control, see Dio Cassius, *Roman History* 69.16.2.

[9] Plato, *Republic* 525d–533a; cf. Alcinous, *Handbook* 7.

[10] Our most reliable sources for Carpocrates, Epiphanes, and Marcellina are Clement, who provides the sole fragment of a Carpocratian (Epiphanes) and Irenaeus. The Refutator, Tertullian, and Epiphanius all depend on Irenaeus. The evidence of Clement's letter to Theodore reputedly discovered by Morton Smith in 1958 must be bracketed due to reasonable suspicions of forgery.

Epiphanes *On Justice*

Epiphanes wrote a "widely acclaimed" treatise *On Justice*.[11] In it, the precocious philosopher distinguished the justice of God from the laws and customs of humankind. God's justice, for Epiphanes, meant "commonality with equality."[12] Equality is a basic principle of the universe.[13] All creatures, according to Epiphanes, ought to experience an equal share of divine benefits, just as all equally enjoy the rays of the sun (Matt. 5:45).

According to Epiphanes, God placed in human beings natural desires for food and sex to fulfil natural law. Animals obey the laws of nature without question. Sparrows peck berries from bushes and cows chomp the grass of the field. They have no notion of property. They do not divvy up lands for high prices and barter their daughters to noble families. These were human-made laws. They introduced inequality and competition for goods that ought by nature to be shared equally.[14]

Accordingly, Epiphanes concluded that the Jewish lawgiver could not have spoken for God. When Moses said, "do not desire your neighbor's possessions" (Exod. 20:17), he contributed to a system that helped generate those desires.[15] The Ten Commandments were not divine, eternal laws; they were human laws and human creations that contradicted the (natural) law of God. Since they supported a system of private ownership, they were by nature invalid. Human legislative systems were in themselves sinful, as the apostle Paul wrote: "through the law I have known sin" (Rom. 7:7).

Carpocrates and his son shared a similar attitude toward Jewish Law. Epiphanes pointed out the inadequacy of Moses's commands (which assumed private ownership, contrary to divine law). According to Carpocrates (or rather Irenaeus's report on Carpocrates), Jesus – though he grew up amidst Jewish Law and customs – recognized their inadequacy and rejected them.[16]

The fragments of Epiphanes help us to evaluate another remark of Irenaeus, that for Carpocrates nothing was naturally evil, but that human "matters" (*negotia*) were

For bibliography from 1974–2008, see Helmut Merkel, "Das geheime Markusevangelium," in *Antike christliche Apokryphen in deutscher Übersetzung*, ed. Christoph Markschies and Jens Schröter, Vol. 1.1 (Tübingen: Mohr Siebeck, 2012), 390–9 at 390–1. A balanced treatment can be found in Tony Burke, ed., *Ancient Gospel or Modern Forgery? The Secret Gospel of Mark in Debate* (Eugene: Cascade, 2013). In my view, neither Clement nor Origen wrote "*Secret Mark*," since the letter depends on the fourth-century testimony of Eusebius, *HE* 2.16.1-2 (that Mark sojourned in Alexandria).

[11] Quotations from the treatise only survive from Clement, *Strom.* 3.2.6.1–3.2.9.3; "widely-acclaimed" (πολυθρήλητος) comes from *ibid.* 3.2.9.2.

[12] Κοινωνία τις μετ᾽ ἰσότητος, Clement, *Strom.* 3.2.6.1; 3.2.8.2.

[13] Cf. esp. Philo, *Special Laws* 4.231-38 (the mother of Justice is equality, with many examples from nature).

[14] Plato depicted private property as the root of social vices (*Republic* 462c; 464c-e). In his latest work (the *Laws*), Plato still upheld the elimination of private ownership as the highest ideal (739b-e).

[15] Clement, *Strom.* 3.2.9.3.

[16] Irenaeus, *AH* 1.25.1.

good or evil (only) in human opinion.[17] This point is in tension with surviving quotes from Epiphanes's *On Justice*. Epiphanes displayed a strong sense of natural and divine Law as opposed to human customs.[18] He questioned central human institutions precisely in order to oppose unjust human conventions (regarding private owner-ship).[19] It is unlikely that Carpocrates and his son would have disagreed on this point, given that Carpocrates was the only known educator of his son.[20]

According to Clement, Carpocrates taught Epiphanes the concept of "monadic gnosis."[21] Although this phrase is cryptic in isolation, it was probably (Neo-) Pythagorean language for the doctrine of a single first principle called "the One" or "Monad," widely known in this period.[22] According to Irenaeus, Carpocrates preached a single first principle, a being whom he called the "unborn Father."[23]

Clement claimed that the followers of Carpocrates and Epiphanes determined that women – or wives – were "common."[24] The charge of holding wives in common was not only hurled at Carpocratians, but at Christians in general.[25] The "communality of wives" idea seems to have come from Plato, who in his *Republic* proposed a system of eugenics in which the best men bred with the best women based on a rotating basis.[26] Later philosophers, such as Zeno the Stoic and Diogenes the Cynic recommended variants of this system as well.[27]

Clement did not say that Carpocratian Christians implemented a system in which wives were held in common. Carpocrates himself did not implement a program of shared wives, since he himself was married to a single, named woman – Alexandria. Epiphanes, who may have claimed that monogamy involved inequality, did not propose – as far as we can tell – concrete guidelines for an alternative (communi-tarian) society, nor did he actually live in such a society.[28]

---

[17] Irenaeus, *AH* 1.25.4. Repeated by Tertullian, *On the Soul* 35.1.

[18] Clement, *Strom.* 3.2.8.3.

[19] *Pace* H. Gregory Snyder, "'She Destroyed Multitudes': Marcellina's Group in Rome," in Terva-hauta et al., ed. *Women and Knowledge*, 39–61.

[20] Epiphanius's claim that Epiphanes was a pupil of Isidore (*Pan* 32.3.2) is based on a misreading of Irenaeus, *AH* 1.11.2. On the fundamental agreement of Epiphanes and Carpocrates, see Izabela Jurasz, "Carpocrate et Epiphane: Chrétiens et platoniciens radicaux," *VC* 71 (2017): 134–67.

[21] Clement, *Strom.* 3.2.5.3. Heracleon also used this Pythagorean lingo, according to Ps.-Tertul-lian, *AAH* 14.

[22] Dillon, *Middle Platonists*, 125–7, 163–4, 283–4, 355.

[23] The language of Epiphanius is more philosophic: *Pan* 27.2.1 (μίαν ἀρχὴν λέγει καὶ πατέρα τῶν ὅλων).

[24] Clement, *Strom.* 3.2.5.1: οἱ δὲ ἀπὸ Καρποκράτους καὶ Ἐπιφάνους ἀναγόμενοι κοινὰς εἶναι τὰς γυναῖκας ἀξιοῦσιν.

[25] Theophilus of Antioch, *Autolycus* 3.4.

[26] Plato, *Republic* 423e–424a; 458e–461e.

[27] Diogenes Laertius, *Lives* 6.72; 7.131; cf. 7.33.

[28] Clement was concerned to suppress an idea which he thought reflected poorly on Christians in general. Not surprisingly, he had fundamental philosophical disagreements with Epiphanes (and, one might add, Plato) on the notions of justice and private property. See further Williams, *Rethinking*, 167–9.

Transmigration

We now turn to information derived solely from heresiological reports. Heresiologists were interested in connecting "heresies" to ancient philosophies, such as Pythagoreanism. Accordingly, they underscored Carpocrates's doctrine of transmigration (souls moving from body to body) – held to be a classically Pythagorean doctrine. Interestingly, Carpocrates and Basilides – both contemporaneous Alexandrian theologians – both upheld a form of transmigration on the basis of biblical texts. Basilideans appealed to Rom. 7:9 and Deut. 5:9 (Chapter 9). Carpocrates, in turn, drew attention to a text of increasing authority – John 1:21 – where the Judean leaders ask John the Baptist, "Are you Elijah?" The form of the question gave Carpocrates pause. The leaders could have asked, "Are you the prophet *like* Elijah?" but they did not. According to Carpocrates, these Judeans assumed that the soul of Elijah had returned to the body of John. Such a theory would explain John's strange behavior, for he wore the same camel-hair clothes as Elijah, ate the same food, and was a desert-dweller like the prophet of old. Christ himself affirmed that "Elijah *has come*" in the person of John – yet unrecognized; and in another passage Jesus said about John: "He is Elijah" – not a prophet "like" him (Matt. 17:12; 11:14-15).[29]

For Carpocrates, however, Jesus incarnated a soul much greater than that of Elijah. The soul that came to indwell Jesus was one of those souls that remembered what it saw when it went around in the great cosmic revolution with the unborn Father.[30] This image alludes to a passage in Plato's *Phaedrus*, where unborn souls circle the outer rim of the universe following the gods and beholding (in Plato's language) the very Form of Beauty.[31]

For Carpocrates, the Beauty beheld was the vision of the unborn Father. Jesus remembered this vision, for his soul was pure and vigorous. So it was that when his soul descended into a body, his limbs perfectly obeyed his sovereign mind. Jesus lived a life of virtue and integrity, uprooting his bodily passions – violent emotions like rage, jealousy, and grief.[32] Such passions were designed to punish human beings.[33] Jesus overcame them and so attained the state of the Stoic sage – *apatheia*, or freedom from negative emotions.

Performing Every Work

The moral virtue of Jesus undermines a charge made by Irenaeus, that the followers of Carpocrates lived licentiously. Jesus was manifestly a moral model for Carpocratian Christians, and Jesus performed no evil work. To the contrary, he lived the life of perfect righteousness. Irenaeus himself expressed disbelief in

---

[29] Cf. Tertullian, *On the Soul* 35.5. Cf. the "Doketai" summarized in *Ref.* 8.10.2.
[30] Irenaeus, *AH* 1.25.1.
[31] Plato, *Phaedrus* 247a-e.
[32] Irenaeus, *AH* 1.25.1; Pseudo-Tertullian, *AAH* 3.1. Among the virtues of Jesus, Epiphanius noted self-control and righteousness (*Pan.* 27.2.2).
[33] For passions as punishments see *CH* 10.20-21; *SH* 23.46.

Carpocratian immorality. He never saw any of their reputed immoral practices. To describe them, he depended on certain remarks in their writings (or rather his interpretations of these writings) – none of which were explicitly quoted.[34]

Carpocrates did, according to Irenaeus, encourage his followers to accomplish "every possible work in the world." Both Tertullian and the Refutator assumed that this meant every work of "sin."[35] But did it? If we analyze Irenaeus's language, he mentions that souls must experience "every life and every act," and participate "in every practice of life."[36] Such language does not refer to wicked deeds. Accordingly, to accomplish every work in the world may have meant little more than to attain the widest breadth of experience. To attain such breadth would convince the soul that earthly life had nothing to offer.[37] In Platonic thinking, it took multiple lives to train the soul for heaven. Philosophic souls required at least three embodiments, and other souls hundreds more.[38] Carpocrations had a distinctive teaching. If, within the space of a single life, one could learn and reject all forms of bodily life, one could take the "fast track" to heaven, as it were, and avoid reincarnation.

There was a Hermetic saying, perhaps current in the time of Carpocrates: "Having supposed that nothing is impossible to you, consider yourself deathless and able to understand everything: all art, all science, the character of every living thing ... times, places, things, qualities, quantities."[39] In this line of thought, to perform every work in the world was in part a work of the imagination. It was the job of the immortal intellect to understand all arts – if only to show that for the soul, all things were possible.

Jesus himself, according to Carpocrates, offered advice for avoiding reincarnation. He counseled his disciples to make peace with their prosecutor even on their way to court. Otherwise, the prosecutor would drag one to the judge, and the judge would hand one to the officer, and the officer would throw one in jail until one paid the last penny (Matt. 5:25-26; Luke 12:58-59). According to Carpocrates, the prosecutor signified the devil, the judge was the creator (or chief angel), and the officer was a subordinate angel. The prison was not hell or Hades, but the human body.[40] Paying the last penny would then refer to living out all the sufferings of the body, which was subject, as every philosopher knew, to the blows of the passions.[41]

---

[34] Irenaeus, *AH* 1.25.5.

[35] Irenaeus, *AH* 1.25.4 (*in omni omnino operatione quae in mundo*); Tertullian, *Soul* 35.4 (*omnium facinorum*) *Ref.* 7.32.7-8 (ὅσον πάντα τὰ ἁμαρτήματα); cf. Epiphanius, *Pan.* 27.2.4-5; 27.3.1.

[36] Irenaeus, *AH* 1.25.4 (*oportere in omni vita et omni actu fieri animas ... in omni usu vitae factae animae*).

[37] Cf. the choice of the soul in Plato, *Republic* 619-20 with Pétrement, *Separate God* 348. Winrich A. Löhr ("Karpokratianisches," *VC* 49, no. 1 [1995]: 23–48) and Williams (*Rethinking*, 167–9) both undermine the claim that Carpocratian Christians were libertine.

[38] Plato, *Phaedrus* 256b.

[39] *CH* 11.20.

[40] Plato, *Cratylus* 400c.

[41] Such allegories were common in early Christian interpretation. Origen interpreted the "adversary" as the devil who delivered the sinful soul to an angelic lord, with the judge as Jesus (*Homilies on Luke* 35.9 in Josef Sieben, ed. *Origenes In Lucam Homiliae*. 2 vols. [Freiburg: Herder, 1991], 2:346–65. Cf. Tertullian *On the Soul* 35.2; Clement, *Strom.* 4.13.95.2.

Imitating Jesus

Jesus was a model for Carpocrates, but in terms of his essence, his soul was not supe-rior to other human souls. Other souls, like that of Epiphanes, had seen the sights of Beauty in the transcendent world. Like Jesus, these souls had come down to earth, born of natural parents. By doing the same works as Jesus – those of righteousness and justice – souls could conform to Jesus.

Heresiographers accused Carpocratians of claiming equality with Jesus.[42] There was, however, some ambiguity in the Greek when one claimed to be "similar" (*homoios*) to Jesus. One could take the Greek adjective *homoios* in the sense of "equal to" or simply "like." Given Jesus's high standing, it is doubtful that Carpocratian Christians claimed anything like natural equality with Jesus. Some Carpocratians might indeed have claimed to be superior to Jesus's disciples. Yet his superiority was left undefined by Irenaeus, and might simply have meant superior in knowledge (as Epiphanius opined).[43]

Irenaeus claimed that some Carpocratians believed themselves "in some respect" (*secundum aliquid*) to be stronger than Jesus. This phrase "in some respect" is ambig-uous.[44] Assuming the accuracy of the language, the Carpocratian claim may go back to a statement of Jesus in John: "the one who believes in me will also do the works that I do, and in fact will do greater works than these" (John 14:12). In the *Secret Book of James* (NHC I,2), Jesus even advised his followers, "Become better than I," and "outdo me, for this is how the Father will love you."[45]

In terms of *works*, the Jesus of these texts invited his followers to be more powerful. In the various Acts of the apostles (novelistic accounts of the first Christian mission-aries), actually, we see this theology worked out: the apostles perform miracles greater and more frequent than Jesus. In the gospel of John, for instance, Jesus performs a single resurrection (John 11). In the *Acts of John* (mid- to late second-century CE), resurrection is one of John's most common miracles – so common, in fact, it becomes almost banal.[46]

Neither Carpocrates nor any of his followers whom we know of actually claimed to have surpassed Jesus in terms of his moral or divine standing. Importantly, Irenaeus used a conditional clause: "*If* there is someone who despises the things of this world more than Jesus, he *can* be better than him."[47] The sentence does not

---

[42] Tertullian, *On the Soul* 23.2.

[43] Epiphanius, *Pan.* 27.2.10.

[44] Unger and Dillon do not translate *secundum aliquid* in their translation of *Against the Heresies Volume 1* (New York: Newman, 1992), 88.

[45] *Secret Book of James* I,2 6.19; 7.13–15. A Hermetic author wrote, "unless you make yourself equal to god, you cannot understand god; like is understood by like. Make yourself grow to immeasurable immensity" (*CH* 11.20).

[46] In *Luke* and *John*, Jesus performs a single resurrection. In the *Acts of John* (Elliott, *Apocryphal New Testament*, 302–45), the apostle *John* performs no less than five.

[47] Irenaeus, *AH* 1.25.2, emphasis added.

actually imply that a Carpocratian Christian had actually claimed to be better than Jesus. The Stoics, interestingly, had a theory that anyone could become a sage by perfecting their virtue and extirpating the passions; but no Stoic, to my knowledge, ever claimed to be a sage.[48]

If a Carpocratian could claim to be stronger than Jesus, this at least shows that Jesus served as an imitable ideal. Imitation, it is said, is the best compliment, and the author of Ephesians encouraged people to imitate even God (5:1). If in terms of just deeds, Carpocratians claimed to be on par with Jesus or – in terms of works – to surpass him in strength, they may well have held this to be Christ's own command (John 14:31).

Marcellina

Epiphanes, echoing a statement of Paul (Gal. 3:28), wrote that God does not discriminate between "rich and poor, ruler and subject, stupid and intelligent, male or female."[49] As Peter Lampe points out, Carpocratians lived up to this ideal at least in their promotion of female leadership.[50] According to Irenaeus, a woman by the name of Marcellina, disciple of Carpocrates, came to Rome and led a Christian movement with considerable success. (As Irenaeus put it: "she exterminated many people"!) Marcellina is the only known woman to have independently led a Christian group in Rome during the second century CE. In fact, outsiders apparently called her group "Marcellinians." This particular name indicates a degree of independence from Carpocrates, especially if Marcellina emphasized teachings from other gospel women like Salome, Mary, and Martha.[51]

Heresiographers did not investigate Marcellina's group in any depth. In fact, both the Refutator and Tertullian completely ignored Marcellina, although they had read Irenaeus. Instead of thinking that they had a different version of Irenaeus's text, more likely they deliberately omitted Marcellina because they were threatened by the very idea of female leadership.[52]

Marcellina had a Roman-sounding name (a female form of Marcellus). Scholars typically see her as coming from Alexandria. Carpocrates himself, like Basilides, stayed in Alexandria; Marcellina evidently had bolder prospects. H. Gregory Snyder calls her an "intrepid lady."[53] In the words of Madeleine Scopello, "She undertook a

---

[48] René Brouwer, *The Stoic Sage: The Early Stoics on Wisdom, Sagehood and Socrates* (Cambridge: Cambridge University Press, 2014), 92–135.

[49] Clement, *Strom.* 3.2.6.2.

[50] Lampe, *From Paul*, 319–20.

[51] Origen, *Cels.* 5.62. Unfortunately the report is garbled. For Salome (Jesus's disciple), see Silke Petersen, *"Zerstört die Werke der Weiblichkeit!" Maria Magdalena, Salome und andere Jüngerinnen Jesu in christlich-gnostischen Schriften* (Leiden: Brill, 1999), 220–2; Snyder, "Marcellina's Group," 47.

[52] *Pace* Snyder, "Marcellina's Group," 48–56.

[53] Snyder, "Marcellina's Group," 39.

long voyage to arrive at the capital, probably with a clear purpose and charged with a defined mission."[54] This is speculation, to be sure, but how else can we explain her success?

Marcellina arrived in Rome during the late 150s or early 160s CE (the heyday of Justin Martyr and Marcion).[55] Between 174 and 189 CE, Hegesippus identified Carpocratians as one of six competing Christian groups at the time (among Menandrians, Marcionites, Basilideans, Valentinians, and Saturninians – though there were probably more).[56] Celsus mentioned Marcellina's group around 175 CE – calling its members "Marcellinians."[57] Irenaeus discussed the group about 180 CE. Possibly Marcellina was still alive and active at the time.

The Name "Gnostic"

Irenaeus reported that Marcellina's group called themselves "gnostics."[58] "Gnostic" means "endowed with (spiritual) knowledge or insight." In antiquity, the label designated spiritually and intellectually mature Christians.[59] Paul had written that "we all have *gnosis*" (1 Cor. 8:1). He referred to these knowers as "perfect people," "initiates," and "spirituals" (1 Cor. 2:6; 3:1). Several other teachers and groups of the second century employed the title "gnostic" (including Clement of Alexandria).[60]

This wide use of the title indicates a certain fluidity in the use of "gnostic" at the time. It was, in the second century, a positive term. In the early to mid-second century, the author of 1 Timothy argued against what he considered to be a "gnosis falsely-so-called" (6:20). Irenaeus was the first author to do battle against falsely called "gnostics," a globalizing term he used to identify a mishmash of his early Christian opponents.[61]

"Gnostic" was probably not the official designation of Marcellina's community. Both Irenaeus and the Refutator accused the Carpocratian Christians of defaming the "divine name of the church."[62] Apparently Carpocratians referred to their group as a "church" or Christian "assembly" (*ekklēsia*). They appealed specifically to secret traditions handed on from Jesus to his disciples.[63] In this sense, their church might be called "apostolic." Eusebius and Epiphanius made explicit that Carpocrations called themselves Christians.[64]

---

[54] Madeleine Scopello, *Femme, Gnose, et Manichéisme. De l'espace mythique au territoire du réel* (Leiden: Brill, 2005), 219.

[55] Irenaeus, *AH* 3.3.4.

[56] Hegesippus quoted by Eusebius, *HE* 4.22.5.

[57] Origen, *Cels.* 5.62.

[58] Irenaeus, *AH* 1.25.6.

[59] Brakke, *Gnostics* 30.

[60] Irenaeus himself did not reject "true gnosis," which he defined as "the doctrine of the apostles" (*AH* 4.33.8).

[61] Smith, *Guilt*, 131–71.

[62] Irenaeus, *AH* 1.25.3; *Ref.* 7.32.6.

[63] Irenaeus, *AH* 1.25.5.

[64] Eusebius, *HE* 4.7.10; Epiphanius, *Pan.* 27.3.3.

Practices

According to Carpocrates, Christians are saved through faith and love.[65] The faith was faith in Christ – the ethical model of the assembly. The love probably included works of Christian charity. These were distinctively Christian virtues lauded by the apostle Paul (1 Cor. 13:13) among early Christian leaders.

In terms of ritual life, Carpocratian Christians do not seem to have been significantly different from competing Christian groups in Alexandria and Rome. Clement mentioned their "*agapē*" (or love feast) – a shared meal which typically included the celebration of the Eucharist.[66] What Clement claims to have happened in the Carpocratian *agapē*, however, recycles baseless rumors that outsiders typically flung at all Christians.[67]

Irenaeus underscored two distinctive Carpocratian practices which probably refer to Marcellina's group in Rome. The first was branding: Marcellinians made a small branding mark behind the right earlobe of their initiates.[68] The mark was called a "seal" and perhaps signified that a member of their church was baptized not only with water but with the fire of the Holy Spirit (Matt. 3:11; Luke 3:16).[69]

Marcellinian Christians also venerated an image of Jesus (apparently a painted picture or statuette) which they thought to have been commissioned by Pilate, the Roman governor who condemned Jesus to death. (According to later Christian legend, Pilate recognized the significance of Jesus and effectively became a Christian.[70]) Carpocratians crowned their images of Jesus, along with the images of other philosophers, namely Pythagoras, Plato, and Aristotle.

Sidelight on Venerating Images. Keeping busts or images of the great philosophers was an established practice in Rome.[71] Reportedly, the emperor Marcus Aurelius kept golden images of revered teachers in his household shrine (*SHA Marcus* 3). According to the same source, the emperor Alexander Severus (ruled 222–235 CE) also venerated a little statue of Jesus among deified emperors and sages like Apollonius of Tyana, Orpheus, and Abraham.[72]

---

[65] Irenaeus, *AH* 1.25.5.

[66] McGowan, *Ancient Christian Worship*, 19–64.

[67] Clement, *Strom.* 3.2.10.1 (note the unattributed use of φάσι, indicating that Clement reported rumour). Cf. Justin, *1 Apol.* 26.7; *Dial.* 10.1; Tertullian, *Apologeticus* 7.1; 8.3, 7; Origen, *Cels.* 6.27; Eusebius, *HE* 4.7.11; Minucius Felix, *Octavius* 9.6-7. See further Mark Edwards, "Some Early Christian Immoralities," *Ancient Society* 23 (1992): 71–82; Williams, *Rethinking*, 163–88. Knust, *Abandoned to Lust* 15–164.

[68] Irenaeus, *AH* 1.25.6; Epiphanius, *Pan.* 27.5.9.

[69] Such branding was also mentioned by Heracleon in connection to the "baptism of fire" prophesied by John the Baptist (reported in Clement, *Ecl.* 25.1).

[70] See the *Gospel of Nicodemus* (*Acts of Pilate*) in Elliott, *Apocryphal New Testament*, 164–228.

[71] Lucian, *Nigrinus* 2.

[72] *SHA Alexander* 29.2.

Heresiographers accused Marcellinian Christians of following Greco-Roman custom (venerating images). From their own perspective, Marcellinians probably felt that they were exalting Jesus by giving him his rightful place among the intellectual and spiritual titans of the time. (Image veneration, as we know from later Christian history, became a standard practice in the Roman Catholic and Eastern Orthodox churches.) Though later Christians typically excluded philosophers from sainthood, Marcellina's contemporary Justin Martyr seems to have viewed Socrates – among other philosophers – as a Christian before Christ.[73]

From what we can tell of their scriptural practice, Carpocrates, Marcellina and their followers made relatively sparse use of Jewish scripture. They were aware of the Judean tradition that angels made the world, but they would not have needed Jewish scripture to conclude this. (It was a common idea among Simonian, Menandrian, Saturninian, and Sethian Christians.)

Carpocratian Christians did, however, make use of at least three gospels. As noted, they interpreted a statement of Jesus that conflates Matthew and Luke (reconciling with one's accuser before paying the last penny). They also used the gospel of John (for John the Baptist as a reincarnation of Elijah). Epiphanes, at least, made use of Paul's epistles (citing the letter to the Romans and alluding to Galatians and probably 1 Corinthians). One suspects that select writings of Plato (the *Phaedrus* and *Republic*) may also have been honored by the group, though none are explicitly cited.

Conclusion

Thanks to the leadership of Marcellina, the movement begun by Carpocrates in Alexandria likely lasted until the end of the century in the imperial capital. Carpocratians may also have existed in Cephalonia if the reports about the veneration of Epiphanes are true. Carpocratians performed Christian rituals (such as the *agapē* meal), but they had some of their own distinctive practices (branding and image veneration of Jesus among other philosophers).

Carpocratian ethics came under heavy scrutiny by heresiologists. In terms of theory, Epiphanes's communitarian ethics seem unconventional. In practice, there is no confirmed evidence of their reputed licentiousness. Carpocratians perhaps distinguished the creating angels from the true God, but they show no disdain for these angels or for this world. For his part, Epiphanes mentioned a single creator as the "father of all."[74] Carpocrates, Epiphanes, and Marcellina were wealthy, cosmopolitan, and educated people – and so were presumably of high social status.

One might suppose that the deification of Epiphanes conflicted with the worship of Christ, but that seems not to have been the case for Carpocratians. The enlightened and pure souls of Epiphanes and Christ existed on the same broad scale. The soul of Christ was the chariot leader forging the path for all pure souls who could attend him

---

[73] Justin, *1 Apol.* 5; *2 Apol.* 10.
[74] Clement, *Strom.* 3.2.7.1.

in the heavenly vision. If Christians did greater works than Christ on earth, then they were not superior to Jesus in every respect. By outperforming Jesus in miracles and virtuous deeds, it seems, they followed Christ's own command.

Further Reading

Kathy L. Gaca, *Making of Fornication: Eros, Ethics, and Political Reform in Greek Philosophy and Early Christianity* (Berkeley: University of California, 2003), 273–91.

Robin M. Jensen, "Visual Representations of Early Christian Teachers and of Christ as the True Philosopher," in *Christian Teachers in Second-century Rome*, ed. H. Gregory Snyder (Leiden: Brill, 2020), 60–83.

Izabela Jurasz, "Carpocrate et Epiphane: Chrétiens et platoniciens radicaux," *VC* 71 (2017): 134–67.

Peter Lampe, *From Paul to Valentinus: Christians at Rome in the First Two Centuries*, ed. Marshall Johnson, trans. Michael Steinhauser (Minneapolis: Fortress, 2003), 319–20.

Winrich A. Löhr, "Karpokratianisches," *VC* 49, no. 1 (1995): 23–48.

Winrich A. Löhr, "Carpocratians," in *DGWE* 240–42.

Madeleine Scopello, *Femme, Gnose, et Manichéisme. De l'espace mythique au territoire du réel* (Leiden: Brill, 2005), 219–21.

H. Gregory Snyder, "'She Destroyed Multitudes': Marcellina's Group in Rome," *Women and Knowledge in Early Christianity*, ed. Ulla Tervahauta et al. (Leiden: Brill, 2017), 39–61.

Guy Stroumsa, *Barbarian Philosophy: The Religious Revolution of Early Christianity*, WUNT 112 (Tübingen: Mohr Siebeck, 1999), 246–57.

Valentinus

Introduction

When Carpocrates and Basilides both flourished in Alexandria, a young theologian named Valentinus reportedly saw a vision. He beheld the Logos of God coming to him in the form of a newborn baby. Valentinus questioned the baby to find out who he was. Endowed with an eloquent tongue, the infant replied that he was the Logos, and related the substance of a "tragic tale."[1]

There is an important parallel to this vision. When Christ first appeared to John in the *Secret Book of John*, he came as a child and told the apostle the mysteries of God, creation, and salvation. The child in the *Secret Book* suddenly becomes an old man and soon manifests himself as a tri-form being.[2] It is nonetheless significant that both Valentinus and the author of the *Secret Book* depicted Christ as a child revealer. Was the author of the *Secret Book* "citing" the vision of Valentinus while taking it in a new direction? Or was Valentinus using a type scene known from the *Secret Book* and elsewhere? In this chapter, we will take a look at what Valentinus did and did not know about traditions later associated with Sethian, Saturninian, and Ophite Christianity based on his genuine fragments (apart from later Valentinian thought).

Life

According to Epiphanius, Valentinus (about 100–165 CE) was born along the nourishing streams of the Nile Delta.[3] While pursuing higher studies at Alexandria,

---

[1] *Ref.* 6.42.2.
[2] See further Karen King, "'In Your Midst as a Child' – 'In the Form of an Old Man': Images of Aging and Immortality in Ancient Christianity," in *Metamorphoses: Resurrection, Body and Transformative Practices in Early Christianity*, ed. Turid Karlsen Seim and Jorunn Økland (Berlin: de Gruyter, 2009), 59–82, esp. 67–73. For Christ's polymorphy, see also *Gospel of Philip* II,3 57.29-35; Clement, *Exc.* 23.4; Origen, *Cels.* 6.77; *Acts of John* 87-90 (Elliott, *Apocryphal New Testament*, 316–17); *Acts of Andrew and Matthias* 18 (ibid., 291); *Acts of Peter* 21 (ibid., 415); cf. *Revelation of Paul* V,2 18.
[3] Epiphanius, *Pan.* 31.2.2-3.

he presumably would have rubbed shoulders with Basilides and Carpocrates – possibly even Marcellina, Isidore, and Epiphanes. As a student, Valentinus drank most deeply from the wells of Platonic and Pythagorean lore. In terms of identity, however, Valentinus was a Christian, and one of the first Christian theologians of whom we know.

Perhaps already in Alexandria, Valentinus led a Christian enclave. We intuit this from the works he left behind. Valentinus preached sermons, published biblical interpretations, and wrote letters, fragments of which were later quoted by Clement of Alexandria. Just as Basilides claimed a kind of apostolic succession from Peter through Glaucias and Matthias, Valentinus apparently claimed to be in the line of Paul through a man called Theudas (who was perhaps the apostle better known as Thaddeus).[4] Even if they were not apostles or apostolic, Glaucias and Theudas may have been two early Christian teachers in Alexandria.

In terms of career, Valentinus set his sights higher than Basilides. Teaching in Alexandria, Basilides secured enduring fame in Egypt. Yet those who sought greater influence set sail for Rome, the beating heart of empire. Artemidorus, a professional dream interpreter, observed that "free men go, even against their will, to Italy. For just as heaven is the house of gods, so Italy is the house of kings."[5] Valentinus was one of several dozen figures, including Marcellina, who debuted in the imperial capital. He stayed there for about twenty-five years (136–166 CE) or at least fifteen (140–155 CE).[6]

Valentinus arrived at around the same time as another ambitious Christian teacher, Marcion. Unlike Marcion, however, Valentinus never separated from the established ecclesial networks. Instead, Valentinus became so famous in one network that he was almost voted its leader.[7] Nothing suggests that Valentinus was disillusioned by losing the election or that he pulled away from established church networks. It seems, rather, that he devoted his energies to developing a church within a church, a small group of tightly knit, intellectually oriented Christians eager to represent their faith as the best all philosophies.[8]

At some point, whether in Alexandria or Rome, Valentinus may have encountered or influenced Sethian and/or Ophite Christian theology. He accepted or developed the idea that the true God unfolded himself in a series of divine thoughts (calling their totality "the Fullness"). He agreed that the world was made through Wisdom (Prov. 8). He also recognized or independently discerned that the creator differed from the true God. At the same time, Valentinus rejected the Sethian and Marcionite idea that the creator was evil. For him, the creator was misguided at most, but not wicked. The world, a dim reflection of the Fullness, was not a terrible place, even if the human spirit would one day transcend it.

---

[4] Clement, *Strom.* 7.17.106.3-4; cf. "Theuda" in *2 Apoc. Jas.* V,4 44.18.
[5] Artemidorus, *Dream Interpretation* 2.68.
[6] Irenaeus, *AH* 3.4.3; cf. Tertullian, *Prescription* 30.2.
[7] Tertullian, *Against the Valentinians* 4.1.
[8] Justin Martyr, *Dial.* 35.6.

How to explore Valentinus's thought and religious practice is one of the thorniest questions in early Christian studies today. In large part, this is because Valentinus's thought was a kind of fullness that spilled over into many different streams. As in the case of Basilides, it is safest to judge Valentinus not by later heresy reports, but by the testimonies and fragments recording the traces of his own voice.

The Creation

Valentinus's original vision included a "tragic tale" (as the Refutator put it). One suspects that this was in part a tale of creation.[9] Like Plato, Valentinus understood our world to be modeled after the Form of a superior world called "the living realm."[10] Valentinus likened the creator to a painter constantly glancing back at his model – a living face – in order to produce this world as a copy of higher realms. The creator received honor by virtue of his creation.[11] Nonetheless, the creation fell short of the beauty of the model. The goal of salvation is to know the model, the true reality of the living realm. One can enjoy the beauty of this world and even honor the creator. But to take the world and the creator as beings of ultimate reality, according to Valentinus, is to mistake reality.

Since creation follows a divine model, it is an ordered system. To express that order, Valentinus composed a "psalm" called *Summer Harvest*:

> Everything by spirit I see suspended,
> Everything by spirit I sense conveyed:
> Flesh suspended from soul,
> Soul hanging on air
> Air suspended from aether.
>> From the depth are borne fruits.
>> From the womb is born a baby.[12]

We know of other psalms of Valentinus, but this is the only one that survives.[13] Possibly these psalms were not simply private musings, but were written to be used in worship.[14] According to *Summer Harvest*, there are five levels of reality all closely

---

[9] It is open to question whether Valentinus spoke in terms of the later Valentinian cosmogonies. See on this point Christoph Markschies, *Valentinus Gnosticus? Untersuchungen zur valentinian-ischen Gnosis mit einem Kommentar zu den Fragmenten Valentins*, WUNT 65 (Tübingen: Mohr Siebeck, 1992), 216–17, 402–7.

[10] Plato, *Timaeus* 29b; Philo, *Creation* 16-19, 25.

[11] Clement, *Strom.* 4.89.6–4.90.1.

[12] *Ref.* 6.37.7.

[13] Tertullian, *Flesh of Christ* 17.1 (Alexander cites psalms of Valentinus as authoritative); cf. 20.3. Origen mentioned other "psalms of Valentinus" (*Ennarations on Job* 21.12 [*PG* 17.80a]). The Muratorian canon mentions a psalm book of Valentinus (lines 81-85). Cf. *Tri. Trac.* I,5 121.25-38.

[14] Andrew McGowan notes that the "dactylic mouse-tails do seem to have been intended for singing" ("Valentinus Poeta: Notes on ΘΕΡΟΣ," *VC* 51, no. 2 [1997]: 158–78 at 159–60). The "I"

intertwined. The highest level is "spirit," the second is "aether," the third is "air," the fourth "soul," and the fifth "flesh." Each level depends on the one above. Flesh depends on soul for its life; soul depends on the air breathed in from the atmosphere; air depends on aether; and aether on invisible spirit. The aether is the highest upper air said to blaze with fire. It is the level of the stars or fiery intelligences. Spirit, then, is something different – probably a bodiless reality like Plato's Forms.

Our material world, for Valentinus, was a place of ordered, interlocking beauty where flesh, though lowest on the chain, was not despised. We might even imagine a situation in which the higher entities give birth to the lower entities: spirit gives birth to aether which gives birth to air which gives birth to soul which gives birth to flesh. It is all one world – one golden chain of life.

The idea of new life is present at the end of the psalm: from the depth are born fruits; from the womb is born a baby. One could imagine the depth as the depth of soil from which the fruits of harvest come. In a deeper sense, one could also envision depth as the ultimate source of reality. Valentinus reportedly called the primal God "Depth."[15]

As for the baby, Valentinus need not have referred to any particular baby. But if Depth is taken in a theological sense, he may have referred to the birth of God's eternal Son. God's Son, the Logos, thus stands over all creation and is ever with God (John 1:1). The depiction of God's Son as a baby dovetails with Valentinus's vision of the Logos as a newborn child.[16]

Humanity

Just like Menandrian, Saturninian, and Sethian Christians, Valentinus believed that angels formed the first human being. Angels were the plural "us" referred to in the phrase, "Let us make humanity according to the image" (Gen. 1:26). The "image" was the higher model of the "preexisting Human."[17] This transcendent "Human," posited by Valentinus, may have adapted Saturninian or Ophite theology (or some combination thereof).

Distinctively, Valentinus compared Adam's creation to the making of ancient cult statues. In ancient workshops, sculptors would make statues of gods gilded in gold and ivory. These statues – like the famous statue of Zeus at Olympia, or the Athena who once towered ten meters tall in the Parthenon – inspired religious dread in the minds of those who drew near to them. Just so, the angelic creators of humanity feared their human creation, espying – if only dimly – a greater power at work in their art.

of the psalm need not be the "I" of Valentinus the lonely visionary, but a group invited to speak as one.
[15] *Ref.* 6.37.5.
[16] The Refutator tried to interpret the poem in terms of later Valentinian reception (*Ref.* 6.37.8).
[17] Clement, *Strom.* 2.8.36.2-4 = Valentinus frag. 1 (Völker – see the primary sources in the bibliography).

According to Valentinus, the first human stood up and talked back to his creators because the "seed of superior reality" was invisibly invested in him (Gen. 2:7). The seed corresponds to the divine spark spoken of by Saturninus.[18] For Valentinus, the seed was a part of the preexisting Human who was established in the first material human. This "preexisting Human" is likely God's Son, the Logos. The Logos is the being who invested the seed. He is also called God's "Name."[19]

Recovering from their shock, the angels attempted to do away with their creation, Adam. Their hostility is based in part on Gen. 3:24, where a cherub – a kind of angel – kept Adam and Eve out of Eden by a whirling sword of fire. The angelic creators of humanity grew jealous (Gen. 3:22) and thereby sought to prevent the first humans from living forever.

From Valentinus's interpretation of Genesis 2–3, we can discern four similarities with Saturninian and later Sethian Christian thought:

1. The human body was made by angels.
2. The existence of a primal Light Man from Gen. 1:3. Valentinus called the Light Man "the Preexistent Human," resembling Ophite language.
3. A divine element inserted into Adam (the spark or seed). This divine element invested into humanity changed the first human being from a worm-like creature (Saturninus) to an upright and audacious speaker (Valentinus).
4. The hostility of the creator angels. According to Valentinus, the angels tried to get rid of – or even destroy – Adam just as Yaldabaoth in Sethian literature tried to destroy Seth's seed.

Such overlaps recall Irenaeus's report that Valentinus adapted elements from the Seed of Seth.[20] Such a report cannot be taken as granted. In fact, it is impossible to determine the direction of influence or to trace it in a straightforward, unidirectional line of genetic connection. Valentinus was early enough to have inspired Sethian Christians in Syria. Alternatively, the overlaps may have been due to a third factor – shared influence from Saturninus and/or Marcion, for instance – or from some other texts or figures now invisible (since they do not survive).

The Nature of Humanity

Valentinus never mentioned Adam's sin in any of his surviving fragments. When he spoke about humans, he apparently assumed that they had never fallen from their pristine state. In a homily, Valentinus declared:

[18] For the seed image, cf. 1 John 3:9 and Numenius, frag. 13 (Des Places): "He that is the seed of every soul sows everything together onto (*or* into) the things that participate in him."
[19] Valentinus frag. 5 (Völker) from Clement, *Strom.* 4.13.89.6–90.1.
[20] Irenaeus, *AH* 1.11.1. Irenaeus folded the Sethians into his "gnostic heresy."

From the beginning you are deathless
and children of life eternal!
You wished to parcel out death among yourselves
so that you could expend and use it up
     and so that death would die in and through you.
For when you dissolve the world, you yourselves do not dissolve.
You rule over the creation and over all corruption!

The declaration is breathtaking. Ruling over creation was humanity's birthright (Gen. 1:28), as was immortality (Wis. 2:23). The first human became subject to death through sin (Rom. 5:12), but Valentinus seemingly ignored the tradition of Adam's fall. Instead of envisioning humans as the passive victims of death, he portrayed them as actively expending and destroying it.

The context of the fragment is lost, yet perhaps we can explain his logic by appealing to "the seed of superior reality" implanted in the first human. If Adam and his children did die – as is obviously the case in a physical sense – then the superior seed did not. In other words, Valentinus assumed that the divine element implanted in Adam was the true (divine) humanity passed on through Adam. This true Human within was deathless and incorruptible.

Valentinus's phrase, "children of life eternal" has a Johannine ring. Christian believers become "children of God" according to John (1:12) and "eternal life" is the characteristic Johannine way of referring to salvation (6:47). Paul said that Christ destroys Death as the last enemy (1 Cor. 15:26). Valentinus said elsewhere that "Jesus produced divinity." Here, "divinity" is probably a synonym of immortality and incorruption (a key characteristic of gods).[21] Corruption had no power over Jesus; neither does it have power over Christians. The work of Christ – to divide and conquer death – becomes the work of the Christian.

How Christians "expend" and "use up" death is not clear. Perhaps Christians give up the part of themselves subject to death – the physical body – allowing their immortal seed to rise incorruptible. For Valentinus, the physical body was the "coat of skin" placed around Adam (Gen. 3:21) – an aspect of humanity not capable of life in "the living realm."[22]

Christians dissolve "the world." This is another Johannine expression referring to the values, systems, and structures of society. "The world" is bound to pass away and dissolve (1 Cor 7:31; 1 John 2:17). Christians play a part in this dissolution by refusing to support the world with its lusts and arrogance (1 John 2:16). By ruling over corruption, believers do the work of, and even attain the incorruptible state of Jesus.

---

[21] Valentinus frag. 3 (Völker) from Clement, *Strom.* 3.7.59.3. Divinity is so understood by [Pseudo-]Basil, *Letter* 366.
[22] *Ref.* 10.13.4.

The Origin of Evil

The underlying problem with humanity is not sin, for Valentinus, but demons. Just as Basilides viewed the unredeemed soul as filled with evil spirits, Valentinus likened the human heart to a hostel crawling with devils.[23] In the ancient world, people were known to be careless of the courtyards of local inns, not cleaning the dung of their pack animals. Just so, demons infest the human heart, filling it with filthy desires.[24]

But God, whom Valentinus called "one" and "good" (Matt. 19:17), works to sanctify the human heart and fills it with light. For Valentinus, both Father and Son are distinct from the malignant angels who made humanity. The Father is good and only good. He redeems the human soul, transforming it from within. The soul, once blind to God, filled with demonic darkness, is enlightened and made fit for seeing God (Matt. 5:8).[25]

View of Christ

Perhaps it is not coincidental that Valentinus depicted demons as those who fill the heart with dung since he depicted Jesus as a man who, quite literally, never defecated. In his letter to a man called Agathopous, Valentinus wrote that Jesus "ate and drank in a particular way, not excreting foodstuffs."

Sidelight on Agathopous. Agathopous was not a common name. Ignatius of Antioch knew a "Rheus Agathopous" from Syria, a deacon whom he called "elect" (*To Philadelphians* 11; *To Smyrneans* 10). That this man "bid farewell to life" probably means that he gave up a worldly career. It is not impossible that he was the same man to whom Valentinus wrote.[26] If so, we would have evidence of a sharing of ideas between Syria and Alexandria through the circulation of letters.

Perhaps this was why Jesus did not seem to eat very much. There is an episode in John where Jesus's disciples beg him to eat but he says that his food and drink is to do the will of his Father (4:34).[27] According to Clement, Jesus did not need to eat, since

---

[23] That souls were dwellings of demons was known from Democritus (DK 68 B171), and the "house of demons" is also mentioned in the (probably Alexandrian) *Epistle of Barnabas* 16:7. According to "Valentinus" in *Ref.*, the "material person" can be the hostel of demons (6.34.6). The "principalities and powers" inhabit the body as a "hostel" in *Interpretation of Knowledge* XI,1 6.30-37. See further Thomassen, *Spiritual Seed*, 455–7.

[24] See further John Whittaker, "Valentinus Fr. 2," in *Kerygma und Logos. Beiträge zu den geistesgeschichtlichen Beziehungen zwischen Antike und Christentum* (Göttingen: Vandenhoeck & Ruprecht, 1979), 455–60.

[25] Clement, *Strom.* 3.7.59.3 = Valentinus frag. 3 (Völker).

[26] Markschies considers it likely due to the double name (*Valentinus Gnosticus*, 88 n. 39).

[27] Heracleon commented on this passage, the remnants of which survive in Origen, *Comm. John* 13.247-48.

his body was held together by "a holy power."[28] He was entirely impassible, impervious to either pleasure or pain. Epiphanius, for all his disagreement with Valentinus, also denied that Jesus eliminated solid waste.[29]

For Valentinus, the reason Jesus did not excrete was because he had profound self-control. His self-control then transformed his physiology (specifically, the process of digestion) from within. Everything he consumed was turned into life-giving energy with zero remainder.

It would be wrong to claim that Valentinus's Jesus was not truly human. Who, after all, has the authority to define humanity? And what kind of humanity are we talking about? The pure, unfallen humanity of Adam in Eden, or the fallen humanity which dies? If humanity was originally created to be deathless (Wis. 2:23), then death is not an essential part of the human condition. And if "to err is human," then Jesus was not human, for he was "without sin" (Heb. 4:15). In short, Valentinus ascribed to Jesus a divine humanity. In other words, he redescribed what true humanity ought to look like.

Culture and Church

In his sermon *On Friends*, Valentinus wrote:

> Many of those things written in publicly available books are found written in the church of God. They hold in common expressions from the heart, a code written in the heart. This is the people of the Beloved, the people who is loved and loves him.[30]

The quote indicates that Valentinus rejected a firm boundary between sacred and secular literature. He was a man ready to accommodate all sorts of Greco-Roman lore and philosophy into his thought. The fragment may even hint at Valentinus's teaching practice. In a study group setting, Valentinus would not have limited himself to scriptural texts, but would have included philosophical and scientific sources from non-Christian authors as well.[31]

For Valentinus, truth was something larger than what is contained in the church. The church is not "the pillar and ground of truth" (1 Tim. 3:15). Truth haunts the human heart by nature and so can, in theory, be found in any book. Perhaps Valentinus was inspired by Paul's statement that there is a law written in the human heart, by which humans know what is good and how to do it (Rom. 2:15).

In his comment, Valentinus also provided an implicit definition of "church." The church is not a special group, isolated from the larger society, holding tightly the

---

[28] Clement, *Strom.* 6.9.71.2.
[29] Epiphanius, *Pan.* 77.15.2. See further Kelley McCarthy Spoerl, "Epiphanius on Jesus' Digestion," *Studia Patristica* 96 (2017): 3–10; M. David Litwa, "Deification and Defecation: Valentinus Fragment 3 and the Physiology of Jesus's Digestion," *JECS* (forthcoming).
[30] Clement, *Strom.* 6.6.52.3–53.1.
[31] We know that this was the case for Origen, about a century after Valentinus (Porphyry in Eusebius, *HE* 6.19.5-8).

reins of truth with eyes narrowed against outsiders. It is not necessarily unified or universal (the ancient sense of "catholic") either. The church is simply the people of "the Beloved" – whom I take to be Christ – and the people who love Christ. Anyone who loves Christ, for Valentinus, is a member of the church. If there is a division of members within the church, there remains a single spiritual body.

Conclusion

Epiphanius claimed that the elderly Valentinus sailed to Cyprus where he was "shipwrecked."[32] One could take this comment literally – Valentinus's vessel was lost. Probably, however, Epiphanius meant to say that Valentinus "shipwrecked" his faith when he taught on the island which became Epiphanius's home. There is no evidence that Valentinus changed his teaching late in life. If Valentinus did teach on Cyprus, he may have died there of old age. Truth be told, however, we do not know how or exactly when Valentinus died.

The fragments of Valentinus reveal him to have been a gifted author, speaker, poet, and interpreter of scripture. He was a visionary who claimed special revelation; yet he also read secular literature, notably Plato. With Plato, Valentinus believed in a creator who made the world according to a higher model – the living, spiritual realm where an infinitely good God abides and who gave birth to his Logos or Son. This Son is the Preexistent Human who sent a seed of his higher reality into the first human being. The body of this human was made by hostile angels who were shocked when their creation stood up and talked back to them. From that time onward, the human essence has been deathless, and those who realize this point take their first step toward overcoming the sinful structures of this world.

Valentinus acknowledged the dangers of this world. The angels hostile to humanity at creation are akin to the demons who invade the human heart, stirring in it a whirl-pool of wicked desires. Yet death is a problem only for those who do not realize that the seed of divinity in them cannot die. Death is expended in the bodily deaths of believers, when they shed their "garments of skin" and rise as purified spirits to the living realm above.

For Valentinus, the Logos of God became incarnate in Jesus, since otherwise he would not have come as a baby or have eaten food. Jesus served as a model of bodily control. In the surviving fragments, Valentinus did not mention Christ's cross, though he did declare that Christ "endured" or "suffered all things."[33]

Most of Valentinus's works are lost, so we cannot hope to reconstruct the structure of his thought. Nevertheless, there is a chance that at least one of his works was recovered at Nag Hammadi, the famous meditation called the *Gospel of Truth*. This work does present an extended interpretation of Jesus's crucifixion, among other important topics, to which we now turn.

---

[32] Epiphanius, *Pan.* 31.7.2.
[33] Clement, *Strom.* 3.7.59.3 = Valentinus frag. 3 (Völker).

Further Reading

Ismo Dunderberg, *Beyond Gnosticism: Myth, Lifestyle, and Society in the School of Valentinus* (New York: Columbia University Press, 2008).

Ismo Dunderberg, "Recognizing the Valentinians – Now and Then," in *The Other Side: Apocryphal Perspectives on Ancient Christian Orthodoxies*, ed. Christopher Tuckett and Joseph Verheyden (Göttingen: Vandenhoeck & Ruprecht, 2017), 39–54.

Ismo Dunderberg, "The School of Valentinus," in *Companion to Second-Century Christian Heretics*, ed. Antti Marjanen and Petri Luomanen (Leiden: Brill, 2005), 63–99.

Peter Lampe, *From Paul to Valentinus: Christians at Rome in the First Two Centuries*, ed. Marshall Johnson, trans. Michael Steinhauser (Minneapolis: Fortress, 2003), 292–318.

Christoph Markschies, *Valentinus Gnosticus? Untersuchungen zur valentinianischen Gnosis mit einem Kommentar zu den Fragmenten Valentins*, WUNT 65 (Tübingen: Mohr Siebeck, 1992).

Christoph Markschies and Einar Thomassen, ed., *Valentinianism: New Studies*, NHMS 96 (Leiden: Brill, 2020).

Geoffrey S. Smith, *Valentinian Christianity: Texts and Traditions* (Berkeley: University of California Press, 2020), 1–16.

Einar Thomassen, *The Spiritual Seed: The Church of the 'Valentinians'* (Leiden: Brill, 2006), 103–18, 417–504.

Part Four

Texts and Figures in Rome

The Gospel of Truth

Introduction

About 180 CE, Irenaeus noted that Valentinian Christians had among them a *Gospel of Truth*. He supposed that if Valentinians honored a *Gospel of Truth*, they thought that the other gospels were false. His inference has been proved false. When the *Gospel of Truth* was discovered in two versions at Nag Hammadi, scholars could see firsthand how the author profoundly valued and mulled over texts from the gospels of Matthew and John.[1] Allusions to Pauline letters, Hebrews, the book of Revelation – among other scriptures – stud the text like diamonds.[2] In short, the author was saturated with writings that would later become part of the New Testament, and used their teaching as a basis for creative thought.

Irenaeus attributed the *Gospel of Truth* to Valentinian Christians. Pseudo-Tertullian claimed that Valentinus himself had his own gospel.[3] The vocabulary, poetic style, and creative imagery all suggest that the *Gospel of Truth* either was this gospel or that Valentinus inspired it.[4] Its author, to be sure, claimed no small authority, professing to have "been in the place of repose," evidently the placeless place of the divine Fullness.[5]

---

[1] For the versions I,3 and XII,2, see Geoffrey S. Smith, "Anti-Origenist Redaction in the Fragments of the Gospel of Truth (NHC XII,2): Theological Controversy and the Transmission of Early Christian Literature," *HTR* 110, no. 1 (2017): 46–74; Katrine Brix, "Two Witnesses, One Valentinian Gospel? The *Gospel of Truth* in Nag Hammadi Codices I and XII," in *Snapshots of Evolving Traditions: Jewish and Christian Manuscript Culture, Textual Fluidity, and New Philology*, ed. Liv Ingeborg Lied and Hugo Lundhaug (Berlin: de Gruyter, 2017), 126–45.

[2] A summary of probable allusions is provided by Jacqueline A. Williams, *Biblical Interpretation in the Gnostic Gospel of Truth from Nag Hammadi* (Atlanta: Scholars Press, 1988), 179–83.

[3] Irenaeus, *AH* 3.11.9; Pseudo-Tertullian, *AAH* 4.6.

[4] Benoit Standaert, "L'Évangile d'Vérité: critique et lecture," *NTS* 22, no. 3 (1976): 243–75. Valentinus need not have written the text himself. Sermons could be taken down by a stenographer and published with or without the author's revisions. Kelhoffer points out that a sermon is not the name of a genre so much as a setting ("If *Second Clement* Really were a 'Sermon' How Would We Know and Why Would We Care?" in *Early Christian Communities between Ideal and Reality*, ed. Mark Grundeken and Joseph Verheyden [Tübingen: Mohr Siebeck, 2015], 83–108).

[5] *Gosp. Truth* I,3 43.2.

The name *Gospel of Truth* comes from the first line of the text and alludes to a passage in a Pauline letter: "you heard this before in the word of truth, namely the gospel" (Col. 1:5). The text of the *Gospel* best resembles a homily. Most likely, it was first preached to a group of Christians whom the author called "children of interior understanding."[6] It was probably originally preached and copied in Rome, where Irenaeus obtained most of his information about Valentinian Christian thought.[7]

Parallels with Valentinus's Fragments

Key parallels exist between the *Gospel of Truth* and Valentinus's fragments. Just as Valentinus depicted the human heart as an inn infested with demons, the author of the *Gospel of Truth* warned people not to become a dwelling place for the devil, but to keep their "house" (evidently the body or perhaps their assembly) pure.[8] Valentinus emphasized the pure goodness of the Father (Matt. 19:17). The *Gospel of Truth* affirmed that the Father is good, perfect, and even sweet.[9] In the fragments, Valentinus spoke of the Son as the "manifestation" and "Name" of the Father. The *Gospel of Truth* also calls the Son the Father's "Name." The name or essence of the Father is revealed through the Son.[10] The Son alone knows the Father and embodies the Father's character. The Son as Name was a succinct metaphor reframing Jesus's own words: "No one knows the Father but the Son and the one to whom the Son reveals him" (Matt. 11:27; cf. John 1:18).

The *Gospel of Truth* mentions "the seed of the Father," associated with the Father's light. Although this seed is in the Father's heart, it is perhaps the same seed implanted in Adam according to Valentinus and passed on generation after generation in the hearts of the elect.[11] By his death, Christ nullified the world, which the author called "the realm of appearance." It is suggestive that dissolving the world is also mentioned by Valentinus.[12] Valentinus once referred to his audience as "children," and this is also a term favored by the author of the *Gospel of Truth*.[13] Finally, the elect in the *Gospel of Truth* are said, through knowledge, to devour matter "like a fire, darkness through light, death through life." In a similar image, Valentinus spoke of the elect expending and exhausting death.[14]

---

[6] *Gosp. Truth* I,3 32.22.
[7] For Valentinians in Rome, see Lampe, *From Paul*, 292–318.
[8] *Gosp. Truth* I,3 33.9-20; 25.23-24.
[9] *Gosp. Truth* I,3 18.38; 27.23-24; 36.34-35; 42.8.
[10] *Gosp. Truth* I,3 38.23-24.
[11] *Gosp. Truth* I,3 43.14-15.
[12] Valentinus frag. 4 (Völker) = Clement, *Strom.* 4.13.89.1-3.
[13] Valentinus frag. 4 (Völker) = Clement, *Strom.* 4.13.89.1. Cf. *Gosp. Truth* I,3 19.28; 32.38; 33.39; 38.28; 43.19-22.
[14] *Gosp. Truth* I,3 25.18-19.

The Problem of Evil

Like Basilides, the *Gospel of Truth* dealt squarely with the problem of evil. The conclusions of both authors were similar: evil has no root.[15] Evil is ignorance, and ignorance is a lack, a gap, a deficiency of knowledge produced by the greatness of the Father. The Father is necessarily unknown because he is infinitely greater than any being who has been born.

The Father has Thoughts which take on their own reality and character. These Thoughts are called "eternities" ("aeons"), and the eternities together make up the "Fullness" of the Father. The eternities are analogous to Platonic Forms (aka Ideas) which exist in the mind of God.[16] In the *Gospel of Truth*, the eternities, individuated in God's consciousness, search to know their Father, unaware that they exist within him.

These eternities, consubstantial with the Father, correspond to elect people on earth. They ignorantly search for God, trying desperately to remember their origin. On high, the Logos reveals the Father's name, just as the Logos, incarnate in Jesus, reveals the Father to the elect.

The chasmic gap of knowledge experienced by the eternities produces a sense of anguish. In the image of the *Gospel of Truth*, the anguish "grew solid like a fog." This fog became the material substrate needed for creating this world. Using the stuff of their own misery, the eternities generated an image of the Father and of themselves. The product of their labors was this world. The direct maker of the world was the creator, here called Error, who vainly tried to make the world according to a higher spiritual model, as in Valentinus's fragments.[17] But the image fell short of reality. At present, ignorance and oblivion pervade this cosmos and infect the human mind like a virus.

The effects of ignorance seem real, just as the scenes of a nightmare. In a nightmare, one can feel the sweat running down one's neck as one flees from a murderer. One can experience the force of a fist against one's jaw; one can sense the terror and disorientation as one falls from a cliff, or is stabbed through the gut, or punches back, looking with horror at one's hands glistening with blood. But when one's eyes flare open, one beholds nothing of the dream, and the memory of the images vanishes in the morning light. The world itself is not a nightmare, but the effects of transcending this world is likened to waking from one.

View of Christ

The Christ of the *Gospel of Truth* does not heal lepers or walk on water or feed thousands on the grassy meadows of Galilee. He is a guide and a teacher, confounding the foolish, turning people away from error, enlightening those who

[15] *Gosp. Truth* I,3 17.29.
[16] Tertullian, *Against the Valentinus* 4.2.
[17] For the image of Error, see Jan Helderman, "Isis as Planē in the Gospel of Truth?" in *Gnosis and Gnosticism: Papers Read at the Eighth International Conference on Patristic Studies (Oxford, September 3rd–8th, 1979)*, ed. Martin Krause (Leiden: Brill, 1981), 26–46.

will hear, showing them the way and the truth – for that is what he is (cf. John 14:6).[18] He is one who opens the eyes of the blind, bestowing knowledge on the ignorant.[19] This Jesus who speaks as if from a lecture hall may hint at the social setting of the author.

The writer of the *Gospel of Truth* knew the parables of Jesus, but modified them in interesting ways. Like the Simonians, he knew the story of the lost sheep who wanders away from the fold of its 99 companions. This sheep is later found by the shepherd who becomes ecstatic with joy (Matt. 18:10-14). The author combined this parable with another saying of Jesus about a man who pulls up his sheep from a pit on the Sabbath (Matt. 12:11).[20]

The author added a parable of his own, imagining human beings as storage jars.[21] When the owner of a house needs to move, he examines the quality and contents of the jars. The jars that are full and sealed tight are retained. The empty jars that are broken, cracked, or leaky are smashed with no loss. This is a parable of judgment. Some people are those full of knowledge. Others are half-full and forgetful of what they have learned. Still others are completely empty, and so perish with the world.[22]

For the author of the *Gospel of Truth*, Jesus suffered and died on a cross.[23] The cross, however, was not dripping with the blood of a slain god, but bursting with the fruit of the tree of knowledge. That is to say, the cross was not a sacrifice of atonement, but an epiphany of knowledge. It did not kill those who ate of its fruit; instead, it allowed mutual self-discovery. Christ discovered the chosen in himself, and they discovered him in themselves.[24]

A Pauline letter spoke of Christ on the cross "erasing the document of debt" that stood against humanity (Col. 2:14). The author of the *Gospel of Truth* changed the image so that Christ, nailed to a post, became a document of redemption, an edict of the Father that was simultaneously the book of life (Rev. 3:5). In effect, Christ's body became a list of heaven's citizens unfurled like a scroll. The book existed from before the foundation of the world.[25] It contained the true names of the elect. When the elect heard their names, they understood who they were and came running to eat the fruit of the Father's knowledge.

In short, the revelation of the name of the believer on the cross was the manifestation of who believers really are, and who Christ is. Christ is a being who took on human form, who suffered and died. He is not the material rag of the body, the garment of skin inherited by Adam. After revealing the book of life on the cross,

---

[18] *Gosp. Truth* I,3 18.19.
[19] *Gosp. Truth* I,3 30.15.
[20] *Gosp. Truth* I,3 32.1-25; cf. Luke 14:5.
[21] *Gosp. Truth* I,3 25.27–26.14.
[22] *Gosp. Truth* I,3 21.34–36.
[23] *Gosp. Truth* I,3 20.11–14.
[24] *Gosp. Truth* I,3 18.20–30.
[25] *Gosp. Truth* I,3 19.34–20.3.

Christ put on the garment of an imperishable body, evidently the same garment with which Paul said that believers will clothe themselves (1 Cor. 15:53).[26]

The author encouraged his hearers to stretch out their hands to the sick, feed the hungry, and give rest to the weary (Matt. 25:35-36). But while taking care of others' physical needs, they were also encouraged to transmit to them the special salvific knowledge they had gained. The author called his hearers "unsheathed swords of intelligence."[27] They were called to pierce the hearts of their hearers with knowledge and so fill them with life.

Conclusion

The *Gospel of Truth* is a homily spoken in the voice of a spiritual master addressed to a group of insiders, saturated with biblical imagery to tell a message about Christ who died on the cross to reveal the knowledge of the Father. The knowledge revealed is an eternal knowledge that saves those who receive it with joy. Salvation is by grace, for God's grace alone allows believers to receive the knowledge. The knowledge is something believers have always had, though they forgot it long ago; for it is knowledge about themselves, knowledge of their true self, knowledge of their belonging inside the true and immortal realm of the Father. Such knowledge helps the elect to nullify the present world, to realize the transitory nature of matter, and with it all bodies, wealth, and material possessions. The world itself is a faded imitation, built from the stuff of ignorance which must inevitably be shattered and discarded like shards of clay.

The *Gospel of Truth* is one of the earliest complete Christian sermons to survive from antiquity. Whoever wrote it had drunk deeply from the books of Platonic philosophy and Christian scripture such that the author no longer realized whether his sentiments were informed more by the "publicly available books" or by those found "in God's church."[28] Determining which sentiments come from scripture and which from philosophy would be a challenging and ultimately artificial task, as they both contained "utterances that come from the heart."[29]

Irenaeus knew the *Gospel of Truth* from Valentinian Christians, evidently those in Rome. The text indicates that Valentinians were meeting together to hear homilies preached by spiritual leaders. There may have been dozens – if not hundreds – of sermons preached by such leaders in mid-second-century Rome. So why was this homily preserved out of them all? The best hypothesis, though surely contested, is that this sermon was preached by the most venerated of all Valentinian preachers, namely Valentinus himself. It was only he who could claim to have gone to the place of repose – the same place, perhaps, where he met the Logos as a newborn babe.

---

[26] *Gosp. Truth* I,3 20.30–34.
[27] *Gosp. Truth* I,3 33.1-9.
[28] Valentinus in Clement, *Strom.* 6.6.52.3-4.
[29] Valentinus in Clement, *Strom.* 6.6.52.3-4.

In Rome, copies of the *Gospel of Truth* were probably few and shared between members of the Valentinian circle. (Irenaeus either could not obtain a copy or did not care to ask for one). All copies of the text in the original Greek eventually perished, probably by the fourth century CE (when Valentinian church meetings were declared illegal by the Roman state). By this time, however, copies of the text had found their way back to Valentinus's homeland in Egypt, where, translated into a different tongue for new settings, they were eventually buried in the side of a sunburnt cliff, waiting to be discovered some 1600 years later.[30]

Further Reading

Harold Attridge, "The Gospel of Truth as an Exoteric Text," in *Nag Hammadi, Gnosticism, and Early Christianity*, ed. Charles W. Hedrick and Robert Hodgson (Peabody: Hendrickson, 1986), 239–56.

J. Helderman, "A Christian Gnostic Text: The Gospel of Truth," in *Gnosis and Hermeticism from Antiquity to Modern Times*, ed. Roelof van den Broek and Wouter Hanegraaff (Albany: SUNY Press, 1997), 53–68.

Anne Kreps, "The Passion of the Book: The *Gospel of Truth* as Valentinian Scriptural Practice," *JECS* 24 (2016): 311–35.

Geoffrey S. Smith, "Constructing a Christian Universe: Mythological Exegesis of Ben Sira 24 and John's Prologue in the *Gospel of Truth*," in *Jewish and Christian Cosmogony in Late Antiquity*, ed. Lance Jenott and Sarit Kattan Gribetz (Tübingen: Mohr Siebeck, 2013), 64–81.

Einar Thomassen, *The Spiritual Seed: The Church of the 'Valentinians'* (Leiden: Brill, 2006), 146–8, 383–5.

Philip L. Tite, *Valentinian Ethics and Paraenetic Discourse: Determining the Social Function of Moral Exhortation in Valentinian Christianity*, NHMS 67 (Leiden: Brill, 2009), 217–84.

[30] Older bibliography on the *Gospel of Truth* can be found in H.-M. Schenke, "Das Evangelium der Wahrheit (NHC I,3)," in *Antike christliche Apokryphen in deutscher Übersetzung*, I/2.1242-43.

Treatise on Resurrection

Introduction

"From the beginning," Valentinus taught, "you are deathless, and children of life eternal!"[1] Such a daring teaching would seem to negate any need for resurrection. Yet in this fragment Valentinus did not deny the reality of death or resurrection. The "you" in "you are deathless" is probably the spiritual seed, the most excellent element donated from the preexistent Human and planted in the soil of Adam's heart. The elect expend and use up death by letting their mortal husks age and die. The part of them that rises again is the spirit which ascends once the mortal coil is left behind.

In the surviving fragments, Valentinus did not expand on the mechanics of resurrection. It is thus our great fortune that a Valentinian *Treatise on Resurrection* was discovered in the Nag Hammadi codices (I,4). It is written in the form of a letter to a "son" (that is, disciple), called Rheginus. Rheginus was a Latin name perhaps deriving from the ancient town Rhegium nestled at the tip of Italy's boot. There is a passing hint that the recipient was an elderly gentleman who had begun to learn more than the basics of Valentinian Christianity.[2]

The author's anti-philosophical rhetoric is beguiling. His learning suggests that he was a Christian intellectual who, like Justin Martyr, wore the garb of a philosopher and competed for both students and patrons. The author wrote to a single man, but likely had a larger audience in mind – a wider circle of disciples open to hearing a spiritual master.

Some scholars who first worked on the letter detected the voice of Valentinus himself. After all, the author spoke with bold imagery, took on a lofty air of spiritual authority, and employed key phrases of the master (such as "from the beginning").[3] Valentinus was a writer of letters, and we know of at least two letters of instruction

[1] Valentinus frag. 4 (Völker) = Clement, *Strom.* 4.13.89.1-3.
[2] *Treat. Res.* I,4 44.17-19; 47.17-18.
[3] *Treat. Res.* I,4 46.28.

he sent.[4] Despite these circumstantial alignments, however, evidence for Valentinus authoring the *Treatise on Resurrection* is much thinner than it is for the *Gospel of Truth*.

Whoever the author was, the Christian scriptures had long sculpted his or her memory. The writer quoted, echoed, or alluded to three (now canonical) gospels and five Pauline letters. Some of his quotes are remembered paraphrases, such as the saying "we suffered with him [Christ], we arose with him, we ascended with him" – mixed quotations from at least three Pauline letters.[5]

Despite working with traditional Pauline texts, the author endeavored to interpret them in bold new ways. Paul, alluding to Isaiah, had written that "Death has been swallowed up in victory" (1 Cor. 15:54). The author of the treatise specified that it was the Savior who swallowed death. This notion is parallel to the notion, found in the *Gospel of Truth*, that the Savior "consumes" (or "eats up") matter within himself like fire, so that death is consumed by life.[6]

Parallels with Other Valentinian Works

There are similarities between the *Treatise on Resurrection* and other Valentinian works. One can begin with the reference to Christ as the "seed of truth." Valentinus had written that a seed from superior reality was implanted in Adam, and that this seed was itself part of the preexistent Human. The seed implanted in Adam and the seed of the preexistent Human are probably one seed, namely Christ (compare Gal. 3:16).

The consubstantiality of the elect who possess the seed and Christ who is the seed is manifest in a brilliant image: "from the Savior we radiate like beams of light." The Valentinian teacher Heracleon (Chapter 16) would say that Christ was the light of believers, as well as the life within them (John 1:4). That life is spirit or mind.[7] Like Heracleon, our author rejected the Platonic immortality of the soul in favor of the resurrection of spirit.

The author of the *Treatise* distinguished three kinds of resurrection: of flesh, of soul, and of spirit.[8] The resurrection of the spirit swallowed up the resurrection of soul (spoken of by Platonists), and the resurrection of the flesh. The distinction between flesh, soul, and spirit probably corresponds to a Platonic tripartite anthropology which became popular among Valentinus's disciples.

In the *Gospel of Truth*, Valentinus used the image of this world as a nightmare that dissolves the moment waking consciousness dawns. The *Treatise on Resurrection* says that this world, when compared to the reality of resurrection, is an illusion.

[4] Valentinus frags. 3, 5 (Völker) = Clement, *Strom.* 3.7.59.3; 4.13.89.6.
[5] Rom. 8:17; Eph. 2:4-6; Col. 2:12.
[6] *Gosp. Truth* I,3 25.15-19.
[7] *Treat. Res.* I,4 46.24.
[8] *Treat. Res.* I,4 45.40–46.2.

Resurrection expresses the fullness of life and being.[9] By comparison, the temporary and corruptible life in the flesh – and of all biological life in this world – is not really life. Human flesh is the "garment of the world," equivalent to the "coat of skin" about which Valentinus apparently spoke.[10]

View of Christ

For the author of our letter, resurrection could not have happened without the incarnation of Christ. He gives perhaps the earliest clear statement of what can be called a "two-nature christology."[11] "The son of God ... was a son of humanity. He embraced them both, possessing humanity as well as divinity so that, on the one hand he might vanquish death through being son of God, and on the other, the restoration to the Fullness might take place through the son of humanity."[12]

Having a divine nature allowed the Savior to conquer and "swallow" death. That is, his divine nature overwhelmed his visible, fleshly nature on the cross (the point at which Christ transcended his flesh). As a child of humanity, the Savior had true flesh. Nevertheless, Christ divested his flesh in the same way that Christians were destined to strip off their worldly garment at death. Christ was the forerunner, the "trial run" of a humanity destined to transcend biological life. By nature, the elect shared in the seed of Christ and Christ participated in their flesh. Thus there was created a mutual participation, allowing the destinies of both parties to intertwine. Christ was the first to expend death and surmount corruption.[13] When believers shed their mortal shells, Christ draws them up like rays retracted into the sun's core, "the Fullness" of life and being.

Conclusion

Since resurrection is resurrection of the spirit, it could be realized now. The author asked Rheginus: "why not look at yourself and see that you already have arisen and have been received in?"[14] Resurrection is not itself salvation, since "we have been saved from start to finish."[15] Resurrection is the "disclosure of those who have arisen."[16] Yet even this understanding of salvation is not yet fully realized, since "restoration to the Fullness" remained a future hope.

---

[9] *Treat. Res.* I,4 48.15–49.9.

[10] *Treat. Res.* I,4 45.30; *Ref.* 10.13.4. Markschies doubted whether the latter text presented a genuine fragment (*Valentinus Gnosticus*, 276–92).

[11] Cf. Ignatius, *Eph.* 20.2; Tertullian, *Praxeas* 27.10-11; Clement, *Paed.* 1.5.15,2; Hermas, *Sim.* 5.6.4b-8; 9.1.7; *Mand.* 10.1.4-5; 1.5.10, 14.

[12] *Treat. Res.* I,4 44.21-33.

[13] See further Thomassen, *Spiritual Seed*, 83–5.

[14] *Treat. Res.* I,4 49.23-25.

[15] *Treat. Res.* I,4 47.28-29.

[16] *Treat. Res.* I,4 48.4-6.

Possibly the author of 2 Timothy responded to our treatise when he wrote against those who said that resurrection has already happened (2:18). Tertullian thought that this verse was directed against Valentinians.[17] The author of 2 Timothy supposed that those who preached present resurrection overturned Christian faith. Yet for the author of the *Treatise*, spiritual resurrection was the deepest understanding of faith. The influence of the *Treatise* might help explain why Tertullian wrote so stridently in support of the resurrection of (material) flesh in the coming generation.[18] (Sometimes the force of the bomb can be understood from the scope of the crater.)

Writing a few decades earlier, however, the writer of our treatise seemed uninterested in intra-Christian controversy about the resurrection. He told Rheginus, "flee from divisions."[19] If the author picked a fight within anyone, it was not with fellow Christians, but with philosophers who required demonstration and argument for their beliefs.[20] Resurrection, for our author, was incapable of demonstration. It demanded pure faith, a faith characteristic of a spiritual person. Spiritual people do not need evidence or signs of truth. They know it within just as they know themselves.

Contemporary writers like Celsus and Galen mocked Christians for preaching a message of simple faith.[21] For them, such advice was the creed of anti-intellectualism. But the author of the *Treatise on Resurrection* had a different theory. Immediate belief, if it is based on innate knowledge, is not stupid, but the result of spiritual maturity. The knowledge that requires evidence from the visible world is itself a lesser form of knowledge. Indeed, this is a well-known teaching of Plato.[22]

Resurrection was one of the most distinctive of Christian doctrines, and would inspire much debate in the coming centuries – even up until the present day. There was great need of teachers who would give an intelligent response to the likes of Lucian who observed, about 180 CE: "These ill-starred [Christians] have convinced themselves that they will be entirely without death and live forever!"[23] The *Treatise on Resurrection* is the gateway for understanding how some early Christians, at least, "convinced themselves" of their resurrection in both rational and suprarational ways.

---

[17] Tertullian, *Pr. Haer.* 33; cf. *Resurrection of the Flesh* 19 (resurrection at baptism); Irenaeus, *AH* 2.48.2 (resurrection with acquisition of truth).

[18] See Tertullian, *Treatise on the Resurrection*, ed. Ernst Evans (London: SPCK, 1960), entire.

[19] *Treat. Res.* I,4 49.11.

[20] Luther H. Martin, "The Anti-Philosophical Polemic and Gnostic Soteriology in 'The Treatise on Resurrection' (CG I,3)," *Numen* 20 (1973): 20–37.

[21] Origen, *Cels* 1.9; Galen, *Use of Parts* 11.4, 14. See further Wilken, *Christians as the Romans*, 68–125; Rebecca Flemming, "Galen and the Christians: Texts and Authority in the Second Century AD," in Lieu and Paget, eds., *Christianity in the Second Century*, 171–87.

[22] Plato, *Republic* 509d–511e.

[23] Lucian, *Peregrinus* 13. See further Victor Schmidt, "Lukian über die Auferstehung der Toten," *VC* 49 (1995): 388–92.

Further Reading

Bentley Layton, *The Gnostic Treatise on Resurrection from Nag Hammadi* (Missoula: Scholars Press, 1979).

Outi Lehtipuu, *Debates over the Resurrection of the Dead: Constructing Early Christian Identity* (Oxford: Oxford University Press, 2015), 16–19, 98–103, 188–93.

Hugo Lundhaug, "These Are the Symbols and Likenesses of the Resurrection: Conceptualizations of Death and Transformation in the *Treatise on the Resurrection* (NHC I,4)," in *Metamorphoses: Resurrection, Body, and Transformative Practices in Early Christianity*, ed. Turid Karlsen Seim and Jorunn Økland (Berlin: de Gruyter, 2009), 187–206.

Thomas D. McGlothlin, *Resurrection as Salvation: Development and Conflict in Pre-Nicene Paulinism* (Cambridge: Cambridge University Press, 2018), 135–60.

Frederik S. Mulder, "The Reception of Paul's Understanding of Resurrection and Eschatology in the Epistle to Rheginos: Faithful Paulinism or Further Development?" in *Authoritative Texts and Reception History: Aspects and Approaches*, ed. Dan Batovici and Kristin De Troyer (Leiden: Brill, 2017), 199–215.

Marcion

Introduction

Marcion of Pontus (about 85–160 CE) became the first Christian leader to break with preestablished Christian networks in Rome.[1] As it turns out, this early Christian thinker accomplished several other "firsts" in Christian history. He is the earliest known author who extensively contrasted both the stories and theologies of the Jewish Bible and what came to be known as the "New Testament." He became the earliest known text critic who tried to discover the original readings of Christian scripture. His text-critical efforts were motivated by a peculiar narrative of the church's fall from apostolic truth.

To put this fall narrative briefly, Marcion believed that certain "Judaizers" who had always nipped at Paul's heels had succeeded in distorting his letters – interpolating passages and even forging some of the letters from scratch.[2] Marcion's role in salvation history was to restore the authentic text of Paul and faithfully to present his (single) gospel (Gal. 1:11). In perhaps the only quote preserved from his writings, Marcion hymned the authentic gospel with a heartfelt cry: "O wonderful wonder, delight, power and astonishment that we cannot speak of it, think of it, or compare it with anything!"[3]

Life

Marcion was born in Pontus, what is today north central Turkey, south of the Black Sea.[4] Although most of his early history (recorded by opponents) is

---

[1] Sebastian Moll proposed a later dating for Marcion's birth (between 100–110 CE) which contradicts Clement's testimony that Marcion was an old man when he started his movement (*The Arch-heretic Marcion* [Tübingen: Mohr Siebeck, 2010], 26). For chronological considerations, see Löhr, "Problems of Profiling Marcion," 125–9.

[2] E.g., Tertullian, *AM* 4.4.1-5.

[3] This line was translated from Syriac by Joseph Schäfers, *Eine altsyrische antimarkionitische Erklärung von Parabeln des Herrn und zwei weitere andere altsyrische Abhandlungen zu Texten des Evangeliums* (Münster: Aschendorff, 1917), 4–5. See further Moll, *Arch-heretic*, 119–20.

[4] The remainder of this chapter selectively adapts, expands, and contracts material published in M. David Litwa, *The Evil Creator: Origins of an Early Christian Idea* (New York: Oxford University Press, 2021), 57–139.

unreliable, it seems secure that he was affluent, evidently because he owned a prosperous shipping business. Marcion was wealthy enough, at least, to make a large donation to a church network in Rome when he arrived there probably in the late 130s CE.[5]

In a tradition attested by the fifth-century church father Jerome, Marcion sent a female teacher to Rome ahead of him to prepare the minds of Roman Christians (compare Marcellina in Chapter 10).[6] If the report is true, Marcion already had a sense of his own distinct brand of Christianity before coming to Rome. Clement of Alexandria dated Marcion's distinctive teachings to the reign of Hadrian (between 117–138 CE).[7] We thus have reason to believe that when Marcion settled at Rome (around the age of fifty), his thought was mature.[8]

In Rome, Marcion met Cerdo, a Syrian apparently with intellectual affinities to Saturninus and the Seed of Seth. The report of Cerdo's teachings and the extent of his influence on Marcion are unclear.[9] Both men distinguished the Judean god from the good, true – and previously unknown – deity revealed by Jesus.[10] Likely, however, Marcion made this distinction before coming to Rome.[11] It is probably no accident that Marcion and the Seed of Seth arrived at the notion of an evil creator around the same time on exegetical grounds. They both understood the Judean deity to be wicked on the basis of stories in Jewish scripture – in particular, the book of Genesis.[12]

Based on his hermeneutics and text-critical activity, we infer that Marcion had a solid education in grammar.[13] Though he probably lacked formal philosophical training, popular philosophical ideas had long seeped into his mind, forming his sense of what was theologically correct.[14]

---

[5] Tertullian, *Prescription* 30.1. See further Lampe, *From Paul*, 241–6; Moll, *Arch-heretic*, 30.

[6] Jerome, *Epistle* 133.4.

[7] Clement of Alexandria, *Strom.* 7.17.106.4–107.1.

[8] Pervo observed: "From the more veiled comments of the Pastor and the less vague observations of Polycarp it is apparent that some of Marcion's ideas were current in Asia Minor and Greece, c. 130, before he went to Rome" (*Dating Acts*, 333). Moll would deny this (*Arch-heretic*, 38–40).

[9] See further G. May, "Marcion und der Gnostiker Kerdon," in *Evangelischer Glaube und Geschichte, Grete Mecenseffy zum 85. Geburtstag*, ed. A. Raddatz and K. Lüthi (Vienna: Oberkirchenrat, 1984), 233–48.

[10] Irenaeus, *AH* 1.27.1; *Ref.* 7.37.1; 10.19.1; Pseudo-Tertullian, *AAH* 6.1; Epiphanius, *Pan.* 41.1.6.

[11] See further Barbara Aland, "Marcion: Versuch einer neuen Interpretation," *Zeitschrift für Theologie und Kirche* 70 (1973): 420–47 at 445; R. Joseph Hoffman, *Marcion: On the Restitution of Christianity: An Essay on the Development of Radical Paulinist Theology in the Second Century* (Missoula: Scholars Press, 1984), 155–84.

[12] See further Litwa, *Evil Creator*, 71–4.

[13] See further Lampe, *From Paul*, 252–6.

[14] Henrik Jan Willem Drijvers, "Christ as Warrior and Merchant: Aspects of Marcion's Christology," in *Studia Patristica* 21 (Leuven: Peeters, 1989), 73–85; John G. Gager, "Marcion and Philosophy," *VC* 26, no. 1 (1972): 53–9; Enrico Norelli, "Marcion: ein christlicher Philosoph oder ein Christ gegen die Philosophie?" in May and Greschat, eds., *Marcion*, 113–30 at 128.

View of God

Marcion agreed with Platonist teaching that God, to be God, must be good – indeed *the* Good and source of all good for all other beings. This Platonized Christian divinity was immensely powerful, but had one limitation: he could not do evil.[15] Indeed, it was sacrilegious to say that God did or caused anything wicked or harmful.[16] Thus whatever intermediate beings cause bad things in the world must not be considered properly divine.[17]

This belief in exclusive divine goodness was the founding assumption for Marcion's critique of the Hebrew deity, whom he dubbed the "creator" and "cosmocrator" (world governor).[18] For Marcion, the creator's character was not – or not exclusively – good. In fact, the creator himself confessed that he "creates evils" (Isa. 45:5, 7).[19]

Today, these "evils" are sometimes translated by the words "woe" or "calamity" (Isa. 45:7). The underlying Hebrew term *rā'* includes disasters like famine, pestilence, and war; but it also encompasses morally perverse actions. There is, for instance, the famous tree of the knowledge of good and *evil* (*rā'*) (Gen. 2:17) – and in this case evil is taken in the broad sense to include moral evil (sin and disobedience against God). This same ambiguity between moral and physical evil is present in the Greek translation of *rā'* known to Marcion, namely *kaka*, "evils" (Isa. 45:7).[20] The lord who makes *kaka* is not only the maker of pestilence and plague, but – at least potentially – of morally wicked actions as well.

From the Judean deity's putatively wicked deeds, Marcion deduced that the creator was himself evil – thus agreeing with Saturninus and the Seed of Seth. It was not simply that the creator did a few bad acts; his many and extensive evil doings revealed his character over time. Marcion oft recalled the saying of Jesus that a bad tree produces bad fruit (Luke 6:43). In short, evil actions are not anomalies;

---

[15] Plato, *Republic* 379b-c; cf. 509b.

[16] Plato, *Timaeus* 29e.

[17] Plato, *Republic* 379b-c; 380b-c; 391e1-2; cf. Plato, *Laws* 672b; 899b; 900d; 941b; Philo, *Decalogue* 176; cf. *Confusion of Tongues* 180; *On the Creation* 74-75; Plutarch, *Obsolescence of Oracles* 423d; *Epicurus Makes a Pleasant Life Impossible* 1102d; Alcinous, *Handbook* 10.3; Numenius frags. 2, 16, 19 (Des Places).

[18] Irenaeus, *AH* 1.27.2 (*cosmocratorem*). Cf. Justin, *1 Apology* 26.5; *Ref.* 7.29.1; 7.30.3. See further René Braun, *Deus Christianorum: Recherches sur le vocabulaire doctrinal de Tertullian* (Paris: Études Augustiniennes, 1977), 374–5.

[19] For Marcion's use of Isa. 45:5, see Tertullian, *AM* 1.11.9. For his use of Isa. 45:7, see Irenaeus, *AH* 1.27.2; Tertullian, *AM* 1.2.2; 2.14.1; 2.24.4. See further Andrew Davies, *Double Standards in Isaiah: Re-evaluating Prophetic Ethics and Divine Justice* (Leiden: Brill, 2000), 193–9; Yuri Stoyanov, *Other God: Dualist Religions from Antiquity to the Cathar Heresy* (New Haven: Yale University Press, 2000), 56–9.

[20] See further Thomas Römer, "The Origin and the Status of Evil according to the Hebrew Bible," in *Die Wurzel allen Übels: Über die Herkunft des Bösen und Schlechten in der Philosophie und Religion des 1.-4. Jahrhunderts*, ed. Fabienne Jourdan and Rainer Hirsch-Luipold (Tübingen: Mohr Siebeck, 2015), 53–66 at 63–5.

they emerge from an evil character.[21] Since the creator was evil, and the true God revealed by Jesus could only be good, they had to be two different beings. This insight may have appeared to be a new revelation, but for Marcion it had always been the case.[22]

A Jealous God

To exemplify the creator's bad character, Marcion used the example of jealousy. In the prevailing philosophy of Marcion's day, God could not be jealous.[23] Plato had written: "There is no jealousy in the divine choir."[24] True deity desires nothing for the simple reason that it lacks nothing. Jealousy assumes a certain insecurity and emotional weakness. But God, according to Platonic theology, did not change.[25] He was perfect, complete, and self-sufficient.[26] Thus it was impossible for God to feel the flame of jealousy – in fact to feel any negative emotions at all.[27]

This enlightened conception of God created a stumbling block for early Christians. A famous passage in the Jewish scripture has the creator declare himself to be a "jealous god." This declaration was memorable, given its place at the opening of the Ten Commandments (Exod. 20:5; Deut. 5:9). It was also emotionally loaded because in context, the creator promised to punish the children of fathers who sinned as far as the fourth generation.[28]

The creator's jealousy was linked with rage. For at the same time he announced himself jealous, he warned his people that – if they worship other gods – he would flare with anger and wipe them from the face of the earth (Deut. 6:15). When the Israelites did trigger the creator's jealousy, he vowed to favor another nation (Deut. 32:21).[29]

---

[21] Tertullian, *AM* 1.2.1; Origen, *First Principles* 2.5.4; *Adamantius* 1.28; 2.20.
[22] Judith M. Lieu, *Marcion: The Making of a Heretic. God and Scripture in the Second Century* (Cambridge: Cambridge University Press, 2015), 256, 400; Matthew J. Thomas, *Paul's 'Works of the Law' in the Perspective of Second Century Reception* (Tübingen: Mohr Siebeck, 2018), 141–2.
[23] Tob. 4:7, 16; 1 Macc. 8:16; 3 Macc. 6:7; Wisd. 2:24; 6:23; 7:13; Sir. 14:10; Philo, *Special Laws* 2.249; *Every Good Person is Free* 13; *On the Creation* 21, 77; *Cherubim* 127; *Allegorical Interpretation* 1.80; 3.164, 203; *Questions on Genesis* 1.55; Irenaeus, *AH* 5.24.2; Clement of Alexandria, *Strom.* 5.4.24.1; 7.2.7.2.
[24] Plato, *Phaedrus* 247a. Cf. *Timaeus* 29e; Musonius Rufus, *Discourses* 17 (Lutz); Celsus in Origen, *Cels.* 8.21; *CH* 4.3.
[25] Plato, *Republic* 380d–382a.
[26] Alcinous, *Handbook* 10.3; Apuleius, *Plato and His Teaching* 1.5.
[27] Tertullian *AM* 4.31.5: "Marcion denies that his god is disturbed (by passions)." Cf. 5.4.14: "the God of Marcion knows neither how to get angry nor take revenge." Cf. Alcinous, *Handbook* 10.4.
[28] Marcion criticized multi-generational punishment (Tertullian, *AM* 2.15.1-2; cf. 4.27.8). On the topic of jealousy, see, e.g., *AM* 1.28.1; 2.29.3; 3.23.7; 4.21.10; 4.25.2-3; 4.27.8; 4.39.18; 4.42.2; 5.5.8; 5.7.13; 5.16.6.
[29] Deut. 32:20-21, quoted by Tertullian in *AM* 4.31.6.

Marcion and his followers pointed up the creator's jealousy in order to undermine his claim to deity.[30] Jealousy indicated that the creator was morally flawed, subject to change, and thus a slave to corruption. If the creator was corrupt and corruptible, then he could not be god.[31]

Two Gods?

Older scholarship maintained that Marcion opposed a *good* and a *just* god. It now seems more likely that Marcion, in line with the Seed of Seth, contrasted a *good* God with an *evil* creator.[32] At the same time, the misconception persists that Marcion believed in two gods (ditheism).[33] Marcion would not have described his theology this way. It was Marcion's opponents who called both Marcion's supreme deity and the creator "gods." Marcion preferred the term "creator" and "cosmocrator" to designate the Judean lord.[34] The creator was an intermediate being, not the true god at all.

It is true that some scholars speak of Marcion's ditheism to affirm his dualism. Marcion was a dualist if by dualism we mean he opposed two superhuman beings. Yet in this sense, Marcion's dualism was not significantly different than the mitigated dualism upheld by a wide range of Christians during his time. Marcion discovered a lower, evil being lurking in what were considered to be scriptural texts (both "Old" and "New" Testaments). For most other Christians of the era, this being was Satan. For Marcion, it was the creator. The true God, however, always had far greater power in reality, and was, furthermore, destined to triumph.[35]

A New Network

When Marcion arrived at Rome the Christian movement there was still a loosely connected network of house churches run by individual presbyters. Individual

[30] Tertullian, *AM* 4.27.8. See further Ekkehard Muehlenberg, "Marcion's Jealous God," in *Disciplina Nostra: Essays in Memory of Robert F. Evans*, ed. Donald F. Winslow (Philadelphia: Patristic Foundation, 1979), 93–114; Miriam von Nordheim-Diehl, "Der Neid Gottes, des Teufels und der Menschen – eine motivgeschichtliche Skizze," in *Emotions from Ben Sira to Paul*, ed. Renate Egger-Wenzel and Jeremey Corley (Berlin: de Gruyter, 2012), 431–50.

[31] Tertullian, *AM* 2.16.3. Cf. Sextus Empiricus, *Against the Physicists* 1.157, 170; Cicero, *Nature of the Gods* 3.32; *Tusculan Disputations* 1.79.

[32] Irenaeus, *AH* 3.12.12; *Ref.* 7.29.1, 7.30.2; Filastrius, *Diverse Heresies* 45. See further Winrich Löhr, "Did Markion Distinguish Between a Just God and a Good God?" in May and Greschat, eds., *Marcion*, 131–46; Moll, *Arch-Heretic* 47–76, 161; Dieter Roth, "Evil in Marcion's Conception of the Old Testament God," in *Evil in Second Temple Judaism and Early Christianity*, ed. Chris Keith and Loren T. Stuckenbruck [Tübingen: Mohr Siebeck, 2016], 340–55 at 354–5).

[33] E.g., Moll, *Arch-heretic*, 47; Todd D. Still, "Shadow and Light: Marcion's (Mis)Construal of the Apostle Paul," in *Paul and the Second Century*, ed. Michael F. Bird and Joseph R. Dodson (London: T&T Clark, 2011), 91–107 at 96; Hoffmann, *Marcion and the Restitution*, 193.

[34] Tertullian, *AM* 1.2.1 (cf. 1.3.1; 1.6.1), possibly following Irenaeus, *AH* 3.12.12.

[35] On Marcion's dualism, see Burns, *Did God Care?*, 137–49.

presbyters jostled for preeminence with no clear winner.[36] Written claims about a single succession of bishops appeared after Marcion's death.[37]

After some years laboring within these ecclesial networks (about 140–144 CE), there was an opportunity for Marcion to present his views to a group of presbyters. A meeting – we do not know how official or how large – was convened. It became clear on this occasion that Marcion's conception of a wicked creator, although based on a biblical principle (Luke 5:36-37; 6:43), was not supported by the majority.

Marcion was not expelled or excommunicated.[38] He left the established ecclesial networks of his own accord. Probably using the cash of his previous donation – dutifully returned to him – Marcion organized his own independent ecclesial network in Rome.[39] From Rome, Marcion began an ambitious recruiting movement to establish his form of Christianity in other parts of the empire. When Marcionite missionaries arrived in Syria, they may have influenced the Seed of Seth and been influenced in return.

Scriptures

Marcion lived in an age of scholarly editions. About 50 BCE, Andronicus of Rhodes had published the works of Aristotle.[40] Thrasyllus (early first century CE) divided the works of Plato into nine groups of four. In the early second century CE, scholarly editions of Hippocrates – antiquity's most famous physician – had appeared, edited by Dioscurides and Artemidorus Capiton.[41]

By Marcion's time, there was already an edition of Paul's letters (written to seven churches).[42] Marcion published his own edition of the letters (the *Apostolikon*) linked to a single gospel (the *Evangelion*), evidently an early form of Luke. Previous scholarship mainly followed the heresiologists in thinking that Marcion changed and omitted portions of Luke to suit his theology. Yet there are many elements of the *Evangelion*, however, that contradict Marcion's theology (e.g., Jesus advocates following Jewish

---

[36] *Shepherd of Hermas* Vision 8 (II.4.3).

[37] Hegesippus in Eusebius, *HE* 4.22. See further Lampe, *From Paul*, 397–408; Robert Lee Williams, *Bishop Lists: Formation of Apostolic Succession of Bishops in Ecclesiastic Crises* (Piscataway: Gorgias, 2014), esp. 91–120.

[38] *Pace* Moll, *Arch-heretic*, 44. See Stephen G. Wilson, "Dissidents and Defectors: The Limits of Pluralism," in *Fair Play: Diversity and Conflicts in Early Christianity, Essays in Honour of Heikki Räisänen*, ed. Ismo Dunderberg, Christopher Tuckett, and Kari Syreeni (Leiden: Brill, 2002), 441–56.

[39] A skewed account of this event can be found in Epiphanius, *Pan.* 42.2.1-8; cf. Pseudo-Tertullian, *AAH* 6.2; Filastrius, *Diverse Heresies* 45. See the comments of Lampe, *From Paul*, 393; Einar Thomassen, "Orthodoxy and Heresy at Second-century Rome," *HTR* 97, no. 3 (2004): 241–56 at 243.

[40] Plutarch, *Sulla* 26.1-2.

[41] Galen, *Commentary on Hippocrates's On the Nature of Man* 15.21.9-10.

[42] Harry Y. Gamble, *Books and Readers: A History of Early Christian Texts* (New Haven: Yale University Press, 1995).

Law, 10:26-28, speaks positively of the prophets, 6.23, and confers with Moses and Elijah, 9:30).[43] Today, many scholars are more open to the idea that what became canonical Luke was not fixed in Marcion's time. Marcion adapted a text that was in turn adapted by his opponents to become what is now the gospel of Luke.[44]

To his *Evangelion* Marcion attached a separate tract called the *Antitheses* (or *Oppositions*). An allusion to the *Antitheses* may already be found in 1 Tim. 6:20: "O Timothy, guard the deposit as you deflect defiled babbling and the antitheses [*Antitheses*?] of falsely named knowledge."[45] Marcion's *Antitheses* itself is lost, but its poignant contrasts are reflected in later literature. In the text called *Adamantius* or *The Correct Faith*, for instance, a Marcionite speaker observes:

> The prophet of the god of generation [Elijah] told a bear to come out of a thicket and devour the children who met him (2 Kgs 2:23-25), but the good Lord says, "Let the children come to me, for of such is the kingdom of heaven!" (*Evangelion* 18:16).[46]
>
> The prophet of the god of generation [Moses], when a battle commenced against his people, climbed to the top of a mountain and extended his hands to his god in order to slaughter masses of people in the battle (Exod. 17:8-9). But our Lord [Jesus], since he is good, stretched out his hands [on the cross] not to slaughter human beings but to save them.[47]

Marcion and his followers mined the "Old" Testament to discover these and other contrasts.[48] Marcion agreed with the Seed of Seth that the Law and the Prophets told the true (if partial) story of a false god. To properly judge the "Old" Testament writings, however, Marcion needed the benchmark of Christ's new revelation. Only by contrasting the God revealed in Christ did the evil of the creator become manifest.[49]

[43] Jason BeDuhn, *First New Testament: Marcion's Scriptural Canon* (Salem: Polebridge, 2013), 75–7; Dieter Roth, "Prophets, Priests, and Kings: Old Testament Figures in Marcion's *Gospel* and *Luke*," in *Connecting Gospels: Beyond the Canonical/Non-canonical Divide*, ed. Francis Watson and Sarah Parkhouse (Oxford: Oxford University Press, 2018), 41–56.
[44] On Marcion's *Evangelion* and its relation to Luke, see Dieter Roth, "The Link between Luke and Marcion's Gospel: Prolegomena and Initial Considerations," in *Luke on Jesus, Paul and Christianity: What Did He Really Know?*, ed. Joseph Verheyden and John S. Kloppenborg (Leuven: Peeters, 2017), 59–80 at 60 n. 7; Daniel A. Smith, "Marcion's Gospel and the Synoptics," in *Gospels and Gospel Traditions in the Second Century: Experiments in Reception*, ed. Jens Schröter, Tobias Nicklas, and Joseph Verheyden (Berlin: de Gruyter, 2019), 129–73; Matthias Klinghardt, *The Oldest Gospel and the Formation of the Canonical Gospels* (Leuven: Peeters, 2021).
[45] Hoffmann, *Marcion*, 281–305; Martina Janßen, "Wider der Antithesen der fälschlich so genannten Gnosis," in *Frühes Christentum und religionsgeschichtliche Schule* (Göttingen: Vandenhoeck & Ruprecht, 2011), 96–109.
[46] *Adamantius* 1.16. Cf. Matt. 19:14; Mark 10:14.
[47] *Adamantius* 1.11.
[48] May, "Marcions Genesisauslegung," 189–98.
[49] Pace Moll, *Arch-heretic*, 58, cf. 82, 106.

View of Christ

Marcion's *Evangelion* preserved the saying of Christ where, in the Last Supper, Jesus took bread, gave it to his disciples, saying, "This is my body which is being given on your behalf" (22:19).[50] If Jesus did not have a real body, he could not have made this statement. Marcion affirmed Christ's incarnation even if – as Tertullian later inferred – he denied Christ's birth. Tertullian made this inference from Marcion's *Evangelion*, which lacked a birth story. Marcion's gospel began with Jesus appearing in Capernaum – a city in Galilee – in the fifteenth year of Tiberius Caesar.[51] On current knowledge, Marcion never explicitly denied that Jesus was born. His *Evangelion*, moreover, stated that Christ truly suffered and died (23:32-46). Such suffering and death implied that he had a fleshly body. Christ evidently transcended this flesh body when he rose from the dead – but even then Christ denied he was a "spirit" (24:37-39).[52]

According to Marcion, Christ came to earth to destroy Jewish Law (Eph. 2:15).[53] He destroyed the Law because the Law was a curse and hostile to humanity (Col. 2:14; Gal. 3:13). Jesus destroyed the Law by breaking it. He touched lepers though the Law forbade it (Lev. 13:45); he touched a bleeding woman though it was prohibited (Lev. 15:19); he transgressed the Sabbath. Sabbath law was not just part of the Ten Commandments, spoken by Yahweh (Exod. 20:8-11) – it was the law of creation, built into the cosmos by the creator himself. Sabbath law was, it was thought, the script of nature, and was performed in deference to the creator's own precedent (Gen. 2:3).[54]

Marcion's *Evangelion* attested three of Jesus's Sabbath violations, two of which are shared with the gospels called Mark and Matthew.[55] In *Evangelion* 6:1-2, Jesus's disciples pick and rub heads of grain on the Sabbath. Some of the Pharisees inform them that this act is unlawful, since it is a form of harvesting, not permitted on the Sabbath.[56] Both Irenaeus and Tertullian agreed that this act of harvesting was unlawful.[57] There was, moreover, no need for the disciples to harvest since they were in no danger of starving.

---

[50] Tertullian, *AM* 4.40.3; *Adamantius* 2.20. See further BeDuhn, *First New Testament*, 185–6.

[51] Some scholars suspect that Luke's birth story was added later (perhaps after Marcion). See, e.g., Ehrman, *Studies*, 351–2.

[52] See further David Wilhite, "Was Marcion a Docetist? The Body of Evidence vs. Tertullian's Argument," *VC* 71 (2017): 1–36.

[53] Tertullian, *AM* 4.36.11; 5.17.15. See further Ulrich Schmid, *Marcion und sein Apostolos: Rekonstruktion und historische Einordnung der Marcionitischen Paulusbriefausgabe* (Berlin: de Gruyter, 1995), 339.

[54] For the connection of Sabbath and creation, see Aristobulus, frag. 5 (*OTP* 2:841-42).

[55] *Evangelion* 6:1-5 // Mark 2:23-28 // Matt. 12:1-8; *Evangelion* 6:6-11 // Mark 3:1-6 // Matt. 12:9-14.

[56] Exod. 34:21: "on the seventh day you shall rest … in harvest you shall rest." Cf. Philo: "it is not permitted [on the Sabbath] to cut any shoot or branch, or even a leaf, or to pluck any fruit whatsoever" (*Life of Moses* 2.22).

[57] Irenaeus, *AH* 4.8.3; Tertullian, *AM* 4.12.5: "They rubbed the plucked grain in their hands, and by preparing food broke the holy festival."

Addressing the Jewish leaders, Jesus stoked the rhetorical fire. He justified his disciples based upon the example of David who took – one might say stole – prohibited bread from the creator's shrine (1 Sam. 21:1-6). And Jesus did not stop there. To ground his allowance of Sabbath violation, he presumed to call himself "Lord of the Sabbath."[58] Tertullian confessed that this claim put Christ in apparent conflict with the Law.[59] Christ was "destroyer of the Sabbath."[60] Epiphanius, for his part, concluded from this episode that "the Sabbath was abolished."[61]

Jesus did not only defend the Sabbath violation of others, he was thought to have transgressed it himself. He performed two Sabbath healings in synagogues before the astounded eyes of Judean leaders. The first was a man with a shriveled hand (*Evangelion* 6:6-11); the second was a crippled woman (13:10-16). Both individuals did not need to be healed on the Sabbath since their conditions were not life-threatening. In spite of this, Jesus publicly healed them in Judean religious spaces. In each case, Jesus ignited a conflict, first by demanding whether one can do good works on the Sabbath (6:9), and second by calling his opponents "hypocrites" because on the Sabbath they untied farm animals (13:15).[62]

To be sure, there was no explicit law against healing on the Sabbath – only against work.[63] But the Sabbath disputes hinged on the idea that Jesus's healings were a form of work. The synagogue leader in *Evangelion* 13:14 declared, "There are six days in which one must *work*; come on these days to be *healed* and not on the Sabbath day" (emphasis added). The Jesus of the *Evangelion* never disagreed that his healings were a form of work. He even agreed with the charge of illegality in the grain-rubbing episode. The disciples did something "unlawful" on the Sabbath, and were justified because David also did something "unlawful" (Luke 6:2, 4). The repetition of "unlawful" and the fact that it is precisely this element of illegality which binds the two incidents together, indicates that Jesus made no attempt to evade the charge that he worked on the Sabbath. He also approved of such transgression when others performed it.

Liturgical Practice

Tertullian complained that Marcion and his followers formed churches like "wasps build nests."[64] The North African helpfully gives a glimpse of what went on in Marcionite churches during his time (the early third century). He observed that Marcionites sang hymns and prayers, drew on their foreheads the sign of the cross, performed baptisms, and offered the "pure sacrifice" (Mal. 1:11) – evidently the

---

[58] Tertullian, *AM* 4.12.11. Irenaeus's claim that David was a priest is inaccurate (*AH* 4.8.3).
[59] Tertullian, *AM* 4.12.1: the question concerning Sabbath violation, he said, "could have no substance if Christ had not proclaimed himself lord of the Sabbath."
[60] Tertullian, *On the Shows* 30 (*sabbati destructor*).
[61] Epiphanius, *Pan.* 30.32.3.
[62] Dieter Roth, *The Text of Marcion's Gospel* (Leiden: Brill, 2015), 414, 425.
[63] A point made by Irenaeus, *AH* 4.8.2.
[64] Tertullian, *AM* 4.5.3.

Eucharist.[65] He also mentions their almsgiving, their habit of raising their hands in prayer, prostrating themselves on the ground, and their thanksgiving over the Eucharistic bread.[66]

These practices more or less conformed to early catholic rites at the time. Augustine indicated that Marcion baptized his initiates "In the name of the Father, Son, and Holy Spirit."[67] Cyprian of Carthage said that their baptism was "in the name of Jesus Christ." He also indicated that in the 250s the bishop of Rome accepted Marcionite baptism as valid.[68] Distinctively, Marcionites allowed women to baptize.[69] They used anointing oil either before or after baptism. They also gave milk and honey to the newly baptized as signs and symbols of the future age.[70] In their Eucharists, Marcionite Christians probably consecrated bread and water (wine was prohibited).[71] Those who were not baptized were invited to the Eucharist meal, though they did not partake of the consecrated elements.[72] Marcionites were allowed to eat fish, but beef and pork were, if not outright forbidden, then discouraged.[73]

Celibacy

In 1 Corinthians 7, Paul advised that it was better not to marry, since Christ's second coming was at hand, and attention to a spouse distracts from devotion to God. Marcion took this advice seriously and discouraged marriage among his followers. Tertullian claimed that Marcion forbade marriage altogether.[74] This seems to have been his own inference. Irenaeus never mentioned such a prohibition. We might accept from Tertullian that Marcion allowed only celibate people to be baptized.[75] But this was not a prohibition of marriage – especially since non-baptized people (called catechumens) were present in Marcionite churches. Tertullian said that

---

[65] Tertullian, *AM* 3.22.7.

[66] Tertullian, *AM* 1.23.9.

[67] Augustine, *Baptism* 3.15.

[68] Cyprian, *Letter* 73.4; 74.7.

[69] Epiphanius, *Pan.* 42.4.5; cf. Tertullian, *Pr. Haer.* 41.

[70] Tertullian, *AM* 1.14.3.

[71] Epiphanius, *Pan.* 42.3.3. So McGowan, *Ascetic Eucharists: Food and Drink in Early Christian Ritual Meals* (Oxford: Oxford University Press, 1999), 164–7. For a different view, see Alistair Stewart-Sykes, "Bread and Fish, Water and Wine: The Marcionite Menu and the Maintenance of Purity," in May and Greschat, eds., *Marcion*, 212–14.

[72] Tertullian, *Pr. Haer.* 41; Epiphanius, *Pan.* 42.3.3; cf. Jerome, *Commentary on Galatians* 6:6.

[73] *Ref.* 7.30.3-4; Tertullian, *AM* 1.14.4; *On Fasting* 15. See further M. Vinzent, "Marcion's Roman Liturgical Traditions, Innovations and Counter-Rites: Fasting and Baptism," *Studia Patristica* 71 (2014): 187–211.

[74] Tertullian, *Pr. Haer.* 33; *AM* 1.29.1, 5; 4.11.8. Cf. Adolf von Harnack, *Marcion: Das Evangelium vom fremden Gott: eine Monographie zur Geschichte der Grundlegung der katholischen Kirche* (Leipzig: Hinrichs, 1921), 277; Moshe Bildstein, *Purity, Community, and Ritual in Early Christian Literature* (Oxford: Oxford University Press, 2017), 164.

[75] Tertullian, *AM* 1.24.

Marcionite Christians baptized married couples who swore not to have children.[76] This report implies that there were married couples in Marcion's community.

The language of 1 Tim. 4:3 (that some people will "prevent marriage") shaped how heresiographers came to describe Marcion's position. This seems particularly true in the case of the Refutator, who quotes the verse in his attack on Marcion: "You 'prevent marriage' and childbearing ... Do you then conceal the fact that you teach the *Purifications* of Empedocles?"[77]

The Refutator may have been on to something when he supposed that Marcion was motivated to discourage marriage in order to attain (spiritual) purity. He was wrong, however, to make Marcion a follower of Empedocles. (Nowhere in his surviving fragments, it should be noted, did Empedocles explicitly forbid marriage.) In the Refutator's later summary, Marcion called marriage "corruption."[78] It seems more likely that for Marcion, it was sex that was perceived as corrupting, not marriage itself (which could, by prior agreement, be without intercourse). Marcion's demand for celibacy aligns him with the ascetic practice of Saturninus, the Seed of Seth, and other celibate Christians zealous in their commitment to Christ.[79]

Conclusion

When Marcion died and under what circumstances are unknown. His church movement, however, lasted several centuries. Epiphanius said that in his day (about 375 CE), Marcionites existed in Rome, greater Italy, Egypt, Palestine, Arabia, Syria, Cyprus, Persia, among other places.[80] Tertullian's five-volume tract against Marcionites (completed by 207 CE) indicates their presence in North Africa. Theodoret in the mid-fifth century speaks of converting over a thousand Marcionites in a Syrian village, and mentions eight entirely Marcionite villages in his diocese.[81] Marcion's theology, his view of the Law, and of the Hebrew scriptures would later influence the Christian movement called Manicheism. The growth and influence of Marcionite Christianity is striking given its emphasis on celibacy. Marcionite Christians were not normally bringing in new members through birth; yet they continued to flourish for centuries.[82]

---

[76] Tertullian, *AM* 4.34.5. Tertullian himself commended Christians who renounced sexuality after baptism (*To His Wife* 1.6.2).

[77] *Ref.* 7.30.3. Cf. Clement, *Strom.* 3.3.12.2.

[78] *Ref.* 10.19.4

[79] Epiphanius, *Pan.* 42.3.3; Irenaeus, *AH* 1.24.2; 1.28.1.

[80] Epiphanius, *Pan.* 42.1.2.

[81] Theodoret, *Letter* 113 in *Correspondence II–III*, ed. Yvan Azéma, SC 111.62 (Paris: Cerf, 1964–65); *Letter* 81 (SC 98.196). See further Adolf von Harnack, *Marcion: The Gospel of the Alien God*, trans. John E. Steely and Lyle D. Bierma (Durham: Labyrinth, 1990), 102–3; E. C. Blackman, *Marcion and His Influence* (London: SPCK, 1948), 3–5; Lieu, *Marcion*, 179–80.

[82] For the later history of Marcionite Christianity, see Harnack, *Marcion*, 99–112.

Their perceived success can be measured in part by the responses toward the Marcionite movement. Between 145 and 200 CE, at least fifteen early Christian writers from all over the empire wrote tracts against Marcionite Christianity.[83] Celsus spoke of Marcionites as if they represented a major branch of Christianity.[84] Evidently Marcion's message proved compelling to many, and in some areas Marcionite Christianity may indeed have been the majority form of Christianity known at the time.[85] An inscription erected by "Paul the presbyter" in 318 CE refers to a "synagogue of the Marcionites" in Lebaba (modern Deir Ali in southern Syria).[86] In the fourth century, Cyril of Jerusalem advised Christians, if they arrive in a new town, always to ask for the *catholic* church, lest someone lead them to the Marcionite community.[87] To outsiders, at least, the Christian identity of Marcionites was not in doubt, and the Marcionite movement produced not a few martyrs who died confessing the name of Christ.[88]

Further Reading

Jason BeDuhn, *First New Testament: Marcion's Scriptural Canon* (Salem: Polebridge, 2013).

Jason BeDuhn, "The Myth of Marcion as Redactor: The Evidence of 'Marcion's' Gospel against an Assumed Marcionite Redaction," *Annali di Storia dell'Esegesi* 29, no. 1 (2012): 21–48.

Matthias Klinghardt, *The Oldest Gospel and the Formation of the Canonical Gospels* (Leuven: Peeters, 2021).

Judith M. Lieu, *Marcion: The Making of a Heretic. God and Scripture in the Second Century* (Cambridge: Cambridge University Press, 2015).

Winrich Löhr, "Problems of Profiling Marcion," in *Christian Teachers in Second-century Rome*, ed. H. Gregory Snyder (Leiden: Brill, 2020), 109–33.

Christoph Markschies, *Christian Theology and its Institutions in the Early Roman Empire: Prolegomena to a History of Early Christian Theology* (Waco: Baylor University Press, 2015), 217–31.

Gerhard May and Katharina Greschat, eds., *Markion und seine kirchengeschichtliche Wirkung. Vorträge der Internationalen Fachkonferenz zu Markion, gehalten vom. 15.–18. August 2001 in Mainz* (Berlin: de Gruyter, 2002).

Sebastian Moll, *The Arch-heretic Marcion* (Tübingen: Mohr Siebeck, 2010).

---

[83] For references, see Harnack, *Marcion*, 314–27 (German text, Beilage VI).

[84] Origen, *Cels.* 5.62; cf. 6.74.

[85] Bauer, *Orthodoxy and Heresy*, 22–32.

[86] W. H. Waddington, *Inscriptions Grecque et Latines de la Syrie* (Rome: L'Erma, 1968), 582, no. 2558.

[87] Cyril, *Catechetical Lectures* 18.26.

[88] Eusebius (*HE* 4.15.46) recorded that a Marcionite presbyter named Metrodorus was burned to death in Smyrna (cf. *Martyrdom of Pionius* 21 in Musurillo, *Acts of Christian Martyrs*, 165). In the Valerian persecution (257 CE), a Marcionite woman was thrown to the wild beasts in Caesarea, Palestine (7.12.1). The successive edicts of 23 Feb. 303–Jan. 304 CE ordering the arrest of Christian leaders resulted in the burning of the Marcionite bishop Asclepius (Eusebius, *Martyrs of Palestine* 10). Cf. Irenaeus, *AH* 4.33.9; Clement, *Strom.* 4.4.17.1-2.

Markus Vinzent, *Marcion of Sinope as Religious Entrepreneur*, Studia Patristica XCIX (Leuven: Peeters, 2018).

Markus Vinzent, *Tertullian's Preface to Marcion's* Gospel, Studia Patristica Supplement 5 (Leuven: Peeters, 2016).

David Wilhite, "Was Marcion a Docetist? The Body of Evidence vs. Tertullian's Argument," *VC* 71 (2017): 1–36.

15

Ptolemy and Flora

Introduction

In a letter written to a Roman matron named Flora, Valentinus's disciple Ptolemy quoted the very same line from the gospel of Matthew once quoted by his teacher: "there is one who is good" (19:17). This single good God is the "Father of the universe" manifested in the person of the Son.[1] In his letter, Ptolemy explained why this Father God is not identical to the creator of this world. Understanding the logic of his position is essential for understanding a key notion of Valentinian Christian teaching. Interpreting this particular letter will also give us occasion for understanding the Valentinian response to Marcion. Along the way, we will introduce what we know about Ptolemy's esoteric teaching about the divine Fullness, which is perhaps the teaching of his disciples.

Life

Where Ptolemy was born is unknown. The fact that he wrote eloquent Greek does not necessitate a birthplace east of Italy, but it may point in that direction. "Ptolemy" was the family name of the Greek kings of Egypt, which may hint at his Egyptian origin. In the 130s or 140s CE, Ptolemy probably became a student of Valentinus in Alexandria or Rome. Presumably by about 140 CE, Ptolemy had settled in Rome along with his teacher. He could thus witness firsthand the controversy surrounding Marcion and the first rumblings of backlash spearheaded by Justin Martyr and other Roman Christian leaders.

Just as Valentinus before him, Ptolemy claimed to be apostolic, to depend on tradition given by the apostles, and to be in their succession.[2] He saturated himself in what he considered to be apostolic writings, in particular the gospels of Matthew and John, along with the letters of Paul. Ptolemy's criterion of truth was the Christian

---

[1] Epiphanius, *Pan.* 33.7.5.
[2] Epiphanius, *Pan.* 33.7.9.

gospel which he viewed as the Savior's verbatim teaching. This is indicated by his interpretive rule, "We shall draw the proofs of what we say from the words of our Savior – for through these alone are we led without stumbling to the comprehension of reality."[3]

We do not know when Ptolemy died. There is a possibility, though not a good one, that our Ptolemy is the same man who died as a Christian martyr. If so, his death would have occurred around 152 CE. The story of the martyr Ptolemy is told by Justin Martyr in a work now known as the *Second Apology*. According to Justin, a Roman aristocrat became infuriated with his wife for refusing his preferred method of sex.[4] His wife, who had previously complied with his wishes, had in the meantime become a Christian, which changed her view on sexual ethics. Tempted to get a divorce, the woman waited to see if her example would change her husband's ways. Yet her hopes were thwarted. While her husband dallied on holiday in Alexandria, she received word of his sexual escapades and successfully sued for divorce. Unable to take revenge in court, her (now former) husband turned against her Christian teacher – a man by the name of Ptolemy.

This Ptolemy was arrested by entrapment on the basis of his Christian profession. He was punished, and perhaps tortured, in jail for some weeks before being brought to trial. There, before the raised chair of the Roman governor Lollius Urbicus (144–160 CE) he professed his Christian faith again and was led away to execution. Two other Christians in the courtroom, inspired by Ptolemy's example, also professed their Christian faith and joined him at the chopping block.[5]

Perhaps it is no coincidence that Ptolemy in his letter to Flora implicitly approved of divorce in order for unhappy ladies to avoid "injustice," "ruin," and "wickedness."[6] Was it such advice that finally convinced Flora, after waiting for her husband to change his ways, to divorce him? We do not know. There were other reasons for Ptolemy to mention the divorce laws in 19:3-9.[7] If the Ptolemy of Justin is the same Ptolemy who wrote to Flora, moreover, Flora is not necessarily the same woman who divorced her husband.[8]

Let us focus on what we know. The way that Ptolemy addressed Flora shows that she was a woman of culture. The fact that Ptolemy called her "sister" indicates that she was already a Christian at the time of writing. If Ptolemy himself did not himself convert her, then at some point he tried to become her advisor. How Flora chose an advisor we can only guess. In her search for deeper understanding, Flora had

---

[3] Ptolemy, *Letter to Flora* 3.8; cf. 7.9.

[4] Justin, *2 Apol.* 2.4.

[5] Justin, *2 Apol.* 2.

[6] Ptolemy, *Letter to Flora* 4.7-8. Quispel took ἀπώλεια here in the sense of "moral ruin" (*Lettre à Flora* [Paris: Cerf, 2006], 59).

[7] David W. Jorgensen, *Treasure Hidden in a Field: Early Christian Reception of the Gospel of Matthew* (Berlin: de Gruyter, 2016), 215–32.

[8] Markschies, "New Research," 247, and Dunderberg, *Beyond Gnosticism*, 92.

probably encountered Marcionite Christian teachers in Rome who rejected or harshly criticized Jewish Law and the "god" who gave it. Probably learning that Christians disputed about these topics, Flora sought advice from another instructor, Ptolemy the Valentinian.

As was traditional at the time, Ptolemy sent Flora a letter of elementary instruction. The letter was designed both to introduce himself and to open the door to further teaching. If Flora was a woman of means, she might subsequently have offered to become Ptolemy's patroness, supplying him with funds for private instruction in her home and perhaps even with lodging.

Sidelight on Patronage. Accepting patronage was a key way in which freelance teachers of all kinds supported themselves in the ancient Mediterranean world. We know, for instance, of a later Valentinian named Paul who lodged in the house of a wealthy woman of Alexandria, providing instruction.[9] Lucian attacked the philosophers who in Roman mansions sold wisdom and virtue for a fee, though he was not averse to accepting such patronage himself.[10]

Assuming for the moment that Flora's Ptolemy was also Justin's, we can date his letter to Flora to about 150 CE. If Ptolemy the Valentinian was not the martyr – as seems more likely – the letter could be dated anytime between about 150 and the year 180 CE. The latter date is when Irenaeus attacked Ptolemy's students since, evidently, their master had died.[11]

If we do identify Ptolemy with the martyr, we should not be surprised that he initially received the praise of Justin Martyr. Justin called Ptolemy "a lover of truth" who, "in awareness of noble things through the teaching from Christ, confessed the teaching of divine virtue," and so proved himself to be a "true Christian."[12] When Christians were under threat of death, distinctions in belief began to pale in comparison. Witness the two other Christians (of unknown variety) who followed Ptolemy to execution. Irenaeus, importantly, did concede that his opponents had "one or two" martyrs to their credit, but he kept them unnamed.[13] Such polemical techniques (subversion and silence) are hardly surprising, since Irenaeus was trying to appropriate the perceived glory of martyrdom for his own church network.

---

[9] Eusebius, *HE* 6.3.2. See further Carolyn Osiek, Margaret Y. MacDonald, and Janet H. Tulloch, *A Woman's Place: House Churches in Earliest Christianity* (Minneapolis: Fortress, 2006), 144–243.

[10] Lucian, *Salaried Posts in Great Houses* 23, 40.

[11] For the identity of the two Ptolemies, see Lampe, *From Paul*, 238–40; Dunderberg, *Beyond Gnosticism*, 90–2 with n. 97.

[12] Justin, *2 Apol.* 2.10, 13-14.

[13] Irenaeus, *AH* 4.33.9. For the argument that Irenaeus wrote *AH* in partial response to the veneration of Ptolemy as a martyr, see Daniel Wanke, "Irenäus und die Häretiker in Rom: Thesen zur geschicthlichen Situation von *Adversus haereses*," *ZAC* 3 (1999): 202–40.

The Creator and the Law

In his surviving fragments, Valentinus said little about the creator. His presence is only implied in the image of the painter who paints according to the model of the living face.[14] Thanks to Ptolemy's *Letter to Flora*, however, we know that Valentinian Christians developed a sophisticated doctrine of the creator, whom they assumed to be the Lawgiver of the Jews. They accepted the Jewish teaching, in other words, that the creator inspired the first five books of the Jewish Bible (or Pentateuch). They accepted this teaching because Jesus had assumed it in the gospels.

In these gospels, Christ made distinctions within the Law. Some of the Law was not given by God, but by Moses. Jesus himself gave the example of divorce. Originally, the creator ordained marriage between a man and a woman, and the marriage ordained by God could not be broken (Gen. 2:23-24). Nevertheless, due to the "hard hearts" of the Israelites, Moses introduced a divorce law (Matt. 19:7).[15]

Similarly, Jesus also spoke of a "tradition of the elders" and "human commandments" (Isa. 29:13) which had taken on the function of divine Law. One of these traditions was that support owed to parents could be dedicated as a gift to the creator. Jesus asserted that his rule contradicted the divine commandment to honor father and mother (Matt. 15:4-5). Thus Jesus acknowledged that at least some of Jewish legal tradition had a human origin and was in tension with God's will.

Ptolemy turned to focus on laws that came directly from the creator. He divided these into three types. Some of these laws, he said, are pure, though imperfect. A key example is the Ten Commandments, one of which was already mentioned: "Honor your father and mother." Another was "Do not kill," a command that Christ "perfected" by forbidding anger (Matt. 5:22). A second group of the creator's laws was interwoven with injustice. The key example here is the law of retaliation, the rule of "eye for eye." This principle is unjust, Ptolemy argued, because it involves cruel and unusual punishment. Finally, Ptolemy agreed with Justin Martyr (among other Christians) that there were symbolic laws. The creator commanded his people not to work on Saturdays (the Sabbath). But this law, said Ptolemy, was only a symbol that people should rest from evil deeds.

From the character of the Law, Ptolemy, like Marcion, deduced the character of the Lawgiver. The Lawgiver, or creator, could not be wholly good, because he did not give a wholly good Law. Some of it was mixed with injustice. Other parts of it were imperfect, needing fulfillment. If the Father who alone is good (Matt. 19:17) gave a Law, it would not have had these imperfections and injustices. Ptolemy deduced that the god of the Law, or creator, could not be the Father of Jesus Christ.

---

[14] Valentinus frag. 5 (Völker) = Clement, *Strom.* 4.13.89.6–4.13.90.1.

[15] Philo spoke of a tradition of the elders (*Life of Moses* 1.1) and distinguished between the laws given by God and those given through Moses (*Decalogue* 175-76; *Life of Moses* 2.187-91).

Despite being different from the Father, Ptolemy's creator was not evil. In fact, he hated evil and his Law (largely) opposed injustice. At the same time, the creator was not entirely good either. Ptolemy concluded that he was an intermediate being, an image of the true Father, from whom all reality flows. In short, Ptolemy subordinated the creator to God. But Ptolemy's subordination was not a denigration. Analogously, the subordination of the Son to the Father was not designed to demote the Son.

Rhetorically, Ptolemy tried to distinguish his group of Christians from two opposing Christian parties at Rome. The first group was Marcionite Christians, who originally depicted the creator as an evil being who gave evil laws. For Ptolemy, this was evidently equivalent to saying that the creator was the devil – a distorted representation of Marcionite teaching. Perhaps Ptolemy wanted to blend Marcionite theology with that of the Sethian school of thought, for some Sethian texts did portray the creator as devilish.[16]

The second group that Ptolemy opposed was the emerging party of early catholics (represented by Justin Martyr and Irenaeus), who accepted the Law in its entirety as coming from the Father, and who were therefore bound to defend the full goodness of the Law and the absolute goodness of the creator, whom they identified with the Father.

Ptolemy aimed to provide a middle way, an intellectually satisfying solution to a persistent theological problem: why is the so-called good Law filled with cruel and imperfect elements? The cruel and imperfect elements express a kind of justice, a justice that describes the character of the imperfect creator. This creator – and his creation – are not ultimate. A higher destiny remains for those who know the truth about the purely good God – for those, that is, who transcend this world.

Ptolemy in Irenaeus

It is reported in the Latin manuscripts of Irenaeus that Ptolemy presented a theory of thirty independent and eternal intellectual beings (aeons) who emerged from the primal Depth of God.[17] This teaching is part of an extraordinary notice that has been called "grand."[18] As is customary in heresy reports, however, there are significant problems.

First, the comment that it was *Ptolemy* who presented a complex drama of thirty aeons is perhaps a gloss in the Latin text of Irenaeus.[19] (Irenaeus originally wrote in Greek, and the Greek manuscripts of his work are lost.) We do not know

---

[16] Dunderberg, *Beyond Gnosticism*, 77–94; Layton and Brakke, eds., *The Gnostic Scriptures*, 437.

[17] Irenaeus, *AH* 1.8.5 (*et Ptolemaeus quidem ita*). Epiphanius, who had a Greek version of *AH*, did not attest this phrase (*Pan.* 31.32.9).

[18] François M.-M. Sagnard, *La gnose valentinienne et le témoignage de saint Irénée* (Paris: Vrin, 1947).

[19] Markschies, "Grand Notice': Einige einleitende Bemerkungen zur Überlieferung des sogenannten Systems der Schüler des Ptolemaeus Gnosticus," in Markschies and Thomassen, eds., *Valentinianism: New Studies*, 29–87 at 52–5. Cf. Thomassen, *Spiritual Seed*, 18.

if Ptolemy actually formulated this system. The system of thirty aeons was a (Neo-) Pythagoreanizing development that tried to explain philosophically how many things come from one.[20] Arguably, however, Valentinians were monists who believed that reality was originally and could be reduced to one single Depth. The question was then how the reality around us – in its near infinite complexity – emerged from the primeval Depth. The Valentinian answer, to put it simply, was that God's thoughts, which are eternal, take on their own reality in ordered array. According to Irenaeus, Ptolemy's followers said that there was first a set of ten individuated thoughts or dispositions (a decad) that emerged from Depth, then a set of twelve (dodecad), which ultimately combined to make a set of thirty co-essential manifestations of the Godhead (a triacontad).[21]

Perhaps Irenaeus intended that his readers believe the story of decads, dodecads, and triacontads was the master narrative ingrained in the minds of all Valentinian Christians. Truth be told, it probably was not. Deep philosophical reflection on the entities in the Fullness may have been the pastime of some Valentinian intellectuals toward the end of the second century CE. Such advanced philosophical learning, however, was likely never considered to be "Valentinian Christianity 101." In fact, this material may have never been introduced to most Valentinian Christians whose interest in Valentinian teaching never went beyond the level of, for example, the *Gospel of Truth*.

When Irenaeus described the various Valentinian versions of the Fullness, he claimed to reveal hidden doctrines.[22] In claiming this, the bishop revealed that he was supplying material that most people – perhaps including most Valentinians – actually did not know about. And this is no surprise. Just as today very few Christians are aware of the advanced Trinitarian speculation of past and present theologians, we cannot expect the average Valentinian Christian to have been aware of the nuances of divine proliferation. This material was meant for initiated and advanced students. As was common, these students wrote down their advanced lessons, the very practice which allowed Irenaeus to obtain them.

In modern scholarly literature, Irenaeus's report on Valentinus is still called "Valentinus's Myth."[23] Intellectually inclined Valentinians, however, would not have described these and other stories as "myths." They should rather be thought of as Christian philosophy in narrative form. Just as Pythagoreans described their primal Monad becoming a Dyad, which further proliferated, Valentinian intellectuals crafted various philosophical narratives of divine expansion. We surmise that these intellectuals lived in the 160s and 170s at Rome, where Irenaeus obtained their documents. By this point, Valentinus had died or departed Rome and Ptolemy – if he was still alive – may or may not have still been in the imperial capital.

---

[20] Thomassen, *Spiritual Seed*, 270–94.

[21] Irenaeus, *AH* 1.1.

[22] Irenaeus, *AH* 1, *pref.* 2.

[23] Layton and Brakke, eds., *The Gnostic Scriptures*, 281.

Conclusion

A major question raised by Ptolemy and his disciples is what degree of separation they envisioned between themselves and other Christian groups in Rome. By the summer of 144 CE, the Marcionites had separated from other ecclesial formations. Did Ptolemy and his disciples also consider their circles at Rome to be organizationally distinct from other Christian networks (between 145–180 CE)?

Two points can be made here. First of all, we cannot assume that all church networks in mid-second-century Rome had firmly bounded identities. Early catholic identity, for instance, was still fluid and in the state of formation. Second, the fact that Ptolemy had his own view of the creator and the Law was not sufficient grounds for what moderns think of as a "church split." There never was a single church, and Ptolemy, though he appealed to a distinct apostolic succession, and possibly had his own practice of fasting, never claimed to have his own particular church.[24] Even if Ptolemy's own teachings were known to Christians like Justin Martyr in the early 150s, no surviving evidence indicates that they were challenged until we come to Irenaeus (about 180 CE).

Irenaeus's attack on Ptolemy's disciples assumes, moreover, that they were still part of Roman ecclesial networks – for Irenaeus wanted them recognized and expelled. Within these networks, Ptolemy and his followers probably led smaller study circles and sought private funding for further instruction. They were not a separate church movement, but an assembly of philosophically informed and theological sophisticated Christians living within larger assemblies.

Further Reading

Ismo Dunderberg, *Beyond Gnosticism: Myth, Lifestyle, and Society in the School of Valentinus* (New York: Columbia University Press, 2008), 77–94.

David W. Jorgensen, *Treasure Hidden in a Field: Early Christian Reception of the Gospel of Matthew* (Berlin: de Gruyter, 2016).

Peter Lampe, *From Paul to Valentinus: Christians at Rome in the First Two Centuries*, ed. Marshall Johnson, trans. Michael Steinhauser (Minneapolis: Fortress, 2003), 238–40.

Winrich Löhr, "La doctrine de Dieu dans la Lettre à Flora de Ptolémée," *Revue d'histoire et de philosophie religieuses* 75 (1995): 177–91.

Christoph Markschies, "Individuality in Some Gnostic Authors: With a Few Remarks on the Interpretation of Ptolemaeus, *Epistula ad Floram*," *ZAC* 15, no. 3 (2011): 411–30.

Christoph Markschies, "New Research on Ptolemaeus Gnosticus," *ZAC* 4 (2000): 225–54.

Einar Thomassen, *The Spiritual Seed: The Church of the 'Valentinians'* (Leiden: Brill, 2006), 119–32, 270–94.

Joseph Verheyden, "Attempting the Impossible? Ptolemy's *Letter to Flora* as Counter-Narrative," in *Telling the Christian Story Differently: Counter-Narratives from Nag Hammadi and Beyond*, ed. Francis Watson and Sarah Parkhouse (London: Bloomsbury, 2020), 95–120.

---

[24] Ptolemy, *Letter to Flora* 5.13; 7.9.

Heracleon

Introduction

Apart from Ptolemy, there were other disciples of Valentinus who began to distinguish themselves at Rome and elsewhere. One of the most gifted was a man named Heracleon, who flourished between 160 and 180 CE.[1] About 200 CE, Clement of Alexandria described Heracleon as the most esteemed in Valentinus's school.[2] He was esteemed in part for his *Commentary on John*, written about 180 CE. This commentary is lost, but almost fifty fragments of it survive in Origen's *Commentary on John*, written between 230 and 248 CE. Two other fragments of Heracleon, perhaps from a commentary on Luke, are provided by Clement.[3]

If Basilides was the first known commentator on "the gospel" (perhaps an early form of Luke), Heracleon was the first known systematic commentator on John. He was also the first, it seems, to systematically apply an allegorical lens to distinctly Christian scripture. The fact that Heracleon's fragments do not record many of the doctrines that Irenaeus ascribed to Valentinians (about 180 CE) should warn us about Irenaeus's selectivity. We need not suppose that Heracleon was concealing information to make his work more inviting. The density of Heracleon's surviving commentary and his omission of supporting arguments suggest that it was directed primarily at Christian insiders.

Life

Heracleon lived in Rome and possibly later in Alexandria. We do not know the place of his birth. His name, reminiscent of the hero Heracles, suggests parents of a

---

[1] Origen, *Commentary on John* 2.14.100. Heracleon received passing mention by Irenaeus (*AH* 2.41) and Tertullian (*Against the Valentinians* 4.2). See also *Ref.* 6.4; Pseudo-Tertullian, *AAH* 4.8; Epiphanius, *Pan.* 36.

[2] Clement, *Strom.* 4.9.71.1.

[3] One other (spurious) fragment is offered by Photius. DeConick asserts that it is "probable" that Heracleon authored the *Tripartite Tractate* (NHC I,5) but offers little evidence (*Gnostic New Age*, 244).

Hellenic or Hellenized background. Based on his precise and detailed commentary, we infer that Heracleon received an advanced form of literary education.

Sidelight on Literary Training. Commentators were trained in various skills like text criticism, character analysis, geography, chronology, and so on – everything that was needed to explain the historical background of a text. They also learned lexicography (the ability to explain obscure words and expressions), and the already well-honed techniques of allegory (how to read persons, objects, and places as symbols of higher realities).[4]

Heracleon was one of the first – perhaps the first – to consistently apply the allegorical method to the gospel of John. In short, he reimagined its characters, places, and objects to represent spiritual realities. When he emphasized the spiritual meanings of John, Heracleon did not deny the historicity of the events, persons, and places of the gospel; he simply saw more value in discerning their deeper meanings.

Heracleon believed that the fourth gospel was written by a "disciple" of Jesus; though he did not mention which one.[5] This disciple, according to Heracleon, had greater spiritual insight than the characters he wrote about. John the Baptist, so Heracleon, cried out that "grace and truth" came with Jesus Christ (John 1:17). But it was the narrator-disciple who declared that no one has ever seen God (1:18). Heracleon was, in a sense, continuing the work of this author-disciple by making unseen spiritual realities seen.

Creation

Heracleon likely began his commentary with John 1:1, but his surviving comments begin with v. 3, where we learn that "everything came about through" the Logos, and "not a single thing apart from him." For Heracleon, the Logos is the true creator because he was the motive force of the (lower) creator. Ptolemy, in his letter to Flora, affirmed this point as well. The Savior made the world in mysterious cooperation with a being called the creator. It was Heracleon, however, who clarified this cooperation. The Logos created the world and its contents *through* the creator, who, in the manner of a construction worker, shaped matter. The creator was not evil, but intermediate (as in Ptolemy). Many Jews and Christians worshiped the creator as the true (that is, highest) God. The true worshipers, said Heracleon, worship "the Father of Truth," a higher being who, incidentally, appears in the opening of the *Gospel of Truth*.[6]

---

[4] Raffaella Cribiore, *Gymnastics of the Mind: Greek Education in Hellenistic and Roman Egypt* (Princeton: Princeton University Press, 2005); Robert A. Kaster, *Guardians of Language: The Grammarian and Society in Late Antiquity* (Berkeley: University of California Press, 1998).

[5] Frag. 3 from Origen, *Comm. John* 6.3.13. Cf. Irenaeus, *AH* 1.8.5.

[6] Frag. 20 from Origen, *Comm. John* 13.95-96.

View of Christ

The Logos came in flesh (John 1:14). This flesh, said Heracleon, was represented by the sandal which John the Baptist thought himself unworthy to untie.[7] Another symbol of Christ's body was the temple (2:21). It was built, according to John, in forty-six years (2:20). The "six" represents matter, thought Heracleon, and thus indicates Christ's entry into matter.[8] Christ came down into the town Capernaum, which Heracleon understood to symbolize the world of matter.[9] The Savior suffered at the festival of Passover; and his flesh was eaten like the meat of the Passover lamb (1 Cor. 5:7).[10]

There was something special about Christ's body. The lower creator could not explain its arrangement.[11] The Refutator claimed that, for Heracleon, Christ's body was made up, not of normal flesh, but of soul substance.[12] Yet the Heracleon of the surviving fragments indicates that Christ truly came into matter. He also said that Christ's body was not perfect, because the lamb, which represents his body, was not a perfect animal. What was perfect was the being "in" Christ's body, namely the Logos.[13]

Three Human Responses

When the Savior came, human beings responded to him in one of three ways. Some rejected him without understanding. Others believed his word without wavering. Still others hesitated, demanding evidence and signs. These three responses sorted people into three permeable groups. The rejectors were "material," the waverers "soulish"; while the quick believers manifested that they were "spiritual."

For Heracleon, these were not fixed classes of people with fixed natures and destinies.[14] People could change their responses to the Savior or even manifest multiple responses. John the Baptist, for instance, was a prophet in terms of his office, and so a symbol of the soulish person. But the Baptist was also "the greatest of those born of women" (Matt. 11:11). In his inner core, he was a spiritual person who knew that the Savior came to take away the sin of the world.[15]

---

[7] Frag. 8 from Origen, *Comm. John* 2.194-203.

[8] Frag. 16 from Origen, *Comm. John* 10.261.

[9] Frag. 11 from Origen, *Comm. John* 10.9.

[10] Frag. 12 from Origen, *Comm. John* 10.117.

[11] Frag. 8 from Origen, *Comm. John* 6.198.

[12] *Ref.* 6.35.5.

[13] Frag. 10 from Origen, *Comm. John* 2.306-7.

[14] Thomassen, "Saved by Nature? The Question of Human Races and Soteriological Determinism in Valentinianism," in *Zugänge zur Gnosis: Akten zur Tagung der patristischen Arbeitsgemeinschaft vom 02.-05.01.2011 in Berlin Spandau* (Leuven: Peeters, 2013), 129–49; and in the same volume, Ismo Dunderberg, "Valentinian Theories on the Classes of Humankind," 113–28; Jean-Daniel Dubois, "Once Again, the Valentinian Expression 'Saved by Nature,'" in Markschies, ed., *Valentinianism*, 193–204.

[15] Frag. 5 from Origen, *Comm. John* 2.109-118. See further Thomassen, "Heracleon," in Rasimus, ed., *Legacy of John*, 179–83.

A key example of a spiritual person, for Heracleon, was the Samaritan woman whom Jesus met by a well (John 4). At first glance, this woman hardly seems a likely candidate for being spiritual. According to Heracleon, this woman had six husbands (five previous husbands and one current). Six, as we already observed, was a sign of the material world. Therefore the six husbands signify the woman's connections to matter. Nonetheless, the woman's former sins were forgiven because she was ignorant. Though ignorant and attached to matter, the woman was actually spiritual. When conversing with the Savior, she understood his word and swiftly believed in him without external evidence. Leaving her water jar behind, she went to preach to the people of her village. These people, since they needed to see the Savior's works, signified the soulish type of response.[16]

Another example of a soulish person is the royal official who met Jesus in Galilee (John 4:46-54). Since this official was a subordinate ruler, Heracleon identified him with the creator. The creator had a sick son, representing soulish people who worshiped the creator. The son was sick, not with disease, but with ignorance about the true God. When Jesus healed the son from afar, the servants of the official, representing the creator's angels, came and announced the healing. The creator inquired carefully as to when the healing occurred, and he discovered that it had occurred exactly when Jesus spoke the healing word. The fact that the creator needed a sign to believe indicated his soulish status.[17]

Those representing the material state, for Heracleon, were the Judeans with whom Jesus spoke in John 8. (Not all Judeans represented material people; elsewhere Heracleon made them symbols of "those in the Fullness."[18]) Some of these materially minded Judeans believed in Jesus (John 8:30). At the same time, because of their focus on matter, they could not – so Heracleon – understand what Jesus was saying (8:43).

When Jesus said that these material people were "from the devil" (8:44), Heracleon denied that they were the devil's natural children. He distinguished three types of offspring: offspring by nature, by inclination, and by merit. The devil cannot have children by nature, because the devil can only destroy and not produce offspring. And since the devil does not have a will, one cannot incline to do his will. There was only one remaining option: material people are children of the devil solely by merit, because they love to do what the devil desires. If their attitude changes, so does their status, a status which corresponds to their "stuff" (*ousia*).[19] The "stuff" of a person is not their fixed and immovable "essence," but their fluid disposition determined by deeds and choice.

In short, Heracleon believed in salvific transformation. He likened material people to an echo, the soulish to a voice, and spirituals to a word. The word is rational communication, the voice is non-rational, and the echo is a reflection of a voice. Just as an echo can become a voice, for Heracleon, a voice can become a word. A soulish

---

[16] Frags. 17-27.
[17] Frag. 40 from Origen, *Comm. John* 13.422.
[18] Frag. 22 from Origen, *Comm. John* 13.114.
[19] Frags. 43-45.

person, in other words, could learn to believe the Savior not through evidence, but simply because they recognized the truth of what he said.[20]

Heracleon also used an image (perhaps from the *Gospel of Thomas* §114), that a woman could change into a man. The woman, for Heracleon, probably symbolized the soulish state, while maleness signified the spiritual state.[21] This was a patriarchal value judgment to be sure. It indicated, however, that moving from a soulish to a spiritual status was possible and encouraged.

The time of the Savior's coming was like a great harvest. The seeds for the harvest, Heracleon said, had been planted long ago. Valentinus envisioned the seed of the superior reality entering the first human at creation. What Adam's descendants did with the seed shaped their later response. Some let the seed remain in dry soil (material people). Some let leaves emerge (the soulish). Others produced fruit and were ready to be reaped when the Savior came (the spirituals).[22] The Child of the Human was the sower who sowed the seed into Adam's heart. When the Savior came in flesh, he began to reap the harvest.

Determinism?

Did people really choose to believe in the Savior, or were they pre-programmed from before the foundation of the world? The gospel of John, interestingly, nowhere speaks of "free will." God's children are born from God (John 1:13). God "gave" spiritual people to Jesus (17:6). These people were "from the truth" (18:37). They did not come to Jesus entirely on their own, we learn, but because the Father "drew" (or possibly "dragged") them (6:44, *helkuō*).

For Heracleon, the seed of God implanted in humans from the beginning represents the innate spiritual potential of all humans. Some humans developed that potential through their choices and acts, while others did not. Therefore some humans were ready for the Savior when he came, while others were not. Most people, it seems, wavered when they encountered God's Logos. For those who did (eventually) come to the Savior, Heracleon did not congratulate them for their works. He knew that salvation was by grace. It was because the Logos created life in spiritual people that they came to him.[23]

Spiritual people were already akin to the Father, but not by virtue of their soul.[24] The human soul is not naturally immortal, otherwise souls would not need God.[25] Spiritual and immortal life was invested by God into souls as a special gift of grace. Those souls who consistently reject the Savior will eventually become material and dissolve like matter. Spiritual people, on the other hand, increasingly share the

---

[20] Frag. 39 from Origen, *Comm. John* 13.363.
[21] Frag. 5 from Origen, *Comm. John* 2.109-118.
[22] Frag. 32 from Origen, *Comm. John* 13.271.
[23] Frag. 2 from Origen, *Comm. John* 2.21.137-38.
[24] Frag. 23 from Origen, *Comm. John* 13.120-21.
[25] Frag. 40 from Origen, *Comm. John* 13.416-26.

deathless nature of the Father, which is spirit.[26] They worship in a spiritual way and after death become pure spirit, ready for entrance into the Father's kingdom, the uncreated realm of the Fullness.

The Savior sent his disciple to reap the spiritual harvest. These disciples represent angels who come to the souls that belongs to them.[27] These angels are the "male" (that is, spiritual) husbands who marry the "female" souls of believers. The Samaritan woman was unaware that she had a spiritual husband, whom Heracleon called her "fullness." For her to receive the fullness of salvation, she needed to unite with her angelic husband.[28] Heracleon likened this spiritual union to a heavenly wedding.[29]

Conclusion

Here one can ask the same question we posed about Ptolemy in the previous chapter: how did Heracleon relate to Christians of other persuasions? It is true that Heracleon implicitly criticized Christians who worshiped the creator as the highest deity. Nevertheless, Heracleon was not pugnacious or supercilious when he referred to "soulish" people. He did not criticize them for being soulish, and did not envision any institutional divisions within the church based on soulish vs. spiritual status. Instead, he envisioned the spiritual transformation of the soulish to a higher mode of perception and status. He believed that spirituals had a duty toward the soulish, "for through the spirit and by the spirit the soul is drawn to the Savior."[30]

Heracleon had a sense that the church must be cleansed. At least this is how he understood the significance of Jesus cleansing the temple with a whip of cords (John 2). For Heracleon, the temple was Jesus's body, the church. The cords signified the power and energy of the Holy Spirit. But the Spirit did not drive out the soulish from the church. Rather, the Spirit expelled the material people and profit lovers who used church services for their own gain.[31]

If material people would eventually be driven out of the church and "consumed," this was not the fate of the soulish. For Heracleon, soulish and spiritual people belonged together in the church. This communion was signified, he believed, by the very architecture of the temple. The temple as a whole is the church; its outer courts are the place of the soulish; the inner sanctum (or Holy of Holies) is the place for spirituals.[32]

In this model, the spirituals were, quite literally, a church within a church. When Heracleon was writing, he evidently thought of himself and his disciples as the spiritual node of pre-established churches. It was this very fact (among others) which

---

[26] Frag. 24 from Origen, *Comm. John* 13.147-50.
[27] Frag. 35 from *Comm. John* 13.322-24.
[28] Frag. 18 from Origen, *Comm. John* 13.67-74.
[29] Frag. 12 from Origen, *Comm. John* 10.117; frag. 38 from *Comm. John* 13.349.
[30] Frag. 27 from Origen, *Comm. John* 13.187.
[31] Frag. 13 from Origen, *Comm. John* 10.212.
[32] Frag. 13 from Origen, *Comm. John* 10.210-15.

annoyed Heracleon's contemporary Irenaeus, and inspired him, at least partly, to write his "refutation and overthrow" of Valentinian Christianity, otherwise known as *Against Heresies.*[33]

If he ever encountered of Irenaeus's *Against Heresies*, Heracleon would probably have hoped for Irenaeus's conversion from a soulish to a spiritual state. We know that Heracleon looked forward to "the resurrection of the church" on the third, or spiritual day.[34] This was the day, apparently, when soulish people would enter the Holy of Holies and become spiritual. Life in the Fullness was not meant solely for an elect few. With humility and grace, the soulish also would learn to fulfill their higher destiny.

Further Reading

Harold Attridge, "Heracleon and John: Reassessment of an Early Christian Hermeneutical Debate," in *Biblical Interpretation: History, Context, and Reality*, ed. Christine Helmer (Leiden: Brill, 2005), 57–72.

Pier Franco Beatrice, "Greek Philosophy and Gnostic Soteriology in Heracleon's 'Hypomnemata,'" *Early Christianity* 3 (2012): 188–214.

Bart Ehrman, *Studies in the Textual Criticism of the New Testament* (Leiden: Brill, 2006), 267–99.

Michael Kaler and Marie-Pierre Bussières, "Was Heracleon a Valentinian? A New Look at Old Sources," *HTR* 99, no. 3 (2006): 275–89.

K. Keefer, *The Branches of the Gospel of John: The Reception of the Fourth Gospel in the Early Church* (London: T&T Clark, 2006), 32–43.

William Lamb, "Johannine Commentaries in the Early Church," in *The Oxford Handbook of Johannine Studies*, ed. Judith M. Lieu and Martinus C. de Boer (Oxford: Oxford University Press, 2018), 416–36 at 424–7.

Titus Nagel, *Die Rezeption des Johannesevangeliums im 2. Jahrhundert* (Leipzig: Evangelische Verlag, 2000), 315–40.

Geoffrey S. Smith, *Valentinian Christianity: Texts and Traditions* (Berkeley: University of California Press, 2020), 31–56.

Einar Thomassen, "Heracleon," in *The Legacy of John: Second-century Reception of the Fourth Gospel*, ed. Tuomas Rasimus (Leiden: Brill, 2010), 173–210.

Einar Thomassen, *The Spiritual Seed: The Church of the 'Valentinians'* (Leiden: Brill, 2006), 103–18.

Annewies van den Hoek, "Heracleon and the Hermeneutics of Prepositions," in *Heretics and Heresies in the Ancient Church and in Eastern Christianity: Studies in Honour of Adelbert Davids*, ed. Joseph Verheyden and Herman Teule (Leuven: Peeters, 2011), 37–50.

Ansgar Wucherpfennig, *Heracleon Philologus: gnostische Johannesexegese im zweiten Jahrhundert*, WUNT 142 (Tübingen: Mohr Siebeck, 2002).

---

[33] Irenaeus was aware of Heracleon, but mentioned him only in passing (*AH* 2.4.1).
[34] Frag. 15 from Origen, *Comm. John* 10.248-50.

Part Five

Christian Leaders in Asia Minor

Marcus and the Rise of Valentinian Churches

Introduction

In Rome, Valentinus, Ptolemy, and Heracleon probably formed small study circles to promote their teaching. Their disciples did not leave pre-existing ecclesial networks, but felt themselves to be the spirit within the soul of the larger body of Christ. Yet change was in the air. By about 160 CE in the province of Asia (western Turkey), Valentinian Christians planted their own independent ecclesial formations. One of the persons responsible for this development was an innovative religious entrepreneur named Marcus.[1]

Marcus was not simply a recruiter who created a temporary audience cult charged with the vibes of his magnetic personality. He passed on a tradition of Valentinian teaching, designed a new order of worship, and trained male and female leaders to speak via inspiration. He created, in short, sustainable church movements that began to compete with other ecclesial formations in Asia Minor, southern Gaul, and eventually Rome. By all accounts, Marcus was, in his time at least, a considerable success.

Life

Who was Marcus? A late source says that he was from Egypt (the city of Memphis), but that may have been because both Egypt and Marcus were both seen as exotic and "magical."[2] As we pointed out with regard to Simon (Chapter 3), Marcus was no more a "magician" than any other Christian ritualist and spiritual entrepreneur. It therefore does not advance scholarship when Marcus is called a "mage" or "magus."

---

[1] Dunderberg notes that "Irenaeus did not call the Marcosians a school ... but a cult society (*thiasos*)" ("The School of Valentinus," in Marjanen and Luomanen, eds., *Companion*, 83, citing *AH* 1.13.4).

[2] Jerome, *Letter* 75.3. See W. Wigan Harvey, *Sancti Irenaei libros quinque adversus haereses*, 2 vols. (Cambridge: Academicis, 1857), 1:126 n. 1; Burrus, *Making of a Heretic*, 126–59. On charges of "magic," see Chapter 3, n. 5.

Irenaeus said that Marcus tried to correct his "teacher," whose name he did not record. The fame of a teacher who did not need to be named hints at Valentinus or Ptolemy. If so, Marcus likely spent some time in either Alexandria or Rome, the epicenters of Valentinian Christianity at the time. From either location, he was sent to Asia Minor or came there as a self-made recruiter.

In the province of Asia, Marcus did not advertise himself as a Valentinian, but as a Christian. That was why he was readily welcomed into the home of a local deacon (more on this below). Using pre-established church networks as a base, Marcus created new social formations with independent ritual practices and doctrines.

Creation and Salvation

Marcus taught that the Father – also called Forefather – generated the Logos.[3] This was fairly standard theology in the circles of Justin Martyr, Irenaeus, and the Refutator. Yet Marcus developed his metaphysics much further. According to him, the Father took a being named Silence as his consort, also called Grace. From them emerged a group of thirty eternities (aeons) – the spiritual church. The lowest of these beings was Wisdom. Wisdom tried to comprehend the Father, but only had a premonition of his greatness. From this premonition came human spirits. The origin of human spirits was not a mistake, but the result of the Father's goodness.[4]

Marcus also told a story of creation and salvation. Wisdom fell from the Fullness of being and produced the creator. The creator wanted to create a world that imitated the infinity and eternity of the higher realm, but he was unable to express its stability and eternity.[5] Tertullian attested that, for Marcus, the human body was the work of angels.[6] In the Fullness of time, the Logos became flesh in Jesus at his baptism. Jesus was a real man of flesh and blood born from Mary. When united with the Logos, Jesus revealed the Father.[7] He was nailed to the cross the Friday before Passover at the hour of noon, and by dying destroyed Death.[8]

Marcus maintained the distinctive idea, based on Matt. 18:10, that each human spirit had an angelic double beholding the face of the Father. The angel was considered to be the spiritual groom, with the human soul as the bride. The key to salvation is the soul's spiritual union with her angel. These angels descended at Jesus's baptism and became his spiritual body. Thus when believers come to know Jesus, they come to know their spiritual selves, their "divine doubles."[9]

---

[3] Irenaeus, *AH* 1.14.1.
[4] Irenaeus, *AH* 1.13.6. Cf. *Valentinian Exposition* (NHC XI,2), and the Valentinian "Lehrbrief" in Epiphanius, *Pan.* 31.5.1–31.6.10; Clement, *Exc.* 43.2-65.
[5] *Ref.* 6.54.1.
[6] Tertullian, *Resurrection* 5.2.
[7] Irenaeus, *AH* 1.15.3.
[8] *Ref.* 6.47.3.
[9] Charles M. Stang, *Our Divine Double* (Cambridge, MA: Harvard University Press, 2016).

Marcus believed that union with one's angel is achievable, at least as a foretaste, while on earth, while final union occurs after death. The human soul who undergoes the ritual of redemption – apparently a form of baptism – becomes invisible and ungraspable to the powers of the lower heaven, including "the judge" – probably a reference to the creator (compare the "Ophites" in Chapter 8).[10] If the creator catches sight of the soul and interrogates it, members of Marcus's congregation were instructed to recite this prayer to Wisdom:

> You who are seated next to God and the mystic Silence before the ages, through you the great ones [angels] ever behold the face of the Father, those who employed you as their guide and encourager to draw their forms [human spirits] above ... Behold! The judge is near and the herald bids me make my defense! You, as one who knows both parties [angel and soul], present the defense of us both as one![11]

Wisdom, Marcus taught, would hear this plea, make the soul invisible, bring it into the bridal chamber, and hand it over to the angelic groom for the consummation in the Fullness.[12]

In early third-century Marcosian practice, a Marcosian bishop would whisper a similar prayer into the ears of the dying, instructing him or her how to pass through the lower heavens.[13] Irenaeus gave a long description of a last-rite ritual in which the initiate memorized responses to be given to the powers surrounding the creator.[14] He did not say that this rite was specifically Marcosian. The words of the rite were later adapted by the author of the *First Apocalypse of James* (NHC V,3). This Last Rites ritual also has a parallel in Ophite Christian practice (Chapter 8).

Baptism

Little is securely known about Marcus's baptismal rite. It is possible that he recommended a second baptism called "redemption." An initial baptism – perhaps received in other churches – was for the forgiveness of sins, but the second baptism granted perfection. Jesus alluded to a second baptism when he said, "I have another baptism to be baptized with" (Luke 12:50).

Irenaeus, our main witness here, did not make clear if he was speaking about distinctly Marcosian practice (he wanted to give the impression that Valentinians were at odds and disorganized). The bishop mentioned "other" Valentinians who used various formulae, for instance "[I baptize you] into the name of the unknown Father of the universe, into Truth, the Mother of all, into him who descended upon Jesus, into

---

[10] Cf. *Apoc. Paul* V,2 22.23–23.28.
[11] Irenaeus, *AH* 1.13.6.
[12] Irenaeus, *AH* 1.13.6.
[13] *Ref.* 6.41.4.
[14] Irenaeus, *AH* 1.21.5.

the union and redemption and participation of the powers."[15] Certain Hebrew phrases were also pronounced, along with a congregational response: "Peace be to all upon whom this Name rests."[16] (Recall that the Son is the Name of the Father in the *Gospel of Truth*.) Irenaeus also noted that Valentinians used fragrant oil in their baptisms and emphasized the importance of knowledge as they underwent the rite.[17]

Excursus: Excerpts from Theodotus

To glean more data on Valentinian baptism, I make a brief detour to study the so-called *Excerpts from Theodotus* (briefly introduced in the Introduction). Valentinus had likened the unredeemed human to an inn infested with demons. The Valentinians of the *Excerpts* recommended baptism as a means of sealing oneself off from demonic invasion.[18] Following Pauline (Eph. 4:30) and Sethian Christian imagery, Valentinians called baptism a "seal." An ancient seal was typically a stamp impressed on heated wax or clay, revealing the name or mark of the owner. A seal quite literally sealed a jar or a letter. It expressed ownership. By being sealed with the name of God, a person or thing became God's servant and protected possession.

The Valentinian baptismal ceremony was thus in part a transfer of ownership from the demons to God. Demons were literally sealed off from entering the human soul. Only the Spirit of God could reside there. All other powers were renounced and trampled.[19] There was, admittedly, a chance that demons could sneak into the waters of baptism and become sealed with the person baptized. Valentinians prevented this danger by exorcizing the waters and by promoting pre-baptismal fasts, vigils, and other acts of mental and physical preparation.[20]

Valentinian Christians emphasized certain baptismal metaphors. Baptism, for instance, signified the death of one's old life (Rom. 6:1-6).[21] Death was important because it freed people from the effects of physical birth. Along with many people of the ancient world, Valentinians believed that at physical birth, astral powers, weak or dominant under particular alignments, gained power over the body and soul of the person born. The combined influence of these powers expressed one's fate.[22] When one dies, however, the astral powers over birth lose control. In this respect, baptism

---

[15] Irenaeus, *AH* 1.21.3; cf. Eusebius, *HE* 4.11.5.

[16] Irenaeus, *AH* 1.21.3.

[17] Irenaeus, *AH* 1.21.3-4.

[18] Clement, *Exc.* 80.3.

[19] The image of trampling snakes and scorpions (i.e. demons) appears also in *Val. Exp.* XI,2 40.15-17.

[20] Clement, *Exc.* 84.1. Cf. Tertullian, *Baptism* 20.1.

[21] Clement, *Exc.* 77.1.

[22] Clement, *Exc.* 69.1. See further Nicola Denzey Lewis, *Cosmology and Fate in Gnosticism and Graeco-Roman Antiquity: Under Pitiless Skies* (Leiden: Brill, 2013), 85–192.

is like death; it breaks the power of demons who are said to shiver in the presence of their former victims.[23]

Valentinians also imagined baptism as a wedding engagement. The baptized soul and her angel were both sealed with the same name, and in this way made one.[24] After baptism, one's angel became one's permanent companion, guaranteeing the safety and security of the baptized person until they fully consummated the marriage in the Fullness.

In order for baptism to work, one required the knowledge gained from the Valentinian story of creation and redemption. But one also needed moral purity and emotional stability.[25] Baptism was thought to help people remove their debilitating emotions (the passions). The Savior was baptized in order to remove the saved from the fires of lust, envy, anger, and grief. He experienced passion (in the sense of suffering) to remove spiritual people from their passions.

Eucharist

Returning now specifically to Marcus, heresiologists noted that his Eucharistic rite differed from other Christian versions. As in traditional eucharists, Marcus presented a loaf of bread as Christ's body and held out a cup of wine representing blood. Distinctively, however, Marcus crafted a lengthy invocation over the cup of wine. He also encouraged women in the congregation to rise and say the blessing over the cup, witnessing firsthand the transformation of the wine into divine blood. The women would say the eucharistic prayer over individual cups, then Marcus would pour their smaller cups into a larger chalice, causing the chalice to overflow. The whole congregation then drank from the chalice.[26]

The Refutator – and only the Refutator – claimed that Marcus secretly used drugs (smeared into the cup beforehand) to change the color of the wine and to make the chalice overflow.[27] It would be hasty, in my opinion, to agree with the Refutator's attempt to debunk Marcosian rituals.[28] Truth be told, we do not know how Marcus performed his rituals or what exactly his congregation saw. What we have are summaries that look more like rumors than eye-witness reports. Parlor tricks were of course known in this period, but we have no insider reports confirming that Marcus used them.[29]

---

[23] Clement, *Exc.* 77.1. Tertullian: the spirit sanctifies water (*Baptism* 4.4-5); Cyprian: the devil lost his powers when he approached baptismal waters (*Letter* 69.15-16). See further Henry Ansgar Kelly, *The Devil at Baptism: Ritual, Theology, and Drama* (Eugene: Wipf & Stock, 2004).

[24] Clement, *Exc.* 22.5-6; cf. Irenaeus *AH* 1.21.3.

[25] Clement, *Exc.* 83.

[26] Irenaeus, *AH* 1.13.2.

[27] *Ref.* 6.39-40.

[28] *Pace* DeConick, *Gnostic New Age*, 251.

[29] The Refutator copied out a manual that debunked "magic tricks" (μάγων ἔργα, *Ref.* 4.42.1). He then used this knowledge to explain Marcus's ritual success.

It might seem strange that Marcus considered the "blood" in the Eucharistic cup to be the blood of Wisdom.[30] But if Wisdom is the Holy Spirit, represented by Christ's blood, then perhaps we can piece together his understanding.[31] The Eucharist, for Marcus, was not only a rite celebrating the sacrificial death of Jesus, a remembrance of Christ's blood shed for sins. It was the experience of participating in the divine Mother, Wisdom, who offered her essence ("blood") to her children, enabling them to reconnect both to her and to their angelic spouses.

Drinking from the chalice provided a "dose" of divine Wisdom. The absorbing of Wisdom led to the proclamation of Wisdom's words. Marcus's Eucharist prepared people, that is, to prophesy. Marcus himself offered revelatory oracles from Wisdom. His oracles were so effective that his enemies accused him of having a superhuman assistant, a personal spirit inhabiting him.[32]

Prophecy

Marcus came to the province of Asia at an interesting time. Between about 157–172 CE, a Christian movement called the New Prophecy came to life in the eastern regions of the province of Asia.[33]

> **Sidelight on the New Prophecy.** The New Prophecy was initiated by a man, Montanus, along with two aristocratic women, Priscilla and Maximilla – all three of whom prophesied ecstatically.[34] In ecstatic prophecy, the prophet's consciousness was put on hold and his or her mind was flooded with Spirit. This Spirit, called Paraclete (John 16:7), spoke the words of God. Notebooks of their prophetic oracles were collected, and a Christian network known for its rigorist ethic (no second marriages) and ascetic practices (food restrictions and fasting) came to flourish in Phrygia (modern west central Turkey), Rome, and North Africa by the late second century.[35]

[30] Note, however, that Irenaeus (*AH* 4.18.4-5) assumes that Valentinians maintain his understanding that bread and the cup re-present the body and blood of Jesus.

[31] *Gos. Phil.* (II,3) 57.6-7 (Jesus's blood is the Holy Spirit); 75.14–21 (the cup is filled with the Holy Spirit).

[32] Irenaeus, *AH* 1.13.3.

[33] Talbert and Bagnall, ed., *Barrington Atlas*, 62.

[34] Jerome, *Letter* 133.4.

[35] For the New Prophecy, see Pseudo-Tertullian, *AAH* 7.2; Eusebius, *HE* 5.3, 16-19; Epiphanius, *Pan.* 48.11.1–48.14.2; Nicola Denzey, "What Did the Montanists Read?" *HTR* 94 (2001): 427–48; Laura Nasrallah, *The Ecstasy of Folly: Prophecy and Authority in Early Christianity* (Cambridge, MA: Harvard University Press 2003); Antti Marjanen, "Montanism, Egalitarian Ecstatic 'New Prophecy' in Marjanen and Luomanen, eds., *Companion*, 185–212; Tabbernee, *Fake Prophecy and Polluted Sacraments: Ecclesiastical and Imperial Reactions to Montanism* (Leiden, Brill, 2007); Markschies, *Christian Theology*, 91–116.

Just as Christian ecstatic prophecy was surging in the interior of the Asian province, Marcus was cultivating his own form of prophecy in the more populous cities on the coast. Marcus theorized that every soul is female and that the source for revelation (Wisdom) was also female. It was no surprise, then, that Marcus encouraged females in his congregation to offer oracles.

Marcus's methods proved controversial. According to Irenaeus, he encouraged hesitant and inexperienced women to come forward before the congregation, say or hear the prayer invoking Wisdom, drink from the chalice, and proclaim what entered their hearts and minds. When Marcus exhorted women to prophesy in front of the group, some of them refused, saying that they did not know how. All the while, Marcus continued to pray and invoke Wisdom until the women reportedly spoke in ecstasy.[36]

Whether Marcus manipulated or empowered these women is up for debate. Perhaps it was a mixture of both. Certainly Marcus proved himself an expert in what has been called "ritual pageantry."[37] Such pageantry stirred the emotions of both men and women. Their intense emotional involvement might have helped them to ascribe – quite reasonably – a particular experience of ritual theater as a spiritual experience. Marcus pushed people, pressuring them to go outside their comfort zones in order to fulfill new and unexpected roles. Women (who were typically socialized to be modest in Greco-Roman society) were at times distressed. Yet after they prophesied, some of them, at least, thanked Marcus for helping them realize their spiritual gifts. Marcus believed that ordinary people could manifest extraordinary talents, and this belief was evidently inspiring.[38]

The Deacon's Wife

According to Irenaeus, Marcus proved so appealing that he drew away the wife of the deacon who once gave him hospitality. We do not know the full story (Irenaeus did not even mention her name). What we do know is that this woman decided to follow Marcus of her own accord. Irenaeus indicated that their relationship was sexual, yet it is highly unlikely that a Christian missionary in an openly adulterous relationship would find a hearing in Greco-Roman society. Marcus attracted this woman because she was convinced by his teachings. Likely he gave her authority as a fellow missionary, teacher, and ritual specialist, as in the contemporaneous story of Paul and Thecla.

---

[36] Cf. the prophetic gift shared without hesitation in *Interpretation of Knowledge* XI,1 15.36-38.

[37] Robert N. McCauley and E. Thomas Lawson, *Bringing Ritual to Mind: Psychological Foundations of Cultural Forms* (Cambridge: Cambridge University Press, 2002), 123. See also Risto Uro, *Ritual and Christian Beginnings: A Socio-Cognitive Analysis* (Oxford: Oxford University Press, 2016), 147–53; Douglas J. Davies, "Ritual, Identity, and Emotion," in *The Oxford Handbook of Early Christian Ritual*, ed. Risto Uro et al. (Oxford: Oxford University Press 2018), 55–73.

[38] For female prophets, cf. Tertullian, *On the Soul* 9.4.

> **Sidelight on Paul and Thecla.** According to *The Acts of Paul and Thecla* (composed in Asia Minor about 170–180 CE), Thecla, a young woman engaged to be married, was so inspired by Paul's message that she broke off her engagement and decided to follow Paul in his missionary journeys. When Paul proved standoffish and unhelpful, she became an independent and successful recruiter herself.[39]

If the deacon's wife did not play some role in the Marcosian network, she would not have stayed in it for so long. When she did, under pressure, finally return to her husband and his ecclesial network, she showed signs of compunction – obligatory in her case if she hoped for reintegration – but she confessed no sexual sin.

It is significant that the Refutator, when he revised Irenaeus's report, excluded any hint that Marcus engaged in illicit sexual behavior. The reason can be inferred. The Refutator had encountered Marcosians – evidently in Rome – who denounced Irenaeus's tale as false.[40] This is one of the only instances we know of where hereticalized peoples "talked back" to heresiographers, leading them to modify their attacks.

To be sure, rich and powerful women were attracted to Marcus, though presumably for social and psychological reasons. Marcus gave women the intellectual and spiritual freedom that they did not have in early catholic networks, which increasingly underscored the priority and authority of single male bishops.[41] These male bishops encouraged women to subject themselves to their husbands and to be silent in the churches.

> **Sidelight on Female "Silence."** In 1 Tim. 2:11-12, a writer impersonating the apostle Paul wrote to a protégé: "Let a woman learn in silence with full submission. I permit no woman to teach or to have authority over a man; she is to keep silent." Compare 1 Cor. 14:34: "women should be silent in the churches. For they are not permitted to speak." The latter passage may be an interpolation.[42] The former may be a polemical response to female prophets active in churches of the early to mid-second century. In short, they do not describe what was happening in the first or second century. Rather, they are prescriptive attempts at social control.[43]

---

[39] Outi Lehtipuu, "The Example of Thecla and the Example(s) of Paul: Disputing Women's Role in Early Christianity," in *Women and Gender in Ancient Religions: Interdisciplinary Approaches*, ed. Stephen P. Ahearne-Kroll et al. (Tübingen: Mohr Siebeck, 2010), 349–78; Stephen J. Davis, *The Cult of Saint Thecla: A Tradition of Women's Piety in Late Antiquity* (Oxford: Oxford University Press, 2001); Elisabeth Esch-Wermeling, *Thekla – Paulusschülerin wider Willen? Strategien der Leserlenkung in den Theklaakten* (Münster: Aschendorff, 2008); Susan E. Hylen, *A Modest Apostle: Thecla and the History of Women in the Early Church* (Oxford: Oxford University Press, 2015).

[40] *Ref.* 6.42.1.

[41] James E. Goehring, "Libertine or Liberated: Women in So-called Libertine Gnostic Communities," in King, ed., *Images of the Feminine*, 329–44 at 334–8.

[42] E.g., Gordon D. Fee, *The First Epistle to the Corinthians* (Grand Rapids: Eerdmans, 1987), 699–708.

[43] See further Ross Shepard Kramer, *Her Share of Blessings: Women's Religions among Pagans, Jews and Christians in the Greco-Roman World* (Oxford: Oxford University Press, 1992), 157–73; Anne

If Marcus targeted women of means, he did no more than any other religious entrepreneur of his time. Ptolemy appealed to Flora, a Roman matron with a keen intellect. Flora represented a kind of woman who had the leisure for higher learning, who could offer her home as a meeting place, who had the means to house teachers and purchase their books. What linked ecclesial nodes together in the ancient world was not so different from what links them today: a steady supply of monetary donations, a shared story creating common identity, and firm social bonds – often maintained by women.[44]

What mattered for community building was not just economic, but symbolic capital. Marcus cashed in his symbolic capital by demonstrating his power to broker the Holy Spirit (aka Wisdom). Marcus's rituals were also characterized by perceptible results. Women prophesied. Wine was thought to become blood. People felt a sense of effervescence and fullness symbolized in the eucharistic chalice overflowing its brim.

Marcus's Vision

Marcus's mastery of ritual pageantry meant no neglect of doctrine. Yet he framed his doctrine in the imagistic framework of personal visions. Marcus claimed to have had a vision of the Tetrad (another name for Silence, the chief feminine reflection of God). The Tetrad revealed to him how language, or words within the Greek language, served as signs and symbols of heavenly realities.[45] Marcus spoke of letters and their meanings, but he imagined the letters in vivid ways, as making up a female body, what he called "the body of Truth."[46] Marcus's vision resembles that of the prophetess Quintilla, a later leader in the New Prophecy, who saw Christ come to her "dressed in a white robe in the form of a woman."[47]

The details of Marcus's vision required knowledge of both grammar and mathematics. But neither the mathematics nor grammar were particularly complex. Any ancient schoolboy knew that Greek letters stood for numbers, and thus one could add up the numbers of words. This activity is sometimes called "gematria" after the later Kabbalistic practice. Yet there was nothing necessarily mystical or mysterious about it; it already had a biblical precedent (Rev. 13:17), and was commonly employed in oracles.[48]

Marcus's disciples also used both grammar and mathematics to reveal the deeper meanings of biblical lore. They were especially fond of attributing symbolic values to numbers in Jesus's parables, such as the single lost sheep who left the 99 (Matt. 18:12;

Jensen, *God's Self-confident Daughters: Early Christianity and the Liberation of Women* (Louisville: Westminster John Knox, 1996), 125–88; Hylen, *Modest Apostle*, 43–70.

[44] Stark, *Rise of Christianity*, 95–128.

[45] Irenaeus, *AH* 1.14-15.

[46] *Ref.* 6.44.1.

[47] Epiphanius, *Pan.* 49.1.3. See further Christine Trevett, *Montanism: Gender, Authority and the New Prophecy* (Cambridge: Cambridge University Press, 1996), 168–70.

[48] Suetonius, *Nero* 39; Artemidorus, *Dream Interpretation* 2.70; 3.34; 4.24. For basic grammar applied to biblical allegory, cf. Philo, *Questions on Genesis* 4.117.

Luke 15:3-10).[49] Their interpretation of the parable had a precedent in the *Gospel of Truth*, where the number 99 represents deficiency, and the completed number of sheep (100) is the sign of the Father.[50]

Heresiographers mocked Marcus's numerical speculations, even as they recorded them at length. One should note, as we mentioned in the case of Ptolemy's disciples (Chapter 15), speculative metaphysics would probably not have been the first lessons related to Valentinian disciples. In his numerological speculations, Marcus assumed a basic and preparatory knowledge of biblical names and stories (such as Jesus's birth, transfiguration, and crucifixion). The aura of secrecy that surrounded Marcus's visions probably heightened their attraction. But the secrecy was also part of the pageantry. Marcus (or his followers) published his visions, making them accessible to all.[51]

Church Order

In the early days of Marcus's movement, the concept of ordination was apparently foreign. All members of the congregation could lead the rituals without long years of schooling or official consecration. Marcus retained his spiritual authority, of course, but he encouraged a mentality in which all members of the church were equal.

Valentinian Christians assumed that the prophetic Spirit had been poured out upon all church members.[52] In Marcus's communities, every member of the congregation exhorted every other to speak with the authority granted by inspiration. In their regular banquets, Marcus's followers used a system of selection (drawing lots) to choose who was to offer a prophetic word, which may have served as something like a modern homily.[53]

Like other Valentinians, Marcus probably wrote other works as well. The record of his liturgical formulas, for instance, are too full and precise to be based on mere oral report. One of Marcus's eucharist prayers went like this: "May Grace who is before all things, unthinkable and unspeakable, fill your inner self and increase in you her own knowledge, by planting the mustard seed in good ground" (Matt. 13:8)[54] Possibly Marcus inscribed these formulas into a sort of prayer book. The fixed prayers and formulas are another indication that Marcus and his disciples formed self-sustaining ecclesial movements.

---

[49] Irenaeus, *AH* 1.16.1.
[50] *Gospel of Truth* I,3 31.35–32.17.
[51] See further Bull, Lied, and Turner, eds., *Mystery and Secrecy*; Hans Kippenberg and Guy Stroumsa, eds., *Secrecy and Concealment: Studies in the History of Mediterranean and Near East Religions* (Leiden: Brill, 1995).
[52] Clement, *Exc.* 24.
[53] Irenaeus, *AH* 1.13.4; cf. Tertullian, *Pr. Haer.* 41.8.
[54] Irenaeus, *AH* 1.13.2. For the invocation of Grace, cf. *Didache* 10.6.

Conclusion

Marcus was an innovator, not only theologically, but in terms of ritual practice and social organization. It was his ability to create rituals with set prayers that helped to maintain independent ecclesial formations. When Marcus left the groups he founded, there were structures in place to maintain them. Group leaders, chosen by lot, would give the message at the communal meals. Men and women would pray, prophesy, and officiate the rites.[55]

The ecclesial character of Marcus's social formations did not entirely replace the study-circle model used by other Valentinians. It did, however, more effectively allow for the spread and stability of Valentinian Christian movements to places like Gaul, Syria, and North Africa. The very fact that Valentinian movements appeared as independent churches probably fueled the sense of threat felt by competing church leaders who lost "sheep" to the Valentinians.

Valentinian Christianity eventually became a successful ecclesial network. In the second and third centuries CE we know of Valentinian groups in Asia Minor, Rome, Gaul, North Africa, Syria, Egypt, and Greece. Epiphanius listed six Egyptian cities where there existed Valentinian communities in his day (around 375 CE): Athribitis, Prosopitis, Arsinoitis, Thebais, Paralia and Alexandria.[56] He claimed that Valentinus retired on the island of Cyprus, which indicates the presence of Valentinians there.[57]

The Refutator claimed that Valentinus's pupils split into an "Italian" school represented by Ptolemy and Heracleon in Rome, and an "Eastern" one led by Axionicus and "Bardesianes" (the manuscript here reads "Ardisianes," apparently by mistake).[58] "Bardesianes" is evidently Bardaisan, the Christian philosopher of Edessa. He was not a Valentinian. Axionicus is an otherwise unknown Christian from Antioch.[59] These easterners, according to the Refutator, said that Jesus had a spirit body from birth (based on Luke 1:35). The "Italian" school, by contrast, believed that the spirit body came into him at baptism.

This theory of two Valentinian "schools" has come under attack in modern scholarship.[60] The Refutator, first of all, was poorly informed about Bardaisan and Axionicus. Assuming there was an internal debate about the nature of Jesus's body, the Refutator presented it in a partial and tendentious way. The Norwegian scholar Einar Thomassen maintains the two-school theory, but on different grounds than the Refutator and with a thorough knowledge of primary texts. For Thomassen, the two schools presented two discrete theories of salvation. The "Italian" branch focused on the salvation of animate people – the mid-level group of Christians who

---

[55] Irenaeus, *AH* 1.13.4.
[56] Epiphanius, *Pan.* 31.7.1.
[57] Epiphanius, *Pan.* 31.7.2.
[58] *Ref.* 6.35.7.
[59] Tertullian, *Against the Valentinians* 4.3.
[60] Joel Kalvesmaki, "Italian versus Eastern Valentinianism?" *VC* 62, no. 1 (2008): 79–89.

underwent moral and spiritual advancement. The "Eastern" school, chronologically prior, proposed a theory of mutual participation in which Jesus becomes what humans are so that they can become what Jesus is – spiritual and divine.[61]

Our extensive treatment of Valentinian leaders is now complete, but we would be remiss to say nothing about other Valentinian leaders contemporary with Marcus. Unfortunately our knowledge about these figures is extremely thin. Heresiologists tend to mention them in a single line. A Valentinian named Secundus, we are told, speculated about the Fullness.[62] Alexander, who made use of syllogisms and Valentinus's hymnbook, reportedly said that Christ assumed an earthly (that is, fleshly) body in order to abolish it.[63] Theotimus explained the "pictures" of the Law (the exact meaning of this remark is uncertain).[64] Theodotus, perhaps from Alexandria, retold the stories of creation and salvation. The author who wrote the *Gospel of Philip* (NHC II,3) provided a treasure trove of meditations on Valentinian spirituality and sacraments.[65] Late in the second century, we find Paul the Valentinian who lived in the same house as the young Origen.

The history of later Valentinian Christians can only be briefly touched on here.[66] Origen's patron Ambrose was originally a Valentinian Christian. Origen disputed with the Valentinian named Candidus around 230 CE in Athens.[67] In the fourth century, Valentinian Christians were still active in Egypt and Syria and certain areas of Asia Minor. We know of one Valentinian church building burned down near the Euphrates River in 388 CE.[68] Traces of Valentinians appear as late as the seventh and eighth centuries.[69] Not all of this evidence indicates a single ecumenical movement. Yet it is certainly fair to say that the Valentinian Christian network had a lengthy career and a measure of success due in part to innovative leaders and organizers like Marcus.

Further Reading

Ellen Bradshaw Aitken, "A Valentinian Response to the Culture of Reclining," in *Meals in the Early Christian World*, ed. D. E. Smith and Hal E. Taussig (New York: Palgrave Macmillan, 2012), 239–44.

Nicola Denzey Lewis, "Apolytrosis as Ritual and Sacrament: Determining a Ritual Context for Death in Second-century Marcosian Valentinianism," *JECS* 17, no. 4 (2009): 525–61.

---

[61] Thomassen, *Spiritual Seed*, 45, 81. A similar theory of mutual participation was proposed by Irenaeus (*AH* 5, *pref.*).

[62] Irenaeus, *AH* 1.11.2; *Ref.* 6.38; Epiphanius *Pan.* 32. See further Thomassen, *Spiritual Seed*, 497–8.

[63] Tertullian, *Flesh of Christ* 16.1; 17.1.

[64] Tertullian, *Against the Valentinians* 4.3.

[65] See further Layton and Brakke, eds., *The Gnostic Scriptures*, 459–63; Smith, *Valentinian Christianity*, 255, Thomassen, *Spiritual Seed*, 90–102, 341–9.

[66] See the useful map in Layton and Brakke, eds., *The Gnostic Scriptures*, 332–3.

[67] Rufinus, *Adulteration of Origen's Books* 7; Jerome, *Against Rufinus* 2.18-19.

[68] Ambrose, *Letter* 40.16.

[69] See further Klaus Koschorke, "Patristische Materialen zur Spätgeschichte der valentinianischen Gnosis," in *Gnosis and Gnosticism*, ed. Martin Krause (Leiden: Brill, 1981), 120–39 at 127–39.

Nicola Denzey Lewis, "Lived Religion among Second-century 'Gnostic Hieratic Specialists,'" in *Beyond Priesthood: Religious Entrepreneurs and Innovators in the Roman Empire*, ed. Richard L. Gordon et al. (Berlin: de Gruyter, 2017), 79–102.

Ismo Dunderberg, "The School of Valentinus," in *Companion to Second-century Christian 'Heretics'*, ed. Antti Marjanen and Petri Luomanen (Leiden: Brill, 2005), 64–99.

Cécile and Alexandre Faivre, "La place des femmes dans le ritual eucharistique des Marcosiens: Déviance ou archaïsme?" *Revue des Sciences Religieuses* 71 (1997): 310–28.

N. Förster, *Marcus Magus: Kult, Lehre und Gemeindeleben einer valentinianischen Gnostik-ergruppe: Sammlung der Quellen und Kommentar*, WUNT 114 (Tübingen: Mohr Siebeck, 1999).

R. J. Hoffmann, "The 'Eucharist' of Marcus Magus: A Test Case in Gnostic Social Theory," *Patristic and Byzantine Review* 3 (1984): 82–8.

Joel Kalvesmaki, "Italian versus Eastern Valentinianism?" *VC* 62, no. 1 (2008): 79–89.

Einar Thomassen, "Baptism among the Valentinians," in *Ablution, Initiation, and Baptism: Late Antiquity, Early Judaism, Early Christianity*, ed. Tor Vegge et al. (Berlin: de Gruyter, 2011), 895–916.

Einar Thomassen, "Going to Church with the Valentinians," in *Practicing Gnosis: Essays in Honor of Birger A. Pearson*, ed. April D. DeConick et al. (Leiden: Brill, 2013), 187–97.

Einar Thomassen, "The Eucharist in Valentinianism," in *The Eucharist – Its Origins and Contexts*, vol. 3, ed. D. Hellholm and D. Sänger (Tübingen: Mohr Siebeck, 2017), 1833–49.

Stephen L. Young, "The Marcosian Redemption: Mythmaking, the Afterlife, and Early Christian Religiosity," *Journal of Early Christian History* 6, no. 2 (2016): 77–110.

Noetus and His Followers

Introduction

When Marcus was enjoying the height of his success in the province of Asia, a man by the name of Noetus was emerging as a Christian leader in the same region. Unfortunately, Noetus's life and thought have long faded from Christian memory. As in the case of Menander, Saturninus, and Carpocrates, no writings from Noetus or his followers survive. We only have heresiographical reports, most importantly a polemical tract *Against Noetus*, which may originally have been part of a larger heresiographical work. The other main treatise informing us about Noetus is the *Refutation of All Heresies*, where Noetus is attacked as the intellectual forefather of the Roman bishop Callistus (served 217–222 CE).

As noted in the Introduction, we do not know the name of the author of the *Refutation*, and the same applies to the writer of *Against Noetus*. Both works were evidently written for different purposes and at different times. *Against Noetus* in particular was adapted for use in fourth-century Christian debates and subtly modified by later editors. In my view, the author of the original *Against Noetus* and the *Refutation* is the same man: a leading Christian intellectual who came to compete with Callistus in early third-century Rome. This unnamed leader first attacked Noetus's scriptural interpretation (in *Against Noetus*) and later tried the strategy of tracing his thought back to pre-Christian philosophy (the *Refutation*). Other scholars have different theories about the authorship of these texts.[1] None of them convince me that we should exclude *Against Noetus* as data for reconstructing the life and thought of Noetus.

Life

Both *Against Noetus* and the *Refutation* report that Noetus was from the city of Smyrna (modern Izmir), the same city in western Turkey that nurtured Polycarp

---

[1] See, e.g., Pierre Nautin, *Hippolyte contre les hérésies* (Paris: Cerf, 1949), 1–70; Josef Frickel, "Hippolyts Schrift Contra Noetum: ein Pseudo-Hippolyt," in *Logos: Festschrift für Luise Abramowski*, ed. Hans Ch. Brennecke, Ernst L. Grasmück, and Christoph Markschies (Berlin: de Gruyter, 1993), 87–123.

and probably Irenaeus as well. Noetus was evidently a close contemporary of
Irenaeus, though he evidently rose to leadership after Irenaeus had left for Italy and
Gaul (southern France).

Some have speculated that Noetus, like Polycarp before him, was in fact bishop
of Smyrna. The evidence for this is thin, but we should consider it nonetheless.
Noetus was said to have sent out his "deacon" Epigonus to Rome in order to spread
his teaching. The word for "deacon" (*diakonos*) can also mean "assistant," but in
ecclesial usage it designates the official assistant of a presbyter or bishop. If Noetus
had a deacon whom he sent in some kind of official capacity, then presumably he
was either a presbyter or bishop – and one must keep in mind that these offices may
not have been (fully) distinct at this time.[2] Polycarp (who died around 155 CE), for
instance, is sometimes spoken of as the sole bishop of Smyrna. Yet when Noetus
was called before a meeting of his congregation (between 160–190 CE), he only met
a group of presbyters with no chief bishop presiding. The solution to this riddle is
probably not that Noetus himself was Smyrna's bishop at the time, but that there
never was a single, monarchial bishop of Smyrna in the mid to late second century
CE.[3]

These church meetings, presuming they occurred, featured a debate about
Noetus's understanding of God. Unfortunately no minutes from these gatherings
survive. All we know is that Noetus understood Christ to be God in the fullest
possible sense. In the first meeting, Noetus reportedly denied having taught what
some accused him of teaching. He said that opponents did not understand the basic
principles of his thought. The indictments were apparently tossed out and no action
was taken. In the meantime, Noetus clarified his thought and gathered a circle of at
least ten close disciples.[4] When a second meeting was called – perhaps months or
even years later – Noetus was purportedly reproved and expelled from "the" church
in Smyrna. Likely, however, there never was "the" church in this thriving city. If
Noetus was expelled, he could have easily joined another Christian group or formed
one of his own.

Why Noetus clashed with fellow presbyters is a matter of debate. He himself seems
to have been exasperated by the opposition. Reportedly he cried out in the second
meeting: "What evil do I do by glorifying Christ?"[5] It was a pressing question. Ignatius
had written to the Smyrneans: "I give glory to Jesus Christ, the God who makes you

---

[2] Hübner, *Paradox*, 72; C. H. Turner, "The 'Blessed Presbyters' Who Condemned Noetus," *JTS* 23
(1922): 28–35 at 30.

[3] Allen Brent, "The Enigma of Ignatius of Antioch," *JEH* 57 (2006): 429–56 at 433; Alistair C.
Stewart, *The Original Bishops: Office and Order in the First Christian Communities* (Grand Rapids:
Baker Academic, 2014), 207–13.

[4] The detail about ten disciples comes from Epiphanius, *Pan.* 57.1.6. For a comparison between
Against Noetus and Epiphanius, *Pan.* 57, see Pourkier, *L'hérésiologie*, 115–46.

[5] *Against Noetus* 1.6. For comments on this text, see Butterworth, *Hippolytus*, 37–8.

so wise."[6] Ignatius had no problem with calling Christ, "God," or "my God," or "our God," and he made no systematic attempt to distinguish him from the Father.[7] He even referred to "the blood of God" and to the "suffering of God" – referring of course to Jesus.[8]

Other early Christian texts follow a similar logic. The first line in the letter called *2 Clement* begins: "Brothers, it is necessary to think about Jesus Christ as we do about God" (1:1). The *Acts of John*, composed in Asia Minor during Noetus's lifetime, refers to "our God, Jesus Christ, higher and loftier than any name and thought."[9] Earlier in the same work, the apostle John addresses "holy Jesus, for you alone are God and none else."[10] The full deity of Jesus – Jesus as God – was, in short, a widespread notion at the time.

Teachings

It is important to discern what exactly Noetus taught about Jesus's divine identity, keeping in mind that any presentation of his thought is a reconstruction. The basic teaching of Noetus was that God is and has always been fundamentally one – a teaching abundantly testified in Jewish and Christian scriptures. Noetus and his followers apparently quoted a mixture of Exod. 3:6 and 20:3: "I am the God of your fathers; there will not be for you other gods beside me." They also cited Isa. 44:6: "I am the first and I am the last, and after me there is no one."[11] The speaker in Isaiah is evidently God the Father, yet in the book of Revelation – a text which includes a letter to Smyrna – Christ is also called "the first and the last" (22:13). These and many other scriptures were available to corroborate the notion of divine unity. Most Christians readily confessed this unity, often in opposition to the polytheism of the majority population.

For Noetus and his disciples, oneness meant a denial of divine plurality. Divine plurality could be conceived of as the "Fullness" emphasized by Valentinian Christians, or it could be conceived in terms of Logos Christology in which God the Father gave birth in some ineffable way to a separate entity called the Logos. This Logos then existed alongside God as a separate being, and could be depicted as the creator (John 1:1-3). Noetus apparently rejected any position in which God is somehow a collective of two, three, or several entities.

---

[6] Ignatius, *Smyrneans* 1.1 (δοξάζω Ἰησοῦν Χριστόν, τὸν θεὸν τὸν οὕτως ὑμᾶς σοφίσαντα).

[7] Ignatius, *Ephesians* Pref. ("our God"); cf. 15:3; 18:2; *To Polycarp* 8:3. A similar phrase occurs twice in the preface to his letter *To the Romans*, but here it is also said that Christ is "Son of the Father." Cf. Rom. 3:3; 6:3.

[8] Ignatius, *Ephesians* 1:1; Rom. 6:3. See further William R. Schoedel, *Ignatius of Antioch: A Commentary* (Minneapolis: Fortress, 1985), 20, 39; Hübner, *Paradox*, 131–206.

[9] *Acts of John* 107.

[10] *Acts of John* 77, cf. 82.

[11] *Against Noetus* 2.1-2.

For Noetus, it seems, "Father" and "Son" were only nominal expressions.[12] They did not refer to different entities, but to the same entity in different modes. The Father became Son not in eternity past, but when he chose to be born from the virgin Mary. "This is your God," says a text attributed to the prophet Baruch: "no other ranks with him … he appeared on earth and conversed with human beings" (3:36, 38). When God was born, he did not change his essence.[13] That is why Jesus could say, "I and the Father are one," and "the one who sees me sees the Father" (John 10:30; 14:9). In brief, Jesus was the Father in a different mode of being. One could only behold the higher mode of Christ if one possessed a higher degree of perception. To quote Noetus's disciples: Christ "did not conceal the fact that he was Father from those who could receive him."[14]

It is one thing to emphasize the oneness of God above all else, it is another to say that God suffers. In the predominant philosophy at the time (Platonism), it was standard doctrine that God could not undergo any suffering because God's essence is bodiless and one requires a body to suffer pain.[15] Yet if Christ was the Father in human form, then the question of the Father's suffering and even death became pressing.

Not long before Noetus, a local bishop called Melito of Sardis, in his work *On the Pascha*, claimed: "He who hung the earth is hanging … he who fastened the universe has been fastened to a tree; … God has been murdered!"[16] This was bold and emotive language which may or may not indicate literally that God suffered. Noetus, for his part, never said anything of the kind. Even in the works that attacked him, Noetus never said that the Father suffered, nor did he cite scriptural support for this view. Moving from (1) the oneness of God in Christ to (2) the Father suffered when he arrived as Jesus was perhaps a logical deduction, but it was not a necessary one. The accusation against Noetus and his circle that their view involved the Father's suffering ("patripassianism") was a common charge among heresiographers to be sure, but it seems to have been their own inference.[17]

---

[12] *Ref.* 9.10.11.

[13] Similar language about God manifest on earth can be found in the *Testaments of the Twelve Patriarchs*, *Testament of Simeon* 6:5; *Testament of Naphtali* 8:3; *Testament of Asher* 7:3.

[14] *Ref.* 9.10.11.

[15] Alcinous, *Handbook* 10.7-8.

[16] Melito, *Pascha* 96; cf. 66. Elsewhere Melito wrote of "God who is naturally God and human": "inasmuch as he begets, Father, inasmuch as he is begotten, Son" (*Pascha* 9). See further Hübner, *Paradox*, 1–38.

[17] *Pace* Paul L. Gavrilyuk, who quotes *Against Noetus* 2.3, 7 as if these excerpts accurately represent Noetus's thought (*The Suffering of the Impassible God: The Dialectics of Patristic Thought* [Oxford: Oxford University Press, 2004], 91–100 at 93–4). Gavrilyuk himself observes: "the state of the sources is such that it is virtually impossible to distinguish the views actually held by the Patripassians themselves from the polemical conjectures of their opponents" (92). On the inaccuracy of the term "patripassian," see Marcel Sarot, "Patripassianism, Theopaschitism, and the Suffering of God: Some Historical and Systematic Considerations," *Religious Studies* 26 (1990): 363–75 at 370; Heine, "Christology of Callistus," 84.

If we can peer behind the polemic, Noetus seems to have maintained a theology of paradox. It was not that God was invisible, then visible in Christ; unborn, then born; undying, then dying. Instead, God in Christ was both visible and invisible, born and unborn, dying and not dying at one and the same time.[18]

This tendency to formulate theology in terms of paradox had precedents. Ignatius called Jesus Christ "fleshly and spiritual, born and unborn, first able to suffer, then unsuffering."[19] Melito wrote that "the invisible is seen ... the incomprehensible is seized ... the immeasurable is measured ... the impassible suffers ... the immortal dies."[20] In the *Acts of Peter*, the apostle Peter testifies that his Lord is both large and small, beautiful and ugly, young and old, "appearing in time, yet utterly invisible in eternity, whom a human hand has not grasped, yet is held by his servants."[21] Monoïmus, a Christian writer from the area of modern Jordan, wrote of God as "uncompounded and compounded, indivisible and divisible, entirely friendly and entirely belligerent, entirely peaceful and entirely hostile."[22]

Sidelight on Monoïmus. Monoïmus explained how God was simultaneously one and many using an analogy from mathematics. In Greek, the letter iota (ι) represented both one (a single downward stroke) and the number ten. In this tiny letter, then, there was both unity and multiplicity at the same time.[23] Father and Son were like an eternal fire plus the light which automatically emerged from that fire.[24] The fire and light are mentally distinguishable but in essence one. Since they were distinguishable, Monoïmus – among other theologians at the time – could limit suffering to the Son.[25]

Finally, the Nag Hammadi text called *Thunder: Perfect Mind* (VI,2) is rich in paradox. Here an unnamed divine figure proclaims: "It is I who am consolation: of my own travail ... Do not neglect to fear my power! ... It is I who am present in all fears: and boldness. In trembling, it is I who am what is feeble."[26]

Noetus and his followers made good use of this paradoxical style of theology. For them, God was "uncontained" when he willed, and by his sovereign counsel contained. Likewise, God is "indomitable and dominated, unborn and born, deathless

---

[18] Most distinctly expressed in *Ref.* 10.26.

[19] Ignatius, *Ephesians* 7.2.

[20] Melito, frag. 13; cf. new fragment II.13 in the edition of *On Pascha and Fragments*, ed. Stuart George Hall (Oxford: Clarendon, 1979).

[21] *Acts of Peter* 20 (trans. Elliott); cf. *Acts of John* 101.6-15.

[22] *Ref.* 8.12.5.

[23] *Ref.* 8.12.6-7.

[24] *Ref.* 8.12.4.

[25] *Ref.* 8.12.2. See further Marcovich, *Studies*, 134–43; van den Broek, "Monoïmus," in *DGWE*, 800–802; Kalvesmaki, *Theology of Arithmetic*, 85–94.

[26] *Thunder* VI,2 13.26; 15.19, 25-27 (trans. from Layton and Brakke, eds., *The Gnostic Scriptures*, 111–13).

and dying."[27] In the Refutator's summary: God is "visible and invisible, born and unborn, dying and deathless."[28]

This paradoxical theology led the Refutator to think that Noetian thought derived from Heraclitus, master of paradox. Heraclitus, a philosopher active around 500 BCE, was also from Asia Minor (the city of Ephesus). It was he who reportedly said that "God is Day Night, Winter Summer, War Peace, Satiety Hunger."[29] The Refutator explained this statement to mean that "God consists of all opposites."[30] This was how the Refutator understood Noetian theology as well.

It would be inaccurate, therefore, to say that for Noetian Christians God suffered and died – for that is only half the paradox. For Noetians, God is "not suffering and deathless when he does not suffer and die, but when he approaches suffering, he suffers and dies."[31] God both suffered and did not suffer in Christ; "he died and did not die."[32] No Noetian explanation of this paradox is ever supplied. If Noetians had their own explanation, it does not survive – nor would we expect it to, since heresiologists were not in the business of explanation but of accusation.

> *Sidelight on Valentinian Christology.* Some Valentinians at the time had their own account for how God in Christ both did and did not suffer at the same time. They made a distinction between several aspects of Jesus: the man who was born from Mary, the Christ sent by the creator, and the spiritual Jesus, the common fruit of the Fullness. All these aspects combined to make up a single person – Jesus Christ – who both suffered in his human nature and could not suffer in his divine nature (Irenaeus, *AH* 3.16.6). Many Christians from the second to the fourth century would have agreed with the basic position that in his human nature Jesus suffered, while his divine nature was untouched.[33]

There is one other mysterious aspect of Noetus's teaching that proves difficult to explain. Reportedly, Noetus called himself "Moses" and his "brother" he named "Aaron." Epiphanius took this report literally, that Noetus had a literal brother named Aaron.[34] In biblical tradition, Moses was God's prophet while his brother Aaron served as spokesperson (Exod. 3–4). Perhaps Noetus had a disciple who had the same function. We know the name of Noetus's disciple Epigonus, who brought Noetus's teaching to Rome. Yet there is no explicit connection between Epigonus and Aaron. The tradition about Noetus's "brother" was later distorted by heresiographers. Filastrius, writing soon after Epiphanius, claimed that Noetus's brother was

[27] *Ref.* 9.10.10.
[28] *Ref.* 10.26.
[29] Quoted in *Ref.* 10.9.8.
[30] Quoted in *Ref.* 10.9.8.
[31] *Ref.* 10.27.
[32] *Ref.* 9.10.11.
[33] See further Hübner, *Paradox*, 95–130.
[34] Epiphanius, *Pan.* 57.1.9.

the prophet Elijah![35] Here, it seems, we are in the echo chamber of heresiological distortion.

Noetus and the New Prophecy

There is a peculiar connection between Noetus and the New Prophecy (introduced in the previous chapter). In the New Prophecy, Christian prophets claimed to be possessed by the Paraclete Spirit.[36] In this state of possession they delivered oracles. The author of *Against Noetus* emphasized not only that Noetus derived his doctrine from scripture, but that an "alien spirit" indwelt him, leading him to teach what he did.[37] It is not impossible that Noetus was influenced by the idea of Spirit possession in the New Prophecy (Smyrna and Phrygia were geographically proximate). Yet Noetus would not have needed the New Prophets to teach him about the dynamics of inspired utterance.[38]

There is, however, another connection between Noetus and the New Prophets. The Refutator testified that a wing of the New Prophecy, evidently in Rome, became proponents of Noetian theology.[39] This is evidence at least for an interchange of ideas between Noetians and the New Prophecy, at least in the capital, a generation after Noetus. The association may have led to the idea that Noetians, including Noetus himself, claimed to speak oracles.

Perhaps Noetus did assert a greater than rational authority for his views, believing that he was inspired by God's Spirit. Unfortunately we have no reliable clue as to how Noetus understood the Spirit. His intellectual heirs – in particular bishop Callistus – were said to have identified the Spirit inhabiting Jesus with the Father himself.[40] On the face of it, this theory resembled Cerinthus's views insofar as Jesus and the Spirit were distinguishable. For Callistus, however, Jesus and the Father-Spirit could not be separated.

Conclusion

If we know little about Noetus himself, we have important information on the impact of his thought. Noetus, it seems, never came to Rome. Instead, he sent one of his disciples there, the aforementioned Epigonus. Epigonus was apparently accepted among early catholic circles in the capital. While there, he taught Cleomenes, a man who became the champion of Noetian thought in Rome. Cleomenes influenced the theology of Callistus, right-hand man to Zephyrinus, who became the catholic leader of Rome in 199 CE. Callistus himself succeeded Zephyrinus as bishop in

---

[35] Filastrius, *Div.* 53.1.
[36] *Ref.* 8.19.1.
[37] *Against Noetus* 1.1-2; cf. Eusebius, *HE* 5.16.7-9.
[38] Nasrallah, *Ecstasy of Folly*, esp. 155–200.
[39] *Ref.* 8.19.3; 10.26.
[40] *Ref.* 9.12.17; Heine, "Christology," 56–78.

the capital in 217 CE. In the early third century, then, variants of Noetian theology were preached from the pulpit of the highest ecclesial official in the west – much to the chagrin of his competitor, the Refutator, who depicted Zephyrinus as a greedy simpleton and Callistus as a conman.[41]

If Zephyrinus and Callistus knew that Cleomenes's thought was Noetian and that Noetus himself had been expelled in a synod at Smyrna, presumably they would not have fallen under the influence of Cleomenes. But such was not the case. We are therefore led to suspect the historicity of both the synods against Noetus and his reputed expulsion. Noetian theology – often called "monarchian" – was simply one theological option in late second-century Christianity. It seems to have been particularly popular in Asia Minor, where the New Prophecy emerged. Noetian theology was only hereticalized, it seems, after Noetus and his immediate followers had died.[42]

Other theologians emphasized the sole monarchy of God, including one Praxeas, a confessor from Asia who also had the ear of the earlier Roman bishop Victor (189–99 CE). We are never told how Praxeas was related to Noetus, Epigonus, or Cleomenes, though we presume there was some connection. Praxeas later left Rome and successfully spread his theology in North Africa.[43]

About 220 CE, another monarchian theologian was expelled from the early catholic fold – by none other than Callistus. His name was Sabellius. Significantly the Refutator – our first witness to Sabellius – did not portray him as a disciple of Noetus. He believed that Callistus's expulsion of Sabellius was a political move. For the Refutator, Callistus was a clandestine monarchian himself. Callistus therefore expelled another monarchian (Sabellius) to cover up the fact that he himself was monarchian.[44] In other words, Callistus – according to the Refutator – engaged in a typical attempt to define "orthodoxy" by cutting off a person further along one's own intellectual trajectory. The expulsion of Noetus may then have been read back into the history of late second-century Smyrna.

As stated previously, however, Noetus's expulsion is unlikely insofar as his own disciples in Rome (Epigonus and Cleomenes) were integrated into the early catholic networks with no hint of controversy. There they served as teachers of Zephyrinus and Callistus, two men who became the highest-ranking church officers in the imperial capital. Epigonus, Cleomenes – and we can add Praxeas – were never asked to leave early catholic networks, nor was their theology attacked – that we know of – until 213 CE (the approximate date of Tertullian's treatise *Against Praxeas*). At that time, Noetus's thought was still apparently being preached from the mouths of two early catholic bishops still venerated today as two of the earliest popes in Rome.

[41] *Ref.* 9.11.1–9.12.26.
[42] Stephen Waers, "Monarchianism and the Two Powers: Jewish and Christian Monotheism at the Beginning of the Third Century," *VC* 70 (2016): 401–29 at 407–15.
[43] Tertullian, *Praxeas* 1.
[44] Hübner views Sabellius as the leader of the Noetian school in the time of the Refutator (*Paradox*, 44).

Further Reading

Wolfgang A. Bienert, "Wer war Sabellius?" *Studia Patristica* XL (2006): 359–65.

Allen Brent, *Hippolytus and the Roman Church in the Third Century: Communities in Tension before the Emergence of a Monarchic Bishop* (Leiden: Brill, 1995), 206–57.

R. Butterworth, *Hippolytus of Rome: Contra Noetum. Text Introduced, Edited and Translated* (London: Heythrop, 1977).

Paul L. Gavrilyuk, *The Suffering of the Impassible God: The Dialectics of Patristic Thought* (Oxford: Oxford University Press, 2004).

Simon Gerber, "Calixt von Rom und der monarchianische Streit," *ZAC* 5 (2001): 213–39.

Ronald E. Heine, "Christology of Callistus," *JTS* 49, no. 1 (1998): 56–91.

Reinhard M. Hübner, *Der Paradox Eine: Antignostischer Monarchianismus im zweiten Jahrhundert* (Leiden: Brill, 1999).

Stephen Waers, "Monarchianism and the Two Powers: Jewish and Christian Monotheism at the Beginning of the Third Century," *VC* 70 (2016): 401–29.

Part Six

Theologians in Later Second-century Rome

Tatian

Introduction

Tatian the Syrian opens up a window into Christianity at Rome in the late 160s and early 170s CE. By about 180 CE, he was labeled a heretic by Irenaeus, who claimed that Tatian related "a myth about invisible aeons similar to those of Valentinus." Irenaeus also linked Tatian's ethics to the ethics of Marcion and Saturninus, insofar as Tatian called marriage "corruption." For some unknown reason – perhaps unknown even to Irenaeus – Tatian was also said to speak against Adam's salvation.[1]

These motley indictments must be tested, as always, against primary sources. Tatian has one advantage over most other targets of heresiography in that a lengthy work survives from his pen (the *Oration against the Greeks*). This work will accordingly serve as our touchstone and main point of reference in our introduction to Tatian. (Tatian's work as a chronographer will be treated in Chapter 23).

Life

By his own report, Tatian was born in the "land of the Assyrians," which in modern topography probably indicates eastern Turkey, Syria, Armenia, and their environs.[2] Tatian claimed not to boast of his good birth, which probably means that he had one.[3] His father was wealthy enough to secure a Hellenic education for his son. Upon reaching adulthood, Tatian became a sophist, or traveling orator and writer.[4] Eusebius wrote that Tatian won "no small glory" lecturing on the subjects of Greek learning.[5] Tatian was a self-proclaimed expert on religious rites, and he claimed to have been initiated into several mystery cults. In this respect, Tatian's profile parallels Lucian of Samosata's (introduced in Chapter 1).

---

[1] Irenaeus, *AH* 1.28.1.

[2] Tatian, *Or.* 42. Tatian is also called "Syrian" (Clement, *Strom.* 3.12.81.1; Epiphanius, *Pan.* 46.1.6). See further Nathanael Andrade, "Assyrians, Syrians, and the Greek Language in the Late Hellenistic and Roman Imperial Periods," *Journal of Near Eastern Studies* 73, no. 2 (2014): 299–317.

[3] Tatian, *Or.* 11.2.

[4] Tatian, *Or.* 35.1 (σοφιστεύσας), followed by Eusebius, *HE* 4.16.7; Theodoret, *Fab.* 1.20.

[5] Eusebius, *HE* 4.16.7.

The high culture of the day was Hellenic, and Tatian had every claim to Hellenicity. He was a master in the Greek tongue, and made his career on the basis of Greek learning (*paideia*). At the same time, Tatian came from an area that most Greeks from Asia Minor and the mainland would have considered "barbarian" in both culture and language.[6]

Perhaps it was this dual identity – Hellenic and Syrian – that encouraged Tatian to examine the "barbarian" writings of the Jewish prophets. Oracle collections had a certain cachet at the time since they promised access to higher knowledge. There were prophetic oracles of Ostanes (a Persian sage), Chaldean oracles, and Sibylline oracles (in polished Greek).[7] Tatian, for his part, became attracted to the rougher style of the ancient Hebrew scriptures, their ethical precepts, and the reputed accuracy of their predictions.[8]

These scriptures, Tatian claimed, made him a Christian. But this self-represented conversion seems overly bookish. The road from sophist to Christian was not a common one at the time. (Tatian himself represented Christians as a despised sect, mocked and abused by the elite.[9]) Tatian called himself "God-taught," but we know that he had other people to guide him in his journey.[10]

Justin Martyr

By about 160 CE, Tatian was in Rome and had sought out an expert in Jewish prophecy, Justin Martyr. Justin, a fellow easterner, taught a small group of disciples in an upstairs apartment above the Baths of Myrtinus.[11] Justin was not drunk on the sweet wine of Hellenicity; he was an active critic of statue cults and competing philosophies. At the time, he was writing his *Dialogue with Trypho*, a work employing Hebrew prophecies to prove the truth of Christianity.

Justin taught Tatian Christianity as a rational system of thought – a philosophy – and the best one on the market. From Justin, Tatian adapted a version of Logos theology: the idea that God's thought was, in eternity past, projected outward and self-differentiated to become a living entity called the Logos. This separate self-manifestation of God then made the world and humankind.[12] Perhaps under the influence of Noetian thought, Tatian deemphasized the independent action of the

---

[6] Daniel S. Richter, "Lucian of Samosata," in *Oxford Handbook of the Second Sophistic*, ed. William A. Johnston and Daniel S. Richter (Oxford: Oxford University Press, 2017), 327–33. On Tatian the "Barbarian," see Antonova Stamenka, *Barbarian or Greek? The Charge of Barbarism and Early Christian Apologetics* (Leiden: Brill, 2018), 146–62.

[7] Cf. Tatian, *Or.* 17.1.

[8] Tatian, *Or.* 29.2.

[9] E.g., Tatian, *Or.* 19.9; 21.1.

[10] Tatian, *Or.* 29.3.

[11] *Martyrdom of Justin* 3 (Musurillo, *Acts*, 45). See further H. Gregory Snyder, "Above the Baths of Myrtinus: Justin Martyr's 'School' in the City of Rome," *HTR* 100, no. 3 (2007): 335–62.

[12] Justin, *1 Apol.* 26; *2 Apol.* 10; Tatian, *Or.* 5, 7, 12. See further Minns and Parvis, *Justin*, 61–5; Mark Edwards, "Justin's Logos and the Word of God," *JECS* 3 (1995): 261–80.

Logos to underscore God's sole rule.[13] From Justin, Tatian may also have learned about the importance of free will in opposition to reputedly Stoic notions of fate. Without free will, God's final judgment would be unjust.[14]

Justin also shaped Tatian's demonology. They both agreed that demons were pulling the strings of Hellenic culture, inspiring the ancient poets, speaking through oracles, inflicting illnesses on people – in general tricking them into believing that they were powerful deities. Justin proudly reported that Christians were the most successful exorcists in the city of Rome, competing with other exorcists who employed incantations and drugs.[15]

In the end, Justin may have convinced Tatian to give up Greek oratory (which philosophers traditionally scorned). Tatian became a "lover of wisdom," donning the philosopher's cloak and possibly sprouting a beard.[16] As a philosopher, Justin taught Tatian to renounce the pretensions of Greek intellectuals – including other philosophers.

Crescens

One of these philosophers was Crescens, a local Cynic who may have taught Stoic wisdom as well. Justin said that Crescens was a "lover of noise" rather than a "lover of wisdom," that he loved to boast, was fond of personal glory, and deserved the name "demagogue" rather than "philosopher."[17] Later, Tatian upped the ante by accusing Crescens of greed and sex with boys. Tatian also said that Justin accused the philosophers – possibly Crescens in particular – of being "gluttons and cheats."[18]

Why such vitriol? Part of it may be explained by the fact that Justin and Crescens appeared similar on the street, offering the same goods in a tight religious market. Both Justin and Crescens preached fearlessness in the face of death, sexual continence, and anti-conventionalism (notably with regard to civic religion).[19] The Refutator called Tatian's lifestyle "rather Cynic."[20] Perhaps Crescens realized the same point: that Justin and his disciple(s) looked more Cynic than he did.[21]

---

[13] Roman Hanig, "Tatian und Justin. Ein Vergleich," *VC* 53, no. 1 (1999): 31–73.

[14] Cf. Justin, *2 Apol.* 7; Tatian, *Or.* 7. See further Michael Frede, *A Free Will: Origins of the Notion in Ancient Thought* (Berkeley: University of California Press, 2012).

[15] Justin, *2 Apol.* 5.6.

[16] On Justin's garb, see *Dial.* 1.2; 9.2; Eusebius, *HE* 4.11.8; Jerome, *Illustrious Men* 23.

[17] Justin, *2 Apol.* 3, quoted in Eusebius, *HE* 4.29.3-6.

[18] Tatian, *Or.* 19.1, quoted in Eusebius 4.16.8-9. Tatian continues to attack Cynics in 25.2. Regarding Crescens, Abraham Malherbe ("Justin and Crescens," in *Light from the Gentiles*, ed. Carl R. Holladay et al. [Leiden: Brill, 2015], 883–94) proves too skeptical. For a more balanced view, see Runar M. Thorsteinsson, "Justin's Debate with Crescens the Stoic," *ZAC* 17, no. 3 (2013): 451–78.

[19] On not fearing death, cf. Lucian, *Peregrinus* 12, 23. The Sophist Aelius Aristides thought that both Cynics and Christians preached atheism, though both groups would deny it (*Oration* 3.671).

[20] *Ref.* 10.18 (κυνικωτέρος).

[21] N. Hyldahl, *Philosophie und Christentum* (Copenhagen: Prostant, 1966), 245–7.

Whatever the case may have been, Crescens went on the attack. He publicly accused Christians of being atheists and irreligious "to win favor," as Justin urged, "with the deluded mob."[22] Crescens's charges were standard at the time, since Christians spoke of an invisible God, and did not participate in state-sponsored rites. In response, Justin interrogated Crescens in public dispute, an exchange written up and published – apparently by Justin or his supporter – and delivered to Marcus Aurelius.

In a later petition addressed to the emperor, Justin sensed his end was near. He announced that Crescens would probably arrange a Roman trial against him. Justin would be murdered and – since he was not a Roman citizen – crucified. Justin had just recently witnessed Ptolemy arraigned by entrapment and executed for confessing Christ (see Chapter 15). Now he expected the same fate.

Crescens did apparently inform on Justin. He "connived," as Tatian put it, "to trap him in death."[23] Justin was brought to court with six students in his circle. The whole group was interrogated, stripped, whipped, and – when they persisted in confessing Christ – beheaded.[24]

It is interesting that Tatian was not among their number. Was Tatian defending himself when he wrote that Crescens also involved him in the death penalty?[25] If Crescens targeted Tatian, it is a mystery how Tatian avoided condemnation, especially since Tatian confessed that he – unlike Crescens – "despised death."[26]

Whatever exactly happened, the death of his teacher and fellow disciples was probably a terrible blow to Tatian. The condemning judge was Rusticus (Roman prefect between 163–168 CE) – the Stoic who had taught Marcus Aurelius.[27] According to the minutes of the trial, Rusticus showed more than usual patience and curiosity, allowing Justin to give a summary of his Christian beliefs, even inquiring about his postmortem heavenly ascent.

After Justin's execution, Tatian set up his own school of Christian philosophy.[28] Some fifteen years later, Irenaeus accused him of leaving "the" church at this time, but there was no "the" church in Rome, only a variety of ecclesial networks.[29] By setting

---

[22] Justin, *2 Apol.* 3.

[23] Tatian, *Or.* 19.1 (τῷ θανάτῳ περιβαλεῖν πραγματεύσασθαι).

[24] Gary A. Bisbee ("The Acts of Justin Martyr: A Form-Critical Study," *Second Century* 3, no. 3 [1983]: 129–57) takes Recension A of Justin's *Martyrdom* (Musurillo, *Acts*, 43–7) to derive from the court proceedings. Cf. Neymeyer, *Christlichen Lehrer*, 21–4.

[25] Tatian, *Or.* 19.2. Trelenberg (following Stephanus and perhaps M. Marcovich, *Tatiani Oratio ad Graecos* [Berlin: de Gruyter, 1995], 39) emends καὶ ἐμὲ ὡς/οῖον to agree with μεγάλῳ in Eusebius, *HE* 4.16.9 (*Tatianos Oratio ad Graecos / Rede an die Griechen* [Tübingen: Mohr Siebeck, 2012], 136).

[26] Tatian, *Or.* 11.1.

[27] Marcus, *Meditations* 1:7.

[28] On Tatian's school and legacy, see Matthew R. Crawford, "The *Problemata* of Tatian: Recovering the Fragments of a Second-century Christian Intellectual," *JTS* 67 (2016): 542–75 at 570–3.

[29] Irenaeus, *AH* 1.28.1.

up his own school with his own teachings, Tatian was probably trying to honor Justin's memory by continuing what he had started. Tatian did not renounce his philosophical brand of Christianity; he advertised it by targeting the competition.

Oration against the Greeks

There was a certain asperity in Tatian's approach. Perhaps Justin's death had radicalized him. Justin had praised philosophy as "most precious" in the sight of God. He believed that philosophy genuinely led to God and that true philosophers were "holy."[30] He lauded Socrates as the deliverer from demons, and imagined him as a forerunner of persecuted Christians.[31] Justin tried to find commonalities with the teachings of the poets. He claimed, for instance, that Menander the comic poet spoke against venerating statues.[32] The Stoics and some of the poets "were honorable at least in their ethical teaching."[33] Justin even theorized that "they who lived with reason (*logos*) are Christians, even though they have been thought atheists; as, among the Greeks, Socrates and Heraclitus."[34]

Tatian, by contrast, wrote with scorn against all Hellenic philosophers and poets. Plato, Socrates's disciple, was a putatively shameless glutton who sailed for Sicilian treats.[35] Heraclitus died in a vat of cow dung. Menander the comic poet was a versifying hack.[36] Stoics foolishly subscribed to eternal recurrence and determinism.[37] The poets sang of immoral acts even among the gods – who were actually demons.[38]

These and other attacks appear in Tatian's *Oration* – a sparkling example of showpiece (epideictic) rhetoric. It is an attack on virtually all fields of Greek learning: against theology, poetry, philosophy, astrology, medicine, theater, (blood) sports, grammar, astronomy, geometry, lawmaking, historiography, and the fine arts. All these systems of learning Tatian discounted as demon-inspired. Yet he did so for a purpose: to turn the hearts of his hearers toward "the Barbarian philosophy" (Christianity).[39]

---

[30] Justin, *Dial.* 2.1.
[31] Justin, *1 Apol.* 5; *2 Apol.* 10.
[32] Justin, *1 Apol.* 20.
[33] Justin, *2 Apol.* 8.
[34] Justin, *1 Apol.* 46.
[35] Tatian, *Or.* 2.1; cf. Diogenes Laertius, *Lives of Philosophers* 6.25.
[36] Tatian, *Or.* 24.1.
[37] Tatian, *Or.* 6.1.
[38] Tatian, *Or.* 1.5; 22.7. See further Josef Lössl, "Between Hipparchian Cynicism and Priscillian Montanism: Some Notes on Tatian *Or.* 3.6," *VC* 74 (2020): 84–107.
[39] On the genre of the *Oration*, see Michael McGehee, "Why Tatian Never 'Apologized' to the Greeks," *JECS* 1, no. 2 (1993): 143–58. Trelenberg discusses why Tatian avoided the terms "Christianity" and "Christ" (*Oratio* 219-24); pointing out the contrast with Justin, who used the name "Jesus" or "Jesus Christ" 97 times in his *Apologies* (222).

From Tatian's education, he was able to quote Homer from memory and allude to Aesop's fables.[40] Most of Tatian's learning, however, seems to have come from handbooks available in Roman bookshops. At the time, there were handbooks of Greek lore treating specialized topics such as the metamorphoses of the gods and figures who had become constellations (such as Callisto the Bear and Virgo the maiden).[41] There were also "reader's digest" versions of philosophy. Some of these were doxographies like that composed by Aetius in the first century CE: lists of leading philosophers with a short summary of their opinions, often arranged by topic.[42] Longer handbooks included biographies. One of these survives complete: the *Lives of Philosophers* by Diogenes Laertius (typically dated to the early third century CE). From such a text, Tatian could have learned his scurrilous rumors about philosophers – that Diogenes, for instance, lived in a tub and died after eating raw octopus.[43]

Diogenes Laertius proposed the opposite thesis as Tatian. According to him, the first philosophers were Greeks.[44] For Tatian, however, the Greeks (like the demons) were robbers who stole from barbarian philosophy – here meaning Judaism. The Greeks had no real claim to originality. They took all the arts and sciences from other nations, coating them with a gilded veneer of Hellenicity.

Scriptural Interpretation

In his *Oration*, Tatian made use of Paul's letters, the gospel of John, and perhaps Hebrews.[45] In a (now lost) work called *Problems*, Tatian dealt with scriptural hard sayings.[46] Similar to the *Homeric Problems* of Heraclitus (a grammarian of the first century CE), Tatian was sensitive to sayings and stories offensive to Hellenized peoples. If the *Homeric Problems* was similar to Tatian's *Problems*, then Tatian probably defended the biblical material to some extent.[47]

Eusebius claimed that Tatian "paraphrased certain sayings of the apostle [Paul]." Thus Tatian probably knew a Pauline letter collection.[48] An expanded corpus of

---

[40] Tatian, *Or.* 26.1 (Aesop).

[41] See Ovid, *Metamorphoses*, trans. A. D. Melville (Oxford: Oxford University Press, 1986); Pseudo-Eratosthenes, *Catasterisms*, trans. Theony Condos, *Star Myths of the Greeks and Romans* (Grand Rapids: Phanes, 1997). See further Grant, *Greek Apologists*, 119, 123; Lampe, *From Paul*, 427–30.

[42] See David T. Runia and Jaap Mansfeld, eds., *Aëtiana V: An Edition of the Reconstructed Text of the* Placita *with a Commentary and a Collection of Related Texts* (Leiden: Brill, 2020).

[43] Tatian, *Oration* 2.1; 3.2; Diogenes Laertius, *Lives* 6.34, 76; cf. Lucian, *Lives for Sale* 10.

[44] Diogenes, *Lives of Philosophers* 1.1-12.

[45] Rom. 1:20 (*Or.* 4); Rom. 7:14 (*Or.* 11.2); Eph. 6:14 (*Or.* 16.2); John 1:1 (*Or.* 5.1); John 1:3 (*Or.* 19.9); John 1:9 (*Or.* 13.2); John 4:24 (*Or.* 4.3); 1 Cor. 7:5 and Matt. 6:24 (Clement, *Strom.* 3.12.81.2); Col. 3:9-10 and/or Eph. 4:22-24 (Clement, *Strom.* 3.12.82.2); Heb. 2:7 and/or Ps. 8:5 (*Or.* 15.4).

[46] Eusebius, *HE* 5.13.8.

[47] See the edition of D. A. Russell and David Konstan, *Heraclitus, Homeric Problems* (Atlanta: SBL, 2005).

[48] Eusebius, *HE* 4.29.6.

thirteen epistles had recently been published including the pseudepigraphic letters
1–2 Timothy and Titus.[49] Jerome claimed that Tatian accepted Titus but rejected the
other two, possibly because he disagreed with their stance on sexuality (for instance,
women "saved" through childbearing in 1 Tim. 2:15).[50]

Tatian knew all four gospels now considered canonical, for he fused them together
into a work he, like Marcion, christened *Evangelion* (the *Gospel*).[51] Scholars call this
work, no longer extant, the *Diatessaron* ("the [one] through four").[52] Recall that
Marcion likely edited an early form of Luke which he promoted as the single and
singular gospel.[53] Perhaps to compete with him, Tatian welded a unified gospel from
four. Marcion was criticized for supposedly making changes to Luke. (How much
Marcion changed or did not change is a matter of debate.) For his part, Tatian needed
to make considerable textual changes to eliminate discrepancies and seamlessly fuse
together four sizeable documents.[54] By harmonizing the gospels, however, Tatian
could make it seem as if he rejected none.[55]

Invisible Aeons?

Irenaeus accused Tatian of preaching "invisible aeons" like Valentinian Christians.[56]
On present evidence, his report cannot be verified. In the *Oration*, Tatian used the
word "aeon" three times: once when "our ages (*aiōnōn*)" reach their end before the
resurrection; once to refer to "worlds (*aiōnes*)" superior to the sky (he mentions

[49] Bart Ehrman, *Forgery and Counterforgery: The Use of Literary Deceit in Early Christian Polemics* (Oxford: Oxford University Press, 2014), 191–229. Tertullian stresses that Marcion (died about 160 CE) did not know the Pastorals. Around 200 CE, Clement reported that some rejected 1–2 Timothy because of 1 Tim. 6:20 (the condemnation of "falsely called gnosis") (*Strom.* 2.11.52.6).
[50] Jerome, *Commentary on Titus*, Pref., in Whittaker, *Oratio*, 82.
[51] Matthew R. Crawford, "Diatessaron, a Misnomer? The Evidence from Ephrem's Commentary," *Early Christianity* 4 (2013): 362–85.
[52] Eusebius, *HE* 4.29.6.
[53] *Adamantius* 1.5 (806c).
[54] For Tatian's opposition to disagreement, see *Or.* 25.4 with Matthew R. Crawford, "Reordering the Confusion: Tatian, the Second Sophistic, and the So-called Diatessaron," *ZAC* 19, no. 2 (2015): 209–36, esp. 213–18.
[55] See further William L. Petersen, *Tatian's Diatessaron: Its Creation, Dissemination, Significance and History* (Leiden: Brill, 1994), 73–6; Tjitze Baarda, "Διαφωνία-Συμφωνία: Factors in the Harmonization of the Gospels, especially in the Diatessaron of Tatian," in *Gospel Traditions in the Second Century*, ed. William L. Petersen (South Bend: University of Notre Dame Press, 1989), 133–54 at 143; Baarda, "The Diatessaron and its Beginning: A Twofold Statement of Tatian," in *The Gospel of Tatian: Exploring the Nature and Text of the Diatessaron*, ed. Matthew R. Crawford and Nicholas J. Zola (London: T&T Clark, 2019), 13–24. For the ascetical bent of the *Diatessaron*, see Hunt, *Case of Tatian*, 146–50; Petersen, *Tatian's Diatessaron*, 76–82, with the critique of Koltun-Fromm, "Re-imagining," 27 n. 58.
[56] Irenaeus, *AH* 1.28.1; cf. *Ref.* 10.18. Trelenberger's discussion "Was Tatian a Gnostic?" (*Oratio* 204-19) is governed by the anachronistic construct of "orthodoxy vs. heresy" and by an outdated typological definition of "Gnosticism."

their climate), and once to mention "eternity (*ton aiōna*) standing still."[57] The usage is diverse, but Tatian never uses "aeon" to refer to a set of divine emanations or intellects unfolding from the Father. When Tatian did refer to the procession of the Logos from the Father, he used language that seemed designed to deny that the Logos was an aeon taken in the sense of an entity divisible from God.[58]

According to Clement, Tatian did refer to a "power" (perhaps an angelic being) set in charge over punishing women who adorned their hair. (Allegedly this "power" also gave strength to the biblical figure Sampson through his hair.[59]) The idea that God used powers or angels to have charge of certain spheres and to punish people was conventional in both Jewish and Christian circles.[60] It did not contradict God's oneness or rule. It certainly did not amount to the idea that Tatian believed in aeons, unless the Logos is considered to be an "aeon."[61] It is interesting that Irenaeus wrote that Tatian reported certain invisible aeons "as if a fable" (*velut fabulam*).[62] Did Tatian in some lost work report on a story of aeons?

Adam not Saved?

On the basis of Irenaeus, later heresiologists claimed that Tatian denied the salvation of the first human Adam.[63] This is a possible reading, but Irenaeus's language could also mean that Tatian "made a dispute (*antilogian*) by his own lights against the salvation of Adam."[64] Everything hangs on the question of "Who or what exactly is Adam?" Is he the first human or some representation of the old self (such as the flesh of the material body)? In a controversy, Tatian cited in support of his view that "In Adam we all die" (1 Cor. 15:22), though his interpretation is not preserved.[65] We need more information to understand Tatian's point of view.

From the *Oration* we can reconstruct how the "dispute" about Adam might have arisen. Tatian wrote that, "in the past, the power of the Logos rejected the founder of

---

[57] Tatian, *Or.* 6.1; 20.2; 26.3. Cf. *Martyrdom of Justin* (Recension C) §3.2 (Musurillo, *Acts*, 57).

[58] Tatian, *Or.* 5.2-3 (γέγονεν δὲ κατὰ μερισμόν, οὐ κατὰ ἀποκοπήν).

[59] Clement, *Eclogues* 39.

[60] Dan. 10:13; 12:1; Ps. 78:4; Prov. 16:14; *1 En.* 40:7; 53:3; 56:1; 62:11; Matt. 25:41. See further Saul M. Olyan, *A Thousand Thousands Served Him* (Tübingen: Mohr Siebeck, 1993), 98–109.

[61] Crawford's hypothesis that Irenaeus (among others) took Tatian's "heavenly beings" (technically, Tatian mentioned only a single "power" over hair) to be "a host of Valentinian-like aeons" is unconvincing ("*Problemata*," 551–2). The "like" in Crawford's "Valentinian-like" aeons hedges too much.

[62] Irenaeus, *AH* 1.28.1 (*aeonas quosdam invisibiles … velut fabulum enarrans*).

[63] *Ref.* 8.16.1 (Ἀδὰμ φάσκει μὴ σῴζεσθαι); Epiphanius, *Pan.* 46.2.1 (φάσκει μὴ σῴζεσθαι τὸν Ἀδάμ).

[64] Irenaeus, *AH* 1.28.1, using the Greek of Eusebius, *HE* 4.29.3 (τῇ δὲ τοῦ Ἀδάμ σωτηρίᾳ παρ' ἑαυτοῦ τὴν ἀντιλογίαν ποιησάμενος). Cf. the Latin: *Adae autem saluti ex se contradictionem faciens.* Ἀντιλογία can mean "controversy," "dispute" (*LSJ s.v.* ἀντιλογέω, ἀντιλέγω), "exchange of arguments," "objection," "disputation" (*Cambridge Greek Lexicon*, ed. J. Diggle et al. [Cambridge: Cambridge University Press, 2021], 1:144).

[65] Irenaeus, *AH* 3.23.8.

madness along with those who followed his way of life; and the one in God's image, when the stronger spirit separated from him, became mortal. On account of his transgression and madness, he is manifested as the firstborn demon."[66]

In this passage, Tatian referred to both Adam and the devil, but a hasty reading may have led one to believe that the Logos rejected a single figure: Adam. Even apart from such hastiness, it remains true that "the stronger spirit" (which ensured Adam's immortality) left him, condemning him to death. Whether the experience of death excluded Adam from final salvation is unknown.[67] Tatian supposed that souls who obeyed wisdom (re-)attracted the "kindred spirit" and re-clothed themselves with the "heavenly spirit" as a garment of immortality.[68] We require more evidence to determine why, for Tatian, Adam did not repent and reclaim his immortality.

May There Be Light

Tatian also wrote a (lost) commentary on Genesis called *The Six Days of Creation* (or *Hexameron*).[69] It was probably in this treatise that he interpreted the saying, "Let there be light" (Gen. 1:3) as a wish: "*may* there be light."[70] In this interpretation, the creator, evidently the Logos, requested light from the Father (possibly called "the superior God"). According to Origen, Tatian wrote that "God was in darkness." What he meant by this remark is itself obscure (perhaps a statement about God's hiddenness?). Origen did acknowledge that taking commands as wishes had biblical precedent.[71]

The Law of Another God?

Clement asserted that Tatian wanted to "destroy the Law since it belonged to another God."[72] This sounds like a charge wielded against Marcionite Christians. In context, Clement agreed with Tatian that the Law represented the "old man" whereas the gospel represented the "new man." Apparently both interpreted the passage in Col. 3:9-10 (cf. Eph. 4:22-24): "Strip off the old person with his practices and put on the new one renewed in knowledge according to the image of his creator."

---

[66] Tatian, *Or.* 7.4-5.

[67] For other theories on Adam's damnation, see Grant, "Heresy of Tatian," 63; Petersen, "Tatian the Assyrian," in Marjanen and Luomanen, eds., *Companion*, 151.

[68] Tatian, *Or.* 13.6; 15.1; 20.6.

[69] Eusebius, *HE* 5.13.8 (εἰς τὴν ἑξαήμερον ὑπόμνημα).

[70] Clement, *Eclogues* 38.1 (ed., Otto Stählin, *Clemens Alexandrinus* III [Leipzig: Hinrichs, 1909], 148).

[71] Origen, *On Prayer* 24.5 in Paul Koetschau, ed. *Origenes Werke* 2. *Die Schrift vom Gebet* (Leipzig: Hinrichs, 1899), 356. Whether Celsus referred to Tatian's doctrine in Origen, *Cels.* 6.51 is not clear.

[72] Clement, *Strom.* 3.12.82.2-4.

To "strip off" the old person would mean stripping off (that is, discounting) the Law. Clement agreed that a certain law was discounted, namely polygamy. In the past, polygamy was permitted. Christ "introduced" monogamy as a new rule. If Tatian concluded that this Old Testament custom (polygamy) was discontinued, this did not amount to a destruction of the whole Law. In his *Oration*, Tatian upheld Moses as "the founder of all Barbarian wisdom" – with no slight against his code of Law (the Torah).[73]

Forbidding Meat and Wine

Tertullian accused Tatian of abstaining from "foods" to destroy the works of the creator – tacking him onto a twin criticism against Marcion.[74] In the *Oration*, Tatian indeed criticized meat-eating, though in the context of animal sacrifice.[75] Since, for Tatian, the creator is the Logos (hardly an evil figure), there is no secure connection to Marcion's theology. If Tatian was ascetic, as seems likely, then his vegetarianism would have been maintained on different grounds than it was for Marcionites.

According to Jerome, Tatian renounced alcohol on the basis of Amos 2:12, where the prophet blamed his audience for giving alcohol to "Nazareans."[76] In Tatian's native Semitic tongue, Christians were likely called "Nazoreans," "Nazorenes," or the like.[77] With a certain license, then, Tatian might have been able to identify ancient Nazirites (those who had taken a special vow to abstain from wine) with Christians. He may, that is, have considered passages about "Nazirites" as prophetic references to Christians ("Nazoreans"). If Tatian rejected alcohol, it confirms a report by Epiphanius and Theodoret that Tatian practiced a Eucharist with water, not wine.[78]

Leader of the Encratites?

Eusebius was the first to make Tatian the founder of Christian ascetic groups who thrived in the eastern Roman Empire from the second to fourth centuries CE. The

---

[73] Tatian, *Or.* 31.1. *Pace* Crawford, the idea that Tatian "attributed the Mosaic law to a lesser divine being in order to deny the ongoing validity of marriage" ("*Problemata*," 575) goes beyond the evidence. It is not clear that Clement was opposing Tatian when he pointed out the use of the definite article in Gen. 4:25 (*Strom.* 3.12.81.6). See further Hunt, *Case of Tatian*, 179–80.

[74] Tertullian, *Fasting* 15.1.

[75] Tatian, *Or.* 23.5.

[76] Jerome, *Commentary on Amos* 2:12 in Whittaker, *Oratio*, 82–3.

[77] The "Aramaic-derived word 'Nazoraean' and its cognates … became the normative terms for believers in Christ in Persia, Arabia, Armenia, Syria and Palestine" (Joan E. Taylor, "The Phenomenon of Early Jewish-Christianity: Reality or Scholarly Invention?" *VC* 44, no. 4 [1990]: 313–34 at 316). See the evidence in Acts 24:5; Tertullian, *AM* 4.8.1; Epiphanius, *Pan.* 29.1.3; 29.6.2-3; Jerome, *Epistle* 112.13. See also H. H. Schaeder, Ναζαρηνός, Ναζωραῖος, in *TDNT*, ed. G. Kittel (Grand Rapids: Eerdmans, 2006), 4:874–9; Andrew Gregory, *The Gospel according to the Hebrews and the Gospel of the Ebionites* (Oxford: Oxford University Press, 2017), 297–300.

[78] Epiphanius, *Pan.* 46.2.3; Theodoret, *Fab.* 1.20; cf. Justin, *1 Apol.* 65-66 (with Mithras parallel). See further McGowan, *Ascetic Eucharists*, 143–74.

groups were called "Encratite" (from the Greek *enkrateia*, or "self-control"). In promoting Tatian to arch-Encratite, Eusebius proved a hasty reader of Irenaeus.[79] Irenaeus had treated so-called Encratites immediately before Tatian, and claimed that both Tatian and the Encratites disputed Adam's salvation.[80] Eusebius apparently inferred that Tatian was the leader of the Encratites. Jerome later called Tatian "prince" and "patriarch" of the Encratites.[81] Such rhetoric shows how far later constructions can veer from reality. Tatian preached self-control and abstention from sex, but he was hardly the single leader of diverse groups later dubbed "Self-controllers."

Departure from Rome

Tatian departed Rome about 172 CE for reasons unknown. A long-lasting plague infected many, but Tatian was probably more concerned about diseases of the soul. Rome was the place where, according to Lucian, "every street and square reeked with delights," where "pleasure is admitted through every gate" of the senses; where "adultery, greed, and perjury met in unison."[82] Lucian called Roman lecture halls "factories and bazaars,"[83] and attacked the philosophers who in Roman mansions sold wisdom for a fee.[84] Perhaps Tatian grew weary of Roman vice, the bread and circuses, and the (quite literally) cutthroat competition (from Crescens). It is unlikely that Tatian was pressured to leave by other Christians. There is no evidence that other Christian leaders in Rome had any problem with Tatian at the time. Tatian's "heresy" was, as far as we know, first aired by Irenaeus and later promoted by Clement, Origen, and Epiphanius.

The place where Tatian had the greatest influence was in the east. Epiphanius said that Tatian's preaching had the most influence in Daphne, a wealthy suburb of Antioch and southeastern Asia Minor (Cilicia and Pisidia). Tatian's school, so Epiphanius, was in Mesopotamia.[85] One scholar claimed that Tatian evangelized the city of Edessa (in modern eastern Turkey).[86] Where Tatian actually ended up, what he did, and when he died are all questions ripe for speculation.

Epiphanius claimed that Tatian spawned a community of "Tatianites."[87] The name, at least, seems invented. Although Tatian did have disciples, tracing them proves elusive. We know of one, Rhodon, who stayed in Rome and debated with Apelles (see the following chapter). Eusebius also connected Tatian with a man called

---

[79] Crawford, "*Problemata,*" 556–7.

[80] Contrast the Refutator, who did not link Tatian and the Encratites (*Ref.* 8.16.1; 10.18.1).

[81] Texts in Whittaker, *Oratio*, 82–3.

[82] Lucian, *Nigrinus* 16.

[83] Lucian, *Nigrinus* 25.

[84] Lucian, *Salaried Posts in Great Houses* 23.

[85] Epiphanius, *Pan.* 46.1.6-8.

[86] F. C. Burkitt, "Tatian's Diatessaron and the Dutch Harmonies," *JTS* 25 (1924): 113–30 at 130.

[87] Epiphanius, *Pan.* 46.4.1.

Severus. Severus led a Christian group – apparently somewhere in the east – in the late second or early third century CE. Like Tatian, Severus rejected alcohol.[88] Unlike Tatian, however, his rejection was based on a particular interpretation of the serpent in Genesis. Severus, unlike Tatian, also rejected all Pauline epistles.[89] Epiphanius testified that Severian Christians survived until the late fourth century CE.[90]

In theory, at least, Tatian's circle of disciples could have been much larger. Acceptance rates in Tatian's school were high. He boasted that he received old men, young men, women, the weak, and the poor – for he did not charge fees for his teachings.[91] Tatian seemed particularly proud of female sages in his school (unless he was referring more generally to women in Christian churches).[92]

Conclusion

In the *Oration*, Tatian spoke with the silver tongue of the Greeks against the Greeks. He picked up the tools he had learned during his rhetorical education and forged them as weapons against their makers. He declared his own Trojan War in which – rhetorically, at least – he took the side of the Barbarians and declared a victory over invading Hellenes. Tatian himself was the Trojan horse, his mind packed, not with soldiers, but with arguments.

Tatian never used the name "Christian" in his *Oration*, probably because the name of this suspect sect would distract from his purpose of making Christianity seem the best of all philosophies. Nevertheless, Tatian was manifestly a Christian, if an idiosyncratic one. He interpreted Christian scriptures, taught Christian disciples, and participated in Christian rituals. He saw Christianity as the one true philosophy, rejected all other philosophies and religions as myth and devilry. He considered himself, like contemporary Cynics, to be a herald of truth.[93] He taught specific disciples (Rhodon and possibly Severus) in a Christian school he had set up in Rome and later (if we credit Epiphanius) somewhere in Mesopotamia.

Although he likely interacted with Valentinian and Marcionite Christians in Rome and elsewhere, these other Christians had little verifiable impact on Tatian. Apart from the *Oration*, Tatian's writings did not survive. The heresiographical tradition, however, focused on isolated terms like "aeon," while discounting the larger structure of Tatian's thought (now admittedly obscure).[94] His name later became a peg on which

---

[88] Eusebius, *HE* 4.29.4-5; Epiphanius, *Pan.* 45.1.6-8. Theodoret, *Fab.* 1.21 only adds that Severians are Encratites and that Mousanos, Clement of Alexandria, Apolinarios, and Origen wrote against them.

[89] Irenaeus, *AH* 1.26.2; Eusebius, *HE* 4.29.4-6.

[90] Epiphanius, *Pan.* 45.1.2; 45.4.9.

[91] Tatian, *Or.* 32.

[92] Tatian, *Or.* 33.

[93] Tatian, *Or.* 17.1.

[94] Here I perceive a tension in Crawford's thought. On the one hand, he emphasizes Tatian's love of order ("Reordering," 213–18), but also posits that Tatian's *Oration* suffers from lack of order

to hang a distinctly Christian ideology of asceticism. In terms of practice, Tatian was only vaguely similar to "Encratite" groups and we can posit no secure sociological connections.

Most of Tatian's enduring influence came through the *Diatessaron*, a text which became the standard form of "the" gospel in Syria for at least two hundred years. Around 450 CE, the Syrian bishop Theodoret gathered more than 200 copies of the *Diatessaron* in his diocese alone to prevent its use in worship.[95] The *Diatessaron* ceased to be copied in Syriac and Greek, but remnants of it survive in harmonies written in many other languages. Tatian's name may be long forgotten in most churches today. Yet his legacy of hostility toward the dominant culture and the cultivation of a stricter morality still survives – indeed, thrives – in a host of Christian movements today.

Further Reading

Matthew R. Crawford, "The *Problemata* of Tatian: Recovering the Fragments of a Second-century Christian Intellectual," *JTS* 67 (2016): 542–75.

Matthew R. Crawford, "Reordering the Confusion: Tatian, the Second Sophistic, and the So-called Diatessaron," *ZAC* 19, no. 2 (2015): 209–36.

Matthew R. Crawford and Nicholas J. Zola, eds., *The Gospel of Tatian: Exploring the Nature and Text of the Diatessaron* (London: T&T Clark, 2019).

Paul Foster, "Tatian," *Expository Times* 120 (2008): 105–18.

Emily Hunt, *Christianity in the Second Century: The Case of Tatian* (London: Routledge, 2003).

Miguel Herrero de Jáuregui, "Tatian *Theodidaktos* on Mimetic Knowledge," in *Christian Teachers in Second-century Rome*, ed. H. Gregory Snyder (Leiden: Brill, 2020), 158–82. Dimitrios Karadimas, *Tatian's Oratio ad Graecos: Rhetoric and Philosophy/Theology* (Stockholm: Almqvist & Wiksell, 2003).

Naomi Koltun-Fromm, "Re-imagining Tatian: The Damaging Effects of Polemical Rhetoric," *JECS* 16, no. 1 (2008): 1–30.

Michael McGehee, "Why Tatian Never 'Apologized' to the Greeks," *JECS* 1, no. 2 (1993): 143–58.

Laura Nasrallah, *Christian Responses to Roman Art and Architecture* (Cambridge: Cambridge University Press, 2011), 213–48.

Heinz-Günther Nesselrath, *Gegen falsche Götter und falsche Bildung: Tatian, Rede an die Griechen* (Tübingen: Mohr Siebeck, 2016).

William L. Petersen, "Tatian the Assyrian," in *Companion to Second-century Christian 'Heretics'*, ed. Antti Marjanen and Petri Luomanen (Leiden: Brill, 2005), 125–58.

Heidi Wendt, *At the Temple Gates: The Religion of Freelance Experts in the Roman Empire* (New York: Oxford University Press, 2016), 129–33.

("*Problemata*," 563–6). We need more surviving works of Tatian to judge the overall structure of his thought.

[95] Theodoret, *Fab.* 1.20.

Lucanus, Apelles, and Philumene

Introduction

Like Valentinus, Marcion had many disciples. Some are named and many more, one suspects, remain unnamed. Men as well as women helped to lead the Marcionite churches that existed in greater Italy, Egypt, Palestine, Arabia, Syria, Cyprus, Persia, and so on. Their histories are unrecorded because their very existence was despised by what became the majority church. Only in rare cases did official ecclesiastical historians and heresiographers take notice of certain independently minded Marcionites – in part because they wanted to show how far they had strayed from their master. In spite of themselves, however, the heresiologists provide us access to three Marcionite figures whose life and thought can here be sketched.

Lucanus

One of these independently minded Marcionites was a man called Lucanus (or Loukianos).[1] Heresiographers admit that, in the main, Lucanus proved faithful to Marcion's teachings.[2] After Marcion died (about 160 CE), Lucanus probably stayed in Rome to help lead the Marcionite ecclesial network. But whether Lucanus was in Rome or somewhere else, he continued to refine his master's text-critical work on the anthology that became known as "the New Testament."[3]

Despite his basic fidelity to his master's teaching, Lucanus did make one important modification. He did not portray the creator as evil, but rather as just or righteous. Lucanus thus distinguished the creator from an unambiguous figure of evil, whom early Christians typically identified as Satan or the devil.[4] Deemphasizing the wickedness of the creator was perhaps an adaptation toward Valentinian Christian thought, which also flourished in Rome in the 160s and 170s CE.

---

[1] *Ref.* 7.37.2; Pseudo-Tertullian, *AAH* 6.3.
[2] Epiphanius, *Pan.* 44.1.3 (κατὰ πάντα … κατὰ τὸν Μαρκίωνα δογματίζει); cf. Filastrius, *Diverse Heresies* 46 (18).
[3] Origen, *Cels.* 2.27.
[4] Epiphanius, *Pan.* 43.1.4.

At the same time, Lucanus maintained Marcion's negative attitude towards the creator. We know that Lucanus emphasized two different prophetic maxims: "The one who serves the Lord is foolish (or impious)" (Mal. 3:14 LXX), and "They opposed god and were saved" (Mal. 3:15 LXX).[5] The "god" and "lord" in these verses was taken to be the creator. Those who worshiped him were foolish; those who defied the (false) deity were redeemed. The fact that Lucanus was reading the prophet Malachi indicates that he was happy to use the "Old Testament" like Marcion. The "word of the Lord" (namely, the Judean deity) could be used against "the Lord."

According to Epiphanius, Lucanus hardened Marcion's ascetic teaching by – not just discouraging – but by actually prohibiting marriage. To enter Lucanus's church, reportedly, one had to be single, divorced, or widowed. Celibacy was required, and Lucanus himself modeled this way of life. His motive for sexual abstinence was not simply moral purity. Producing children was the creator's will ("Be fruitful and multiply!" Gen. 1:28). By cutting off reproduction, Lucanus evidently aimed to oppose the creator's designs.[6]

Lucanus's philosophical education shines through his doctrine of resurrection. With Aristotle (and Plato), Lucanus proposed three basic human components: the body (made by the creator), the soul (also made by the creator), and the mind or *nous* (coming from the good God).[7] In the resurrection, both body and soul are dissolved. Only mind, the true self, rises pure and free to heaven.[8]

Aristotle was one of the first to develop a theory of a perduring human *nous*, but Lucanus was probably more directly dependent on second-century Platonists. Plutarch, for instance, told a myth of two deaths. The first death occurs when the soul separates from the body on earth. The second death happens on the moon, when the *nous* separates from the soul and goes to live in the sun (symbol of the intelligible world).[9] The sole survival of the *nous*, which early Christians called *pneuma*, became a widespread idea among Christian intellectuals of the time.

By about 185 CE, Lucanus had probably died or departed from Rome, for he is not mentioned as a Marcionite leader by Rhodon, who wrote against Marcionites in the capital around that time.

Apelles

Lucanus was an important disciple of Marcion, but he was outshone by Apelles. Apelles was perhaps a fellow student with Lucanus in the late 140s or early 150s CE.

---

[5] Epiphanius, *Pan.* 43.1.4.

[6] Cf. *Testimony of Truth* IX,3 29.26–30.17.

[7] This basic division can already be seen in Plato, *Timaeus* 30b.

[8] Tertullian, *Resurrection* 2.12.

[9] Plutarch, *Face in the Moon* 941a–945d. See further William A. Beardslee, "De Facie quae in Orbe Lunae Apparet (*Moralia* 920A-945D)," in *Plutarch's Theological Writings and Early Christian Literature*, ed. H. D. Betz (Leiden: Brill, 1975), 286–8; Deuse, "Plutarch's Eschatological Myths," in *On the* Daimonion *of Socrates*, ed. Günther Nesselrath (Tübingen: Mohr Siebeck, 2010), 184–6.

Yet Apelles, assuming he was in Rome with Marcion, did not remain there. After instruction from his teacher, he traveled to Alexandria, perhaps on a defined mission. There he remained for as long as twenty years, absorbing the intellectual culture of the Egyptian metropolis – one-time home of Valentinus, Carpocrates, and Basilides. In Alexandria, Apelles possibly encountered Pantaenus, reputed teacher of Clement of Alexandria.

Perhaps it was due in part to Alexandria's vibrant intellectual culture that Apelles pushed Marcion's thought in new directions. In line with the prevailing Christian theology of his time, Apelles strongly emphasized the oneness and single rule of the good God, the Father of Jesus Christ. He specifically categorized the creator as an angel, not a god. This angel, Apelles agreed with Lucanus (and the Valentinians), was not evil but just.[10] The just creator was associated with fire, probably on the basis of Deut. 4:24, "The Lord … is a consuming fire."[11]

According to Apelles, the creator made both the world and the human body.[12] The soul (or perhaps *nous*, as in Lucanus) was a creation of the good and true God. Souls were preexistent and heavenly. They were enticed by the material delights of this world sometime before or after the creator fused them to flesh.

Although the creator-angel attempted to make the world according to the model of the transcendent realm above (as in Plato's *Timaeus*), his work fell short of perfection. Thus the whole creation became dyed with the maker's remorse.[13] This notion apparently builds on the creator's repentance in Gen. 6:6.

Apelles did not blame the creator for inspiring evil. A renegade angel flew loose in the heavens, namely the devil. Apparently as a result of the devil's terrorism, the creator requested the good God to send his Son to correct the world.[14] According to Apelles, Christ alone, not the Hebrew prophets, was sent by the true God to redeem humanity.[15] For this notion, Apelles may have leaned on the gospel of John (10:7-8), which depicted Christ alone as the good shepherd while his predecessors are branded as brigands.

[10] *Ref.* 7.38.1. Cf. Tertullian, *Pr. Haer.* 34; *Resurrection* 5; *On the Soul* 23.
[11] *Pace* Katharina Greschat (*Apelles und Hermogenes: Zwei theologische Lehrer des zweiten Jahrhunderts* [Leiden: Brill, 2000], 90–6) and Meike Willing ("Die neue Frage des Marcionschülers Apelles – zur Rezeption marcionitischen Gedankenguts," in May and Greschat, eds, *Marcion*, 221–31 at 221), it is not advisable to follow the Refutator (*Ref.* 7.38.1; 10.20.1) and distinguish the angelic creator from yet another fiery angel who created the human body. The Refutator shows a tendency to multiply divine beings unnecessarily (in *Ref.* 10.20, he counts five: the good God, the creator, a fiery god, an evil being, and Christ).
[12] Tertullian, *Resurrection* 5.2; *Flesh of Christ* 8.
[13] Tertullian, *Flesh of Christ* 8.1.
[14] Origen *Epistle to Titus* via Pamphilus, *Apology* 33 in René Amacker and Éric Junod, *Pamphile et Eusèbe de Césarée apologie pour Origène suivi de Rufin d'Aquilée Sur la falsification des livres d'Origène*, SC 464 (Paris: Cerf, 2002), 80.
[15] Origen, *Cels.* 5.54; Origen, *Commentary on Titus* via Pamphilus, *Apology* 33.

Christ's Body

Like the Valentinians, Apelles theorized about the nature of Jesus's body. When Christ descended through the heavens, he generated his own body out of stellar substance (namely, aether).[16] With this starry body, Christ blended in with heavenly beings.[17] When he arrived on earth, he wove his body from the four "essential constituents of the universe (that is, from the hot, cold, moist, and dry)."[18]

These teachings resonate with the medical literature of the day. Athenaeus the first-century CE physician wrote: "The elements of medicine are, as some of the ancients supposed, the hot, the cold, the wet, and the dry. From these simplest of elements … humanity is composed and into these … humanity is dissolved."[19] Apelles's Jesus, in short, employed a body with the same elements as all human bodies. His flesh was true flesh which dissolved after death.

Because Christ generated his own body, there was no need for him to be born from a virgin. Though Jesus was not an angel, he appeared in flesh just as angels appeared to Abraham of old (Gen. 18).[20] (They could eat and drink but they were not born.) The fact that Jesus did not have a mother was proved by the story of those who told Christ that his mother and brothers were standing outside. Jesus asked: "Who are my mother and brothers?" (*Evangelion* 8:20-21).[21] The statement proved, according to Apelles, that Jesus did not recognize any physical kin.

After Jesus died on the cross, he returned to life on the third day and showed his disciples the marks of the nails and the hole in his side (John 20:20, 25, 27; *Evangelion* 24:39). For Apelles, "Christ allowed himself to suffer in that very same body, was truly crucified and truly buried and truly arose, and showed that very flesh to his own disciples."[22] The resurrection body was no phantom; but when Christ rose to heaven, he stripped away the earthly elements of his body and rose as a pure spirit on high.[23]

Return to Rome

Probably after Lucanus's death, Apelles returned to Rome – perhaps intending to take up Marcion's mantle.[24] He likely arrived about 180 CE, since Irenaeus,

---

[16] Tertullian, *Flesh of Christ* 6.3; 8.5.

[17] *Ref.* 7.38.3. Cf. *Ascension of Isaiah* 10; *Epistle of the Apostles* 13:1-2; Simon of Samaria in Epiphanius, *Pan.* 21.2.4.

[18] *Ref.* 7.38.3; Epiphanius, *Pan.* 44.2.3. Heresiologists tend to conflate Christ's sidereal and elemental bodies. For the two conceptions of Christ's body (which probably refer to two different bodies adapted to two different ecologies), see Greschat, *Apelles*, 102–9.

[19] In Galen, *Medical Definitions* 31 in K. G. Kühn, ed., *Claudii Galeni Opera Omnia*, 20 vols. (Leipzig: Knobloch, 1821–33), 19:356.

[20] Tertullian, *Flesh of Christ* 6.3.

[21] Tertullian, *Flesh of Christ* 7.1; cf. *AM* 4.19.7.

[22] Epiphanius, *Pan.* 44.2.7.

[23] *Ref.* 7.38.4-5; Pseudo-Tertullian, *AAH* 6.5. Cf. Philo, *Life of Moses* 2.288.

[24] Rufinus called Apelles Marcion's "successor" (*On the Falsification of Origen's Books* 7 [SC 464:302]).

who wrote *Against Heresies* about this time, did not mention Apelles. While in Rome, Apelles attracted many followers. Yet his new teachings and ideas proved controversial, and he had to compete with already-established Marcionite leaders.

The Marcionite church in Rome, like the early catholic church of the time, was diverse. Different house churches supported a variety of leaders with diverse views. About 185 CE, Rhodon identified what he thought were three different Marcionite branches in Rome. The first was led by Apelles. Apelles emphasized a single God as the principle from whom all reality developed. A second church was co-led by Potitus and Basilicus. Reportedly, they emphasized a more dualistic system in which good and evil were opposing principles. Syneros, a third Marcionite leader, putatively proposed three principles.[25]

Rhodon aimed to make Marcionite Christians seem hopelessly conflicted. When one looks under the surface, however, one finds basic theological continuities among the Marcionite leaders. The "three principles" of Syneros, for instance, seem to be nothing more than the good God, just creator, and evil angel (that is, devil) proposed by Apelles and Lucanus.[26] One could combine, that is, pseudo-divine entities (the creator and the devil) with a true God existing on a higher plane. They were not co-equal "principles."

Heresiographers made it seem as if Apelles rebelled against Marcion and set up an opposing church, but neither point seems accurate. Apelles formed his own ecclesial network, to be sure, but he showed no antagonism toward Marcion; nor did he oppose pre-established Marcionite churches in Rome. Apelles agreed with Marcionite teaching on major points. For instance, the good God and Father of Jesus Christ was different than the creator; the creator was not good; Christ truly suffered, and so on. Apelles employed Marcionite scriptures, maintained Marcionite asceticism, and practiced Marcionite sacraments.[27] He continued Marcion's policy of discouraging marriage.[28] Like Marcion, Apelles ate no meat and remained celibate.[29] He did not despise the flesh, but rejected its final salvation. In line with Lucanus, he preached that resurrected humans, following Christ, ascend to heaven in spirit bodies.[30]

---

[25] Rhodon in Eusebius, *HE* 5.13.2-4.

[26] Marcionite three principal systems appear in *Adamantius* 1.2; Epiphanius, *Pan.* 42. Cf. the good God, just Sabaoth, and evil Yaldabaoth in *Nat. Rulers* II,4 86.27–96.17.

[27] Cyprian referred to the baptisms of Marcion and Apelles in a single breath (*Epistle* 74.7). Almost two hundred years after Apelles died, Marcellus of Ancyra "quoted" Apelles to the effect that Marcion deceived people by introducing two principles (*On the Holy Church* 17 in Alistair H. B. Logan, "Marcellus of Ancyra (Pseudo-Anthimus), 'On the Holy Church': Text, Translation and Commentary," *JTS* 51, no. 1 [2000]: 81–112 at 93).

[28] Tertullian, *Pr. Haer.* 33, claimed – I think wrongly – that Apelles forbade marriage.

[29] Rhodon in Eusebius, *HE* 5.13.

[30] Attempts to emphasize a firm break between Marcionite and Apellian theology depend on Harnack's reconstruction of Marcionite thought. Willing claims that Marcion's "split between the creator and the redeemer god" and his "differentiation of the just Law and good gospel" are not transmitted by Apelles, but there is no evidence that Apelles disagreed with these points ("Die neue Frage," 231).

Philumene

At some point during his ministry, Apelles met a virgin prophetess named Philumene. So pure was this woman that she was likened to an angel of light.[31] It was thought that, due to her spiritual and physical purity, Philumene saw visions. She said that at times a young man appeared to her, identifying himself sometimes as Jesus and sometimes as Paul. Apparently this young man gave interpretations of scriptures, interpretations which were thought to come from Jesus and Paul themselves. Philumene was also said to predict the future by divine inspiration which she received either in sleep or in a trance state. Apelles would report her prophecies in private to those with specific inquiries in the manner of an oracle.[32]

Apelles inscribed some of Philumene's prophecies into a (now lost) book called *Manifestations*.[33] His activity resembled the practice of literate members in the New Prophecy: educated men compiled oracle collections of venerated female prophets like Priscilla, Maximilla, and Quintilla. Such collections (now in fragments) give the lie to the claim that it was forbidden for a woman to speak in church (2 Tim. 2:18). Female prophets like Philumene probably spoke in religious settings on a regular basis.[34]

In addition to being a prophetess, Philumene reportedly worked miracles.[35] It was said that she lived on a single large loaf of bread. She preserved this bread by pushing it into the narrow neck of a glass bottle. When she desired to eat, she would extract the bread undamaged by pulling it through the bottleneck with her fingertips.[36] It is difficult to know what to make of this story. We might easily credit the idea that Philumene preserved her bread in glass and ate only scraps. The fact that she could pull the bread out by dexterity may or may not seem miraculous today.

Philumene's influence on Apelles's theology was evidently considerable. It was she, according to Tertullian, who taught Apelles that Christ was clothed in "true and solid flesh."[37] She showed him that even souls are gendered; male bodies receive their gender by being joined with male souls and vice versa for females.[38] Tertullian

---

[31] Tertullian, *Pr. Haer.* 6.5-6; *Flesh of Christ* 24.3.

[32] Augustine, *Heresies* 24 in R. Vander Plaetse and C. Beukers, eds., *De Haeresibus* (Turnholt: Brepols 1969), 301.

[33] Tertullian, *Pr. Haer.* 30.

[34] Denzey Lewis is correct to say that heresiographical portraits of women are "polemically-charged"; but to state that they are "not historical" in the end devalues real women of the past by removing them from the stage of history ("Women and Independent Religious Specialists in Second-Century Rome," in Tervahauta, ed., *Women and Knowledge*, 21–38 at 36).

[35] Tertullian, *Pr. Haer.* 6 (end).

[36] Augustine, *Heresies* 24.

[37] Tertullian, *AM* 3.11; *Flesh of Christ* 6.1.

[38] Tertullian, *On the Soul* 36.3. See further Roman Hanig, "Der Beitrag der Philumene zur Theologie der Apelleianer," *ZAC* 3 (1999): 241–77.

scorned Apelles for following Philumene. Interestingly, however, Tertullian also described the vision of a prophetess in North Africa who claimed to see human souls, solid to the touch, in the shape of fleshly bodies.[39]

Debate with Rhodon

When Apelles was old (between 180–195 CE), he joined in debate with the afore-mentioned Rhodon. How long the debate lasted is unknown (ancient debates were known to extend over several days). At some point during the exchange, Apelles refused to be caught up in the captious doctrinal differences among Christians at Rome. Instead, he called upon Rhodon to recognize the common core of their religion: faith in the crucified one. This belief alone can save, Apelles confessed, if it is joined with good works.[40]

When Rhodon demanded that Apelles prove on rational grounds his doctrine of a single God – a view that Rhodon himself held – Apelles professed that such a point could not be proved by logic. The transcendent God was not an object of rational knowledge. Believing in such a God was the ground of Christian thought, not an inference based on other principles.[41] Either one accepted an unborn, good God as a first principle, or one did not.

In response, Rhodon "laughed and condemned" Apelles because he could not establish his theology with rational arguments.[42] Rhodon's attitude here resembles that of Galen and Celsus. These Platonically minded intellectuals scorned Christians for believing things not based upon rational demonstration.[43] Apelles's own position seems to have been closer to that of Clement of Alexandria, who wrote: "Knowledge is a state concerned with demonstration, but faith is grace (coming) from indemonstrables."[44] A similar sentiment also appears in the *Treatise on Resurrection* (Chapter 13).[45]

---

[39] Tertullian, *On the Soul* 9.

[40] Rhodon in Eusebius, *HE* 5.13.4.

[41] Greschat, *Apelles*, 124.

[42] Rhodon in Eusebius, *HE* 5.13.7.

[43] Celsus in Origen, *Cels.* 5.14; 6 (entire); Galen, *Use of Parts* 11.14. Galen wrote a fifteen-book treatise *On Demonstration* (*On My Own Books* 19.39; cf. *Doctrines of Hippocrates and Plato* 2.2) with a one-book summary of it; he wrote three books on Aristotle's mode of interpretation, and eight on syllogistic proof (*On My Own Books* 19.39-42 in I. Müller, *Galeni Pergameni scripta minora* [Leipzig: Teubner, 1891], 2:115–21). See further Wilken, *Christians as the Romans*, 83–93.

[44] Clement, *Strom.* 2.4.13.4–2.4.14.3; cf. 2.2.8.4; 7.16.95.4-6; 8.7.1-2; Ps.-Justin, *Resurrection* 1.5-7; *Treat. Res.* 46.3-19. Cf. the followers of Basilides 2.6.27.2. See further Lilla, *Clement*, 118–42. Galen acknowledged that some premises are primary, unprovable and convincing by themselves (*Method of Healing* 1.4.6). What is apparent to reason does not require proof (ibid., 1.4.12), but essences cannot be perceived and certain premises ought not to be allowed as self-evident.

[45] *Treatise on Resurrection* I,4 46.3-8.

The Syllogisms

Yet Apelles was no stranger to rational argument. He wrote at least 38 books of *Syllogisms* proving that the prophecies of the Old Testament were inconsistent, self-canceling, and unworthy of God.[46] A syllogism, to define it simply, was a set of propositions from which other propositions logically follow.[47] Apelles argued that if the stories and prophecies of the Old Testament were taken as true, absurd conclusions about God would follow.[48]

Apelles's *Syllogisms* was dependent on a long tradition of literary criticism in antiquity.[49] Most educated Greeks of the time could not believe everything in ancient mythology. It was incredible, for instance, that the Trojan horse contained 3,000 soldiers, as was reported in poetry.[50] It was ridiculous that so many men would go undetected, piled up and fully armed in a mobile wooden contraption.[51]

Apelles launched a similar critique of the Hebrew scriptures. The book of Genesis, for instance, spoke of Adam and Eve in the garden of Eden. According to Gen. 2:7, the creator enlivened Adam by breathing into him the breath of life. Later, the creator drove Adam and Eve out of the garden to prevent them from eating the tree of life (3:22–23). Apelles asked why the tree of life had more power to bestow life than the creator's own breath. What more could the true God have given to bestow life other than his own breath? If the Judean creator was the true God, his breath should have provided eternal life at the beginning – but it did not. The Hebrew god – in fact no god at all, but an angel – intentionally made humans vulnerable to death.[52]

The first couple died because they ate of a tree. But it was not the tree that killed them. If this was the case, then a tree would have more power than the vivifying breath of the creator. It was the creator who killed Adam and Eve by his own punishment. Given this fact, either the creator was devoid of goodness – since he refused to pardon the first couple's fault – or he was morally weak because he found himself unable to forgive.[53]

---

[46] The name of this work is preserved in Pseudo-Tertullian, *AAH* 6.6; book 38 is mentioned by Ambrose, *Paradise* 5.28.

[47] Cf. Alcinous, *Handbook*, 6.3.

[48] Éric Junod's idea ("Les attitudes d'Apelles, disciple de Marcion a l'égard de l'Ancien Testament," *Augustinianum* 22 [1982]: 113–33 at 131–3) that Apelles changed his view of the Old Testament between the writing of the *Syllogisms* and the *Manifestations* is not based on sufficient data. We do not have fragments of the *Manifestations* to adequately judge its contents, nor do we have hard evidence that it was written later than the *Syllogisms*.

[49] Greta Hawes, *Rationalizing Mythology in Antiquity* (Oxford: Oxford University Press, 2014), entire; Litwa, *How the Gospels Became History: Jesus and Mediterranean Myths* (New Haven: Yale University Press, 2019), 1–21.

[50] This is the figure given in the *Little Iliad*, frag. 22 in W. W. Allen and D. B. Monroe, *Homeri opera* (Oxford: Clarendon, 1912–46).

[51] Dio Chrysostom, *Oration* 11.123, 125, 128.

[52] Apelles in Ambrose, *Paradise* 5.28.

[53] Apelles in Ambrose, *Paradise* 7.35.

The creator forbade the first couple from eating the fruit of knowledge (Gen. 2:17). From this story, Apelles inferred that the creator himself knew both good and evil. He reasoned that if it was good for the creator to know good and evil, then it was good for human beings as well. Nevertheless, the creator prohibited humans from sharing this knowledge. The prohibition indicated that the creator not only made an unfair ruling, but also begrudged humanity a positive good.[54]

The creator, according to Apelles, wrongly condemned Adam and Eve. These freshly created humans had no idea what good and evil were. Like children, they had no notion that disobeying a command was evil. A true (good) God, according to Apelles, would never have punished Adam and Eve with the extreme penalties of banishment, affliction, and death.[55]

The pain and suffering inflicted on humanity's first parents was only an example of a broader phenomenon. The continuing and uncorrected disorders of the world (death, plague, natural disaster), Apelles urged, showed either that the creator was physically weak or – if he had the power – was evil because he did not care to rid the world of these catastrophes.[56]

All these are theological criticisms; but Apelles made historical ones too. He censured, for instance, the story of Noah's ark (Gen. 6–7). How could the ark, Apelles asked, contain two of *every* unclean animal on earth and fourteen of *every* clean animal? Aristotle distinguished at least 550 species of animals in his works (as we know today, there are millions more). How could so many animals be fed over the course of a year? Apelles estimated, rightly or wrongly, that the ark, despite its large dimensions, could only store enough food to feed about four elephants over the course of a year.[57]

Apelles's criticisms might lead one to think that he rejected everything in the Hebrew scriptures – but that is not so.[58] Apelles prided himself on following Christ's reputed advice to "be approved money changers" – to detect, that is, the good and discard the bad.[59] Following Marcion's example, Apelles trained himself to preserve

---

[54] Apelles in Ambrose, *Paradise* 6.30. See further Greschat, *Apelles*, 54–6. Cf. Theophilus of Antioch, *Autolycus* 2.25-26. Cf. Irenaeus ("god did not envy him the tree of life, as some dare to declare," *AH* 3.23.6). Cf. *Life of Adam and Eve* 18:4 (the serpent speaking to Eve): "god knew that you would be like him, envied you and said not to eat from it" in J. Tromp, ed., *The Life of Adam and Eve in Greek: A Critical Edition* (Leiden: Brill, 2005); *Testimony of Truth* IX,3 47.14–48.4: by begrudging Adam the fruit of the tree of knowledge, the creator proves himself to be a malicious envier. See further May, "Marcions Genesisauslegung," 89–98; Williams, *Rethinking*, 68–72.

[55] Apelles in Ambrose, *Paradise* 6.31-32.

[56] Apelles in Ambrose, *Paradise* 8.41.

[57] Origen, *Homilies on Genesis* 2.2; cf. Origen, *Cels.* 4.41. See further Grant, *Heresy and Criticism*, 85–8.

[58] *Pace* Moll, *Arch-heretic*, 152, 155–6, who reinscribes Pseudo-Tertullian, *AAH* 6.6; *Ref.* 7.38.2. See Origen, *Commentary on Titus* via Pamphilus, *Apology for Origen* 33.

[59] Epiphanius, *Pan.* 44.2.6; cf. *Ref.* 7.38.4. Ps.-Clementine *Homilies* 2.51.1 (1.55.17 Rehm/Strecker) See further J. S. Vos, "Das Agraphon 'Seid kundige Geldwechsler!' bei Origenes," in *Sayings of Jesus: Canonical and Non-Canonical. Essays in Honour of T. Baarda*, ed. W. L. Petersen et al.

what was useful in Hebrew prophecies, even if he rejected the Jewish Bible as scripture. In this position, he was probably in agreement with Lucanus.

As for his own scriptures, Apelles adopted Marcion's text (the *Evangelion* and *Apostolikon*), though he never ceased to purify (that is, edit) it.[60] From what we can tell, Apelles seems to have been more open to influence from the gospel of John and to other floating maxims of Christ (such as the moneychangers maxim).[61]

Conclusion

We do not know when Apelles died, although it was probably not long after the death of the emperor Commodus (December 31, 192 CE). The Christian movement inspired by Apelles spread from its epicenters in Rome and Alexandria. By about 200 CE, it was established in North Africa and Palestine. Tertullian wrote a lost treatise against the followers of Apelles about 205 CE. Between 200 and 250, Origen undertook journeys in order to combat Apellian Christianity in various cities of the east.[62] He also wrote against Apelles's *Syllogisms*, as did Ambrose in Milan about 375 CE.[63] In Rome between 254–257 CE, bishop Stephen I did not require former Marcionite or Apellian Christians to be rebaptized – a stance that indicates their continued presence in the capital.[64]

To formulate his theology, Apelles used both heart and head. He believed in progressive revelation and supported the leadership of a female prophet, Philumene. Perhaps it was Apelles's interactions with Philumene that convinced him that the existence of the solely good God could not be proved by reason alone. The good God could only be met in the revelation of Jesus Christ, the crucified one. Marcion, I surmise, would have concurred.

What unites Lucanus and Apelles was their attempt to make Marcionite theology intellectually respectable and thus authoritative. They succeeded in softening the harsh "good God vs. evil creator" paradigm of Marcion. They depicted the creator as a just being mediating between the good God and an evil figure (the devil). For Lucanus and Apelles, there was one true God – the Good. They therefore preserved the rule of a single divine being, while handily explaining the origin of evil, which was an increasingly pressing question for Christians as time rolled on.

(Leiden: Brill, 1997), 227–302; Giovanni Bazzana, "Be Good Moneychangers," in Brakke et al., eds., *Invention*, 297–312.

[60] Rufinus, *On the Falsification of Origen's Books* 7.

[61] Tertullian's remarks in *Flesh of Christ* 7.8 do not say that Apelles rejected John. Jerome's statement that Apelles wrote his own gospel (preface to Jerome's *Commentary on Matthew*, CCSL 77.1.1, ed. Hurst/Adriaen) cannot be substantiated and is contradicted by Pseudo-Tertullian, *AAH* 6.6. See further Greschat, *Apelles*, 31–3.

[62] Arnobius iunior, *Praedestinatus* 1.22. The success of the church movement fostered by Apelles indicates that he did not form a mere school (*pace* Greschat, *Apelles*, 38–44, 123).

[63] Origen, *Homilies in Genesis* II.2, ed. Baehrens, 27–8.

[64] Cyprian, *Letters* 74-75, ed. Hartel, 810–13.

Further Reading

Katharina Greschat, *Apelles und Hermogenes: Zwei theologische Lehrer des zweiten Jahrhunderts* (Leiden: Brill, 2000).

Matyáš Havrda, "Intellectual Independence in Christian and Medical Discourse of the 2nd–3rd Centuries," in *The Rise of the Early Christian Intellectual*, ed. Lewis Ayres and H. Clifton Ward (Berlin: de Gruyter, 2020), 81–100.

Anne Jensen, *God's Self-confident Daughters: Early Christianity and the Liberation of Women* (Louisville: Westminster John Knox, 1996), 194–225.

Lautaro Roig Lanzillotta, "The Envy of God in the Paradise Story according to the Greek *Life of Adam and Eve*," in *Flores Florentino: Dead Sea Scrolls and Other Early Jewish Studies in Honour of Florentino García Martínez*, ed. Anthony Hilhorst, Émile Puech, and Eibert Tigchelaar (Leiden: Brill, 2007), 537–50.

Jean-Pierre Mahé, "Le traité perdu de Tertullien 'Adversus Apelleiacos' et la chronologie de sa triade anti-gnostique," *Revue des études augustiniennes* 16 (1970): 3–24.

Christoph Markschies, "Das Evangelium des Apelles," in *Antike christliche Apokryphen in deutscher Übersetzung*, Vol. 1/1, ed. Christoph Markschies and Jens Schröter (Tübingen: Mohr Siebeck, 2012), 471–5.

Madeleine Scopello, *Femme, Gnose, et Manichéisme. De l'espace mythique au territoire du réel* (Leiden: Brill, 2005), 229–34.

Brad Windon, "The Seduction of Weak Men: Tertullian's Rhetorical Construction of Gender and Ancient Christian 'Heresy,'" in *Mapping Gender in Ancient Religious Discourses*, ed. Todd Penner and Caroline Vander Stichele (Leiden: Brill, 2007), 457–78.

21

Theodotus, Florinus,
and "Melchizedekian" Christians

Introduction

Theodotus was from the city of Byzantium (modern Istanbul), the prosperous metropolis spanning Europe and Asia.[1] He was active in the last quarter of the second century. There was a rumor, passed on by Epiphanius, that Theodotus was arrested for being a Christian in Byzantium but failed to persevere in his confession.[2] Unfortunately, we cannot test Epiphanius's claim here. We do not know why Theodotus came to Rome. One suspects, however, that it had something to do with the attack of the city by the emperor Severus in 193 CE.

We already met Severus in Chapter 1. As this industrious emperor swooped to defeat his rival, the Syrian governor Niger, in late 193 CE, he besieged Byzantium. The city would only fall over a year later. Stripped of its walls, theaters, and baths, Byzantium was reduced to the status of a village and forced to pay reparations. The economic impact in the region must have been devastating. Theodotus, if he was wise, had gauged the situation and migrated long before the siege. Whatever his reasons for moving, he chose to go to the imperial capital.

In Rome, Theodotus would have met several early catholic groups, now increasingly centralized under a leading bishop, Victor (about 189–199 CE). He would have also met at least three Marcionite Christian branches, one led by Apelles. There was probably one, if not several groups influenced by the New Prophecy. Asian-inspired communities that celebrated Easter on the date of the Jewish Passover were soon to be excluded from the early catholic fold. There were also Valentinian circles led by Heracleon and the heirs of Ptolemy. These are only the Christians of whom we know.

[1] The historian Herodian attested the prosperity of Byzantium "in population and money" at the time (*History* 3.1.5).
[2] Epiphanius, *Pan.* 54.1.4; Filastrius, *Diverse Heresies* 50.

The Pursuits of Theodotus

Theodotus was a leather worker by trade. Since leather was the ancient material used for shoes, Theodotus is sometimes called "Shoemaker" or "Cobbler." Yet leather was used in a variety of ways, including tentmaking. Heresiographers mocked Theodotus for his supposedly low-brow profession, ignoring the fact that the apostle Paul worked in leather as well.[3] Another famous leatherworker was Simon the Athenian cobbler, who conversed as an equal with Socrates.[4] Leatherworking was a recognized, if not an illustrious, profession in Rome, where there was an organized guild established for decades.[5] Occasionally leatherworking proved lucrative. The poet Martial (early second century CE) knew of a rich shoe-maker called Cerdo who sponsored entertainment shows.[6] Surviving monuments show that rich shoemakers had the means to memorialize themselves in lavish ways.[7]

Like Paul of Tarsus, Theodotus was a knowledgeable man. Epiphanius called him "learned in oratory" (or "in scripture").[8] From what we know of his work, we can infer that Theodotus enjoyed a decent education in grammar. Yet Theodotus and his circle went far beyond grammar. It was said that they studied Euclidean geometry, syllogistic logic, the scientific works of Theophrastus (Aristotle's successor), and the medical works of Galen (still alive in Rome at the time and at the height of his fame).[9]

Galen is a good indicator of the intellectual currents in the capital at the time. He was a man of reason who valued scientific demonstration. He recommended the practice of Euclidean-style proofs, wrote several commentaries on Aristotle's works of logic, and a long commentary on Theophrastus's textbook *On Affirmation and Denial*.[10] He even published his own works of logic: *On Syllogisms from Mixed Propositions* and *On the Use of Syllogisms*.[11] If one wanted to win an argument – and the world of intellectuals was notoriously argumentative at the time – a sound knowledge of logical demonstration was required.

---

[3] Ronald F. Hock, *The Social Context of Paul's Ministry: Tentmaking and Apostleship* (Philadelphia: Fortress, 1980).

[4] Diogenes Laertius, *Lives of Philosophers* 2.122-23; Plutarch, *A Philosopher Ought to Converse with Rulers* (*Moralia*) 776b. See further Snyder, "Shoemakers and Syllogisms," 190–3.

[5] Plutarch, *Numa* 17.2.

[6] Martial, *Epigrams* 3.59. See further Lampe, *From Paul*, 344.

[7] See further Snyder, "Shoemakers and Syllogisms," 195–9.

[8] Epiphanius, *Pan.* 54.1.3 (πολύμαθὴς δὲ τῷ λόγῳ); cf. 54.1.7.

[9] Eusebius, *HE* 5.28.14-15. See further Jared Secord, "Galen and the Theodotians: Embryology and Adoptionism in the Christian Schools at Rome," *Studia Patristica* LXXXI (2017): 51–63.

[10] Galen, *Use of Parts* 3.830.

[11] Galen, *On My Own Books* 19.39-42; cf. Karl Kalbfleisch, *Galeni Institutio Logica* (Leipzig: Teubner, 1896), 32.13-17; 8.7-9, 16 (English translation by John Spangler Kiefer, *Galen's Institutio Logica* [Baltimore: Johns Hopkins University Press, 1964]); Aulus Gellius, *Attic Nights* 16.8.9-14. See further Ben Morison, "Logic," in *Cambridge Companion to Galen*, ed. R. J. Hankinson (Cambridge: Cambridge University Press, 2008), 66–115.

The followers of Theodotus applied logic as an aid to scriptural interpretation. One heresiographer quipped, "If someone holds up to them [Theodotean Christians] a passage from divine scripture, they investigate to see whether it is allowed to apply a conditional [if ... then] or disjunctive [either ... or] syllogism."[12] Theodotus may have been mocked for his precision, but he was hardly the only Christian who employed the tools of logic. The Chicago historian Robert Grant noted long ago that "syllogistic arguments had been used at Athens by the apologist Athenagoras and would be used at Alexandria by Clement and Origen."[13] Recall also that Apelles wrote a work of scriptural interpretation called *Syllogisms* which probably used similar tools of logical demonstration.

Text Criticism

Theodotus had a partner in ministry, another man, as it turns out, named Theodotus. This latter Theodotus was a banker by trade.

> **Sidelight on Banking.** Banking was a lucrative occupation in antiquity.[14] Although it was despised by the elite, we know of the future catholic bishop, Callistus, who practiced banking as a slave in the late second century. Unfortunately for Callistus, banking for a Christian master carried all the same pressures as secular banking. The Refutator claimed that, when Callistus lost the deposits of certain investors, he was so terrified that he fled to the port of Rome and – when caught on board a ship – tried to kill himself by diving headlong into the harbor.[15]

The two Theodotuses worked with three other men named Asclepiodotes, Hermophilus, and Apolloniades.[16] All five performed text-critical work on Christian scripture, repairing the text so that it showed better readings. Unfortunately, we can no longer detect their accomplishments, although we can learn from contemporaneous procedures. In the same city, Galen was performing text criticism on the works of Hippocrates. Hippocrates's great fame as a doctor had encouraged later medical writers to attribute their works to him. Galen had a sense for which works of Hippocrates were spurious and which genuine.[17] He opposed other text critics for introducing new readings into the Hippocratic corpus based on stylistic concerns and Hippocrates's supposed "intent."[18] Following text-critical practice, Galen either used an obelus mark (†) in the margins to indicate what he thought were forged passages, or he relegated the passage to the upper or lower margin.

[12] Eusebius, *HE* 5.28.18. For syllogisms, see Diogenes Laertius, *Lives of Philosophers* 7.71-73.
[13] Grant, *Heresy and Criticism*, 69.
[14] Lampe, *From Paul*, 344–5.
[15] *Ref.* 9.11-12.
[16] Eusebius, *HE* 5.28.17.
[17] See further Grant, *Heresy and Criticism*, 61–7.
[18] Galen, *Commentary on Hippocrates's Surgery* (Kühn 18B:630-632). See further Wesley Smith, *The Hippocratic Tradition*, 2nd electronic ed. (Ithaca: Cornell University Press, 2002), 235–6.

Text-critical practice had long been part of the Christian tradition. In the decades before Theodotus, Marcion, Lucanus, and Apelles had performed text criticism on Christian scriptures. The Theodoteans, however, formed what might be called the first text-critical team that ever worked on Christian scripture. They often differed, to be sure, on how to repair the text. What is striking is that, already by their time (the late 190s CE), there was significant disagreement in the biblical manuscripts themselves, let alone about how to correct them.[19]

The Theodotean Church

From the description of their practices, one might be tempted to call the Theodotean circle the first Christian grammar school. But it was more than that. We know this because by 199 CE, the Theodotean community was large and prosperous enough to support its own bishop. They offered the post, with a sizeable salary, to a man named Natalius. Natalius was a confessor, and so duly respected by other Christians. He may not have been a teacher (no intellectual credentials are mentioned), but he was apparently a recognized leader. Natalius, as we learn, took up the charge of directing the Theodotean community with no recorded reservations.

Natalius did eventually resign his post, but not because he was self-motivated. Reportedly, Natalius had strange and disturbing dreams which he interpreted as omens. He thought that he felt an angel whipping him at night. For a long time, he ignored the dreams until he could bear the suffering no more. He made his way to the place of the early catholic bishop Zephyrinus (Victor's successor). Upon reaching him, Natalius reportedly wailed and rolled on the ground until he was accepted back into early catholic networks.

The vividness of this story does not secure its truth. In fact, it recycles a well-known type scene in Roman literature. Roman historians, for instance, told the story of Titus Latinius, an ancient Roman peasant. One night, he dreamed that Jupiter told him to enter the Senate chamber and demand that the Roman Games (an important state-funded spectacle) be restarted. The next day, Titus neglected the command out of fear. The second night, the same order came in stricter terms. When Titus lingered, his son suddenly took ill and died. On the third night, Jupiter told Titus that heavier punishment awaited him if he disobeyed. When Titus still hesitated, he fell ill. Finally, he arranged to be brought into the Senate chamber on a litter to inform the heads of state. When Titus did so, he was instantly cured and walked out of the chamber whole.[20]

---

[19] Bart Ehrman concluded that evidence for the Theodotean corruption of scripture "is neither extant nor, when it comes down to that, perhaps even credible." The accusation of corruption could more effectively be turned on the "proto-orthodox party" (*Studies*, 300–306 at 304, 306).
[20] Cf. *SHA Hadrian* 25.1.

To outline the structure of this type scene: (1) a superhuman being appears to a person in a dream, (2) the superhuman being makes a demand, (3) the person resists the demand, (4) the person is punished, yet (5) eventually complies and escapes a divinely inflicted ailment. The outline can be filled out with concrete "historical" details, though the underlying schema survives.

The histrionic repentance of Natalius was deemed plausible due in part to the actions of Victor. An anonymous third-century writer claimed that bishop Victor had "publicly denounced" and "rejected" Theodotus.[21] This report, however, is at loggerheads with another report that the purveyors of Theodotus's doctrine in the third century did not blame Victor for opposing them. In their minds, the opposition began with Victor's successor Zephyrinus (199–217 CE). It was Zephyrinus who departed from the reputedly apostolic teaching that Christ was a deified man, not a god-man from conception.[22] One suspects that it was Zephyrinus who successfully attracted Natalius into the early catholic ecclesial network.

Excursus: Florinus

During the episcopacy of Victor thrived a certain Florinus, a Roman presbyter. Irenaeus, for his part, considered Florinus (also from Asia Minor) to be a Valentinian. He wrote to Florinus at least twice.[23] From surviving quotes, Irenaeus implored Florinus to change his views. Irenaeus then wrote a letter to Victor warning him that Florinus had composed books which Irenaeus considered blasphemous. Irenaeus recommend that the books, not Florinus himself, be rejected.

We do not know how Victor responded to this advice. It is Eusebius who, much later, reported that Florinus "fell" from office.[24] It seems more plausible, however, that Eusebius made his own inference. It would have been anathema to Eusebius that Florinus held high rank in the Roman church. Yet Florinus shows that Christians with Valentinian leanings were in fact integrated in catholic networks even late in the second century CE. It is inadequate to say that Florinus only *appeared* to be catholic. He was a catholic *presbyter* – in the church hierarchy for several years. To imply that he was insincere reinscribes the heresiological cliché about "heretical" wolves in sheep's clothing.[25]

---

[21] The anonymous opponent of Artemon cited in Eusebius, *HE* 5.28.6.

[22] Eusebius, *HE* 5.28.3.

[23] Eusebius, *HE* 5.15, 20; cf. Irenaeus, *AH* 3.15.2.

[24] Theodoret indicated that Irenaeus wrote *AH* against Florinus and Blastus, two Valentinian presbyters (*Fab.* 1.21.1).

[25] *Pace* DeConick, who writes, "One of the strategies that most bothered Irenaeus was the willingness of some Gnostic groups to appear to be Apostolic Catholic by using the same liturgies in their rituals and catechisms" (*Gnostic New Age*, 286).

Seven hundred and fifty years after Florinus, Agapius of Hierapolis, a Christian chronicler writing in Arabic, provided an entirely new account about Florinus's beliefs. He asserted that Florinus preached three interconnected deities who made the world and made the first humans dwell in a heavenly paradise. A jealous angel who became Satan cast the first humans out of paradise. In response, the lowest of the deities took on human form, cast out Satan, and restored the human race to paradise.[26]

We have no idea from whence Agapius derived this story; nor do we have good reason to trust it. There is nothing distinctly Valentinian about it. Agapius was, more importantly, not a particularly accurate reporter. He often related heresiological slurs as if they were history. If he had access to a heresiology that no longer survives, it was not earlier than Eusebius and has little claim to accuracy.

A Human Christ

If Victor was prepared to tolerate theological diversity in Florinus, he may have done the same with Theodotus. According to later reports, Theodotus accepted the (by now popular) tradition of the virgin birth. For this idea, he depended on the Lukan tradition, where the angel Gabriel said to Mary, "a spirit of the Lord shall come upon you and power of the Most High shall overshadow you" (1:35). As virgin-born, Jesus was no "mere" human, but he was still human. Jesus grew up as the most righteous and pious man (compare Luke 2:52 and the teachings of Cerinthus and Carpocrates).[27]

Theodotus made use of several scriptures to affirm the humanity of Jesus. He cited John 8:40, where Christ said to his opponents, "Now you seek to kill me, a *human being*." Jesus said, "Whoever speaks a word against the *Child of the Human* [that is, Christ] will be forgiven" (Matt. 12:32). In context, Christ distinguished himself from the Holy Spirit; if someone speaks against the Spirit, there is no forgiveness. In Deuteronomy, Moses said that God would raise up from the Israelites "a prophet like me" (18:15). Since Moses was a man, so was Christ. Jeremiah prophesied of Christ: "He is a *human being*, and who shall know him?" (17:9 LXX). Isaiah called Christ "a *man* of wounds, knowing how to bear weakness" (53:3 LXX). Peter, when he preached Christ to the people of Jerusalem did not call him a god, but a "*man* proved by signs and wonders" (Acts 2:22). According to the letter called 1 Timothy, "there is one God and one mediator between God and humans, the *man* Christ Jesus" (2:5).[28]

From what we can tell, the scriptural canon of Theodotean Christians was virtually identical to the early catholic one. Both Theodotean and early catholic Christians

---

[26] The text appears with translation and commentary in Niclas Förster, "Florinus – ein valentini-anischer Gnostiker in Rome?" in Markschies, ed., *Valentinianism*, 171–92.

[27] *Ref.* 7.35.1 (most pious); Pseudo-Tertullian, *AAH* 8.2 (righteous). Cf. Epiphanius, *Pan.* 54.5.

[28] These scriptural texts derive from Epiphanius, *Pan.* 54.2-6; cf. Tertullian, *Flesh of Christ* 15. See further Grant, *Heresy and Criticism*, 70–3; Daniel A. Bertrand, "La argumentation scripturaire de Théodote le Corroyeur (Epiphane, Panarion 54)," in *Lectures anciennes de la Bible* (Strasburg: Center of Analysis, 1987), 153–67.

accepted the Hebrew scriptures and saw them as prophetic. Theodoteans apparently accepted all four gospels. Although we possess no direct evidence of the Theodotean use of Mark, it is hard to deny Mark's influence on Theodotean Christology (see below). Epiphanius implied that Theodoteans rejected John, but that is evidently not the case if they cited John 8:40.[29]

The Point of Deification

According to Theodotus, the human Jesus was united with divine Spirit at his baptism (an attested theological position since the days of Cerinthus). At that moment, he was empowered to perform miracles. Some of the followers of Theodotus said that Jesus, after receiving the Spirit, became divine. Others said that his divinity was realized after his resurrection.[30] There was no Theodotean tradition, however, of Christ separating from Jesus before his death. The union was real: Christ and Jesus were the same person.

The dispute about when Jesus became divine illustrates the growing preference for Lukan over Marcan christology. In the gospel of Mark (widely considered today to be the earliest narrative gospel), Jesus's birth is not highlighted as significant – indeed, there is no birth story at all. What is important is when a dove, representing the Spirit, enters Jesus at his baptism (Mark 1:10). At that point, Jesus was empowered to become the Messiah or Christ.[31]

The author of Luke, together with Matthew, pushed the union of humanity and divinity back to the point of Jesus's conception. Jesus became divine when the Spirit overshadowed Mary.[32] But the Theodoteans – precise interpreters of scripture – pointed out that Mary's fertilization by a divine entity does not mean that Jesus was a divine entity at birth. He was called "son of God" in the same sense that the (fully human) David was called "son of God" in Jewish scripture (Ps. 2:7) – a righteous man chosen to fill a divine office.[33]

The gospel of John agrees with Mark in omitting a birth story and by presenting Jesus as endowed with Spirit at his baptism. We saw how Cerinthus developed this reading in Chapter 2. Cerinthus may or may not have accepted the virgin birth, but Theodotus did. As virgin-born, Jesus was hardly a "mere" man. For whatever reason,

---

[29] Epiphanius, *Pan.* 54.1.1, 9.

[30] *Ref.* 7.35.1. See further Winrich Löhr, "Theodotus der Lederarbeiter und Theodotus der Bankier – ein Beitrag zur römischen Theologiegeschichte des zweiten und dritten Jahrhunderts," *ZNW* 87 (1996): 10–25.

[31] The Spirit entering Jesus is present in Luke 3:22, Codex Bezae. See further Michael Peppard, *The Son of God in the Roman World: Divine Sonship in Its Social and Political Context* (Oxford: Oxford University Press, 2011).

[32] The gospel of John is less helpful here than one would think. For even though it says that "the Logos became flesh," it did not say when (John 1:14).

[33] See John Collins and Adela Yarbro Collins, *King and Messiah as Son of God: Divine, Human and Angelic Messianic Figures in Biblical and Related Literature* (Grand Rapids: Eerdmans, 2008), 1–24.

however, it was important for Theodotus that Jesus *remain* human, despite his later deification. Perhaps it was to avoid the sense that Christ's body, as theorized by Apelles and the Valentinians, somehow transcended normal humanity. In the Sethian treatise *Melchizedek*, we read of a dispute about Jesus put in the mouth of unnamed opponents:

> "He is without birth" – though he was born;
> "He does not eat" – though he does indeed eat;
> "He does not drink" – he does indeed drink
> "He is not circumcised" – he was circumcised;
> "He is without flesh" – he existed in the flesh;
> "He did not suffer" – he did endure suffering;
> "He did not rise from corpses" – he did rise from corpses.[34]

The Importance of Melchizedek

This quote from *Melchizedek* is relevant because later followers of Theodotus – perhaps led by the Banker[35] – attributed great importance to the ancient figure of Melchizedek. They had read in the letter to the Hebrews that Melchizedek was king of righteousness and peace, "without father, without mother, without beginning of days or end of life, he remains a priest forever, assimilated to the son of God" (7:3). Melchizedek without parents or origin would seem to be an eternal, heavenly being, not just the priest of Salem who met Abraham on his way from battle (Gen. 14:18). Some Theodoteans reportedly called Melchizedek "a heavenly power of special grace."[36]

From the letter to the Hebrews, Theodotean Christians took the idea that Jesus came "according to the likeness of Melchizedek." Jesus, like Melchizedek, became an eternal priest raised into heaven to sit at the right hand of God (Heb. 7:15; 8:1). From there he intercedes with God on behalf of humanity. This intercessory role was important for Theodotean Christians. According to them, "what Christ does for people, becoming their intercessor and advocate, Melchizedek does for the heavenly angels and powers."[37]

Heresiographers claimed that for this (second) group of Theodoteans, Melchizedek was superior to Christ. If this report is accurate, it should be understood, as Epiphanius did, in light of the Theodotean interpretation of scripture. According to Epiphanius, Theodoteans read the statement that Christ was "in the order of Melchizedek" (Ps. 110:1; Heb. 5:6, 10; 6:20) to mean that he was subordinate to Melchizedek in rank. Perhaps it was the application of simple logic: if Christ was in the order of Melchizedek, then Melchizedek was prior in terms of position.[38] Certainly if Christ

---

[34] *Melchizedek* IX,1 5.2-11.

[35] *Ref.* 7.36.1.

[36] Pseudo-Tertullian, *AAH* 8.3; cf. Epiphanius, *Pan.* 55.1.1.

[37] Pseudo-Tertullian, *AAH* 8.3. Cf. *11QMelch.*

[38] Epiphanius, *Pan.* 55.1.2-4.

was Jesus – a man born of Mary – then Melchizedek was before Christ. In the order of salvation, Christ came to save humans, while Melchizedek had a role in redeeming "heavenly angels and powers."[39] These are distinct roles, yet evidently complementary in the divine plan.

Epiphanius went on to claim that some "who are members of the church" identified Melchizedek with the Holy Spirit on the basis of Rom. 8:26 ("the Spirit makes intercession for us").[40] Other Christian sects identified Melchizedek with the son of God.[41] Some others reportedly made offerings in Melchizedek's name, saying that he gives access to God.[42] Still another group was said to identify Melchizedek with the Father.[43] Even if there were no reason to doubt these reports (and one must be cautious), these views likely present developments in the third and fourth centuries CE. Assuming they are accurately reported, Epiphanius did not take time to explain the logic of each position. My inclination, however, is to think that Epiphanius reported a combination of hearsay and his own inferences.[44]

We should at least try to test what Epiphanius says against genuine Melchizedek speculation, such as we find in the treatise *Melchizedek*. In its present form, this is a Christian document found in the ninth Nag Hammadi codex (preceding the *Thought of Norea* and the *Testimony of Truth*). The treatise presents an angelic revelation to the priest Melchizedek. It begins with the prophecy of Christ's death at the hands of demons (1 Cor. 2:8). It goes on to show how the experience of Melchizedek in the past corresponds to Christ's in the future.[45] Scholars debate whether in this work the figure Melchizedek is identified with Christ or merely prefigures him.[46] If the work was written around 200 CE, it could have influenced or have been influenced by Theodotean Christians, even if the work was later revised by Sethian Christians.

Conclusion

The beliefs of Theodotean Christians might seem incoherent or peculiar today, but most of them, it seems, emerged from a reading of Christian scripture. Theodotean Christians, despite their theological differences, formed an ecclesial network in Rome. At the turn of the third century, they had their own bishop, Natalius,

[39] Pseudo-Tertullian, *AAH* 8.3.

[40] Epiphanius, *Pan.* 55.5.1-3 (Hieracas); 55.7.3 ("members of the church").

[41] Epiphanius, *Pan.* 55.7.3.

[42] Epiphanius, *Pan.* 55.8.1.

[43] Epiphanius, *Pan.* 55.9.11.

[44] On Melchizedek, see further the *Second Book of Jeu*, 46 (Schmidt-MacDermot, *The Books of Jeu*, 110); *Pistis Sophia* 1.25-26; 2.86; 3.112, 128-131.

[45] For dating, see J. P. Mahé in *Melchisédek* (Laval: Laval University Press, 2001), 56–9. See further Pearson, *Gnosticism, Judaism*, 108–23.

[46] Pearson argues for identification in *Nag Hammadi Scriptures*, 597. Cf. Wolf-Peter Funk, Jean-Pierre Mahé, and Claudio Gianotto, eds., *Melchisédek*, 109, 159; Hans-Martin Schenke, "Melchisédek (NHC IX,1)," in *Nag Hammadi Deutsch*, ed. Hans-Martin Schenke, Hans-Gebhard Bethge, and Ursula Ulrike Kaiser, 2 vols. (Berlin: de Gruyter, 2003), 2:677–90 at 681.

although by this time they were in competition with the larger catholic network in Rome, Theodoteans still considered themselves to be Christians and were noteworthy for their learning in logic and textual criticism.

Theodotean Christians made a significant impact in Rome. The Refutator turned his rhetorical guns on the Theodotean community about 222 CE, since he thought Theodotean ideas had influenced the Roman bishop Callistus (reigned 217–222 CE).[47] Epiphanius attacked the Theodoteans about 375 CE. His report – written so long after Theodotus and his namesake had died – indicates that Theodotean theology had raised enduring theological questions.[48] It was possibly as a result of Theodotean exegesis that the Roman presbyter Gaius rejected the epistle to the Hebrews (for its high view of Melchizedek).[49] Skepticism about Hebrews persisted in Roman catholic networks until at least the fourth century.

After Theodotus, the humanity of Christ was a common emphasis among theologians. We see a general decline in separationist christologies during the third century, as well as any idea that Christ had a divine "spirit body" rather than a human body during his earthly ministry. Christ's humanity was here to stay, both before and after his resurrection. And – as Epiphanius indicated – Christian speculation relating Christ and Melchizedek had only just begun. The Seed of Seth, for instance, would turn the Melchizedek-Christ typology into something more daring: Melchizedek was not just a forerunner of Jesus, but an incarnation of Christ long before Christianity was born.

Further Reading

Dylan M. Burns, "Jesus' Reincarnations Revisited in Jewish Christianity, Sethian Gnosticism, and Mani," in *Portraits of Jesus: Studies in Christology*, ed. Susan E. Myers (Tübingen: Mohr Siebeck, 2012), 371–92.

Bart Ehrman, "The Theodotians as Corruptors of Scripture," in *Studies in the Textual Criticism of the New Testament* (Leiden: Brill, 2006), 300–306.

Robert M. Grant, *Heresy and Criticism: The Search for Authenticity in Early Christian Literature* (Louisville: Westminster John Knox, 1993), 61–73.

Peter Lampe, *From Paul to Valentinus: Christians at Rome in the First Two Centuries*, ed. Marshall Johnson, trans. Michael Steinhauser (Minneapolis: Fortress, 2003), 344–8.

Birger Pearson, "Melchizedek in Early Judaism, Christianity, and Gnosticism," in *Biblical Figures Outside the Bible*, ed. M. Stone and T. Bergren (Harrisburg: Trinity International Press, 1998), 176–202.

H. Gregory Snyder, "Shoemakers and Syllogisms: Theodotus 'the Cobbler' and His School," in *Christian Teachers in Second-century Rome*, ed. H. Gregory Snyder (Leiden: Brill, 2020), 183–204.

---

[47] *Ref.* 9.12.19; 10.27.4.
[48] Epiphanius, *Pan.* 54-55 at 55.9.17.
[49] Eusebius, *HE* 6.20.3.

Justin, Author of *Baruch*

Introduction

In antiquity, several kinds of ritual experts proffered sacred books (*hieroi logoi*), in both poetry and prose. These texts contained putatively secret lore about the birth of gods, directions for the afterlife, mysteries about the origin of the world, and much more.[1] Some of these writings really were hoary with age. Others were of more recent vintage, although still attributed to ancient mystagogues like the Thracian Orpheus and Hermes Thrice Great of Egypt. For instance, the Hermetic text *Korē Kosmou* (the *Pupil of the Cosmos*) relates a story (or stories) of creation whose ultimate source was reputed to be Hermes.[2] The *Chaldean Oracles* spoke of the creation of matter through a "great god."[3] The Orphic *Rhapsodies* contained stories about the origin of the gods and the world through a cosmic egg.[4] A small minority of religious experts attached their own name to their sacred tales. One of these was a man named Justin.

Justin is sometimes called "Justin the Gnostic" to distinguish him from Justin Martyr. If our Justin called himself a gnostic, however, it was not in a technical sense to designate a defined group. Justin certainly does not fit the modern category of

---

[1] R. Baumgarten, *Heiliges Wort und Heilige Schrift bei den Griechen: Hieroi Logoi und verwandte Erscheinungen* (Tübingen: Mohr Siebeck, 1998), 122–43; Albert Henrichs, "'Hieroi Logoi' and 'Hierai Bibloi': The (Un)written Margins of the Sacred in Ancient Greece," *Harvard Studies of Classical Philology* 101 (2003): 207–66.

[2] M. David Litwa, *Hermetica II: The Excerpts of Stobaeus, Papyrus Fragments, and Ancient Testimonies in a English Translation with Notes and Introductions* (Cambridge: Cambridge University Press, 2018), 100–129. See further Christian H. Bull, "The Notion of Mysteries in the Formation of the Hermetic Tradition," in Bull, Lied, and Turner, eds., *Mystery and Secrecy*, 399–425.

[3] Majercik, *Chaldean Oracles* 62, frag. 34; cf. 57, frag. 25.

[4] M. L. West, *The Orphic Poems* (Oxford: Clarendon, 1983), 70–5, 230–46; Baumgarten, *Heiliges Wort*, 97–121; Radcliffe G. Edmonds III, *Redefining Ancient Orphism: A Study in Greek Religion* (Cambridge: Cambridge University Press, 2013), 139–91; Jennifer Eyl, *Signs, Wonders, and Gifts: Divination in the Letters of Paul* (Oxford: Oxford University Press), 152–6.

Gnosticism. He did not reject the world or the institution of marriage. He did not believe in an evil creator. He did not despise his body or say that Christ did not have a real body.[5] For the Refutator, who is our sole informant, Justin was "gnostic" insofar as *all* the Refutator's opponents grouped with Justin (namely, the Naassenes, Peratics, and his "Sethians") called themselves gnostics.[6] Whether they actually did so is open to debate.

Justin, to be sure, did claim to have secret knowledge. He did not say where his knowledge came from, but from his sacred story we learn that his source was an angel called Baruch (Hebrew for "Blessed One"). Baruch revealed a creation story, or cosmogony, never told before. The last tradent of the story was Jesus, whose secret teaching somehow reached Justin. Justin inscribed his story in a volume called *Baruch*.[7] Most of the story seems to be Justin's creative invention. We possess no close antecedents of his account, nor does it seem to have had a reception history. All we have is Justin's insistence that the story contained things "unutterable," a *mystērion* – or secret teaching – accessible only to those who had undergone Justin's rite of initiation.[8]

To guard the secrecy of his story, Justin framed it with "hair-raising oaths."[9] He thereby compelled – or tried to compel – the reader to maintain secrecy and not to apostasize from the true God.[10] If the oaths were not kept, then divine punishments would be meted out.[11] Ideally, simple respect for the gods was enough to tie the tongues of initiates.[12] Oaths, however, added an extra layer of protection.[13] By means of oaths, initiates of all sorts of cultic groups were ordered to guard the secrets of the lore they learned in their initiations. We surmise that Justin also sponsored some particular rite of initiation (we will return to this issue below). For now, we sketch the content of his sacred tale.[14]

---

[5] Williams, *Rethinking*, 18–23; Williams, "Uses of Gender Imagery in Ancient Gnostic Texts," in *Gender and Religion: On the Complexity of Symbols*, ed. Caroline Walker Bynum, Stevan Harrell, and Paula Richman (Boston: Beacon, 1986), 196–227 at 203; Jorunn Jacobsen Buckley, "Transcendence and Sexuality in the *Book Baruch*," *History of Religions* 24 (1985): 328–44.

[6] *Ref.* 5.23.3.

[7] *Ref.* 5.24.3.

[8] *Ref.* 5.24.1-2 (ἄρρητα, ἄλ<α>λα μυστήρια); cf. 5.27.2.

[9] *Ref.* 5.23.2 (φρικτοῖς ... ὅρκοις).

[10] *Ref.* 5.23.2 (μήτε ἀποστῆναι)

[11] Alan H. Sommerstein and Isabelle C. Torrance, *Oaths and Swearing in Ancient Greece* (Berlin: de Gruyter, 2014), 6–59, 295–303.

[12] *Homeric Hymn to Demeter* 478-80.

[13] Bernabé, *Poetae Epici Graeci* 1B. Cf. Majercik, *Chaldean Oracles*, 100, frag. 132. Walter Burkert. *Antike Mysterien: Funktionen und Gehalt*, 3rd ed. (Munich: Beck, 1994), esp. 56–74; Burkert, *Griechische Religion der archaischen und klassischen Epoche*, 2nd ed. (Stuttgart: Kohlhammer, 2011), 376–81; Bremmer, *Initiation*, 90, 105.

[14] For what follows, see *Ref.* 5.26-27; 10.15.

Justin's Sacred Tale

In the beginning, there were three entities: the Good, the creator, and the earth.[15] The Good is the wholly transcendent God. The creator, called Elohim (Hebrew for "God" or "gods"), is a heavenly being also called "our Father."[16] The earth, also called Edem, is depicted as a half-female, half-serpentine creature.[17] Sometime in the deep past, Elohim married Edem. Thus there was a sacred marriage between heaven and earth. The fruits of this marriage were twenty-four angels, twelve associated with Elohim, and twelve with Edem. The married couple then made human beings out of a mixture of soul from Edem and spirit (*pneuma*) from Elohim.[18]

All was well – or seemed to be well – until Elohim rose to inspect his creation. Rising to the highest heaven, Elohim discovered a superworldly light and a majestic gate he had never beheld before. After Elohim was deemed righteous, the gate opened and ushered him into the transcendent world of the Good. There, Elohim swore an oath and was initiated into the rites of the Good. Thereupon he realized the folly of binding his spirit to human souls. Yet it was impossible for him, now assimilated to the Good, to dissolve his creation. It was also impermissible, having attained his ultimate good, for him to return to earth.

Edem, uninformed and feeling jilted, struck back at Elohim by punishing his spirit inside human beings. She used her angels and particularly her angel called Naas ("Snake") to trick human beings into sexual sins. The plan worked even as Elohim's angel Baruch, the counterpart of Naas, tried to inform the Jewish prophets, along with the Greek hero Heracles, about the reality of the Good. Yet the prophets, Heracles among them, were all led astray by Naas. Heracles specifically was led astray by the vice of lust, represented by his slavery to a woman called Omphale ("Navel").[19]

Finally, Baruch appeared to a twelve-year-old shepherd boy named Jesus, revealing the mysteries of creation.[20] Jesus lived a life of complete obedience in accordance with the revelation of Baruch. When Jesus was crucified by the conniving of Naas, Jesus returned both his body and soul to Edem, and rose in spirit form to the Good. Jesus thus followed the path forged by Elohim, while at the same time proving that human beings could successfully discover and live according to their spiritual natures, rising through heaven after death, and entering the realm of the Good.[21]

---

[15] J. Montserrat Torrents relates the three principles to the philosophy of Numenius ("La philosophie du *Livre de Baruch* de Justin," *Studia Patristica* 18, no. 1 [1985]: 253–61 [255–6]).

[16] *Ref.* 5.24.1. ὁ πατὴρ ἡμῶν.

[17] See further Daniel Ogden, *Drakōn: Dragon Myth and Serpent Cult in the Greek and Roman Worlds* (Oxford University Press, 2013), 68–115.

[18] *Ref.* 5.26.8-9.

[19] *Ref.* 5.26.27-28. For Heracles and Omphale, see Ps.-Apollodorus, *Bibl.* 2.6.3; Ovid, *Fasti* 2.319-26). Cf. Omphale among the Peratai (*Ref.* 5.14.8).

[20] Cf. Moses in Exod. 3:1 and David in 1 Sam. 16:11; 17:15 (both of whom tend sheep before being called). Jesus is also twelve in the temple scene of Luke 2:42. According to Josephus, Samuel began to prophecy at age twelve (*Ant.* 5.348). See further van den Broek, "Gospel Tradition," 375–7.

[21] *Ref.* 5.26.29-32.

Then we learn of a particular ritual – a kind of baptism that imitates the heavenly ascent of both Elohim and Jesus. The ritual apparently involved two separate dunkings or dousings with water. The dunkings represented two sorts of waters: the waters below the firmament (or sky dome) and the waters above it (Gen. 1:7). After passing through the two heavenly seas, the initiate is said to stand before the gate leading to the realm of the Good. He or she then swears an oath: "I swear by the one over all things, the Good, to keep these mysteries and to tell them to no one, nor will I backslide away from the Good toward creation."[22] At this point the initiate was imagined to become pure spirit and thus prepared to enter the transcendent realm. In that realm, one perceived sights which eyes of flesh never behold (1 Cor. 2:9).

Such was Justin's account, and it is one of the most striking fusions of Mediterranean lore known from antiquity. The story of Heracles and Omphale stands side by side with the Jewish prophets. The marriage and separation of Heaven and Earth was known from the poet Hesiod.[23] The snake form of Edem could come from Greek or Egyptian lore.[24] The idea of a transcendent Good is a leaf taken from the pages of Plato.[25] Justin allegorized the amorous relations of Zeus with human women to refer to the union of Elohim and Eden. He even saw the Good symbolized by Priapus, the godling whose erect phallus was draped with summer fruits (symbol of fertility).[26]

Yet Justin's story was most patently a riff on the book of Genesis with other phrases and characters of Jewish scripture woven in. Elohim stars as himself (the creator). Edem is the garden of Edem. The angels are the trees in paradise. Naas is the snake in Genesis 3 who fools Adam and Eve. Moses and the Jewish prophets make their appearance as well. Then come the obviously Christian elements: Jesus is the Nazarene prophet, but he is not apparently Christ (the Messiah). He is not divine from birth. He dies but does not rise in flesh. Instead, he shed his mortal platform (compare Cerinthus and Apelles). He ascends to heaven and shows the way of salvation to the elect who – in their spirit form – are not essentially different from Jesus himself.

Justin's creator is distinct from the high deity, as he is for Menander, Saturninus, the Seed of Seth, Valentinus, Marcion, Apelles, among others. Justin's creator is not, however, evil as in Sethian thought; nor is he providentially involved in the world as in Valentinian and Basilidean thought. Rather, Elohim checks out of creation rather early. He does not have foreknowledge, but he is righteous as in Valentinian and later Marcionite thought. The snake (Naas) is not associated with Jesus or heavenly

---

[22] *Ref.* 5.27.2.

[23] Hesiod, *Theogony* 126-210. For an allusion to Pherecydes, see R. M. Grant, "Gnosis Revisited," *Church History* 23 (1954): 36–45 at 41.

[24] Roelof van den Broek, "The Shape of Edem according to Justin the Gnostic," *VC* 27 (1973): 35–45; Marcovich, *Studies in Graeco-Roman Religions and Gnosticism* (Leiden: Brill, 1988), 97.

[25] Plato, *Republic* 506e–509b.

[26] *Ref.* 5.26.32-34. See further Maurice Olender, "Éléments pour une analyse de Priape chez Justin le Gnostique," in *Hommages a Maarten J. Vermaseren*, ed. Margreet B. de Boer and T. A. Edridge, 2 vols. (Leiden: Brill, 1978), 2:874–97; Marcovich, *Studies*, 114–19; Buckley, "Transcendence," 338–43.

Wisdom. Jesus is human, as emphasized by Theodotus the Shoemaker, but the Spirit never enters him, as in Cerinthus, because Jesus – along with all human beings – are naturally endowed with spirit.

Justin's story – although it combines a bevy of old elements and parallels other streams of Christian thought – still sparkles with innovation. His genius was to combine various streams of Greek and Jewish lore to create a new story of salvation. There were precedents for this kind of storytelling. The Jewish writer Cleodemus Malchus, for instance, presented Heracles fighting alongside the literal sons of Abraham in Africa.[27] Justin's story is no whimsical yarn, but a polished account of creation wherein the stakes – human salvation – are incredibly high. The story was not advertised as creative fiction, but as a "mystery" – secret information passed on to Jesus by an angel.

Justin's Profile

Since we only know Justin's persona from his story, our inferences about him are necessarily limited. Justin's use of Hebrew names and idioms hint that he knew some Hebrew, which would indicate a Jewish background.[28] Yet Justin's use of gospel traditions and his focus on Jesus for his story of salvation indicates a Christian identity as well. We can call Justin a virtuoso expert in Jewish scripture and Greek cultural lore, although he did not advertise his dependence on any previous litera-ture. It was left to the Refutator to claim that Justin was dependent on a story about Heracles having sex with a half-viper woman in Herodotus.[29] Yet the Refutator, in his attempt to forge genetic links between texts, only scratched the surface of Justin's inculturation in Greek wisdom. Justin was manifestly a man of overlapping cultural domains: possibly a Judean by birth with an impressive Hellenic education and expertise in gospel literature.

Justin's knowledge of scripture is notable. He focused on three texts of Jewish scripture dear to early Christians: Genesis, the Psalms, and Isaiah. He alluded to and adapted the gospels of Matthew, Luke, and John which he seamlessly interwove – almost as if he was using a gospel harmony. He knew a Pauline letter collection, citing 1 Cor. 2:9, alluding to Gal. 5:17 and likely 3:19.[30] He seems to have known Valentinian lore, since he used the Valentinian name for Wisdom, Achamoth.[31] His interpreta-tion of Priapus may have been inspired by the reflections of the Naassene preacher (Chapter 25).[32] All these data indicate that Justin was not an early "missing link"

---

[27] *OTP* 2:887, from Josephus, *Ant.* 1.239-41.

[28] Abramowski, "Female Figures," 143.

[29] *Ref.* 5.25, summarizing Herodotus, *Histories* 4.8-10.

[30] *Ref.* 5.24.1; 5.26.24, 25.

[31] *Ref.* 5.26.4.

[32] Marcovich, *Studies*, 118.

between "Jewish monotheism and full-blown gnosticism."[33] To know what Justin knew, he must have written late in the second century or very early in the third. Unfortunately, we cannot locate Justin anywhere in the Mediterranean world, except perhaps Rome where his story was discovered.[34]

Justin was deeply familiar with Jewish scripture, but he did not feel himself bound to it. He did not openly correct Moses, as in the *Secret Book of John*. The most that Justin said was that Moses did not know the whole truth.[35] This is not a rejection of Jewish scripture. Indeed, Justin created a new tapestry from the threads of Jewish scripture, a story that he held to be more true. His revisionary stance toward Judean sacred writings resembles a literary phenomenon known as rewritten Bible.[36]

Perhaps the key question is: Was Justin simply some kind of short-story writer with his own quirky take on Christianity, or was he actually some kind of leader propounding a sacred tale to a real circle of initiates? If we only had his story of Elohim and Edem, we might judge Justin simply to be a good story teller. But his story was also a sacred tale (a *hieros logos*). That is to say, it encodes a ritual, or serves, rather, as the basis of a ritual. This ritual apparently involved a double baptism representing an ascent to heaven and a proleptic entrance into the unspeakable realm of the Good (compare the Valentinian "Fullness"). The first baptism symbolically represented the shedding of one's material and "soulish" form. The second baptism, called the drinking of living water, was meant only for those who were entirely spiritual.[37] The description of the ritual and the oath suggests that Justin did in fact sponsor some sort of two-level Christian initiation.

This theory involves speculation, of course. The devil's advocate might rise and say that Justin's "ritual" is itself part of his literary representation. Justin depicted a ritual because he wanted to portray himself as some kind of authoritative leader. Maybe he intended by his story to create a group consciousness or audience cult. His literary depiction of a ritual is not a reliable witness to actual practice.

Perhaps the only solid evidence of Justin's circle is the Refutator's response to it. He treated Justin as a kind of mystagogue leading a sect (a *hairesis*), which he also called a "school" (*didaskaleion*).[38] He indicated that Justin's *Baruch* was only one of many books that Justin used to promote his particular group.[39] He imagined people coming

---

[33] *Pace* Marvin Meyer and Willis Barnstone, *The Gnostic Bible* (Boston: Shambhala, 2003), 119. Roelof van den Broek tried to connect Justin to traditions of "Jewish Christianity" ("Gospel Tradition and Salvation in Justin the Gnostic," *VC* 57 [2003]: 363–88), but the usefulness of this category is doubtful. See the Introduction to this volume, n. 32.

[34] Van den Broek argued for Justin's Alexandrian provenance ("Shape of Edem," 43), but see Marcovich, *Studies*, 96–7.

[35] *Ref.* 5.26.6.

[36] For rewritten Bible, see, e.g., *Jubilees*, the *Life of Adam and Eve*, and Pseudo-Philo's *Biblical Antiquities*. All these texts can be found in Charlesworth, *OTP*, vol. 1.

[37] *Ref.* 5.27.2-3.

[38] *Ref.* 5.27.5; 5.24.3.

[39] *Ref.* 5.24.2; 5.27.5.

to be catechized by Justin and initiated into the "mystery" of the Good.[40] Here again, however, one could argue that the Refutator is no reliable guide. Using polemical techniques, he was prone to convert texts into movements and to see individuals as communities. Thus anything inferred about Justin's circle by the Refutator must be taken with a grain of salt.

It is also challenging to say anything concrete about Justin's ethical directives. He seems to have cherished marriage, but to have despised adultery, divorce, and lust – a standard position among Christian moralists. In his oath, Justin bid his initiates to swear that they would not veer from the Good toward creation.[41] This stance probably involved ascetic commitments aimed to focus one's attention on the Good, not on the material pleasures of this world. Justin did not despise creation by any means, but he did demand that it not be made an end in and of itself. True humanity is spirit, therefore the destiny of humanity is to become entirely spirit to transcend this world of birth and change.

Conclusion

In closing, one can ask how the Refutator gained access to Justin's *Baruch* (and possibly other literature written by Justin). On this point, unfortunately, we are completely in the dark. We might imagine a scenario in which Justin, to enhance his religious authority, planted his sacred story in a church setting (it had the same name as a biblical book).[42] In this way, Justin self-advertised his "secret" knowledge, perhaps gaining interested readers. If Justin followed this plan, its inefficiency would have soon become apparent, for the only known discoverer of his story was the Refutator, who called it the worst evil he had ever found, a sewer filled with unscourable filth.[43]

More likely, Justin wrote his creation story for a group that was already initiated into his teachings. One of his initiates then carried the book from the inner circle and allowed it to slip into enemy hands. Perhaps, however, Justin actually aimed for his initiates to export his tale. Writing was a way to get the word out. Justin's oaths of secrecy might have been "hair-raising," but they were also a common rhetorical trope. By advertising his work as secret, Justin aroused interest in the readers who suddenly felt privileged to learn his tale. Once a secret was learned, a social interest was created to protect it. This shared social interest, in turn, could have fueled or maintained at least a minimal sense of group coherence.

---

[40] *Ref.* 5.27.1.
[41] *Ref.* 5.27.2.
[42] William A. Johnson, *Readers and Reading Culture in the High Roman Empire: A Study of Elite Communities* (Oxford: Oxford University Press, 2010).
[43] *Ref.* 5.27.6.

In this scenario, Justin's "secret" tale was intentionally crafted for a wider audience.[44] How else, we might ask, could Justin expand his clientele? Justin led an initiatory group, inscribed his sacred tale explaining the divine model of his rites, and so created a sacred text. This text was a creation and salvation story that would have appealed to those of Greek and broadly Judeo-Christian background. Little did Justin know that his story would fall into the hands of a heresiographer who took unsubtle delight in defiling the mystery. Justin's sacred tale became an open secret. Yet open secrets are sometimes the most attractive. We cannot rule out that Justin would have been covertly pleased or even bemused with the Refutator's exposé of his work. After all, in "refuting" Justin's *Baruch*, the Refutator preserved it for all time.

Further Reading

Luise Abramowski, "Female Figures in the Gnostic *Sondergut* in Hippolytus's *Refutatio*," in *Images of the Feminine in Gnosticism*, ed. Karen L. King (Philadelphia: Fortress, 1988), 136–52.

Jorunn Jacobsen Buckley, "Transcendence and Sexuality in the Book of Baruch," in *Female Fault and Fulfillment in Gnosticism* (Chapel Hill: University of North Carolina Press, 1986), 3–19.

Karen King, "Mystery and Secrecy in the *Secret Revelation of John*," in *Mystery and Secrecy in the Nag Hammadi Collection and Other Ancient Literature: Ideas and Practices*, ed. Christian H. Bull et al. (Leiden: Brill, 2012), 61–85.

Miroslav Marcovich, *Studies in Graeco-Roman Religions and Gnosticism* (Leiden: Brill, 1988), 93–119.

Christoph Markschies, "Esoteric Knowledge in Platonism and in Christian Gnosis," in *Christian Teachers in Second-century Rome*, ed. H. Gregory Snyder (Leiden: Brill, 2020), 45–59.

Georg Simmel, "The Sociology of Secrecy and of Secret Societies," *American Journal of Sociology* 11 (1906): 441–98, esp. 464–7.

Roelof van den Broek, "Gospel Tradition and Salvation in Justin the Gnostic," *VC* 57 (2003): 363–88.

Roelof van den Broek, "Justin the Gnostic," in *DGWE*, ed. Wouter Hanegraaff, 656–8.

Roelof van den Broek, "The Shape of Edem according to Justin the Gnostic," *VC* 27 (1973): 35–45.

Michael Williams, "Secrecy, Revelation, and Late Antique Demiurgic Myths," in *Rending the Veil: Concealment and Secrecy in the History of Religions*, ed. Elliot R. Wolfson (New York: Seven Bridges Press, 1999), 31–58.

---

[44] Stroumsa observed: "there is no better way to publicise a text than to prohibit its publication, strongly limit its readership, or insist that it reveals deep and heavily guarded secrets" ("From Esotericism to Mysticism?" in Kippenberg and Stroumsa, eds., *Secrecy and Concealment*, 289–310 at 297). Similarly Karen King: "The strategies employed … in the name of mystery and secrecy ultimately are aimed not at concealing the truth from other people, but at revealing it" ("Mystery and Secrecy," in Bull, Lied, and Turner, eds., *Mystery and Secrecy*, 83).

Part Seven

Later Theologians in Alexandria

23

Julius Cassianus

In ancient Mediterranean culture, a married woman who committed adultery risked loss of status, banishment, and even her life. Men who committed the same crime with slaves and prostitutes could typically avoid such harsh penalties. Nevertheless, there was a general sense that manliness (Roman *virtus*, whence the English word virtue) was proved by control over one's passions, including sexual passions.[1] Extreme sexual license led to public disrepute, which is why rumors about clandestine orgies among Christian groups proved so damaging in the second century CE. Christian teachers such as Marcion, Justin Martyr, and Tatian sought to heighten their credibility and deflect criticism by promoting an ethic, not just of sexual control, but of complete sexual abstinence – the cutting off of sexual desire, insofar as it was possible.

Justin Martyr, for example, opposed any pleasure "contrary to the law of nature," and railed against "adulteries, acts of uncontrol, and all evil."[2] He equated lust and remarriage with adultery and recommended sexual abstinence. He proudly mentioned Christians who "renounced marriage" and "disciples of Christ" who from childhood remained virgin until seventy.[3] One of Justin's female disciples, Charito, confessed before a Roman judge that she kept herself "pure and unstained by the taints of the flesh."[4]

Another Christian promoter of abstinence was Julius Cassianus, an Alexandrian typically dated between 160–180 CE. He may, however, have been active somewhat earlier. We know from Justin Martyr that sometime between 150 and 154 CE a young Alexandrian petitioned L. Munatius Felix, then governor of Egypt, to have his testicles removed by doctors (who, due to anti-castration laws, required government approval).[5] The young man did not simply send the governor a short request. He sent Felix a small tract (a *biblidion*) to show that early Christians were not licentious and to lay out his logic for castration.

[1] Knust, *Abandoned to Lust*, 15–50.
[2] Justin, *2 Apol.* 2; 4.4.
[3] Justin, *1 Apol.* 15, 29; cf. Athenagoras, *Embassy* 33.
[4] *Martyrdom of Justin* (Recension C) §3.4 (Musurillo, *Acts*, 57).
[5] Justin, *1 Apology* 29.1-2. See further Brown, *Body and Society*, 168–70.

Now we know that Cassianus wrote a work called *On Self-Control*, also known as *On Being a Eunuch*. Only a few fragments and summaries of it survive. From what we can tell, the book argued on the basis of biblical texts that people should abstain from sex and pursue the ideal of androgyny (a state in which, theoretically at least, one transcends gender). There is a small chance that this work *On Being a Eunuch* is the very treatise to which Justin Martyr referred. This would make Cassianus the man who pled for his own castration in the 150s. More likely, however, Cassianus was a different man who composed a different, though analogous treatise. In this scenario, Cassianus was part of a larger cultural field in which learning from Jewish and Christian scriptures helped him to formulate an ethic of abstention

Clement of Alexandria called Cassianus a former Valentinian.[6] It is hard to evaluate this claim. Clement might simply have noticed vague similarities between Cassianus and Valentinian Christians. Both Cassianus and Valentinians, for instance, used the *Gospel according to the Egyptians* (introduced below).[7] We also know from an offhand comment by Tertullian that some Valentinians were voluntary eunuchs.[8] In general, however, Valentinians supported marriage while Cassianus did not. Cassianus also exhibits no distinctive Valentinian ideas or practices. On the question of sexual ethics, it seems best to compare Cassianus with his contemporary Tatian. Both Cassianus and Tatian have been called "Encratites" ("Self-controllers"), though they supported different rationales for their ethics of self-control. As it turns out, Cassianus and Tatian also overlap in their study of Christian chronography, an overlap which we can treat only briefly here.

Tatian on Sex

It was Irenaeus, as we saw, who made the accusation that Tatian called marriage "corruption" and "fornication" (*porneia*).[9] There was a similar charge hurled against Marcion.[10] In the case of Tatian, we are in a better position to evaluate the indictment, since we have an excerpt from Tatian's work *On Perfection according to the Savior*. In this treatise, Tatian interpreted Paul's advice to married couples in 1 Cor. 7:5: "Do not deprive each other unless by mutual agreement for a time in order to pray; then come together again [for sex] so that Satan does not tempt you due to your lack of control." On this verse Tatian commented:

Agreement molds [married couples] for prayer. Participation in corruption dissolves intercession. [Paul], shaming them, excluded [sex] in permitting [it]. He permitted them to be together on account of Satan and their lack of control, but declared that the one who succumbed would serve two masters (Matt. 6:24): God when there is agreement; but when there is disagreement: lack of control, fornication, and the devil.[11]

[6] Clement, *Strom.* 3.13.92.1.
[7] Clement, *Exc. Theod.* 67.2.
[8] Tertullian, *Against the Valentinians* 30.4
[9] Irenaeus, *AH* 1.28.1.
[10] *Ref.* 10.19.4.
[11] Clement, *Strom.* 3.12.81.1-2. The translation "succumbed" is Crawford's ("*Problemata*," 559).

Here Tatian apparently called sex – and specifically sex *within* marriage – "participation in corruption." Sexually active married couples who are in conflict serve "fornication" and the "devil." Perhaps it was from this very excerpt that Irenaeus inferred that Tatian called marriage "corruption."

The Refutator claimed that Tatian did not much differ from Marcion with regard to "legislation on marriages."[12] Whatever his report means exactly, it is important to recall that Marcion never forbade marriage outright.[13] At the same time, Tatian's position on sex as "participation in corruption" does indeed resemble that of Marcion and Saturninus. Marcionite (and possibly Saturninian) Christians were in Rome during Tatian's sojourn there (about 155–172 CE). If Tatian agreed with them on sexual ethics, we do not know how much he agreed with them theologically.

According to Jerome, Tatian also used Gal. 6:8 to link sex and corruption.[14] According to this verse, "the man who sows into his own flesh from the flesh will reap corruption." Tatian took "flesh" here to refer to a man's wife, perhaps on the basis of Gen. 2:24, "and the two [the married couple] shall be one flesh." Paul, in this reading, was not just making a metaphor about farming; he was talking about sex. Accordingly, even inseminating one's wife leads to "corruption" – according to Tatian – though it is unclear whether corruption here refers to the act of sexual intercourse, the children produced from it, or both.

Cassianus on Sex

We turn to compare Tatian with his contemporary, Julius Cassianus. In *On Being a Eunuch*, Cassianus wrote:

> Let no one think that since we have sexual organs shaped in a male and female way, the female to receive, the male to inseminate, that sex is conceded to come from God. For if this design was from God, to whom we hasten, he would not have blessed eunuchs, nor would the prophet have said that eunuchs "are not a dry tree" (Isa. 56:3), referring by means of the tree to the person who makes himself a eunuch from such thinking.[15]

This quote has a parallel in the *Testimony of Truth* found at Nag Hammadi (IX, 3):

---

[12] *Ref.* 10.18. Crawford follows Markovich's unnecessary emendation (*Hippolytus: Refutatio omnium haeresium* [Berlin: de Gruyter, 1986], 398), resulting in the translation: "slander … against [κατὰ added by Markovich] the legislation concerning marriages" ("*Problemata*," 562).

[13] See further Koltun-Fromm "Re-imagining," 11–12. Gaca depicts Tatian as unbiblical (*Making of Fornication*, 240). To the contrary, Tatian interpreted the Bible in his own way. On the heresiological construction of Tatian's asceticism, see Knust, *Abandoned to Lust*, 160–1; Clark, *Reading Renunciation*, 31–2, 40, 137, 217–18.

[14] Jerome, *Commentary on Galatians* 3 (on 6:8), trans. Thomas P. Scheck, *St. Jerome's Commentaries on Galatians, Titus and Philemon* (Columbia: University of Notre Dame Press, 2010), 262. Jerome initially referred to Cassianus, but I take "the heresiarch of the Encratites" to refer to Tatian (cf. Jerome, *Epistle* 48.2, where we also find the phrase *princeps encratitarum*).

[15] Clement, *Strom.* 3.13.91.1-2.

But those who receive him [Christ, the Child of the Human] to themselves with ignorance, the pleasures which are defiled prevail over them. It is those people who used to say, "God created members for our use, for us to grow in defilement, in order that we might enjoy ourselves." And they cause God to participate with them in deeds of this sort; and they are not steadfast upon the earth. Nor will they reach heaven.[16]

In both passages, Cassianus and the author of the *Testimony of Truth* undercut the argument from "nature" that the presence of genitals guaranteed the lawfulness of their use. The passage from the *Testimony of Truth* is damaged, so we do not know if this author immediately appealed to scripture (as we see Cassianus appealed to the prophet Isaiah). Interestingly, the author of the *Testimony of Truth* later appealed to the story of Isaiah sawn in two, taken to symbolize the separation of males from females.[17] On the basis of these and other similarities, Birger Pearson hypothesized that the author of the *Testimony of Truth* was Julius Cassianus himself.[18] The jury is still out on this question, mostly due to lack of evidence.

Returning to the quotes from Clement, Cassianus claimed that "someone" (he did not say who) reasonably asked the Savior whether he "reshaped" Christians, removing them from error, genital coitus, and shameful appendages (the genitals themselves).[19] This "someone" was probably Jesus's disciple Salome who appeared as a main speaker in the (no longer extant) text called the *Gospel according to the Egyptians*.

Sidelight on the Gospel according to the Egyptians. This gospel is not the same as the *Egyptian Gospel* (more properly: *Holy Book of the Great Invisible Spirit*) used by the Seed of Seth and recovered at Nag Hammadi (III,2; IV,2). The *Gospel according to the Egyptians* was evidently written in Greek during the early second century CE. It featured a dialogue between Jesus and Salome (a female disciple mentioned in Mark 15:40; 16:1; *Gos. Thom.* 61; *1 Apoc. Jas.* V.3, 40.25–26).[20] It contained three other sayings that would have appealed to Cassianus:
1. Jesus said, "I have come to bring female works to an end."
2. Salome said, "How long will humans die?" Jesus said, "As long as women give birth."
3. Salome said, "I did well, then, by not giving birth?" Jesus said, "Eat every plant, but do not eat one that has bitterness."[21]

---

[16] *Test. Truth* IX,3 38.27–39.15, trans. Pearson, all emendations accepted.

[17] *Test. Truth* IX,3 40.28–29.

[18] Pearson, ed., *Nag Hammadi Codices IX and X* (Leiden: Brill, 1981), 118–20.

[19] Clement, *Strom.* 3.13.92.1.

[20] See further Richard Bauckham, *Gospel Women: Studies of the Named Women in the Gospels* (Grand Rapids: Eerdmans, 2002), 234–47.

[21] Clement, *Strom.* 3.9.63.1; 3.6.45.3; 3.9.66.1; cf. *Dial. Sav.* III.5, 144.19–20. See further S. Petersen, *"Zerstört die Werke der Weiblichkeit!" Maria Magdalena, Salome und andere Jüngerinnen Jesu in christlich-gnostlichen Schriften* (Leiden: Brill, 1999), 208–20; H.-J. Klauck, *Apocryphal Gospels: An Introduction* (London: T&T Clark, 2003), 55–9; Christoph Markschies, "Das Evangelium nach den Ägyptern," in *Antike christliche Apokryphen* I/1, 661–82.

Cassianus quoted the *Gospel according to the Egyptians*, and specifically the saying of Jesus that there will be a time when his disciples "trample on the garment of shame, when the two become one, when male and female are neither male and female."[22]

This saying resembles one found in the *Gospel of Thomas* 37: "His disciples said, 'When will you appear to us and when shall we see you?' Jesus said, 'When you strip without being ashamed and you take your clothes and put them under your feet like little children and trample them, then [you] will see the child of the living one and you will not fear.'"[23]

In both texts, stripping off clothes would seem to be a metaphor for leaving the fleshly body. One tramples this body only to receive a new, redeemed body which is not sexually differentiated. The time when male and female were not distinguished was in the garden of Eden when God made the first human prior to distinguishing Adam from Eve (Gen. 1:26). Cassianus may have thought that this was the original state of human beings. In this blessed state, humanity could not have sex, since there was no distinction between male and female.

Humans were split into male and female not by the omnibenevolent God, but by some lower being, perhaps an angelic creator, such as we see in the *Apocalypse of Adam* (NHC V,5). Here Adam reports to his son Seth: "Then god the ruler of the aeons and powers angrily divided us. Then we became two aeons, and the glory in our hearts abandoned your mother Eve and me."[24]

There is not enough evidence to say whether Cassianus was influenced by Sethian readings of Genesis. But if he did not think that the true God designed human genitals, then some other being who is not the true God did. This false god may be the being who commanded Adam and Eve to "be fruitful and multiply" (Gen. 1:28).

However it was that Cassianus thought that males and females were formed, the practice of sex and birth, he believed, was introduced later by deceit. For this idea, he appealed to Paul in 2 Cor. 11:3: "I fear that, just as the snake deceived Eve, so your thoughts are corrupted from the simplicity that is in Christ."[25] The snake of Genesis 3 (widely taken to be the devil) deceived Eve into partaking of the tree whose fruit, for Cassianus, probably represented sex or sexual desire. Once Eve felt the impulse of sexual desire, she and her husband enjoyed the "fruit" together. According to some Jewish traditions, Eve and the snake had sexual intercourse.[26]

Carnal intercourse led to punishment, including the first couple's being clothed with "tunics of skin" (Gen. 3:21). Like Philo and Valentinus, Cassianus understood

---

[22] Clement, *Strom.* 3.13.92.2. A version of this saying is also found in the *Gos. Thom.* 22 and the letter of *2 Clem.* 12:2.

[23] Cf. *Gos. Thom.* 21a. See further J. Z. Smith, "The Garments of Shame," *History of Religions* 5 (1966): 217–38; April D. DeConick and Jarl Fossum, "Stripped before God: A New Interpretation of Logion 37 in the Gospel of Thomas," *VC* 45 (1991): 125–50; Simon Gathercole, *The Gospel of Thomas: Introduction and Commentary* (Leiden: Brill, 2014), 362–6.

[24] *Apoc. Adam* V,5 64.20-26.

[25] Clement, *Strom.* 3.14.94.1.

[26] *2 Enoch* (J) 31:6; *4 Macc.* 18:7-8; *Targum Pseudo-Jonathan* Gen. 4:1; cf. Tertullian, *On Patience* 5.15; *Gospel of Philip* II,3 61.5-10.

these tunics to refer to fleshly bodies.[27] They are evidently synonymous with "the garments of shame" which Jesus commanded his followers to trample. In short, bodies with genitals were given to humans as a punishment for sin, not as part of God's original plan. Genitals are "appendages" that humans instinctively hide because they do not in fact belong on their bodies.

Therefore, according to Cassianus, it is only "those ruled by earthly things who give birth and are born, whereas 'our citizenship is in heaven, from which we eagerly expect a savior' (Phil. 3:20)."[28] Cassianus apparently meant that the "citizens of heaven" (his brand of ascetic Christians) did not engage in the practice of sex and procreation. They made themselves eunuchs for the kingdom of heaven, according to Jesus's saying in Matt. 19:12: "there are eunuchs who castrate themselves for the sake of the kingdom of heaven."

Cassianus may also have disparaged birth on the basis of Jeremiah 20:14, where the prophet cries out, "Cursed be the day of my birth!" The prophet who said this could not, according to Cassianus, have agreed with the being who commanded Adam and Eve to have sex (Gen. 1:28).[29]

On the basis of this discussion, Clement of Alexandria concluded that Cassianus held that Jesus was not truly born but only appeared on earth.[30] This claim appears to have been his own inference. The truth about Cassianus's view of Christ is difficult to recover, largely because Clement did not quote any actual material from Cassianus about the constitution of Christ's body.[31]

Comparison

We can better judge the worth of Clement's other comparison. After he quoted Cassianus to the effect that the Savior removed his followers from error and coitus, Clement indicated that in this respect Cassianus taught "very similar things" to Tatian.[32] It is indeed true that Tatian called sex – and specifically sex within marriage – "participation in corruption." Tatian, then, would presumably have agreed with the position advocated by Cassianus, namely that Christians, in order to attain perfection, should refrain from sex and its result (procreation).[33]

---

[27] Clement, *Strom.* 3.14.95.2; Philo, *QG* 1.53; cf. *Allegorical Interpretation* 2.55-56; *Ref.* 6.13.4.

[28] Clement, *Strom.* 3.14.95.2.

[29] Clement, *Strom.* 3.16.100.1; 3.16.101.2.

[30] Clement, *Strom.* 3.17.102.3; cf. 3.13.91.1 (ὁ τῆς δοκήσεως ἐξάρχων Ἰούλιος Κασσιανός).

[31] There are not enough data to determine whether for Cassianus Jesus possessed a penis with testicles (for which see Christoph Markschies, *Gottes Körper: judische, christliche und pagane Gottesvorstellungen in der Antike* [Munich: Beck, 2016], 384–6). On the defunct category "docetism," see Joseph Verheyden, Reimund Bieringer, Jens Schröter, and Ines Jäger, eds., *Docetism in the Early Church: The Quest for an Elusive Phenomenon* (Tübingen: Mohr Siebeck, 2018); Hoklotubbe, "What Is Docetism?" 62–3.

[32] Clement, *Strom.* 3.13.92.1.

[33] Clement, *Strom.* 3.12.81.1-2.

Nevertheless, it is not clear that Tatian would have made the additional move that human genitalia were not created by God, that fleshly bodies were given as a primeval punishment, and that Christ reshaped human bodies (into something transcending flesh). Tatian and Cassianus (along with Marcion and Saturninus) agreed on sexual renunciation, though their rationales differed. On current evidence, we do not have any indication that Tatian appealed, like Cassianus, to an original and "natural" androgynous state of humanity to justify his ethic of abstention. He may have in some way blamed Adam (and Eve) for introducing (sexual) sin, yet we lack the data to say anything more definite.

An appeal to primitive androgyny does appear in other texts, notably sayings of Jesus in the *Gospel of Thomas* (*NHC* II,2):

> 11.4: On the day when you were one, you became two. But when you become two, what will you do?

> 22.4–7: When you make the two one ... and when you make the male and the female one and the same, so that the male not be male nor the female ... then you will come into [the kingdom].

Compare the remarks of the anonymous *Gospel of Philip* (*NHC* II,4):

> 68.24–26: When Eve was in Adam, there was no death. When she was separated from him, death came. If <she> enters into him again and he receives <her>, death will not arise.   .

> 70.10–17: If the female had not separated from the male, the female and the male would not have died. The separation of male and female became the beginning of death. For this reason, Christ came to heal the separation that was from the beginning and join the two, in order to give life to those who died through separation and join them.

If Cassianus and Tatian followed the logic of these passages, they were trying to use the ethic of abstinence through Christ to overcome death. There was a connection, based on a reading of Genesis, between sexual desire, corruption, and death. By overcoming sexual desire – not just refraining from sex – humans could take steps to transcend gender (Gal. 3:28) and bodily corruption.

A similar ideology appears in the *Testimony of Truth*. According to its author, "no one who is under Law will be able to look up to the truth; they cannot serve two masters. For the impurity of the Law is clear ... The Law bids (one) to take a husband (or) a wife and to bear children, to abound like the sands of the sea (Gen. 1:28; 22:17). But passion which is sweet to them constrains the souls of those who are born in this place – those who defile and are defiled."[34]

---

[34] *Test. Truth* IX,3 29.23–30.9.

Here again there are overlaps with Tatian: the language of serving two masters, the defiling nature of sex within marriage, and – if it be admitted – Clement's charge that Tatian "destroyed" (or simply undermined?) Jewish Law. Such parallels do not allow us to determine the authorship of the *Testimony of Truth*. They do helpfully show, however, the spread of early Christian ascetic ideas. They also lead us to question how close Tatian and Cassianus actually were in terms of theology. There is much about Tatian's theology that we do not know; yet any Christian who rejected sex – especially sex within marriage – had to deal with the Judean deity whose Law commanded sex and marriage. If sex was defiling, then the "god" who commanded it was to some degree suspect.

Chronography

One other point on which to compare Tatian and Cassianus regards chronography. According to Clement, both men independently did work on the chronology of Moses with the purpose of proving Hebrew wisdom more ancient than any competing tradition (Greek, Babylonian, and so on). Tatian set forth his chronology in a section of his *Oration against the Greeks*, and Cassianus did likewise in the first book of a work called *Exegetica*.[35]

It is interesting to ask who first employed the tools of chronography in the service of Christian wisdom. Recent scholarship has dated Cassianus's *Exegetica* to between 173–176 CE.[36] This makes it roughly contemporary to Tatian's *Oration*, which is typically dated between 166–178 CE.[37] It is difficult to determine, then, who was first. Even if one author wrote earlier than the other, they were not necessarily dependent. Complete independence, however, would be striking since both authors obtained their key chronological anchor from the writings of the first-century CE Egyptian polymath, Apion.

It was Apion who, following the *Chronicles* of Ptolemy of Mendes, said that the Egyptian king Amosis lived in the time of the Greek (more specifically, Argive) king Inachus. According to Greek king lists, there were eighteen Argive kings who reigned between Inachus and Agamemnon, the Greek commander in the Trojan war. Tatian and Cassianus could thereby date Moses, a contemporary of Amosis, to about four centuries prior to the Trojan war.

Cassianus and Tatian concluded that Moses lived long before the flowering of Greek culture – indeed before the invention of the Greek alphabet. Tatian specifically

---

[35] Clement, *Strom.* 1.21.101.2. Jerome referred to Cassianus's work as χρονογραφία (*Illustrious Men* 38).

[36] Nikos Kokkinos, "Julius Cassianus, Pseudo-Thallus and the Identity of Cassius Longinus in the Chronographia of Eusebius," *Scripta Judaica Cracoviensia* 8 (2010): 15–28 at 16–17.

[37] Josef Lössl, "Date and Location of Tatian's *Ad Graecos*: Some Old and New Thoughts," *Studia Patristica* 74 (2016): 43–56. Marcovich opted for 166–70 CE (*Tatiani Oratio* 1-5). Grant's date of 177–178 CE (*Greek Apologists*, 113–15) was undercut by G. W. Clarke, "The Date of the Oration of Tatian," *HTR* 60, no. 1 (1967): 123–6.

inferred that Moses's chronological priority meant that Greek "sophists" were all later and derivative. In fact, they had pilfered the writings of Moses without giving him credit.[38]

At present, we can no longer tell what were Cassianus's distinctive contributions to chronography since his *Exegetica* does not survive. Clement cited both Tatian and Cassianus at the start of his own mini-treatise on chronology (*Strom.* 1.21). We might deduce that they were Clement's chief sources, or at least chief inspirations. It would, however, be overly neat to say that everything Clement said in *Strom.* 1.21 which does not come from Tatian derived from Cassianus. In this section, Clement synthesized a small library of (often conflicting) historians and chronographers, so there is no secure way to discern Cassianus's distinctive contributions.[39]

Conclusion

For most Christians, it must be admitted, the name of Julius Cassianus is unknown and unsung. In the late second century CE, however, his thought and writings were well known, utilized, and critiqued by Clement of Alexandria and perhaps by others unknown to us. It would be easy to depict Cassianus as a radical Christian intellectual on the fringe, a man who argued for the impossible ideal of androgyny through castration. We will never know whether Cassianus was the young man who petitioned Felix, the Egyptian governor, to have his testicles removed. In the end, it is not important. What is significant is that, when his petition was refused, the young man, along with "those of like mind" (*tōn homognōmonōn*) lived the life of eunuchs with their testicles intact.[40] If they could not literally reshape their bodies, they could transform their minds to attain a sexless ideal. Cassianus, if he did not belong to an actual group of ascetics, was one of those "of like mind."

Some Christians, it should be said, did succeed in becoming literal eunuchs for the kingdom. It was said that Melito of Sardis (died about 180 CE) was a eunuch, though we do not know if he made himself one.[41] Tertullian said that some Valentinians (apparently in North Africa) were eunuchs.[42] Shortly after 200 CE, the budding Christian theologian Origen successfully removed his testicles, at least according to Eusebius's report.[43]

Radical asceticism was certainly "in the air" – and not just in Egypt. If we are fair to the likes of Cassianus, castration – whether by physical removal of flesh or mental removal of lustful thoughts – was not perceived as extreme. It was based on Christ's

---

[38] Tatian, *Or.* 38-41. Apion himself dated Moses and the Exodus to the seventh Olympiad (the mid-eighth century BCE), long after the Trojan War (Josephus, *Against Apion* 2.17).

[39] The presence of Cassianus in Clement, *Strom.* 1.21.141.5 is based on Gutschmid's conjecture: <ὑπὸ> Κασσιανοῦ (Stählin, *Stromata Buch I-VI*, 88). See further *FGrH* 723 F4.

[40] Justin, *1 Apol.* 29.3.

[41] Eusebius, *HE* 5.24.6 (citing Polycrates of Ephesus).

[42] Tertullian, *Against Valentinians* 30.4.

[43] Eusebius, *HE* 6.8; Jerome, *Epistle* 84.8.

own observation that some make themselves eunuchs for the kingdom (Matt. 19:12). It expressed the seriousness of one's intent to serve God and Christ. In his own words, Cassianus felt himself to be "hastening" toward God with other people.[44] If he did belong to a group of like-minded celibates, one might dare to call him a forerunner of urban monastics who would appear in third- and fourth-century Egypt. To call Cassianus an "encratite" (a person engaged in practices of radical self-control) would perhaps be accurate as long as one does not envision "the Encratites" as a formal, organized group with a defined character at this time. In addition to being ascetic, moreover, Cassianus was also a scholar whose chronological findings were incorporated by Clement and later by better known chronographers, in particular Eusebius, Julius Africanus, and Jerome.

Further Reading

William Adler, "Moses, the Exodus, and Comparative Chronology," in *Essays on Early Judaism and Christianity in Honor of Carl R. Holladay* (Leiden: Brill, 2008), 47–66 at 52–3.

Peter Brown, *The Body and Society* (New York: Columbia University Press, 1988), 83–102.

Richard W. Burgess, "Apologetic and Chronography: The Antecedents of Julius Africanus," in *Julius Africanus und die christliche Weltchronistik*, ed. Martin Wallraff (Berlin: de Gruyter, 2006), 17–42.

Daniel F. Caner, "The Practice and Prohibition of Self-castration in Early Christianity," *VC* 51 (1997): 396–415.

Elizabeth A. Clark, *Reading Renunciation: Asceticism and Scripture in Early Christianity* (Princeton: Princeton University Press, 1999).

Matthew R. Crawford, "Tatian, Celsus, and Christianity as 'Barbarian Philosophy' in the Late Second Century," in *The Rise of the Early Christian Intellectual*, ed. Lewis Ayres and H. Clifton Ward (Berlin: de Gruyter, 2020), 45–80.

Arthur J. Droge, *Homer or Moses? Early Christian Interpretations of the History of Culture* (Tübingen: Mohr Siebeck, 1989), 82–101.

B. Lang, "No Sex in Heaven: The Logic of Procreation, Death and Eternal Life in Judaeo-Christian Tradition," in *Mélanges bibliques et orientaux en l'honneur de M. Mathias Delcor*, ed. A. Caquot, S. Légasse, and M. Tardieu (Neukirchen-Vluyn: Neukirchener, 1985), 237–53.

Richard Valantasis, *Making of the Self: Ancient and Modern Asceticism* (London: James Clark & Co., 2008).

Martin Wallraff, "The Beginnings of Christian Universal History from Tatian to Julius Africanus," *ZAC* 14 (2011): 540–55.

---

[44] Clement, *Strom.* 3.13.91.1-2 (θεοῦ εἰς ὅν σπεύδομεν).

Prodicus and His Disciples

Introduction

In the last chapter, we spoke of the unsung Alexandrian ascetic theologian Julius Cassianus. Another largely unknown and unstudied theologian – though apparently not ascetic – was Cassianus's near contemporary and fellow Alexandrian, Prodicus. Unlike Cassianus, it is not clear that Prodicus wrote any treatise. If he did, it has long since perished. What we can know about Prodicus, then, is meager. There is, however, some information about his followers (whom we can call Prodican Christians) thanks to the – admittedly hostile – reports of Clement and, to a lesser extent, Tertullian.[1] These authors offer a window, albeit a narrow one, into the thought of yet another Alexandrian Christian leader and group which reached its acme from the mid- to late second century CE.

Beliefs and Practices

Clement represented Prodicus's followers as a coherent group who called themselves "gnostics."[2] They did so, evidently, in the common, non-technical sense of "knowers." (Recall that Marcellina's group in Rome also called themselves "knowers" in this sense.[3]) Prodicans were "gnostics" in part because they claimed knowledge of God. This God they called the "primal God," a being far above the creator.[4] Prodicans believed themselves to be children of this primal God. This perceived status as God's children reportedly fostered a sense of spiritual worth. Prodican Christians viewed themselves as "royal children." According to Clement, Prodicans

---

[1] It is possible that Clement referred to Prodicus when he attacked a man who claimed to be gnostic in *Strom.* 2.20.117.5-6. This man, according to Clement, claimed to fight pleasure by using pleasure. Clement then accused him of following the opinion of Aristippus the Cyrenaic philosopher. Clement also mentioned the Cyrenaics when he opposed Prodicans in *Strom.* 7.7.41.2.

[2] Clement, *Strom.* 3.4.30.1.

[3] Irenaeus, *AH* 1.25.6.

[4] Clement, *Strom.* 3.4.30.1; Tertullian, *Scorpion's Sting* 15.6.

did not think that they were subject to the regulations of Jewish Law. They were, like Jesus (Matt 12:8), "lords of the Sabbath" and obeyed an unwritten – apparently divine – ordinance.[5]

The disciples of Prodicus affirmed that they had arrived into this world as strangers.[6] This belief may imply a doctrine of the soul's preexistence before entering the body (compare Basilides and Carpocrates). We are told, furthermore, that Prodicans discouraged martyrdom for theological reasons: to oppose the view that God is bloodthirsty and to promote the idea that Christ's sacrifice is sufficient.[7] Finally, Prodicans reportedly understood petitionary prayer as unnecessary, at least for the "knowers" who truly recognized God's will.[8] Prodican Christians wished to present themselves as foreigners to this world. Virtually all the material comes from Clement.

To a certain extent we can test Clement's claims by asking how Prodican notions stack up against data appearing in contemporaneous Christian scripture. Although not all Christians referred to themselves as "knowers," to be sure, they did think that they – unlike their "idol-worshiping" neighbors – knew the living and true God (1 Thess. 1:9). They considered themselves to be the children of the true God (Gal. 3:26; Rom. 8:14). Moreover, they refused to be "under [Jewish] law" (Gal. 5.18), since, for them, some or all of Jewish Law had been annulled (Eph. 2:15). They could conceive of an internalized law written in their hearts (Rom. 2:14-15). They viewed themselves as strangers and sojourners upon the earth (1 Pet. 2:11). Many Christians lauded martyrdom, but would have denied that God was bloodthirsty and that Christ's sacrifice was insufficient. They would have encouraged petitionary prayer, not the babbling censured by Jesus himself. The heavenly Father, after all, already knew his children's needs (Matt. 6:7-8). Most Prodican teachings, in short, at least have analogues in what have become biblical texts.

Deepening the Comparison

Yet there are certainly places where one could argue that Prodicans forged their own distinctive path. A God above the creator, a sense of royal privilege, and the superfluity of petitionary prayer all seem to go beyond scripture, at least how it is read today. Yet even in the case of these doctrines one can, with some charity, see how they could also have emerged from readings of biblical texts. Take, for instance, the Prodican sense of royal privilege. The apostle Paul shamed those Corinthian Christians who "reigned as kings" apart from him, yet he did not reprimand their sense of royal prerogative. Rather, he fostered it: "would that you had reigned as kings," he confessed, "so that we too might reign together with you!" (1 Cor. 4:8). Paul was not being entirely ironic. In fact, the idea that Christians considered

---

[5] Clement, *Strom.* 3.4.30.1.
[6] Clement, *Strom.* 3.4.31.3.
[7] Tertullian, *Scorpion's Sting* 15.6.
[8] Clement, *Strom.* 7.7.41.1.

themselves to be children of God and a "royal priesthood" (1 Pet. 2:9) was well-known. Co-reigning together with Christ in a heavenly kingdom was a common Christian hope (2 Tim. 2:12; Rev. 21-22). Christians who expected the kingdom of God also expected to rule in it – and even, as Paul claimed, to judge angels (1 Cor. 6:2).

As for believing in a God above the creator, we have already seen – for instance in our chapters on Marcion and Saturninus – how such a view could have emerged from a reading of scripture. Prodican Christians agreed with Saturninus, Valentinus, Marcion, and the Seed of Seth that the creator was not the highest deity. We do not know how Prodicans in particular arrived at this conclusion, and whether in their view the creator was evil or just. Regardless, distinguishing the creator from the true God was a well-known option for Christians in the second century. A variety of Christian groups (for instance, Marcionites and the Seed of Seth) advertised their knowledge of the true God above the creator, a notion contributing to their sense of election and higher knowledge.

Like the Seed of Seth, Prodicans reportedly used secret books attributed to Zoroaster.[9] Interestingly, the author of the *Secret Book of John* refers to a *Book of Zoroaster* which contained the names of angels who designed human body parts.[10] This putatively Zoroastrian source is quoted in the longer version of the *Secret Book of John*.[11] We also know of an "apocalypses of Zoroaster" used by Christians in mid-third-century Rome.[12] These apocalypses might have included *Zostrianos*, a work that partially survives in Nag Hammadi codex VIII. Generally speaking, we can infer that Prodicans were interested in what they took to be ancient wisdom coming from Persia and evidently believed that it witnessed to their Christian faith. In this respect, they resembled Isidore, Basilides's son, who commented on the wisdom of the prophet Parchor, who was evidently a Persian sage.

Agreeing with Basilides, Prodican Christians did not promote martyrdom as an intrinsic good, a "baptism of blood" that secured a heavenly reward. Basilides, the reader will recall from Chapter 9, conceived of martyrdom as punishment for a person's sin. It had no other redemptive value.[13] Clement, by contrast, believed that one could suffer and die for one's own salvation.[14] The disciples of Prodicus, for their part, urged that martyrdom had no salvific benefit, even for the one martyred. In their theory of salvation, Christ's sacrifice was all-sufficient. No more blood was needed to satisfy God or to pay for human sin (one's own or another's).

---

[9] Clement, *Strom* 1.15.69.6.
[10] *Secret Book of John* II,1 19.8-10.
[11] *Secret Book of John* II,1 15.27–19.10.
[12] Porphyry, *Life of Plotinus* 16.5.
[13] Clement, *Strom.* 4.12.81-83 = Löhr, *Basilides*, frag. 7.
[14] Clement, *Strom.* 4.7.43.2 (διὰ τὴν ἰδίαν ἔπαθε σωτηρίαν ὅ τε αὖ διὰ τὴν ἰδίαν ἀποθνῄσκων σωτηρίαν).

Together with the Prodicans, Basilides and his circle emphasized that Christians were aliens upon the earth. In support of this view, Basilides quoted Abraham's words in Gen. 23:4 (cf. Ps. 38:13 LXX): "I am a stranger and sojourner among you." The feeling of being alien was likely correlated with the sense of being special or elect. Clement accused the Basilideans of claiming to be "superworldly by nature."[15] It is not clear whether they used such language. Yet if they did consider themselves to be strangers and aliens, then both Basilidean and Prodican Christians apparently felt that they belonged to another world which they imagined to be higher than this one. They were, as Paul put it, "citizens of heaven" (Phil. 3:21).

We noted how Prodicans and Marcellinians both called themselves "gnostics." There may be another connection between Prodican and Carpocratian Christians, for the ideal Prodican Christian resembled the Carpocratian Christ. Jesus, according to Carpocrates, came into his (Jewish) world as a stranger. He discovered that the regulations of Jewish Law were unjust and so rejected them.[16] He lived according to another, natural and higher law, ruling over his passions and attaining perfect self-control.[17] Prodicans, for their part, arrived as strangers in this world. They considered themselves to be above human laws. Still, they endeavored to rule over all sins and passions by virtue of knowing and living according to a higher, unwritten law.

For both Carpocratian and Prodican Christians, their life above human law was taken by their enemies as a sign of lawlessness.[18] But this was a manifestly polemical conclusion.[19] Prodican Christians – according to their own ethical ideal – needed no written law because they had already attained a state of bodily and mental control. There was a common notion that those who had been perfectly formed or matured would not need written directions to achieve moral excellence. Philo, for instance, wrote: "There is no need, then, to give injunctions or prohibitions or exhortations to the perfect person formed after the Image [of God]."[20] The law is designed to restrain the lawless and uncontrolled. As Clement testified: "the law is not enacted for a just person."[21] Those with perfect self-control have no need of human laws. Accordingly, Prodican Christians considered themselves "mastered by nothing."[22] This would apparently mean that Prodicans felt themselves to be above human law since they managed to rule over their sinful desires.[23]

---

[15] Clement, *Strom.* 4.26.165.3 = Löhr, *Basilides*, frag. 12.

[16] Irenaeus, *AH* 1.25.1.

[17] Irenaeus, *AH* 1.25.1; Pseudo-Tertullian, *AAH* 3.1; Epiphanius, *Pan.* 27.2.2.

[18] Theodoret, *Fab.* 1.6.

[19] Williams, *Rethinking*, 172–3.

[20] Philo, *Allegorical Interpretation* 1.94.

[21] Clement, *Strom.* 7.2.10.1; cf. 1 Tim. 1:9.

[22] Clement, *Strom.* 3.4.30.1 (κρατηθῆναι ὑπ' οὐδενὸς νενομιχότες).

[23] Cf. Clement, *Strom.* 3.7.57.1-2. See further Jean-Baptiste Gourinat, "*Akrasia* and *Enkrateia* in Ancient Stoicism: Minor Vice and Minor Virtue?" in *Akrasia in Greek Philosophy: From Socrates to Plotinus*, ed. Christopher Bobonich and Pierre Destrée (Leiden: Brill, 2007), 215–47.

We do not know how Prodicans thought that they attained the state of perfect control, but if they were readers of Paul, as seems likely, they would have known that endowment with the divine Spirit annulled the desires of the flesh (Gal. 2:16). The Spirit produced virtues "against which there is no law" (3:23). All Christians, in fact, were expected to "crucify" their old self "with its passions and desires" (3:24). In this light, Prodican Christians were nothing special. They aimed to live according to a scriptural ideal. Whether or not they lived up to their ideal in all cases is of course another question. It is noteworthy, however, that Clement never accused them of specific sins.

Comparison with Clement

Clement is our main source for Prodican Christians, and he only mentioned them in passing. It would accordingly be daring to claim any robust Prodican influence on Clement. One can hypothesize, however, that Clement was motivated more broadly to oppose the Prodican vision of the Christian gnostic. For his part, Clement made a striking claim about gnosis. Every baptized believer, according to Clement, received enlightenment, a kind of perfection in the knowledge (gnosis) of God.[24] Were Prodican claims to gnosis so different? According to Clement, the Prodican Christian gnostic had special characteristics: (1) he or she knew the true (primal) God, (2) received divine benefits without asking, and (3) was subject to no written law. Throughout his *Stromata*, I suggest, Clement combatted the Prodican gnostic with his competing portrait of what he thought the Christian gnostic should be. Clement's *Stromata* is massive, of course, and his view of the Christian gnostic is too vast a topic to deal with here in full.[25] Nevertheless, we can trace the ways in which the Clementine gnostic resembles the Prodican counterpart in order to reconstruct some of the implicit dialogue between Prodicans and Clement.

The Primal God

With regard to point (1), that Prodicans claimed to know the primal God, Clement indicated something similar. He believed that God cannot be taught by humans or expressed in speech. Knowledge is a gift, and this gift comes from God through God's Son.[26] Only the gnostic has this knowledge, a knowledge which Clement

---

[24] Clement, *Pedagogue* 1.6.25.1; 1.6.26.3.
[25] See further Walther Völker, *Der Wahre Gnostiker nach Clemens Alexandrinus* (Berlin: Akademie, 1952); André Méhat, "'Vraie' et 'fausse' gnose d'après Clément d'Alexandrie," in *The Rediscovery of Gnosticism: Proceedings of the International Conference on Gnosticism at Yale*, ed. Bentley Layton, 2 vols. (Leiden: Brill, 1980), 1:426–33; André Guillaumont, "Le Gnostique chez Clément d'Alexandrie et chez Évagre le Pontique," in ALEΞANΔRINA: *Héllenisme, Judaïsme et christianisme à Alexandrie. Mélanges offerts à Claude Mondésert* (Paris: Éditions du Cerf, 1987), 199–201.
[26] Clement, *Strom.* 5.11.71.2.

defines as a "sure comprehension leading up through true and sure reason to the knowledge of the Cause," here referring to God.[27] The Clementine gnostic "comprehends what seems to others to be incomprehensible, believing that nothing is incomprehensible to the child of God."[28] Here, incidentally, Clement's reference to his "gnostic" as God's child resembles the Prodican confession that they, as "gnostics," were children of the primal God. We also note that although Clement did not call his gnostic Christians "royal servants/children," he did see as their ultimate goal the state of becoming "royal friends of God."[29]

Apparently Clement emphasized God's unity whereas Prodicans, we are led to believe, envisioned a multitude of divine powers.[30] Clement even quoted a supposedly secret writing, a text he seems to link with Prodican thought:

> All things were one. When, however, the One resolved not to be alone, a Conception went out from him. He became intimate with her and made the Beloved. From the Beloved came forth a Conception. When he [the Beloved] was intimate with her, he made Powers unable to be seen or heard … each with its own name.

Such (Neo-)Pythagorean speculation (theorizing how many things come from One) was a common mode of intellectual exploration at the time.[31] Christians differed regarding how they viewed the emergence of entities like the Son, Wisdom, and the Spirit from the primal deity (or Father). Somehow they emerged as distinct (hypostatic) entities. In Valentinian thought, for instance, God as the "Pleroma" or "Fullness" was not a denial of God's unity – nor should we assume such was the case for Prodicans. Christian thought has typically found a way to combine divine plurality and unity.

Clement, for his part, articulated his own position on divine proliferation: "the unspeakable part of God is Father and the part that has sympathy with us has become Mother. By loving, the Father became female, and a great proof of this is he whom he bore from himself," namely the Son.[32] Granted, this is an idiosyncratic way of discussing divine proliferation. Yet one can still employ it in a thought experiment: assume for a moment that we lacked complete texts from Clement and only had at our disposal a hostile summary of his views along with the above quote to the effect that, according to Clement, God became "Mother" and produced a Son. From this de-contextualized excerpt, we might receive the impression that Clement's emphasis was on divine plurality – that God actually became female and produced a Son as a

---

[27] Clement, *Strom.* 6.18.162.4.

[28] Clement, *Strom.* 6.8.70.2.

[29] Clement *Strom.* 4.7.52.2 (βασιλικῷ τε φίλῳ τοῦ θεοῦ).

[30] Tertullian, *Praxeas* 3.6.

[31] Whittaker, "Self-generating Principles in Second-century Gnostic Systems," in Layton, ed., *Rediscovery*, 1:176–89.

[32] Clement, *Rich Man* 37.2.

separate entity. Clement acknowledged on several occasions the reality of multiple divine powers, although he saw the Son as their collective center.[33]

This thought experiment raises a question about what Prodicans emphasized when it came to their own presentation of theology (and divine proliferation in particular). They might have spoken about divine plurality while still, in the manner of Clement, simultaneously pushing for a form of more basic unity or monism – a nuance which would be lost in heresiological attacks.[34]

Petitionary Prayer

Our comparison regarding point (2) can be dealt with more briefly. Clement's gnostic, unlike the Prodican gnostic, does indeed make petitions to God. But the petitions are in a sense a formality, since Clementine gnostics, endowed with special knowledge of God, always make their petition according to God's will. Logically, then, the Clementine gnostic always receives what is fitting and according to God's will, whether or not it is vocally pronounced.[35] The Clementine gnostic's thoughts are inspired by God because the will of God is conveyed to his soul.[36] The gnostic is not "wordy in his uttered prayers, since he has been taught by the Lord what to ask."[37] Prayer is not a laundry list of requests, but a permanent state of contemplation.[38] "Accordingly the gnostic will pray in every place ... in every sort of way his prayer ascends, whether he is walking or in company or at rest or reading or engaged in good works; and though it be only a thought in the secret chamber of the heart, while he calls on the Father in groanings which cannot be uttered, yet the Father is near at hand even before he is done speaking."[39] The idea of immediate petition through thought by a kind of synchronism of will is of course different from the Prodican position. In practice, however, the Clementine and Prodican gnostic may

---

[33] Clement, *Strom.* 7.2.5.5-6; 3.17.103.1; 6.16.148.2; *Ecl.* 57.1 (multiple Powers); 4.25.156.1-2 (Son as center of the Powers). See further Annewies van den Hoek, "God Beyond Knowing: Clement of Alexandria and Discourse on God," in *God in Early Christian Thought: Essays in Memory of Lloyd G. Patterson*, ed. Andrew McGowan, Brian E. Daley, and Timothy J. Gaden (Leiden: Brill, 2009), 37–60; Henny Fiska Hägg, *Clement of Alexandria and the Beginnings of Christian Apophaticism* (Oxford: Oxford University Press, 2006), 207–37.

[34] See further Barbara Aland, "Gnostischer Polytheismus oder gnostischer Monotheismus? Zum Problem von polytheistischen Ausdrucksformen in der Gnosis," in *Was ist Gnosis*, 274–90.

[35] Clement, *Strom.* 7.7.41.4 (οὕτως πᾶν ὃ ἄν [ὁ] αἰτήσῃ γνωστικὸς λαμβάνει). See also Völker, *Wahre Gnostiker*, 546–9.

[36] Clement, *Strom.* Strom 6.17.157.4.

[37] Clement, *Strom.* 7.7.49.6 (trans. Oulton and Chadwick, adapted).

[38] Clement, *Strom.* 7.2.10.2-3; 7.9.56.5; 7.9.57.1.

[39] Clement, *Strom.* 7.7.49.6-7 (trans. Oulton and Chadwick, adapted). See further Jana Plátová, "The Gnostic's Intercessory Prayer according to Clement of Alexandria," in *The Seventh Book of the Stromateis: Proceedings of the Colloquium on Clement of Alexandria (Olomouch, October 21–23, 2010)*, ed. Matyáš Havrda Vít Hušek and Jana Plátová (Leiden: Brill, 2012), 185–98.

have been more similar with regard to prayer than Clement would have liked his readers to believe. Both the Clementine and the Prodican gnostic, I propose, did not need to use verbal (or discursive) requests, for the thought and will of the gnostic was already aligned with God.

No Written Law

Point (3), that the Prodican gnostic is subject to no written law, has a rather more robust parallel in Clement. Clement affirmed that gnostics should follow the law of God. He nevertheless urged that this law was inscribed on the heart.[40] The law, Clement agreed with the Stoics, is "right reason" (*orthos logos*) which is not necessarily instantiated in a written code.[41] Clement agreed with the biblical statement (1 Tim. 1:9) that for a righteous person there is no law.[42] The law "from above," he wrote in the same context, is simply the voluntary choice of virtue.[43] In upholding these views, Clement was no more lawless, it seems, than the Prodicans whom he criticized.

The overall point is that Clement harshly criticized his Christian competitors – in this case, the Prodicans – not because they were radically different from his views, but because they were (dangerously for Clement) all too similar. I suspect that this similarity was in part deliberate. Clement, in his depiction of the gnostic, was responding to the Prodican version of the gnostic, and his response incorporated and adapted certain elements of the Prodican position.

Conclusion

What, in sum, can we infer about Prodicus and his followers? First, Prodican Christians were likely based in Alexandria, since their beliefs are mentioned by an Alexandrian (Clement) who seems to have been familiar with their movement by personal encounter. We infer this because Clement mentioned no writings of Prodicus or his followers, but was familiar with their ideas. He evidently knew Prodicans as real people.

When did Prodicus himself flourish? To determine this point, we must work backwards. Evidently, Clement did not know Prodicus, but his followers. We can infer that Prodicus had died by the time Clement was writing (about 200 CE). On the other hand, Prodicus was seemingly unknown by Irenaeus. We might then set his *floruit* between 140 and 180 CE. If so, Prodicus was a contemporary of Cassianus, Tatian, Apelles, and Theodotus the Valentinian.

[40] Clement, *Protrepticus* 11.114.4-5.
[41] Clement, *Strom.* 1.25.166.5.
[42] Clement, *Strom.* 7.2.10.1.
[43] Clement, *Strom.* 7.2.10.1.

Clement assumed that Prodicus left behind a movement – a sect (*hairesis*) with its own stamp. Although Clement pointed out what he thought was distinctive – and negative – about Prodicans, there are in fact substantial overlaps between Prodican and other Christian beliefs and practices at the time – including considerable overlaps with Clement himself.

It seems safe to say that Clement felt himself to be in competition with a group of Prodicus's followers in Alexandria, some of whom were teachers like Clement. As a hostile rival, Clement was not motivated to represent their views accurately and his clipped summaries do them little justice. At the same time, it seems that the Prodican vision of the Christian gnostic conditioned Clement's thought and motivated him to create his own full-scale portrait of the "gnostic" (that is, the spiritually mature Christian).

How far did Prodican Christian influence spread? Tertullian is another roughly contemporary writer to mention Prodicans (with reference to their view of martyrdom and their putatively plural notion of Godhead).[44] How Tertullian derived his information is unknown. Yet if Prodicus never wrote anything, we might infer that his followers spread west from Alexandria to Carthage. Tertullian evidently assumed that his North African readers knew Prodicus and his disciples, since he felt no need to explain their identity.

Beyond the early third century, however, there is no mention of Prodican Christians until Theodoret in the fifth century. For some reason, Theodoret connected Prodicus with "Adamian" Christians who – if one can believe Epiphanius – held their church services in the nude.[45] One can surmise, however, that Theodoret had never actually met a Prodican or an "Adamian" Christian. Their connection – and in fact Theodoret's entire report on Prodicus – shows rather how information passing from one heresy report to another can swiftly, and seriously, degrade.

Further Reading

Peter Karavites, *Evil, Freedom, and the Road to Perfection in Clement of Alexandria* (Leiden: Brill, 1999), 139–74.

Judith L. Kovacs, "Divine Pedagogy and the Gnostic Teacher according to Clement of Alexandria," *JECS* 9 (2001): 3–25.

Salvatore R. C. Lilla, *Clement of Alexandria: A Study of Christian Platonism and Gnosticism* (Oxford: Oxford University Press, 1971), 142–89.

G. Salmon, "Prodicus," in *A Dictionary of Early Christian Biography*, ed. Henry Wace and William C. Piercy (London: John Murray, 1911), 863–4.

Roelof van den Broek, "Prodicus," in *DGWE*, ed. Wouter Hanegraaff, 974–5.

Michael Williams, *Rethinking "Gnosticism": An Argument for Dismantling a Dubious Category* (Princeton: Princeton University Press, 1996), 172–3.

---

[44] Tertullian, *Scorpion's Sting* 15.6; *Praxeas* 3.6.

[45] Epiphanius, *Pan.* 52.

The Naassene Preacher

Introduction

About 222 CE, the Refutator introduced yet another Christian group who reputedly called themselves "gnostics."[1] The Refutator called them "Naassenes" ("Snake people"), apparently due to their allegorical interpretations of Greco-Roman snake imagery. This heresiographer wanted to make it seem as if they worshiped the snake, but his report is marred by distortion.[2] Although the Refutator wanted to group together a series of "snake heresies," he did not identify Naassenes with Ophite Christians, whom he also knew.[3] (Ophites, as we know from Chapter 8, were a distinctive Christian group with their own rites and stories.) The term "Naassene" highlights the distinctive nature of the group. Nevertheless, this label is hardly optimal, since, on present evidence, they neither offered an exposition of the serpent in Genesis, nor was the snake indisputably central to their thought and practice.[4]

It is better to refer to these people as Christians, since that is how they referred to themselves. In fact, they claimed to be the only true Christians.[5] Other signs of their Christian identity are evident. First, they traced their tradition back to Jesus, whose

---

[1] Ref. 5.6.4; 5.11.1; cf. 5.23.3. Clement of Alexandria makes a similar use of "the depth of gnosis" (cf. Rom. 11:33) in Strom. 5.8.54.3.

[2] Ref. 5.9.11; pace van den Broek, "Naassenes," in DGWE, 820; see further Rasimus, Paradise, 210–23. Apart from the Refutator's initial comments, the snake only appears at the end of the Naassene report (Ref. 5.9.12-13). Here the Naassene author related the word naas to naos ("temple" or "shrine"). He also allegorized the snake to mean "watery substance," relating it to the river which flowed from Paradise.

[3] Ref. 8.20.3. See Rasimus, Paradise, 26, 82–3, 214–15.

[4] Two massive chapters in the Refutation intervene before the "Naassenes" even mention "naas." See further Lancellotti, Naassenes, 37–55. DeConick's statement that "The Naassenes believed the God from which everything originates is a serpent living in the moist essence of the primordial universe" goes beyond the evidence (Gnostic New Age, 216). Only from a series of inferences could one identify the snake with the divine Human Adamas. Theodoret wrongly identified Naassenes with Ophites in Questions on the Book of Kings 49.

[5] Ref. 5.9.22: ἡμεῖς Χριστιανοὶ μόνοι.

teaching was passed on through two apostolic figures: James the brother of Jesus, and "Mariamme" (apparently Mary Magdalene).[6] Second, they practiced Christian rituals like baptism and anointing. Third, they read Christian scriptures using well-honed techniques of Christian allegory.

The "Naassenes" were not the only Christian group to refer to themselves as "gnostics" (compare the followers of Marcellina and of Prodicus), and they probably did not intend "gnostic" as a technical group designation. As noted in our chapter on Justin, the Refutator claimed that *all* the "snake heresies" called themselves gnostics.[7] In the Naassene report itself, the main speaker refers rather to his group of "spirituals," "perfect people," and "elect."[8] For lack of a clearer and more specific term, I will refer to this group as "Naassene Christians" and to their spokesman as the "Naassene Christian preacher," or for short, "the preacher."[9]

I emphasize the Christian identity of this group in light of attempts to challenge it. One scholar theorizes that the name "Naassene" goes back to an "eponymous founder of pagan mysteries" named "Naos" ("Mr. Church" [*sic*]) and that when Naassenes employed Christian texts, these texts ceased to be Christian insofar as Naassenes endorsed other cults.[10] The first hypothesis is speculation (we have no inkling who founded the movement) and the second gives the wrong impression. The Naassene preacher was not endorsing other cults. If anything, he or she Christianized them by seeing in them manifold symbols of an exclusive Christian truth.[11]

Provenance

The Refutator came to know Naassene Christians after obtaining one of their documents in Rome. The document was apparently a kind of sermon addressed

---

[6] *Ref.* 5.7.1. See further Karen King, *Gospel of Mary of Magdala: Jesus and the First Woman Apostle* (Salem: Polebridge, 2003).

[7] *Ref.* 5.23.3 (οὗτοι δὲ ἰδίως οἱ πάντες γνωστικοὺς ἑαυτοὺς ἀποκαλοῦσιν).

[8] *Ref.* 5.9.21; 5.8.5.

[9] By contrast, Josef Frickel sees at least two authors behind the Naassene document: an "Anthropos Gnostic" and a "Pneuma Gnostic." The Anthropos Gnostic was a universalist who took over a commentary on an Attis hymn. The Pneuma Gnostic was a Christian believer in exclusive salvation, heavily influenced by Pauline and Johannine literature. Frickel reconstructed what he thought was the original text of the Anthropos Gnostic, which originated about 150 CE (*Hellenistische Erlösung in christlicher Deutung. Die gnostische Naassenerschrift: Quellenkritische Studien, Strukturanalyse, Schichtenscheidung, Rekonstruktion der Anthropos-Lehrschrift* [Leiden: Brill 1984], esp. 164–71). See the evaluation of Lancellotti, *The Naassenes: A Gnostic Identity among Judaism, Christianity, Classical and Ancient Near Eastern Traditions* (Münster: Ugarit-Verlag, 2000), 24–5.

[10] Mark Edwards, "The Naming of the Naassenes: Hippolytus, Refutatio V.6-10 as Hieros Logos," *Zeitschrift für Papyrologie und Epigraphik* 112 (1996): 74–80 at 78 ("Mr. Church") and 80.

[11] Lancellotti, *Naassenes*, 10–29; Rasimus, *Paradise*, 187–8. The representatives of these other cults did not realize the full import of their own myths (*Ref.* 5.9.7). Hence the Naassene preacher took it upon himself to unveil their true meaning.

by a preacher to a group of insiders.[12] But Rome was probably not their native city. The Naassene preacher showed no interest in specifically Roman deities or rites. His world was that of the Hellenized east, from where most of his illustrations derive. The Italian scholar Maria Grazia Lancellotti locates the Naassenes in Syria because they practiced anointing, asceticism, and authorized their tradition through James and Mariamme.[13] Yet neither these practices nor authorities are specifically Syrian.

The Naassene Christian preacher was highly educated, as we shall see, but what he learned by direct experience came from Egypt. He spoke of ritual objects in Egypt "within everyone's purview."[14] The remark implies an Egyptian audience. Alexandria – or some other Egyptian metropolis – is thus a better guess for his locale. An Egyptian provenance is also supported by the author's use of the *Gospel according to the Egyptians*, a text likely composed in Egypt and quoted, as we have seen, by Julius Cassianus (Chapter 23).[15]

Author

The Naassene preacher was a religious polymath, who by his learning rivaled his older contemporaries Plutarch and Apuleius. We surmise that he received a solid education in rhetoric. He could cite a range of poets and philosophers including Anacreon (*Ref.* 5.8.6-7), Aristotle (5.7.25), Empedocles (5.7.30), Heraclitus (5.8.42-44), Homer (5.7.30-38; 5.8.3, 36), and Parmenides (5.8.43).[16]

He knew cultural and religious lore stemming from diverse places like Syria, Libya, Samothrace, and Phrygia. Given the specificity of the author's religious knowledge, we might speculate that he, before becoming a Christian, was initiated into several mystery cults, as Tatian claimed to be (Chapter 19). Alternatively, he might simply have been bookish – well-read in the literature of various Mediterranean religions.[17] His sermon jibes well with the interests of showpiece (epideictic) rhetoric, characteristic of the Second Sophistic. It is a piece of extraordinary learning, a kaleidoscope of scriptural texts, poetic tags, and cultic lore that washes over readers, threatening to overwhelm them at every turn.

---

[12] Richard Reitzenstein, *Poimandres: Studien zur griechisch-ägyptischen und frühchristlichen Literatur* (Leipzig: Teubner, 1904), 82; Lancellotti, *Naassenes*, 10–29.

[13] Lancellotti, *Naassenes*, 74. For Syrian anointing practices, see *Acts of Thomas* 26-27, 49, 120-21, 131-32; cf. *Gos. Philip* II,3 83; *Didascalia* 3.12 [16]. See further Bryan D. Spinks, *Early and Medieval Rituals and Theologies of Baptism* (London: Routledge, 2006), 14–36.

[14] *Ref.* 5.7.28.

[15] *Ref.* 5.7.9; Clement, *Strom.* 3.6.45.3; 3.9.63.2. See further Ian Phillip Brown, "Where Indeed was the Gospel of Thomas Written? Thomas in Alexandria," *JBL* 138, no. 2 (2019): 451–72.

[16] *Ref.* 5.7.10; 5.9.4.

[17] Lancellotti, *Naassenes*, 245, 258–9, 265–6, 283–4.

Date

Irenaeus, writing about 180 CE, apparently knew nothing about Naassene Christians – likely because no information had come to him. Accordingly, we can imagine them thriving between 180–220 CE. The Refutator, one should note, considered them to be significantly earlier. According to him, the Naassenes were the first "gnostic" group, earlier even than Simon of Samaria (thus disagreeing with Irenaeus). This is not likely, since the Naassene preacher quoted the *Great Declaration Commentary* (Chapter 3).[18] The author also quoted Plutarch, who lived until about 125 CE. The preacher used, furthermore, key terms from Valentinian theology (the "Fullness") and a specific self-designation from the Seed of Seth (the "kingless generation").[19] Use of the terms "Human" and "Child of the Human" may also derive from Ophite Christian influence or even from Monoïmus (briefly introduced in Chapter 18).[20] In short, the Naassene preacher was an intellectual magpie picking from a variety of second-century Christian thinkers. Accordingly, he lived toward the end of this century.

Individual or Group?

The Refutator possessed a speech written by a single preacher, but did this preacher belong to a larger group? The evidence for this hypothesis can only be judged from the Naassene report itself. For his part, the Refutator assumed that the Naassene document was addressed to a group.[21] When he quoted the document, he almost always cited it as "they say." The preacher speaking in the document also assumed he addressed a community, for instance when he said that "*we* are the only true Christians,"[22] and "*we* alone know the unspeakable mysteries."[23] If the Naassene preacher did not actually address a collective, he at least imagined one.

The Refutator called the Naassene authorities "leaders and priests."[24] Even if this was partial sarcasm, it indicates some sort of leadership structure. The organizational structure of the group probably included persons of greater perceived holiness (those who made more ascetic commitments) – probably including the Naassene preacher himself. The Refutator likened certain Naassenes to castrated priests of Cybele.[25] This point hardly indicates that Naassenes worshiped the goddess. What it does hint at is that some members of the group practiced celibacy or even castration (compare Julius

---

[18] *Ref.* 5.6.4; 5.9.5.
[19] *Ref.* 5.8.2 (kingless generation); 5.8.30 (Fullness).
[20] The same terminology appears in Monoïmus (*Ref.* 8.12.1-4).
[21] *Ref.* 5.6.5 (τὸν αὐτῶν λόγον).
[22] *Ref.* 5.9.22.
[23] *Ref.* 5.8.26.
[24] *Ref.* 5.6.3.
[25] *Ref.* 5.10.10-11.

Cassianus). Perhaps dependent on the Valentinians, the Naassene preacher referred to his group as the "angelic church" – though we cannot assume everyone in his "church" agreed with their preacher in everything.[26]

Ritual Practice

The Naassene preacher assumed the practice of Christian rituals, namely baptism and anointing. Naassene baptism occurred in "living" water; and the ointment he used was called "ineffable."[27] "Living water, often meant the running water of a stream or river.[28] Yet even if "living" was metaphorical (as the life-giving spring in John 4:10, 14), then "living water" was thought to differ from the baptismal waters available in other churches. Being baptized in "living" water, according to the preacher, led the initiate into "unfading pleasure," namely the non-fleshly pleasure experienced by spirit.[29]

Similarly, the Naassene preacher contrasted his "ineffable" ointment with what was available in other churches. These churches were said to possess only the ointment of Saul, ancient king of Israel and friend of "fleshly lust."[30] Naassene Christians, by contrast, had ointment from the "horn of David," which made them rulers over their bodies (1 Sam. 16). Apparently this was an implicit criticism of other churches, who anointed people but did not deliver them from lust. Naassene Christians may also have supplied milk and honey, like the Marcionites, to those who received their sacraments.[31]

Scriptural Practice

The Naassene Christian preacher used scriptural texts common in other ecclesial formations. In contrast to figures like Carpocrates, the preacher made extensive use of the Hebrew scriptures. In the space of a single discourse, there are at least eight quotations or allusions to Genesis, ten to Isaiah, two from Proverbs, three from Exodus, ten from the Psalms, one from Daniel, one from Joshua, two from Jeremiah, and three from Deuteronomy.[32]

The preacher also employed gospels that were standard by the late second century, including Matthew (eleven quotations or allusions) and John (at least sixteen), along with six Pauline letters (twenty-four Pauline references in all). But the Naassene

---

[26] *Ref.* 5.6.7.
[27] *Ref.* 5.7.19; cf. *Ref.* 5.9.21. "Ineffable" (ἀλάλῳ) is a manuscript emendation of ἄλλῳ ("other").
[28] *Didache* 7.1-2.
[29] *Ref.* 5.7.19.
[30] *Ref.* 7.9.22.
[31] *Ref.* 5.8.30 (quoting Deut. 31.20). DeConick speculates about other Naassene sacraments (*Gnostic New Age*, 217–20).
[32] See the index in Litwa, *Refutation*, 811–16.

scriptures were broader. The preacher used the *Gospel according to the Egyptians* at least once and a version of the *Gospel of Thomas* at least twice. Both documents are attested in Egypt and were used by second-century Christians.[33]

All these points indicate that, although the Naassene preacher was idiosyncratic, he was speaking to and for a group of fellow Christians. He was a universalist of sorts, a wide-ranging allegorizer who saw truth lurking in all religions. At the same time, he aimed to generate an exclusive community ethos to reinforce group solidarity in an environment of competing religious claims. The rites, hymns and poems of all religions, he thought, proclaimed Christian truth, even if the very hymnists and poets did not know it. Likewise, other churches did not know the deeper scriptural mysteries revealed by the preacher's interpretations.

Cosmopolitanism

The Naassene author manifested an outlook on the world which we can call cosmopolitan.[34] Valentinus remarked, "Many of those things written in publicly available books are found written in the church of God."[35] The Naassene preacher took this insight to a whole new level. He found truth glittering like diamonds on every street corner. He saw all reality as a symbol system for Christian truth. As the Refutator put it, "all creation attests to their teaching."[36] The Refutator later observed (with apparent frustration), "They claim that everything said and done by all human beings comes about spiritually in accord with their particular understanding."[37] The Naassene author based this outlook on Rom. 1:20: "from the creation of the world, God's invisible workings have been understood and observed in his created products."[38]

But if the Naassene preacher delighted in the creative transformation of all sorts of knowledge, he was not a "seeker."[39] The preacher had found the truth, and was certain of it. His certainty opened him up to seeing truth in places that other Christians, for instance Tatian, thought were haunted by demons.

[33] Anne Marie Luijendijk, *Greetings in the Lord: Early Christians and the Oxyrhynchus Papyri* (Cambridge, MA: Harvard University Press, 2008), 21; Nongbri, *God's Library*, 216–46.
[34] On cosmopolitanism, see Daniel S. Richter, "Cosmopolitanism," in *The Oxford Handbook to the Second Sophistic*, ed. Daniel S. Richter and William A. Johnson (Oxford: Oxford University press, 2017), 82–93.
[35] Clement, *Strom.* 6.6.52.3–6.6.53.1.
[36] *Ref.* 5.7.16.
[37] *Ref.* 5.9.7.
[38] Quoted in *Ref.* 5.7.17.
[39] *Pace* April D. DeConick, "Crafting Gnosis: Gnostic Spirituality in the Ancient New Age," in *Gnosticism, Platonism and the Late Ancient World: Essays in Honour of John D. Turner*, ed. Kevin Corrigan and Tuomas Rasimus (Leiden: Brill, 2013), 287–305 (301).

Using the versatile tool of allegory, the preacher converted classical literature into the substance of Christian truth. He effectively scripturalized Homer, transformed the sense of Greek myths, and reinvented the meaning of foreign rites. Nothing was off limits. He saw symbolic truth in the castration of the Phrygian god Attis;[40] he theorized about the meaning of erect phalluses in Egyptian and Greek iconography,[41] he re-envisioned the spiritual or psychological meaning of eroticized gods such as Aphrodite and Priapus.[42] For the preacher, the whole world was an open book of spiritual symbols, and he accrued authority by unveiling their meanings.

View of God

Though bursting with intertextual complexity, the preacher's basic thesis is clear: Christ, called Child of the Human, is symbolized in a host of other religious rites and songs. The preacher seems to have taken over this idea from a priest of Attis, who sang about his own deity revealed in other gods and rites. With daring one-upmanship, the Naassene preacher used a preexisting hymn sung to Attis as the basis for his own Christian allegory.

Sidelight on Attis. According to one Phrygian tradition, Attis was born from a virgin, exposed as a baby, but miraculously saved by being tended by a goat. He grew into a beautiful boy and was pledged to the king's daughter. On their wedding day, however, a jealous lover drove Attis mad. In a wild fit, Attis sliced off his own genitals and bled to death under a pine tree. But from his blood, a violet emerged, which entwined the tree. Zeus granted that Attis's body never decay, that his hair continue to grow, and that his little finger twitch for all time.[43] In another traditions, the deified Attis became an astral being called "Shepherd of gleaming white stars."[44]

The Naassene preacher explained Attis's names and symbols in light of his own Christian theology. According to this theology, there was in the beginning a divine

---

[40] *Ref.* 5.7.13-15.
[41] *Ref.* 5.7.27-29.
[42] For Priapus, cf. Justin in *Ref.* 5.26.32-33.
[43] Pausanias, *Description* 7.17.9-12; Arnobius, *Against the Nations* 5.5-7; cf. Lucian, *Syrian Goddess* 15; Ovid, *Fasti* 4.179-90, 221-44, 333-72. See further Lynn E. Roller, *In Search of God the Mother: The Cult of Anatolian Cybele* (Berkeley: University of California Press, 1999), 237–59; Philippe Borgeaud, *Mother of the Gods: From Cybele to the Virgin Mary*, trans. Lysa Hochroth (Baltimore: Johns Hopkins University Press, 2005), 102–7; Maria Grazia Lancellotti, *Attis: Between Myth and History: King, Priest and God* (Leiden: Brill, 2002), 16–118; Jaime Alvar, *Romanising Oriental Gods: Myth, Salvation and Ethics in the Cults of Cybele, Isis and Mithras*, trans. Richard Gordon (Leiden: Brill, 2008), 63–74. For Attis's castration allegorized, cf. Clement, *Protrepticus* 19.4.
[44] *Ref.* 5.9.9.

Human and a Child of the Human corresponding to the godhead of Father and Son. The Father deity is unknown and indeterminate. The Child of the Human is the determinate Logos identified with Christ.[45] Both the Human and Child of Human were called "Adamas" (a heavenly being who appears in Sethian lore) and were thought, somehow, to be one.[46] Evidently the preacher maintained the consubstantiality of Father and Son.[47]

For the preacher, the binitarian Godhead was distinct from the creator. He called the creator "Esaldaios" (apparently a form of the Hebrew divine name "El Shaddai").[48] He is identical to the Judean deity insofar as he is a fiery god (Deut. 4:34; 9:3).[49] This fiery god made the world and physical bodies of humans from mud (Gen. 2:7). He rules the world with a rod of iron (emphasizing his harsh justice).[50] He is basically similar to the angelic creator theorized, among others, by Apelles (Chapter 20).

Also similar to Apellian thought is the fact that the creator did not make human souls. Souls are fragments of the Child of the Human, Adamas.[51] The creator dragged down these souls from heaven so that the divine Human became enslaved in bodies and subjected to negative emotions.[52]

View of Humanity

Human souls in bodies take one of three paths. They can be earthly, following the needs and desires of the body; they can be animate, following the impulses of their souls; or they can be noetic, following their higher minds. These three groups of people find themselves in three "churches": the earthly, animate, and angelic. Naassene Christians viewed themselves, like the Valentinians, as the angelic church, also called "elect." We can surmise that competing Christians made up the animate church (the "called," Matt. 22:14).[53] All other people, presumably, made up the earthly church, called "captive."

---

[45] *Ref.* 5.6.4; 5.7.33.

[46] *Ref.* 10.9.1.

[47] Hans-Martin Schenke argued that both the Human and Child of the Human in Naassene thought are called Human, but only the Child of the Human was enclosed in human bodies (*Der Gott "Mensch" in der Gnosis* [Göttingen: Vandenhoeck & Ruprecht, 1962], 57–8). For Lancellotti, only the Naassene "second God" is the Human, but split into two aspects: one unformed, one trapped in matter (*Naassenes*, 75–7, 80, 82).

[48] Cf. Ἠσαδδαῖος in *Ref.* 5.26.3 (Justin). Lancellotti, who provides a discussion of his name (*Naassenes*, 116–20), believes that he is parallel to Plutarch's Typhon in *Is. Os.* 40 (367a).

[49] Cf. *Ref.* 6.9.3 ("Simon"); 6.32.7-8 ("Valentinus"); 7.38.1 (Apelles); 8.9.7 ("Doketai"); *PGM* XII.115 (ὁ [π]ύρινος θεός).

[50] *Ref.* 5.7.32.

[51] *Ref.* 5.7.30.

[52] *Ref.* 5.7.7-8.

[53] *Ref.* 5.6.7.

The fact that all humans belong to "churches" indicates at least their potential to be saved. After all, each human soul is a portion of the divine Human.[54] Since the divine Human has three aspects – earthly, animate, and spiritual – so does the human soul.[55] The divided soul is understandably pulled in different directions. Whatever direction one primarily follows determines one's overall character. If one changes one's orientation, attaining higher knowledge, one can pass from one "church" to another.[56]

View of Christ

All human beings incarnate fragments of the divine Human. But the divine Human in his fullness inhabited Jesus, born of Mary.[57] When this inhabitation occurred is uncertain. It could have happened when Jesus was conceived, or at his baptism, or at some other time. In a Naassene Christian hymn, the Child of the Human is already called Jesus. In this hymn, Jesus begs his Father to take note of his fractured self, wandering in human souls.[58]

Although the Refutator glides over this point, the fact that Jesus was born from Mary is significant. According to the Naassene preacher, Jesus had a physical birth and was genuinely human. Evidently, the physical birth was also a virgin birth, because the preacher, like Tatian (and probably Marcion), viewed sex as impure.

The divine Human in Jesus encompassed three different aspects – earthly, animate, and spiritual. Jesus could thus speak to all members of the three churches who understood him according to three different levels of maturity.[59] Only the angelic church received "the hidden things of the holy path … called *gnosis*."[60] This model of revelation is close to Valentinian thought as indicated, for instance, by Heracleon.

In sum, even though Naassene Christians considered themselves to be the only true Christians, they acknowledged other "churches" (in a theological, not a sociological sense) and thought that all people were capable of salvation. Though in the end few are saved (Matt. 7:13-14), even those blind from birth can recover their spiritual sight (John 9).[61]

---

[54] *Ref.* 5.8.4; cf. 5.8.23. See further Lancellotti, *Naassenes*, 130; Theo K. Heckel, *Der Innere Mensch: Die paulinische Verarbeitung eines platonischen Motivs* (Tübingen: Mohr Siebeck, 1993), 82–8, 221–6.

[55] *Ref.* 5.7.13.

[56] Lancellotti, *Naassenes*, 139–40.

[57] *Ref.* 5.6.7. Cf. Irenaeus, *AH* 1.8.3. See further Antonio Orbe, *Cristología Gnóstica: Introducción a la soteriología de los siglos II y III.*, 2 vols. (Madrid: Biblioteca de Autores Cristianos, 1976), 1:416–17.

[58] *Ref.* 5.10.2.

[59] *Ref.* 5.6.7.

[60] *Ref.* 5.10.2.

[61] *Ref.* 5.8.45; 5.9.20.

Ethics

Salvation requires spiritual rebirth which for the Naassene preacher meant birth out of flesh. He took seriously Jesus's statement in John: "What is born of flesh is flesh; what is born of Spirit is spirit" (3:6).[62] That is to say, what is born of flesh dies again; what is born of Spirit is everlasting and eternal. Salvation requires moral effort to separate from the works of the flesh (erotic practices); but it is also the work of God. The higher, noetic nature of the supercosmic beings calls up the male power of the soul (the *nous* or mind), and cuts it off from the forces of fleshly generation (sex and procreation).[63]

Like Saturninus, Marcion, and Cassianus, the Naassene preacher forbade sexual intercourse, calling it the work of pigs and dogs.[64] He demonized fleshly lust. He depicted an ongoing war in the body, evidently between spirit and flesh (Gal. 5:17).[65] Spiritual people were those who triumphed over flesh. At the same time, the desire to transcend the flesh did not mean hatred of it. Even the divine, for the Naassene preacher, had an earthly aspect.

The Naassene preacher based his sexual ethics in part on his peculiar reading of Rom. 1:27: "Likewise the males, after abandoning the natural use of the female, were fired in their yearning for one another – males with males performed the work of formlessness (*aschēmosunē*)."[66] This final Greek word is usually understood as "disgrace," "shame" or the like. The Naassene preacher took it in the etymological sense of "form-less" (*a-schēm*) activity. "Formlessness" is identified with "the primal and blessed Being."[67] Yet what is the work of formlessness? In context, the preacher had just finished allegorizing the myth of Attis cutting off his penis. For the preacher, the penis signifies "the male power of the soul" (that is, the mind) which can ascend to the "supercosmic beings" when it is cut off from the "female" (the fleshly body and lower soul).[68] The supercosmic realm is the realm of formlessness where only "males" (that is, minds) abide. For the "males," then, to do the work of formlessness is for them to feel the "unfading pleasure" of "formless" (evidently fleshless) activity.[69]

Deification

Death for the Naassene preacher meant departure from the body. He interpreted the saying, "the dead will leap out of the graves" (compare John 5:28) to mean "out

---

[62] Quoted in *Ref.* 5.7.40.
[63] *Ref.* 5.7.13.
[64] *Ref.* 5.7.14; 5.8.33; 5.9.11.
[65] *Ref.* 5.8.19, quoting Job 40:32 LXX.
[66] *Ref.* 5.7.18.
[67] *Ref.* 5.7.18.
[68] *Ref.* 5.7.13.
[69] Cf. *Ref.* 5.8.44-45; 5.9.11. Cf. the interpretation of Cahana-Blum, *Wrestling*, 94–6. See further Frickel, *Hellenistische Erlösung*, 49; Lancellotti, *Naassenes*, 164–77.

of earthly bodies." When the saints leap out of earthly bodies, they "are reborn as spirit, not as flesh."[70] In supporting this line of thought, the preacher believed he was following the footsteps of Paul, who soared to the third heaven, passing through three heavenly gates.[71] The final gate was Jesus himself, through whom only spiritual people find passage.[72]

Beyond the third gate, spiritual people become gods (that is, immortal spirit beings). They do so on the basis of Ps. 82:6, where God himself performatively proclaims: "you are gods!" The preacher did not envision the angelic church as simply absorbed into the divine Human. He made a distinction between the supreme God and the future deified selves of the elect, called "the kingless generation."[73]

Conclusion

To sum up: the Naassene preacher addressed a Christian group that probably existed in Egypt between 180–220 CE. He tried to cultivate a mentality that was both universalistic (all could be saved), but also exclusive ("we" are the only true Christians). He saw the truth of his brand of Christianity gleaming in all Mediterranean religions, though he did not endorse these other religions or their practices as such.

His group of self-identified knowers had their own rites (baptism and anointing), a leadership structure, a communal gathering (at least a setting for sermons), an exegetical practice, and a corporate aim: to transcend the flesh while living in it; to be angelic (celibate) even on earth (Luke 20:36). Christ, the Child of the Human, inhabited all people. But he had given true knowledge to the elect alone.

Armed with this knowledge, Naassenes Christians evidently spent their lives trying to attain physical and moral purity so that after death they could ascend past the third heaven. In doing so, they thought they followed in the footsteps of Jesus and Paul, and with them hoped to become immortal spirits – fleshless beings called angels or gods, experiencing eternal pleasure far above this cosmos.

Further Reading

R. Scott Birdsall, "The Naassene Sermon and the Allegorical Tradition: Allegorical Interpretation, Syncretism, and Textual Authority" (Ph.D. diss., Claremont, 1984).
Steven R. Johnson, "Hippolytus's *Refutatio* and the *Gospel of Thomas*," *JECS* 18, no. 2 (2010): 305–26.
Maria Grazia Lancellotti, *The Naassenes: A Gnostic Identity among Judaism, Christianity, Classical and Ancient Near Eastern Traditions* (Münster: Ugarit-Verlag, 2000).

[70] *Ref.* 5.8.23.
[71] *Ref.* 5.8.25-26.
[72] *Ref.* 5.7.24. The Naassene version of the *Gospel of Thomas* mentioned fourteen aeons, but it is not clear if they belong to the cosmic level.
[73] *Ref.* 5.8.2, 30.

M. David Litwa, "You Are Gods: Deification in the Naassene Writer and Clement of Alexandria," *HTR* 110, no. 1 (2017): 125–48.

Miroslav Marcovich, *Studies in Graeco-Roman Religions and Gnosticism* (Leiden: Brill, 1988), 80–8.

Tuomas Rasimus, *Paradise Reconsidered in Gnostic Mythmaking: Rethinking Sethianism in Light of the Ophite Evidence*, NHMS 68 (Leiden: Brill, 2009), 64–102, 210–23.

W. R. Schoedel, "Naassene Themes in the Coptic Gospel of Thomas," *VC* 14 (1960): 225–34.

Roelof van den Broek, "Naassenes," in *DGWE*, ed. Wouter Hanegraaff, 820–2.

"Sethian" Christians of the *Refutation*

Introduction

Along with the Naassene sermon, the Refutator also obtained a document in Rome called the *Paraphrase of Seth*. From this document, he concluded that there was a competing group of Christians called "Sethians." Apparently, his sole reason for calling them "Sethians" was because of the title of their treatise – the *Paraphrase of Seth*. Ironically, Seth only once appears in this treatise (from what the Refutator quotes of it): he is part of a group of three, illustrating a scriptural preference for groups of three.[1] As far as we know, Seth was of no independent importance to the author of the *Paraphrase of Seth*. I will therefore refrain from calling this author and his hypothesized group "Sethian," except when the name is enclosed in quotation marks. This will help to distinguish those treated in the present chapter from the Sethians (aka the Seed of Seth) treated in Chapter 7. The "Sethians" of the *Refutation* and the Seed of Seth were different people. There was, of course, a basic commonality: both the author of the *Paraphrase of Seth* and the Seed of Seth were Christians interested in revising the stories of creation. But the author of the *Paraphrase*, as we can see from the remains of his text, forged his own path.

Creation and Salvation

Let us begin with the remains of the document as we have it. From the Refutator's report, we gather that the *Paraphrase of Seth* was an allegorical and revisionary telling of Gen. 1:1-3. This passage can be translated as follows from the Septuagint:

> In the beginning God made the heaven and the earth. The earth was invisible and unformed; darkness was over the abyss, and a wind of God was borne over the waters. God said, 'Let there be light,' and light arose.

According to the author of the *Paraphrase of Seth*, these verses introduced several figures: (1) the primeval waters of creation, (2) a wind (*pneuma*, also meaning "spirit")

---

[1] *Ref.* 5.20.1-3.

whipping over the waters, (3) God's Word or command, and (4) an original light shining in the darkness. The author interpreted these figures to be cosmogonic entities in the abysmal past. The waters signified the waters of nature – the physical world of birth and death, symbolized by a womb. The Light was the divine Word of God (or Logos), a ray from the true God or Father. The wind was the creator or "lower father" who caused nature to give birth to all sorts of creatures.[2] The wind of the creator created serpentine trails on the waters. The creator himself, represented by violent wind, was said to have a serpentine form.[3]

All would have been well if the light had not mixed with darkness. But the light shone onto the dark waters and became trapped. Allegorically, this was taken to mean that the son of God, the "perfect mind," was blended with the waters of matter. He entered the waters (the process of physical birth) and was locked by the creator into "the variegated blend" of human bodies.[4] From these mortal shells, the son of God, though deathless, cried out for redemption.[5]

According to the *Paraphrase*, the divine redeemer of God's son came in the person of the "Logos of God," also called "the perfect Human." The Logos, in order to enter the waters of creation, assumed the snake form of the creator. This serpentine form was called "the form of the slave" (Phil. 2:7). The Logos as Snake is not a positive image (as it was for Peratic Christians). The snake form of the Logos was, in the *Paraphrase*, a ruse – a necessary evil designed to deceive Nature into letting the Logos enter her "womb" (namely this world) with the overall goal of redeeming the light-mind trapped in human bodies.

This story of creation and redemption in the *Paraphrase* was probably told at greater length. (We are not informed about the deeds of the incarnate Logos, for instance, though we know he was born of a virgin.[6]) What we possess is a tendentious summary of the Refutator, who chose to excerpt material based on his primary thesis. He believed that the *Paraphrase* was inspired not by scripture, but by philosophers – specifically Epicureans and Aristotelians – along with mystery cult leaders, most prominently Orpheus.

Sidelight on Orpheus. Orpheus, son of the Muse Calliope, was an ancient bard from Thrace (northern Greece). According to legend, Orpheus founded certain mysteries of the god Dionysus.[7] In the fifth and fourth centuries BCE, a "hubbub" of books were fathered on Orpheus and his son Musaeus.[8] Some of these books

---

[2] *Ref.* 5.19.16.
[3] *Ref.* 5.19.18.
[4] *Ref.* 5.19.16.
[5] *Ref.* 5.19.16. Cf. *Ref.* 5.8.15.
[6] *Ref.* 5.19.20.
[7] Ps.-Apollodorus, *Library of Mythology* 1.3.2; Diodorus of Sicily, *Library of History* 3.65.6.
[8] Plato, *Republic* 364e.

included a poem (or poems) about the birth of the gods (called a "theogony"). Others included spells for healing diseases, purifications for expunging guilt, as well as instructions for bloodless sacrifice and other rituals. The point of undergoing purification was to avoid dire punishments in Hades like lying in mud, carrying water in a sieve, and so on.[9] One of the books Orpheus reputedly wrote was called *Descent to Hades*. Excerpts of the content of this book—or one like it—may also have been incised into extant "Orphic" gold tablets, along with ritual formulae.[10] Making Orpheus the author of such formulae was apt, since—according to widespread legend—he had visited Hades and returned.[11]

The author of the *Paraphrase* described a painting showing an old man with an erect penis chasing a dog-shaped or dog-faced woman.[12] For a long time this depicted old man was identified with the Orphic creator Phanes. In part, this is because the author of the *Refutation* tried to derive "Sethian" thought from the traditions of Orpheus. It is more likely, however, that the old man represents a form of Hermes, while the woman (mysteriously called "Phikola") is a version of the goddess Hekate.[13]

The "Sethian" writer's source for the painting was Plutarch's ten-volume study *On Empedocles* (now lost).[14] It was Plutarch who presumably visited an apparently Athenian sanctuary in the early second century and described the paintings in its portico. The rites performed in the sanctuary were ascribed to Orpheus.[15] The Refutator saw fit to ascribe all of "Sethian" thought to Orpheus. Yet a mere description of a so-called Orphic painting hardly made the author of the *Paraphrase* dependent on "Orpheus" – at least not in any thorough-going way.

[9] Plato, *Phaedo* 69b–d (lying in mud); *Gorgias* 493b–c (water in sieve).

[10] Miguel Herrero de Jáuregui, "Orphic Ideas of Immortality: Traditional Greek Images and a New Eschatological Thought," in *Lebendige Hoffnung—ewiger Tod?! Jenseitsvorstellungen im Hellenismus, Judentum und Christentum*, ed. Michael Labahn and Manfred Lang (Leipzig: Evangelische Verlagsanstalt, 2007), 289–314 at 300.

[11] Euripides, *Alc.* 357-62; Plato, *Symposium* 179d; Isocrates, *Busiris* 7-8. See further Claudia Klodt, "Der Orpheus-Mythos in der Antike," in *Der Orpheus-Mythos von der Antike bis zur Gegenwart*, ed. Claudia Maurer Zenck (Frankfurt am Main: Peter Lang, 2004), 37–98 at 57–8. A readable introduction to Orphic thought and practice is Robert Parker "Early Orphism," in *The Greek World*, ed. Anton Powell (London: Routledge, 1995), 483–510. For the Orphic tablets, see Alberto Bernabé, ed., *Poetae Epici Graeci: Testimonia et Fragmenta Pars II, Orphicorum et Orphicis Similium Testimonia et Fragmenta* (Teubner: Leipzig, 2003–2007). An English translation of the tablets can be found in Alberto Bernabé and Ana Isabel Jiménez San Cristóbal, *Instructions for the Netherworld: The Orphic Gold Tablets*, trans. Michael Chase (Leiden: Brill, 2008).

[12] *Ref.* 5.20.7.

[13] See further M. David Litwa, "Phikola: A Mysterious Goddess at Phlya," *Religion in the Roman Empire* 2, no. 2 (2016): 279–93.

[14] *Ref.* 5.20.6. See further Osborne, *Rethinking Early Greek Philosophy*, 92–4.

[15] *Ref.* 5.20.5.

First Principles

If the *Paraphrase of Seth* seems to have a philosophical air, it accords with the Refutator's designs. The Refutator made it appear as if the author spoke of three philosophical principles – Light, Darkness, and Spirit – which interact according to an Epicurean theory of collision. The Refutator also gave the impression that the theory of mixture presupposed in the *Paraphrase* was Aristotelian. Philosophical ideas may indeed have been present in the original *Paraphrase*, but one wonders whether they were as prominent as the Refutator urged. For the Refutator, tracing the philosophical background of an idea in effect de-Christianized it. Yet the *Paraphrase* manifestly presents Christian ideas and characters.

The three principles of creation, for example, should not distract from the fact that the author of the *Paraphrase* conceived of the primal God as a Father with a Son, who are also described as a perfect Light giving birth to a ray of light.[16] Furthermore, the author believed in a Spirit (counterpart to the wind or creator) which he likened to a wondrous fragrance fumigating all creation.[17] Here, as with Peratic Christian theology, we have a triadic structure of Godhead analogous to other early theories of the Trinity.

The Refutator had an interest in connecting his opponents with snakes. He knew that snakes were associated with Greek mystery cults, and he had just finished culling every hint about snakes he could find in Naassene and Peratic lore. Understandably, the eyes of the Refutator were trained on a single episode in the *Paraphrase*: the Logos entering the "womb" of Nature in snake form. The Refutator was hardly interested in acknowledging the differences between the Logos as snake for Peratic Christians, who depended, not on the text of Gen. 1:1-3, but on John 3 and Numbers 21. For Peratic Christians, the snake form of the Logos was positive (he was the "universal snake") whereas for the author of the Paraphrase, the snake form was a temporary costume, the assumption of a slavish form (Phil. 2:7) – evidently a reference to the human body of the Logos.[18]

Scriptural Practice

The author of the *Paraphrase of Seth* used several scriptural texts. His main text was of course Gen. 1:1-3, combined with a reading of John 1:1 (the Logos). Yet he also referred to Genesis 2–3; Exod. 10:22 (or Deut. 5:22); Exodus 20 (or Deut. 5), Ps. 28:3 (LXX), Matt. 10:34; John 4:4, 10, Phil. 2:7; 3:20, and possibly Acts 2:24 – at least six scriptural texts, three of them distinctly Christian.[19] He also appealed to

---

[16] *Ref.* 5.19.17. In the *Paraphrase of Shem* VII,1 6.30–7.1, the Father God is called "Majesty," and the "Son of Majesty" is also likened to "a ray of bright light."

[17] *Ref.* 5.19.3.

[18] *Ref.* 5.19.21.

[19] See the scriptural index in Litwa, *Refutation of All Heresies*, 811–16.

well-known classical authors, namely Plutarch, Homer, and Herodotus.— He was indeed philosophically informed, citing Andronicus of Rhodes (flourished around 60 BCE).[21] Yet one would be hard pressed to describe him as a philosopher pure and simple. The author of the *Paraphrase* was, rather, a skilled Christian exegete. He had a cosmopolitan mentality akin to the Naassene preacher. He created a theology characterized by Christian preoccupations: the presence of the divine in matter, rescue through a redeemer figure (the incarnate Logos, John 1:14), and the attempt to transcend the physical body and its desires.

Little would indicate that the author of the *Paraphrase* was a member of the already known social formation called the Seed of Seth. The author of the *Paraphrase* did seem to believe in an evil creator (the violent "wind"), but this was not a distinctive Sethian belief. The author referred to none of the major characters of Sethian thought (for instance, Barbelo, the Four Luminaries, Yaldabaoth). He forged his own revisionary take on creation which was based on his own distinctive allegorical interpretation of scripture.

Group or Individual?

Is the *Paraphrase of Seth* the work of an idiosyncratic Christian intellectual trying to advocate his own peculiar teaching? Or did he speak to a larger Christian group? The Refutator, for his part, assumed a larger "Sethian" community with "leaders" and "boundless treatises."[22] Was this mere guesswork?

There is only one point in the *Paraphrase*, or what remains of it, where the author addresses a wider circle. When the author spoke of the separation of the blended elements of the cosmos, he or she referred to a single "place of separation." "No one," the author wrote, "knows this place except for us alone, the spirituals who have been reborn. We are not fleshly, since we have a 'commonwealth in heaven.'"[23]

This sentence, which assumes an "us" and a set of "spiritual" people, indicates that the author at least imagined that he was speaking to a larger group. This implied group was apparently familiar with the Christian scriptures cited or alluded to as authoritative texts. Both Paul (1 Cor. 2:13, 15; 3:1) and the Naassene preacher (among others) had referred to mature Christians as "spirituals."[24] Being "reborn" alludes to Jesus's discourse in John 3:7 – that one must be born again (or "from above"). The "commonwealth in heaven" is a phrase found in Phil. 3:20. Apparently the writer's audience was expected to recognize or at least appreciate these allusions to Christian scripture. The assumption seems to be that they, along with the author of the *Paraphrase*, were spiritually mature Christians already.

[20] *Ref.* 5.20.8-10 (Homer); 5.20.4-9 (Plutarch); 5.21.10-12 (Herodotus).
[21] *Ref.* 5.21.1.
[22] *Ref.* 5.20.1.
[23] *Ref.* 5.21.6.
[24] *Ref.* 5.9.21.

Ritual and Ascetic Practice

More hints about the group's Christian identity appear in a passing reference to ritual. The author of the *Paraphrase* describes what seems to be a baptismal and eucharistic rite. The Logos, after his incarnation, "washed himself clean and drank the cup 'of living, bubbling water'" (John 4:10, 14). This cup is drunk, however, not only by the Logos. He is the model, to be sure, but the cup is meant for "everyone ... who is destined to strip off the slave form [the material body] and be robed with the celestial garment."[25] The fact that the eucharistic cup is filled with water, not wine, suggests a group that forbade alcohol. A wineless eucharist was characteristic of Christian communities in Syria and Asia Minor, and is attested among Marcionite Christians, Severus, Tatian's reputed disciple, and possibly by Tatian himself.[26]

Forbidding alcohol raises the question of other ascetic practices. Sex is never openly prohibited in the *Paraphrase*, though it is apparently demeaned.[27] The serpentine creator repeatedly enters the "womb" of nature to produce different creatures. One does not need Freud to see the snake as a penis; the Greek word for "womb," moreover, was sometimes a euphemism for "vulva."[28] The sexual innuendo of the story becomes explicit when the author illustrates it by means of an ancient painting – an old man with an erection chasing a dog-woman.[29]

In short, the creation of this physical world happens in the way that humans are born – through sex and procreation. The creator encourages human sex (Gen. 1:28) because he is himself sexually active. He is a vibrant "wind" who mixes with water (wet nature). Sex is defiling and results in death (all creatures who are born also die). To escape the creator's realm – the kingdom of birth and death – one must presumably reject sex, allowing the divine element in oneself (the "perfect mind") to ascend out of this wet platform (the material body). When the perfect mind ascends, it leaves behind – presumably like Christ – "the form of the slave," which refers to fleshly bodies.

Such ascetic rejection of sex was characteristic of Saturninian, Marcionite, and Naassene Christians. Although one cannot call this position popular (in the sense of practiced by many people), it was certainly commonplace among a variety of early Christian groups, especially in the eastern Mediterranean. It should be emphasized again that the desire to transcend the present fleshly body does not necessarily mean hatred of it. Virtually all Christians believed that the present physical body destined to die would somehow be transcended or upgraded so as to surmount death and corruption in the "kingdom of heaven." The present body is enslaving since it limits and imprisons the perfect mind within.

---

[25] *Ref.* 5.19.21.

[26] McGowan, *Ascetic Eucharists*, 143–217.

[27] The later *Paraphrase of Shem* has a more open polemic against sexual intercourse ("impure rubbing," VII,1 38.9).

[28] Note the use of "impure womb" in *Ref.* 5.19.19-20.

[29] *Ref.* 5.20.6.

As with Ophite and Naassene Christians, final salvation was envisioned as an ascent. The author of the *Paraphrase* used a particular metaphor ~~~~~~~~~~~~~~~~ aged his audience to be clothed with "the celestial garment." The garment could allude to a parable told by Jesus in Matt. 22:11, where the redeemed are clothed in wedding garments. Probably, however, the "celestial garment" is a nod to Paul's discourse on the resurrection: "this mortal [body] must put on immortality" (1 Cor. 15:53). An even closer intertext is 2 Cor. 5:2: "We yearn to be robed over with our permanent dwelling from heaven." In other words, Paul envisioned the resurrection body as a kind of heavenly overcoat. The "celestial garment" in the *Paraphrase of Seth* is what enables resurrection. Those resurrected will dwell above this cosmos in a heavenly commonwealth (Phil. 3:20).

From these (admittedly sparse) data, we can hypothesize that the author(s) who composed the *Paraphrase* (and potentially other documents attested by the Refutator) probably addressed a pre-existing group of Christian initiates. Where this group existed is unknown. Some have suggested Mesopotamia because of suspected Persian influence. But this idea is based on the assumption that a dualism between Light and Darkness must be Persian in origin. Significantly, when the author speaks of a famous well in Persia, he is completely dependent upon Herodotus.[30] It is better to place the author's circle some place in Alexandria, Syria, or Asia Minor where there were ascetic Christian groups that rejected both alcohol and sex. I favor Alexandria due to the intensely cosmopolitan outlook, but one cannot be certain. Wherever the group was located, it probably existed, like Naassene Christians, between 180–220 CE.

Despite the name of one of their books, the *Paraphrase of Seth*, the users of this text probably did not call themselves "Sethians." The *Paraphrase of Seth*, at least as cited by the Refutator, only once mentions Seth, son of Adam, in passing, and never his heavenly counterpart (a distinctive character among the Seed of Seth). The patriarch Seth may conceivably have been reputed as the author of the document.

We know that later Christian groups attributed books to Seth.[31] The Nag Hammadi writing called *Paraphrase of Shem* (its surviving Coptic version probably composed in the fourth century CE) may be a radical revision and expansion of the creation story in the *Paraphrase of Seth*. Both documents portray three entities involved in creation: Light, Darkness, and Spirit.[32] Both feature the formation of a primeval womb.[33] Both present a savior figure who takes on serpentine form to enter the womb.[34]

---

[30] *Ref.* 5.21.10-11.

[31] Epiphanius, *Pan.* 39.5.1 ("Sethians"); 40.7.4-5 ("Archontics").

[32] *Ref.* 5.19.2-3; *Paraphrase of Shem* VII,1 1.25-28.

[33] *Ref.* 5.19.11; *Paraphrase of Shem* VII,1 4.24.

[34] *Ref.* 5.19.20; *Paraphrase of Shem* VII,1 19.23-35. M. Roberge (*Paraphrase of Shem*, 84–93), points out systemic differences, concluding that "Neither text could have served as the basis for the other. It is equally futile to appeal to a common source" (93). I believe this conclusion to be too rigid, and am inclined to agree with Hans-Martin Schenke, who spoke of a common "mythological matrix and metaphoric presupposed in both documents" ("Die Paraphrase des Sēem," in *Nag Hammadi Deutsch*, 2 vols. [Berlin: de Gruyter, 2003], 2:547).

But major differences also abound. Most obviously, the *Paraphrase of Shem* is much larger, more complex, and shows fewer Christian features. (Evidently this was deliberate, since "Shem" lived long before Christ.) Perhaps the two *Paraphrases* shared a common textual ancestor. Whatever the case may have been, the person who copied the *Paraphrase of Shem* into Nag Hammadi codex VII may have been aware of its earlier association with Seth, since the same codex includes a *Second Discourse of Great Seth* (VII,2) and *Three Steles of Seth* (VII,5). Quite possibly, what mattered was not so much the name (Seth or Shem) as the authority residing in the name, an authority that supported an "ancient" (pre-Mosaic) truth.

Conclusion

To sum up: the author of the *Paraphrase of Seth* was a Christian reader and allegorizer of scripture. He had also read a work of the Aristotelian Andronicus, and was familiar – via Plutarch – of an obscure painting used in an Athenian mystery cult. He recommended Christian rituals including baptism and the eucharist. He demeaned sex, at least implicitly, and thought of the body as enslaved to corruption. He was a theological innovator whose ideas evidently had a significant reception history (in the *Paraphrase of Shem*). The "Sethian" author thus fits the cosmopolitan, entrepreneurial profile of the Naassene preacher who also rejected sex, used allegory, appealed to mystery cults, cited Plutarch, and knew classical poets.

The Naassene preacher and the writer of the *Paraphrase of Seth* were not, to be clear, the same person. The commonality of their thought is indicative – not of identity or direct influence – but of a shared cosmopolitan mentality with a mutual interest in explaining the "mysteries" of creation (a common pastime of religious entrepreneurs in this period). What is striking among these early Christian entrepreneurs is their ability to assimilate all the gifts of Hellenic education (*paideia*) while apparently spurning key pillars of mainstream Greco-Roman society (marriage and childbearing). Both authors provide evidence of late second-century Christian movements fully engaged with the broader Hellenic culture, with leaders intent on parading their knowledge of elite religious and philosophical culture in order to transform the meaning of Jewish and Christian scriptures.

Further Reading

Daniel A. Bertrand, "Paraphrase de Sem et Paraphrase de Seth," in *Les textes de Nag Hammadi: Colloque du Centre d'Histoire des Religions*, ed. J. E. Ménard (Leiden: Brill, 1974), 146–57.

Dylan M. Burns, "μίξεως τινι τέχνη κρείττονι: "Alchemical Metaphor in the Paraphrase of Shem (NHC VII,1)," *Aries* 15 (2015): 81–108.

Carsten Colpe, *Einleitung in die Schriften aus Nag Hammadi* (Münster: Aschendorff, 2011), 219–25.

Werner Foerster, *Gnosis: A Selection of Gnostic Texts*, trans. R. McL. Wilson, 2 vols. (Oxford: Clarendon, 1972), 1:299–305.

Birger Pearson, *Ancient Gnosticism: Traditions and Literature* (Minneapolis: Fortress, 2007), 200–209.

Michel Roberge, *The Paraphrase of Shem (NH VII,1): Introduction, Translation, and Commentary* (Leiden: Brill, 2010), 84–93.

Herbert Schmid, *Christen und Sethianer: Ein Beitrag zur Diskussion um den religionsge-schichtlichen und den kirchengeschichtlichen Begriff der Gnosis* (Leiden: Brill, 2018), 40–56.

Frederik Wisse, "Stalking Those Elusive Sethians," in *The Rediscovery of Gnosticism*, ed. Bentley Layton, 2 vols. (Leiden: Brill, 1981), 2:563–76.

Conclusion

Imagine for a moment what it would be like to walk into second-century Antioch, Alexandria, or Rome in search of a Christian teacher to light the way of salvation. In the Syrian metropolis of Antioch, one might find Ignatius struggling to prove himself as sole manager of his riven Christian community. Yet one could also find Saturninus and Sethian teachers offering more ascetical and philosophical variants of Christianity on different streets of the same city. In early second-century Alexandria, the only Christian teachers we know of were Valentinus, Basilides, Isidore, Carpocrates, and Epiphanes. By about 175 CE, Pantaenus had joined their ranks, but he and his reputed disciple Clement had to compete with Apelles, Prodicus, Julius Cassianus, and likely the Naassene preacher, among – potentially many – others whose names, unrecorded, we will never know.

Perhaps the greatest variety of Christians, however, could be found in the eternal city of Rome, where Valentinus settled to teach a gifted generation of Christian intellectuals, namely Ptolemy, Heracleon, and possibly Marcus. By about 160 CE, one could find in the imperial capital a network of Simonians, Carpocratians under Marcellina, and flourishing branches of Marcionite churches. Marcion, that tireless organizer, had perished by this time, but able leaders were present to take his place: Lucanus, Syneros, Potitus, and Basilicus. Apelles returned from Alexandria and pushed Marcion's thought in new directions. By the end of the second century, the early catholic ecclesial network had incorporated, as it were, under bishop Victor – a development that sharpened already existing divisions between Victor's party, adherents of the New Prophecy, the disciples of Tatian, Ptolemy, Noetus, Theodotus the Shoemaker, and so on. By the turn of the third century, heresiographers – some of them soon to be labeled heretics themselves – produced lengthy treatises blacklisting Christians whom they thought should be ostracized from Christian networks.[1]

Heresiographers aimed to de-Christianize competing Christian groups, pushing them beyond the boundaries of the faith so that they would be ignored and forgotten. And indeed, some early Christian groups probably did perish without us ever even knowing even their names. The memories of other Christian teachers and societies survived, ironically, only on the pages of heresiography. Still others we have come to know through the discovery of manuscripts, inscriptions, and artifacts that have more recently come to light. At this very hour, we know not what the archaeologist's

---

[1] Origen, *Cels.* 5.61-62.

spade (or the Egyptian farmer's mattock) will uncover. Further discoveries – and certainly further interpretations – are bound to come, and they will further inform and complexify our understanding of early Christianity.

It is time now to ask what de-Christianized Christian groups actually contributed to the development of early Christian culture and thought. Many of the impacts may have been subtle; some are now unclear or hard to prove. Nevertheless, it is possible to sketch the main outlines of their contribution under six headings: (1) scriptural formation and interpretation, (2) view of God, (3) view of Christ, (4) view of humanity, (5) ritual and ethics, and (6) leadership and organization.

Scriptural Formation and Interpretation

There was a time when scholars argued that Marcion created the concept of the New Testament as a canon (or closed list) of sacred writings.[2] Although this viewpoint is now seen as anachronistic (a closed list – or rather lists – only solidified in the late fourth century), we can still vouch for the idea that Marcion helped to stabilize the form of the New Testament with the basic structure of at least one gospel plus a set of Pauline letters.[3] By Marcion's time, there was probably already a ten-letter edition of these letters in circulation. Marcion published his own edition (the *Apostolikon*) linked to his single gospel (the *Evangelion*), which was likely an earlier form of what is now called the gospel of Luke. Apelles's later use of scriptural texts shows that Marcion's canon was not in fact closed. It was certainly not closed for other Christian groups. Early catholics expanded their Pauline collection with at least three pseudepigraphical letters (Titus, 1–2 Timothy) – perhaps in partial response to Marcion, whose asceticism and acceptance of female leadership was resented.[4]

Work on Marcion's scriptural edition, moreover, did not cease with the master's death. His disciples Lucanus and Apelles continued the work of text criticism in their own ways. Sometime later, Theodoteans formed the first team of text critics that worked on Christian scripture. Their work did not stabilize the text of the New

[2] Harnack, *Marcion: Das Evangelium*, 71–72; John Knox, *Marcion and the New Testament: An Essay in the Early History of the Canon* (Chicago: Chicago University Press, 1942), 19–38; Hans von Campenhausen, *The Formation of the Christian Bible*, trans. John Austin Baker (London: A. & C. Black, 1972), 163; Jason BeDuhn, "New Studies of Marcion's *Evangelion*," ZAC 21 (2017): 8–24 at 22; Michael Satlow, *How the Bible Became Holy* (New Haven: Yale University Press, 2014), 251–2.
[3] John Barton, *Holy Writings, Sacred Text: The Canon in Early Christianity* (Louisville: Westminster John Knox 1997), 35–62; Enrico Norelli, "Of Books and Bishops: The Second Century as a Key to the Process that Led to a New Testament Canon," *Zeitschrift für Religionswissenschaft* 18 (2010): 179–98 at 191–5; Enrico Norelli and Averil Cameron, *Markion und der biblische Canon* (Berlin: de Gruyter, 2016), 1–27; Markschies, *Christian Theology*, 217–31; David Brakke, "Scriptural Practices in Early Christianity: Towards a New History of the New Testament Canon," in Brakke et al., eds., *Invention*, 263–80; Matthias Klinghardt, "Marcion's Gospel and the New Testament: Catalyst or Consequence?" NTS 63 (2017): 318–34.
[4] Tyson, *Marcion and Luke–Acts*, 124–5.

Testament by any means, but they did recognize the problem of textual fluctuation, developed theories to explain it, and proposed a variety of textual solutions.

When Marcionite textual criticism was in full swing, Tatian was weaving together the text of the four gospels into a single macro-text now called the *Diatessaron*. He could thus achieve the Marcionite ideal of upholding a single written gospel even if considerable adjustments were made in the process of seamlessly fusing four texts together. Gospel harmonies – many of them based on Tatian's work – proved enormously influential in the history of the church.

The Simonian author of the *Great Declaration Commentary* explored the genre of the allegorical commentary on Genesis 1 later known as the *hexameron*. This genre would later be developed by Tatian, Rhodon, Basil of Caesarea, Ambrose, Augustine, among many others.[5] Allegorical interpretation was employed extensively in the second century by the author of the *Paraphrase of Seth* and by Heracleon in his *Commentary on John*. Origen and Augustine are perhaps the most famous Christian allegorists of the early church, but the techniques they used had long been tested and honed by the Christians discussed in this volume.

Heracleon and Basilides are the first known commentators on Christian scripture. Basilides possibly commented on a form of Luke while Heracleon tackled John. Both wrote academic commentaries of considerable length and sophistication. The commentary genre would become prevalent among Christian intellectuals of all times. Indeed, writing biblical commentaries is still a cottage industry today.

With the benefit of hindsight, we know that the Christians discussed in this book worked on many texts that later became books of the New Testament. Nevertheless, they also give a glimpse of the great variety of Christian literature in the second century that influenced Christian thought. Reportedly, Basilides made use of prophetic writings attributed to Barkabbas and Barkoph. His son Isidore commented on the writings of the prophet Parchor and knew a text called the *Prophecy of Ham*.[6] Julius Cassianus is a key witness to the *Gospel according the Egyptians*. The Naassene preacher quoted both the *Gospel according the Egyptians* and a version of the *Gospel of Thomas*. Both the author of the *Secret Book of John* and Prodicus used a book attributed to Zoroaster.

Some figures and groups composed their own scriptures, scriptures that preserved alternative Christian traditions and memories. The Seed of Seth, for instance, composed almost a dozen scriptural or quasi-scriptural works – for instance the *Secret Book of John*, the *Holy Book of the Great Invisible Spirit*, the *Apocalypse of Adam*, and *Melchizedek*. Several of these texts were recovered at Nag Hammadi. Justin wrote the book of *Baruch*, and we have excerpts from a *Paraphrase of Seth* which was perhaps extensively reworked as the *Paraphrase of Shem* found at Nag Hammadi. Christians would write what they aimed to be authoritative (typically pseudepigraphical) texts well into Late Antiquity.

[5] Jerome, *Illustrious Men* 37.
[6] Clement, *Strom.* 6.6.53.2-5 = Löhr, *Basilides*, frag. 15.

View of God

The unnamed writers representing the Seed of Seth were pathbreakers when it came to what today is called "apophatic" or "negative" theology. Adapting terminology from the Pythagoreans, Sethians posited a supreme principle called "Monad," described as higher than divinity, illimitable, unsearchable, unnamable, and so on.[7] The author of *Eugnostus*, who offered the first recognizably Ophite Christian theology, called God "immortal," "without birth," "without a beginning," "undominated," "unnamable," "formless," "infinite," "incomprehensible," "immeasurable," "untraceable," and so on.[8] In the *Gospel of Truth*, the unknowability of the Father is the very problem that kickstarts creation. The idea of the unknown primal God higher than any national god – including the Judean deity – is one of the most persistent notions in the early Christian laboratory of ideas.[9]

The second century saw the first extensive forays into Christian trimorphic theology (later called Trinitarianism). Simonians spoke of three modes of Godhead, with Simon as the underlying essence. From Jewish Wisdom speculation, Simonians developed the character of Thought (*Ennoia/Epinoia*), as the feminine – and fallen – aspect of the divine. Noetus in Smyrna and his followers in Rome believed that Father and Son shared the same essence even if they appeared as different manifestations. Ophite Christians envisioned a Trinity of three Humans: the First Human or Father, the Child of the Human, and Christ (or the Savior). The Naassene preacher and Monoïmus used similar language in a binitarian way (Human and Child of the Human). The Seed of Seth put forward a more familial model – God as Father, Mother, and Son. In Valentinian Christian thought, the role of the feminine divine was expanded so that the ancient figure of Wisdom, reimagined as the creatrix, took center stage.

Stories about Wisdom as the creatrix sometimes involved the idea that the high deity and the creator were different beings. In an important stream of Wisdom theology, Wisdom was creatrix *because* she gave birth to the creator. The creator's subordination to true deity was a common Platonic idea, but the creator's reputed ignorance and wickedness, it seems, was a Christian innovation. A variety of early Christian theologians championed an angelic creator identified with the Judean deity, although they differed on how to view the chief creator's character. Saturninus, Marcion, and the Seed of Seth inferred from Jewish scripture that the creator was jealous, violent, and thus wicked. Later Marcionites emphasized the creator's strict justice, while Valentinian theologians made room for his moral and intellectual improvement.[10]

Valentinian intellectuals speculated about the "Fullness" of divine reality split into ten, twelve, thirty – or even an infinite number of – distinguishable emanations, all apparently consubstantial with the primal deity. Due to the fact of consubstantiality, it

---

[7] *Ap. John* BG 22.16–26.14.
[8] *Eug.* III,3 71.18–73.5.
[9] See further John Whittaker, "Basilides on the Ineffability of God," *HTR* 62 (1969): 367–71.
[10] Origen, *Comm. John* 13.422.

would be wrong to think of these emanations as separate "divinities."[11] They are rather the Father's individuated, eternal thoughts and were duly called "eternities" ("aeons"). The eternities were analogous to Platonic Forms that exist in or out of the divine mind.[12] Thus the claim that some Christians believed in twelve, thirty, or 365 gods is not accurate.[13] Despite the accusations and counter-accusations of polytheism, virtually all early Christians would have insisted that they worshiped a single Godhead. In this way, early Christians revealed their intellectual debts to Judaism and adapted their theology to the philosophical currents of their time.[14]

View of Christ

Cerinthus was among the first known Christians to theorize a baptismal incarnation – the idea that the divine Spirit, sometimes called Christ, joined with Jesus at his baptism. This Spirit energized Jesus so that he, a Jewish peasant, could perform miracles and preach heavenly wisdom. Most later Christians never denied that Jesus was empowered by the Spirit, even if the point at which Jesus became divine was increasingly traced back to his conception (Luke 1:35).

Both Valentinus and Apelles theorized about the properties of Jesus's body. Valentinus and Epiphanius agreed in denying that Jesus eliminated solid waste.[15] Such waste was viewed as corruption, which Jesus did not produce. According to Apelles, when Christ descended through the heavens, he generated his own body out of stellar substance.[16] When he arrived on earth, he wove his mortal body from the "essential constituents of the universe."[17]

Saturninus said that Jesus in his divine nature was "unborn and formless." Christ came in a real body, but in his divine nature, he was bodiless and unborn – just like his Father. The *Treatise on Resurrection* gives perhaps the earliest clear statement of two-nature christology: "The son of God ... was a son of humanity. He embraced them both, possessing humanity as well as divinity."[18] These theologies could explain how, when Jesus died, the divine in him remained unsuffering.

[11] *Pace* DeConick, *Gnostic New Age*, 247.
[12] Tertullian, *Against the Valentinus* 4.2.
[13] *Pace* Ehrman, *Lost Christianities*, 2. Such a belief was ascribed to Orpheus, though he was also a reputed monotheist (Theophilus of Antioch, *Autolycus* 3.2).
[14] See, e.g., Oskar Skarsaune, "Is Christianity Monotheistic? Patristic Perspectives on a Jewish/Christian Debate," in *Studia Patristica* 29 (1997): 340–63; Michael Mach, "Concepts of Jewish Monotheism During the Hellenistic Period," in *The Jewish Roots of Christological Monotheism*, ed. James Davila, Carey C. Newman, and Gladys Lewis (Leiden: Brill, 1999), 21–42; Stephen Mitchell and Peter van Nuffelen, eds., *One God: Pagan Monotheism in the Roman Empire* (Cambridge: Cambridge University Press, 2010); Mitchell and van Nuffelen, *Monotheism between Pagans and Christians in Late Antiquity* (Leuven: Peeters, 2010).
[15] Epiphanius, *Pan.* 77.15.2.
[16] Tertullian, *Flesh of Christ* 6.3; 8.5.
[17] *Ref.* 7.38.3; Epiphanius, *Pan.* 44.2.3.
[18] *Treat. Res.* I,4 44.21-33.

Christological conflicts became more sharply defined later in the second century. Noetus and his followers argued that the Son was somehow the Father in flesh. Theodotus the Leatherworker demanded that Jesus was human and remained human even after his deification (whether at his baptism or resurrection). It was widely debated whether Jesus after his resurrection reassumed solid flesh or took on a spirit body (1 Cor. 15:45) that transcended earthly matter. Thinkers like Apelles, the Naassene preacher, and Justin (author of *Baruch*) explored how Jesus, after his resurrection, became a more subtle body (*pneuma*) which naturally soared to heaven.

View of Humanity

Many Christians in this book experimented with a tripartite anthropology introduced by Plato and his heirs. They envisioned humans as combinations of bodies, souls, and minds (also called "spirits"). The mind (*nous*) or spirit (*pneuma*) was the entity that communicated directly with God during prophetic inspiration. It was also the entity that survived death and could ascend past the planets. Its natural home, in fact, was heaven and the divine world. The spirit, for many early Christian thinkers, was a little piece or emanation of God metaphorized as a spark or seed (among other things). It was not necessarily immaterial, but it was not a coarse or corruptible entity like flesh either. The human spirit could in fact move from one corruptible body to another in a scheme of transmigration, a notion promoted by Basilides, Carpocrates, and the Naassene preacher. The idea of transmigration eventually faded in Christian thought, but the notion of an immortal soul or spirit that can exchange an earthly for a heavenly body still perdures.

When it came to human sin, moral evil was acknowledged by the vast majority of the figures treated in this book. At the same time, evil was often traced to demonic inspiration or even possession. Unbaptized persons were called hostels for demons (Valentinus). Evil is the demon-inspired choice to live according to one's earthly nature. As such, evil has no root, for matter was but the distant outflow of the divine. It has no substance in itself. To choose it was to opt for what has no being in itself, a stuff that will eventually dissolve into nothing. The denial of evil as a substance, famously championed by Augustine, would have a long history in Christian thought.[19]

Ritual and Ethics

Simonian Christians are the first known Christian group to engage in statue veneration. They venerated a statue in Rome putatively representing Simon. Simonians were also said to venerate statues of Helen in the form of Athena. Marcellinian Christians venerated an image of Jesus (apparently a painted picture) along with pictures (or perhaps statuettes) of other philosophers, namely Pythagoras, Plato, and Aristotle. Statue or icon veneration still persists in many forms of Christianity today.

---

[19] Augustine, *Confessions* book 7 (entire).

Reportedly, Basilidean Christians first celebrated the holy day of Christ's incarnation. On the night prior to January 6th or 10th, they listened all night to (apparently scriptural) texts.[20] At dawn, they celebrated the moment of incarnation, possibly with song. Basilides was known as a songwriter,[21] and Valentinus published the first known Christian psalm book made of his own compositions.[22]

There were many variations on the Christian baptismal rite and different ideas about the benefits it bestowed on believers. For Valentinians, the baptismal ceremony was a transfer of ownership from demons to God. Demons were literally sealed off from entering the human soul. Valentinians exorcized the baptismal waters and promoted pre-baptismal fasts, vigils, and other acts of mental and physical preparation.[23] Many variations on baptism included a rite of anointing. Several of these practices – anointing, exorcism, disrobing, and so on – had a long afterlife in Christian worship.

The most enigmatic baptismal rite, perhaps, was the Five Seals promoted by Sethian Christians. The seals may refer to five steps in the ritual, five dunks in the water, or five anointings with oil.[24] *Three Forms of First Thought* mentions five steps: robing, baptizing, enthroning, glorifying, and rapturing. The last three steps, though they might have had earthly symbols, probably refer to what happened in an imagined heavenly ascent. Sethian baptism "surpassed the heavens," changing one's status in heaven as well as on earth.[25] In later Sethian thought, a series of heavenly baptisms made the ideal Christian into an angel and even a god.[26] Mysterious as it was, the Five Seals ritual is one example of a common phenomenon: the tendency of Christians to go "one up" on competitors when it came to conceptualizing their rite of initiation.

Ophite and Marcosian Christians pioneered what can be called a practice of Last Rites. In Marcosian ritual of the early third century, a bishop would whisper a prayer into the ears of the dying, instructing him or her how to pass through the lower heavens. Similar was an Ophite Christian ritual which instructed the dying how to ascend past the planetary rulers with short formulas and prayers spoken aloud by an officiant or "father."[27]

Saturninus is the first known Christian who embraced and preached a radical Christian asceticism. His ban on sex and procreation foreshadowed later Sethian and Marcionite directives. Sex was also prohibited – or at least strongly discouraged – by the likes of Tatian, Julius Cassianus, and the Naassene preacher, among others. Some

---

[20] Clement, *Strom.* 1.21.145.6–146.4 = Löhr, *Basilides*, frag. 1.

[21] Origen, *Enarrations on Job* 21.12 (PG 17 80a) = Löhr, *Basilides*, Testimony 11.

[22] Tertullian, *Flesh of Christ* 17.1; cf. 20.3. Origen mentioned other "psalms of Valentinus" (*Ennarations on Job* 21.12; PG 17.80a). The Muratorian canon (lines 81-85) mentions a psalm book of Valentinus.

[23] Clement, *Exc.* 84.1. Cf. Tertullian, *Baptism* 20.1.

[24] *Tri. Prot.* XIII,1 48.15-25.

[25] *Gosp. Eg.* III,2 63.24-25; 65.25.

[26] Litwa, *Posthuman Transformation*, 133–50.

[27] *Ref.* 6.41.4.

of these figures also discouraged the consumption of meat and/or wine. Each of these thinkers was a pioneer of an ascetic tradition that informed, directly or indirectly, Christian monastic ideals.

Valentinians were perhaps the first to theorize about marriage as a sacrament. For them, marriage was a holy rite that symbolized the union of the female soul with the male angelic consort in the Fullness. In this way, the horizontal dimension of marriage to a human partnership corresponded to the vertical dimension of spiritual union with an angel, a union that allowed one to enter the Fullness after death.

Leadership and Organization

Many of the figures discussed in this book were the first to experiment with the institution of the Christian school. They advertised themselves as teachers, assigned a meeting place, and gathered disciples. Their students, in turn, continued the teaching of their masters, often in new ways. Some figures – even as they led scholastic formations – were also connected to ecclesial networks. Others experimented with forming churches of their own. Basilideans had their own rituals, and so evidently their own assemblies. Marcionites made churches "like wasps build nests."[28] Marcus created ecclesial formations in Asia Minor and Gaul. Marcellina and Theodotus also formed their own independent assemblies in Rome. Others – like Valentinus, Tatian, Florinus, and Noetus's disciples – were integrated into incipient catholic networks at least until the early third century.

Ideals of female leadership go all the way back to stories about Norea, the sister of Seth, as well as to apostolic figures like Mary Magdalene and Salome. Salome starred in the *Gospel according the Egyptians* as a dialogue partner with Jesus. Mary Magdalene played a similar role in the *Gospel of Mary*, a text partially preserved today in Greek and Coptic. The Simonian leader Helen was said to be venerated along with Simon, and some Simonians were called "Helenians."[29] Female Marcionites officiated the rite of baptism.[30] Ptolemy appealed to Flora as a patroness and intellectual equal. Marcellinians were the first known Christian group in Rome said to be solely led by a woman. Philumene's prophecies influenced the thought of Apelles. Marcus inspired several female prophets in Asia Minor. They spoke boldly in the meetings and exercised leadership at banquets. We can thus verify the reality behind Tertullian's complaint that his opponents allow women a wide scope of leadership in their assemblies.[31]

[28] Tertullian, *AM* 4.5.3.
[29] Origen, *Cels.* 5.62.
[30] Epiphanius, *Pan.* 42.4.5.
[31] Tertullian, *Pr. Haer.* 41. See further Madeleine Scopello, "Jewish and Greek Heroines in the Nag Hammadi Library," in King, ed., *Images of the Feminine*, 71–90; and in the same volume Luise Abramowski, "Female Figures in the Gnostic *Sondergut* in Hippolytus's *Refutatio*," 136–52; Margaret Y. MacDonald, "Was Celsus Right? The Role of Women in the Expansion of Early

All the Christians discussed in this book worked to some extent to integrate Christian thought into the intellectual culture of their time. Julius Cassianus and his contemporary Tatian were the first Christian chronographers who paved the way for more famous chronographers like Julius Africanus, Eusebius, and Jerome. The Naassene preacher used the tools available to him from epideictic rhetoric. Peratic Christians used astronomy to see Christ in the stars. The Simonian author of the *Great Declaration Commentary* combined his knowledge of Genesis with the latest theories of embryology. Theodoteans adapted text-critical tools and Aristotelian logic.

Some early Christian formations were open societies that allowed members to be fully involved in the larger culture; others were closed conventicles that – even as they selectively borrowed elements from mainstream culture – forbade involvement with Greco-Roman temples, state holidays, banquets, and sporting events. Yet there was no way for any Christian group to be completely sealed off from the broader society, since most Christians – whether Jew or Greek, slave or free – were already socialized in Greco-Roman cultural formations. It is no wonder that they experimented with elements from classical literature, philosophical culture, and Greco-Roman education.

To sum up, the "found" Christianities discussed in this book had much to contribute to Christian thought and life – and not only in the tender years of the Christian movement(s). Truth be told, we have barely scratched the surface of their impact. Some of the practices and beliefs discussed here would be carried forward in new forms. Others would be scrapped and forgotten. The second century was an age of experimentation, an era with only incipient creeds, no closed canon, and no elaborate ecclesial hierarchy. The tradition of the apostles – much of it invented, revised, and debated during this period – was at most two or three generations old. Christian leaders tried hard to carve out a space for their own authority in what sometimes proved to be a hostile political environment. Many of them succeeded in laying the groundwork for long-lasting Christian ideas and institutions. To understand their contributions is important for understanding Christianity as a whole.

Of course, even as we bring to light these figures and groups typically unsung in ecclesiastical history, it is important not to heroize them or to conform them too closely to modern movements (some of which claim the "gnostic" title and spirituality). The fact that some of the Christian groups discussed in this book called themselves "gnostics" does not mean that they were unchristian.

It would be nice to say that the "knowing" Christians treated in this book always had open minds and open hearts. For many, however, that does not seem to have been the case.[32] To claim special knowledge was in many cases to claim transcendent and unchanging truth. Some of the figures discussed in this book claimed to have gained

Christianity," in *Early Christian Families in Context: An Interdisciplinary Dialogue*, ed. David L. Balch and Carolyn Osiek (Grand Rapids: Eerdmans, 2003), 157–84.
[32] *Test. Truth* IX,3 69.3-4.

this truth by special revelation, others by apostolic tradition. They would not have tolerated others experimenting in theology even if they were daring experimenters themselves. Most early Christians, it seems, believed in truth as a zero-sum reality – either one had it or not. There was no gray area. Truth was not just a viewpoint or an opinion. Those who had the truth were saved; those who did not were lost. The stakes were high, which is why most Christians were willing to fight for their beliefs and a few even died for them.

Many of the figures here introduced believed in a transcendent deity of pure goodness, but this being was not necessarily the "God of love" preached from many modern pulpits. Indeed, it is doubtful that a transcendent deity could have anything resembling human emotion. Ironically, although Ophite and Sethian Christians viewed God as the ultimate Human, this figure was typically far beyond human feelings and traits. God was so great as to be beyond gender, knowledge, and even divinity itself. God was not love, to put it bluntly, but something beyond it – something beyond even God.

Several of the Christian leaders discussed here used the language of secrets and mysteries, but by and large they were not very secretive about their beliefs. The secret knowledge they spoke of was often written down and to that extent accessible. They preached sermons revealing so-called secrets to the elect, promising the revelation of even greater mysteries. The unknown God preached by Valentinus among others was not so much secret as ineffable – unable, that is, to be understood by the human mind. The fact that God was unknown was in fact widely known and accepted (John 1:18).

In terms of ethics, the Christians here treated did not emphasize tolerance or mutual acceptance. Several of them were quite judgmental about the practices and beliefs of the majority culture. They mocked Greek philosophers and intellectuals, and condemned what they considered to be immoral sexual practices. Some even forbade sex *within* marriage. Others demanded vegetarianism. Watching games and sports events was condemned as frivolous and immoral. In sum, most early Christians seemed to have fashioned oppositional attitudes in conflict with the majority sentiments of many ancient Mediterranean peoples.

It is of course true that most of the figures discussed in this book were the victims of heresiographical attacks, but they also engaged in vigorous polemic themselves.[33] Indeed, there was no other way to survive in the intellectually competitive environment of the second century. Early Christians of all stripes mocked each other, demeaned each other's rituals, and even expelled one another. Broadmindedness, dialogue, and mutual acceptance were not well-known or persistent features in early Christian subcultures or in Greco-Roman culture at large.

There was indeed an early Christian emphasis on healing and the therapy of emotions.[34] But to say that the figures in this book supported something analogous

---

[33] Origen, *Against Celsus* 5.63.
[34] Ismo Dunderberg, *Gnostic Morality Revisited* (Tübingen: Mohr Siebeck, 2015), 19–136; DeConick, *Gnostic New Age*, 17, 21.

to modern therapeutic holism seems wide of the mark.[35] Many of them vigorously asserted the need to separate from bodily urges and ultimately from the mortal flesh itself. They did not necessarily hate the current bodily platform, but they did not seem to love it either. Negative emotions were considered "appendages" that could be cut off.[36] Julius Cassianus – among other Christians – recommended that men actually cut off their testicles in order to attain a higher spiritual state. The point was not to integrate body and spirit, but to *become* spirit (*pneuma*) which was itself conceived of as a higher, subtle, and deathless body.[37]

There is no doubt that to some degree the voices of Christians described here were countercultural and antitraditional. Here we can cite the *Wisdom of Jesus Christ* (NHC III,4) where Jesus himself lampoons the creator of this world and his angels: "Therefore tread upon their tombs, bring low their providence and break their yoke … I give you authority over all things as children of light that you tread upon their power!"[38] Yet in the very same text we read of the redeemed, who are "full of every imperishable glory and unspeakable joy. They all are at rest in him [the Unknowable God] … in his unchanging glory and his measureless joy."[39] The story here is not one in which Christians are in constant battle with lower powers. Their struggle against demons and the creator is real, to be sure, and sometimes violent; but eventually Christians transcend these lower powers to enjoy the peace and rest of the supernal realm.

Thus to play up the element of transgressiveness, making it a key element in the "gnostic" orientation seems to press too firmly on one particular key.[40] In fact, there is a danger here that emphasizing transgressiveness might in fact reinforce a preexisting emphasis in heresiological rhetoric – the rebellious spirit of supposed "gnostics" who were putatively lawless and licentious. It is this emphasis on rebellion as determining a persistent orientation – not individual instances of transgression under certain circumstances – that I highlight as problematic. Many Christians looked forward to the time when they would crush Satan – and his father Ialdabaoth – underneath their feet. They considered life to be a struggle, for which they wore the full armor of God (Eph. 6:12-18). Yet they also knew that, deep down, they had a spark of the divine in them, that they were in fact unbeatable, and members of an "indomitable generation." Such beliefs would have afforded them at least a foretaste of the rest and joy they looked forward to experiencing in the transcendent realm. Disobedience to the lower authorities would finally and even necessarily yield to joy and everlasting rest.

---

[35] *Pace* DeConick, *Gnostic New Age*, 343–4.

[36] Clement, *Strom.* 2.20.112.1–114.2 = Löhr, *Basilides*, frag. 5.

[37] T. Engberg-Pedersen, *Cosmology and the Self in the Apostle Paul: The Material Spirit* (Oxford: Oxford University Press, 2010).

[38] *Wisd. Jes. Chr.* III,4 119.1–8.

[39] *Wisd. Jes. Chr.* III,4 100.9-12.

[40] DeConick, *Gnostic New Age*, 13. It should be noted that DeConick's "ideal cognitive model," presents five traits of the Gnostic orientation, including the direct experience of the transcendent, a seekership outlook, innate spiritualness, and the possession of Gnosis (DeConick, "Crafting Gnosis").

In this discussion, much depends on the lens through which we choose to see the figures studied in this book. Some scholars choose the lens of modern counterculture or post-structuralist critical theory.[41] In both lenses, the image of the early Christian as a critic or renegade is to some degree valorized. Thus the portrayal of "gnostics" as the ancient counterculture is also a mode of valorization. This valorization ostensibly performs the opposite function as heresiological discourse, which attempts to delegitimate and denigrate "gnostic" Christians as subaltern, marginal, and dangerous to ("real") Christianity.

Ironically, however, the modern attempt to counter heresiological portraits actually reinforces the content of a heresiological emphasis (namely, "gnostics" as deviants). This emphasis I think is wrong – not just because it potentially reinscribes heresiological discourse – but because it does not fit the data as a whole. Relative to elite Greco-Roman culture, virtually *all* Christians were coded as transgressors, though this is generally not how they viewed themselves.[42] Relative to the *truly* divine world, however, Christians were not rebels at all, and their need to transgress cosmic structures to attain the true Father can be viewed as an act of obedience and submission to true (albeit hidden) Reality as they conceived it. Transgressivity, in brief, is a relative term. If a group of ancient Christians is said to be transgressive, we must always ask – transgressive with respect to what and under what circumstances? If in this cosmos one had to be on constant guard, in the transcendent realm – often accessed through mystical or spiritual experience – everything was peace and joy.

One final point before closing. The fact that some Christianities are "lost" to memory today has a lot to do with what later Christians *chose* to remember. Today, scores of books and dictionary articles have been written on how one group of Christians, the early catholics, became the imperial church in the fourth-century CE and beyond.[43] In my view, the reception of imperial patronage does not mean that the politically sponsored Christians "won" while the others (namely, the figures discussed in this book) "lost." Early Christianity, to borrow an image from David Brakke, was not a horse race – meaning that early Christian groups were not discrete and bounded entities like horses that can be said to win or lose.[44] In the second century, at least, they were loosely bounded systems open to all sorts of interaction, borrowing, and negotiation.

What became known as early catholicism was a conglomerate of early Christian ideas and practices tested and re-tested in the laboratory of the second century. It never existed in any pure state and never attained the coherence and intellectual dominance that it advertised. The idea (or ideology) of a "great church" did, to be sure, became a social fact for some early observers.[45] In reality, however, there were

---

[41] DeConick, *Gnostic New Age*; Cahana-Blum, *Wrestling with Archons*.

[42] For general Christian transgressiveness, see Hurtado, *Destroyer of the Gods* (Waco: Baylor University Press, 2016).

[43] See, e.g., Paul Veyne, *When Our World Became Christian 312–394* (Cambridge: Polity, 2010).

[44] Brakke, *Gnostics*, 7–8.

[45] Origen, *Cels.* 5.59.

always various churches filled with various people with various practices and various ideas.

It would concede too much to the religion of intellectuals to say that everyone had the same basic notions as regards the "essence" of Christianity (summed up in creeds, for instance). Strictly speaking, there never was an essence of Christianity. Even if many Christian intellectuals argued vigorously for what were considered to be essential truths, these truths were always understood in different ways by different people of different nations and genders in different times. Despite the reality of later forms of state-sponsored Christianities, the control of thought and practice was never such that all Christians in the Roman empire – not to mention those outside it – were forced to think and practice in the same ways, especially in the privacy of their own hearts and homes.

To be sure, there are forms of ancient Christianity that are generally not remembered or memorialized today. We might wish to call these forms of Christianity "lost." What I would emphasize here, however, is that due to the discoveries of recent times, many of the "lost" Christianities of the second century CE now have the capacity to be "found." Indeed, we have done our best to rediscover and re-present some of them here in an accessible way.

Allowing the forms of Christianity discussed here to *continue* to be "lost" is no longer due simply to lack of data. The data – though still fragmentary and contested to be sure – are greater now than perhaps they have ever been since the fourth century CE. So today, allowing some forms of earliest Christianity to continue to be "lost" is, to a significant extent, a matter of will. Many modern people, truth be told, probably care less about finding lost forms of Christianity. They believe that they were lost for a reason and ought still to be marginalized in memory or categorized as small and threatening – if they need to be acknowledged at all.

For those serious about understanding early Christianity, however, going after the "lost sheep" (who is often the black sheep) is a necessary and rewarding task. Despite the continued patchiness of the data, we now have the means to imagine responsibly what many previously de-Christianized Christians lived – and in some cases died – for. We have the ability to lay aside the worn-out discourse of who "won" and "lost" for the sake of gaining insight into what happened in their assemblies, what they felt and what they believed. To put it briefly: we have the power – using both new and old tools of historical reconstruction – to make what is lost *found*, and in so doing recover important truths about what has become the largest – and arguably the most diverse – religion on earth today.

Select Bibliography

Primary Sources

Note: Coptic texts of Nag Hammadi and related literature can be found in James Robinson, ed. *Coptic Gnostic Library, A Complete Edition of the Nag Hammadi Codices*, 5 vols. (Leiden: Brill, 2000). Many newer editions of Coptic texts (with French translations) can also be found in the series published by Laval University Press series, *Bibliothèque Copte de Nag Hammadi.*

Alcinous. *Enseignement des doctrines de Platon.* Edited by John Whittaker. Paris: Belles Lettres, 1990.

Apostolic Fathers. Translated by Bart Ehrman. LCL 25. Cambridge: Harvard University Press, 2003.

Apuleius. *Metamorphoseon Libri XI.* Stuttgart: Teubner, 1992.

Apuleius. *Opuscules philosophiques: Du Dieu de Socrate, Platon et sa doctrine, Du Monde, Fragments.* Edited by Jean Beaujeu. 3d printing. Paris: Belles Lettres, 2018.

Augustine. *De Haeresibus.* Edited by R. Vander Plaetse and C. Beukers. CCSL 46. Turnhout: Brepols, 1969.

Brankaer, Johanna. *The Gospel of Judas.* Oxford: Oxford University Press, 2019.

Charlesworth, James, ed. *The Old Testament Pseudepigrapha.* 2 vols. New York: Doubleday, 1985.

Clement of Alexandria. *Paedagogus, Stromata, Excerpta ex Theodoto, Eclogae Propheticae.* Edited by Otto Stählin and Ludwig Früchtel. 4 ed. Berlin: Akademie, 1985.

Copenhaver, Brian P. *Hermetica: The Greek Corpus Hermeticum and the Latin Asclepius in a new English Translation with Notes and Introduction.* Cambridge: Cambridge University Press, 1992.

Cyril of Jerusalem. *Opera quae supersunt omnia.* Edited by W. K. Reischl and J. Rupp. 2 vols. Hildesheim: Olms, 1967.

Epiphanius. *Ancoratus* and *Panarion.* Edited by Karl Holl, Marc Bergermann, Christian-Friedrich Collatz, and Jürgen Dummer. 2d ed. 4 vols. Berlin: Akademie, 1980–2013.

Eusebius, *Histoire ecclésiastique.* Edited by Gustav Bardy. 4 vols. SC 31, 41, 55, 73. Paris: Cerf, 1952–60.

Irenaeus. *Contre les hérésies.* 10 vols. Edited by Adelin Rousseau and Louis Doutreleau. SC. Paris: Cerf, 1974.

Josephus. Translated by H. St J. Thackeray et al. 10 vols. Loeb Classical Library. Cambridge, Mass.: Harvard University Press, 1926–65.

Justin Martyr. *Dialogus cum Tryphone.* Edited by Miroslav Marcovich. Berlin: de Gruyter, 1997.

Kasser, Rudolphe and Gregory Wurst. *Gospel of Judas Critical Edition Together with the Letter of Peter to Philip, James, and a Book of Allogenes from Codex Tchacos.* Washington DC: National Geographic, 2007.

Lactantius. *Institutions divines.* Edited by Pierre Monat. SC 236. Paris: Cerf, 1984.

Litwa, M. David, ed. *Refutation of All Heresies.* WGRW 40. Atlanta: SBL Press, 2016.

Litwa, M. David. *Hermetica II: The Excerpts of Stobaeus, Papyrus Fragments, and Ancient Testimonies in a English Translation with Notes and Introductions.* Cambridge: Cambridge University Press, 2018.

Lucian. *De morte Peregrini.* Edited by Jacques Schwartz. Paris: Belles Lettres, 1963.

Minns, Denis and Paul Parvis, ed. *Justin, Philosopher and Martyr, Apologies.* Oxford: Oxford University Press, 2009.

Nock and A.-J. Festugière, ed., *Hermès Trismégiste.* 4 vols. Paris: Belles Lettres, 1946–2008.

Numenius. *Fragments.* Edited by Édouard des Places. Paris: Belles Lettres, 2003.

Origen. *Commentaire sur Saint Jean.* Edited by Cécile Blanc. 5 vols. Paris: Cerf. 1966–92.

Origen. *Contra Celsum Libri VIII.* Edited by M. Marcovich. Leiden: Brill, 2001.

Philo. *Opera.* Edited by Leopold Cohn and Paul Wendland. 7 vols. Berlin: de Gruyter, 1962–63.

Photius. *Bibliothèque Tome II, Codices 84-185.* Edited by René Henry, ed., 2d ed. Paris: Belles Lettres, 2003.

Plato. *Opera.* Edited by E. A. Duke, W. F. Hicken, W. S. M. Nicoll, D. B. Robinson, J. C. G. Strachan. 5 vols. OCT. Oxford: Clarendon, 1995.

Plutarch. Translated by Frank Cole Babbit, Paul A. Clement, Herbert B. Hoffleit, Lionel Pearson, F. H. Sandbach, Harold Cherniss, William C. Helmbold, Benedict Einarson, and Phillip H. de Lacy. 28 vols. LCL. Cambridge, MA: Harvard University Press, 1914–2004.

Preisendanz, K. and A. Henrichs, ed. *Papyri Graecae magicae.* 3 vols. 2d ed. Stuttgart: Teubner, 2001.

Pseudo-Clement. *Die Pseudoklementinen. Homilien; Rekognitionen in Rufins Übersetzung.* Edited by Bernhard Rehm and Georg Strecker. Berlin: Akademie 1992–94.

Ptolemy. *Lettre a Flora.* Edited by Gilles Quispel. 2d ed. SC 24. Paris: Cerf, 1966.

Rahlfs, Alfred and Robert Hanhart. *Septuaginta, id est Vetus Testamentum graece iuxta LXX interpretes.* 2d ed. Stuttgart: Deutsche Bibelgesellschaft, 2006.

Schmidt, Carl ed. and Violet MacDermot, trans., *Pistis Sophia.* Leiden: Brill, 1978.

Schmidt, Carl ed. and Violet MacDermot, trans., *The Books of Jeu and the Untitled Text in the Bruce Codex.* Leiden: Brill, 1978.

Sextus Empiricus. *Opera.* Edited by Hermann Mutschmann and J. Mau. 4 vols. BSGRT. Leipzig: Teubner, 1912–61.

Tatian. *Oratio ad Graecos, Rede an die Griechen.* Edited Jörg Trelenberg. Beiträge zur historischen Theologie 165. Tübingen: Mohr Siebeck, 2012.

Tertullian. *Opera.* Edited by A. Kroymann and E. Evans. 2 vols. CCSL 2/1-2. Turnholt: Brepols, 1954.

Theodoret. *Haereticarum fabularum compendium,* ed. Benjamin Gleede. GCS NF 26. Berlin: de Gruyter, 2020.

Theophilus. *Ad Autolycum.* Edited by Robert M. Grant. Oxford: Clarendon, 1970.

Tuckett, Christopher. *Gospel of Mary.* Oxford: Oxford University Press, 2007.

Völker, W. *Quellen zur Geschichte der christlichen Gnosis.* Sammlung ausgewählter kirchen- und dogmengeschichtlicher Quellenschriften, new ser., no. 5. Tübingen: Mohr Siebeck, 1932.

Key Reference Works

Crum, Walter Ewing. *A Coptic Dictionary.* Oxford: Clarendon, 1939.

Evans, Craig A., Robert L. Webb and Richard A. Wiebe. *Nag Hammadi Texts and the Bible: A Synopsis and Index.* Leiden: Brill, 1993.

Foerster, Werner. *Gnosis: A Selection of Gnostic Texts.* Ed. R. McL. Wilson. 2 vols. Oxford: Clarendon, 1972.

Hanegraaff, Wouter, ed. *Dictionary of Gnosis and Western Esotericism.* Leiden: Brill, 2006.

Layton, Bentley and David Brakke, eds. *The Gnostic Scriptures Translated with Annotations and Introductions.* 2d ed. Anchor Yale Bible Reference Library. New Haven: Yale University Press, 2021.

Marjanen, Antti and Petri Luomanen. *A Companion to Second-Century Christian 'Heretics.'* Supplements to *VC* 76. Leiden: Brill, 2005.

Markschies, Chr. and Jens Schröter, ed. *Antike christliche Apokryphen in deutscher Übersetzung. 1 Band: Evangelien und Verwandtes.* 2 parts. Tübingen: Mohr Siebeck, 2012.

Rudolph, Kurt. *Gnosis: The Nature & History of Gnosticism.* Trans. R. McL. Wilson. New York: HarperSanFrancisco, 1987.

Schenke, Hans-Martin, Hans-Gebhard Bethge and Ursula Ulrike Kaiser, ed. *Nag Hammadi Deutsch.* 2 vols. Berlin: de Gruyter, 2001.

Simonetti, Manlio. *Testi gnostici cristiana.* Bari: Editori Laterza, 1970.

Smith, Geoffrey S. *Valentinian Christianity: Texts and Traditions.* Berkeley: University of California Press, 2020.

Major Studies

Note: In what follows, I cite only monographs and essay collections, preferring studies of the past quarter century. Most earlier secondary literature can be found in three separate volumes edited by David Scholer, *Nag Hammadi Bibliography 1948–1969, 1970–1994, 1995–2006* published by Brill between 1971 and 2009. The most recent secondary literature can be explored using Brill's Nag Hammadi Bibliography Online (https://bibliographies.brillonline.com/browse/nag-hammadi-bibliography).

Aland, Barbara. *Was ist Gnosis? Studien zum frühen Christentum, zu Marcion und zur kaiserzeitlichen Philosophie.* WUNT 239. Tübingen: Mohr Siebeck, 2009.

Bauer, Walter. *Orthodoxy and Heresy in Earliest Christianity.* Philadelphia: Fortress Press, 1971.

BeDuhn, Jason D. *The First New Testament: Marcion's Scriptural Canon.* Salem OR: Polebridge, 2013.

Buckley, Jorunn Jacobsen. *Female Fault and Fulfilment in Gnosticism.* Chapel Hill: University of North Carolina Press, 1986.

Burns, Dylan M. *Apocalypse of an Alien God: Platonism and the Exile of Sethian Gnosticism.* Philadelphia: University of Pennsylvania Press, 2014.

Cahana-Blum, Jonathan. *Wrestling with Archons: Gnosticism as a Critical Theory of Culture.* Lanham, MD: Lexington Books, 2018.

DeConick, April D. *The Gnostic New Age: How a Countercultural Spirituality Revolutionized Religion from Antiquity to Today.* New York: Columbia University Press, 2016.

Franzmann, Majella. *Jesus in the Nag Hammadi Writings.* Edinburgh: T&T Clark, 1996.

Goehring, James E., Charles W. Hedrick, Jack T. Sanders with Hans Dieter Betz, ed. *Gnosticism and the Early Christian World in Honor of James M. Robinson.* Sonoma, CA: Polebridge, 1990.

Greschat, Katharina. *Apelles und Hermogenes: Zwei theologische Lehrer des zweiten Jahrhunderts.* Supplements to *VC* 48. Leiden: Brill, 2000.

Hedrick, Charles, and Robert Hodgson Jr., ed. *Nag Hammadi, Gnosticism & Early Christianity.* Peabody: Hendrickson, 1986.

Holzhausen, Jens. *Der "Mythos vom Menschen" im hellenistischen Ägypten.* Bodenheim: Athenäum, 1994.

Hübner, Reinhard. *Der Paradox Eine: Antignostischer Monarchianismus im zweiten Jahrhundert.* Supplements to *VC* 50. Leiden: Brill, 1999.

Iricinschi, Eduard, Lance Jenott, Nicola Denzey Lewis and Philippa Townsend, ed. *Beyond the Gnostic Gospels: Studies Building on the Work of Elaine Pagels.* Tübingen: Mohr Siebeck, 2013.

Iricinschi, Eduard and Holger M. Zellentin, ed. *Heresy and Identity in Late Antiquity.* Tübingen: Mohr Siebeck, 2008.

King, Karen L. *Images of the Feminine in Gnosticism.* Philadelphia: Fortress Press, 1988.

King, Karen L. *What is Gnosticism.* Cambridge, MA: Harvard University Press, 2003.

Klinghardt, Matthias. *The Oldest Gospel and the Formation of the Canonical Gospels.* Leuven: Peeters, 2020.

Krause, Martin, ed. *Gnosis and Gnosticism: Papers read at the Eighth International Conference on Patristic Studies.* Leiden: Brill, 1981.

Layton, Bentley, ed. *The Rediscovery of Gnosticism: Proceedings of the Conference at Yale March 1978.* 2 vols. Leiden: Brill, 1980.

Litwa, M. David. *Desiring Divinity: Self-deification in Ancient Jewish and Christian Mythmaking* (Oxford: Oxford University Press, 2016).

Litwa, M. David. *Posthuman Transformation in Ancient Mediterranean Thought: Becoming Angels and Demons.* Cambridge: Cambridge University Press, 2021.

Litwa, M. David. *The Evil Creator: Origins of an Early Christian Idea.* New York: Oxford University Press, 2021.

Logan, Alastair H.B. *The Gnostics: Identifying an Early Christian Cult.* London: T&T Clark, 1996.

Löhr, Winrich A. *Basilides und seine Schule: Eine Studie zur Theologie- und Kirchengeschichte des zweiten Jahrhunderts.* WUNT 83. Tübingen: Mohr Siebeck, 1996.

Luttikhuizen, Gerhard P. *Gnostic Revisions of Genesis Stories and Early Jesus Traditions.* NHMS 58. Leiden: Brill, 2006.

Mahé, Jean-Pierre, Paul-Hubert Poirier and Madeleine Scopello, ed. *Les Textes de Nag Hammadi: Histoire des religions et approches contemporaines.* Paris: AIBL, 2010.

Marjanen, Antti, and Petri Luomanen. *A Companion to Second-century Christian 'Heretics'.* Supplements to *VC* 76. Leiden: Brill, 2005.

Marjanen, Antti. *The Woman Jesus Loved: Mary Magdalene in the Nag Hammadi Library and Related Documents.* NHMS 40. Leiden: Brill, 1996.

Marjanen, Antti. *Was There a Gnostic Religion?* Helsinki: Finnish Exegetical Society, 2005.

Markschies, Chr. *Valentinus Gnosticus? Untersuchungen zur valentinianischen Gnosis mit einem Kommentar zu den Fragmenten Valentins.* WUNT 65. Tübingen: Mohr Siebeck, 1992.

Markschies, Chr. *Gnosis und Christentum.* Berlin: Berlin University Press, 2009.

Markschies, Chr. *Gnosis: An Introduction.* London: T&T Clark, 2003.

Markschies, Chr. and Einar Thomassen, ed. *Valentinianism: New Studies.* NHMS 96. Leiden: Brill, 2020.

Nicklas, Tobias, Candida R. Moss, Christopher Tuckett, and Joseph Verheyden, ed. *The Other Side: Apocryphal Perspectives on Ancient Christian "Orthodoxies."* Göttingen: Vandenhoeck and Ruprecht, 2017.

Painchaud, Louis and Paul-Hubert Poirier. *Coptica-Gnostica-Manichaica. Mélanges offerts à Wolf-Peter Funk.* Leuven: Peeters, 2006.

Pearson, Birger A. *Gnosticism, Judaism, and Egyptian Christianity.* Philadelphia: Fortress, 1990.

Pearson, Birger A. *Gnosticism and Christianity in Roman and Coptic Egypt.* London: T&T Clark, 2004.

Pearson, Birger A. *Ancient Gnosticism: Traditions and Literature.* Minneapolis: Fortress, 2007.

Petersen, Silke. *"Zerstört die Werke der Weiblichkeit!" Maria Magdalena, Salome und andere Jüngerinnen Jesus in christlich-gnostischen Schriften.* NHMS 48. Leiden: Brill, 1999.

Pétrement, Simone. *A Separate God: The Christian Origins of Gnosticism.* New York: Harper & Row. 1990.

Petrey, Taylor G., ed. *Re-making the World: Christianity and Categories: Essays in Honor of Karen L. King.* Tübingen: Mohr Siebeck, 2019.

Rasimus, Tuomas. *Paradise Reconsidered in Gnostic Mythmaking: Rethinking Sethianism in Light of the Ophite Evidence.* NHMS 68. Leiden: Brill, 2009.

Schmid, Herbert. *Christen und Sethianer: Ein Beitrag zur Diskussion um den religionsgeschichtlichen und den kirchengeschichtlichen Begriff der Gnosis.* Supplements to *VC* 143. Leiden: Brill, 2018.

Schröter, Jens and Konrad Schwarz, ed. *Nag Hammadi Schriften in der Literatur und Theologiegeschichte des frühen Christentums.* Tübingen: Mohr Siebeck, 2017.

Snyder, H. Gregory, ed. *Christian Teachers in Second-century Rome: Schools and Students in the Ancient City.* Supplements to *VC* 159. Leiden: Brill, 2020.

Stroumsa, Gedaliahu A. G. *Another Seed: Studies in Gnostic Mythology.* Leiden: Brill, 1984.

Tardieu, Michel. *Trois mythes gnostiques. Adam, Éros et les animaux d'Égypte dans un écrit de Nag Hammadi (II,5).* Paris: Augustinian Studies, 1974.

Thomassen, Einar. *The Spiritual Seed: The Church of the 'Valentinians.'* Leiden: Brill, 2008.

Trompf, Gary, ed. *The Gnostic World.* London: Taylor & Francis, 2018.

Turner, John D. and Anne McGuire, ed. *The Nag Hammadi Library After Fifty Years: Proceedings of the 1995 Society of Biblical Literature Commemoration.* NHMS 44. Leiden: Brill, 1997.

Turner, John D. *Sethian Gnosticism and the Platonic Tradition.* BCNH Études 6. Leuven: Peeters, 2001.

Van den Broek, Roel. *Gnostic Religion in Antiquity.* Cambridge: Cambridge University Press, 2013.

Verheyden, Joseph, Reimund Bieringer, Jens Schröter, and Ines Jäger, ed. *Docetism in the Early Church: The Quest for an Elusive Phenomenon.* WUNT 402. Tübingen: Mohr Siebeck, 2018.

Verheyden, Joseph, Tobias Nicklas, and Elisabeth Hernitscheck, *Shadowy Characters and Fragmentary Evidence.* WUNT 388. Tübingen: Mohr Siebeck.

Verheyden, Joseph and Herman Teule, eds. *Heretics and Heresies in the Ancient Church and in Eastern Christianity. Studies in Honour of Adelbert Davids.* Leuven: Peeters, 2011.

Williams, Michael A. *Rethinking "Gnosticism": An Argument for Dismantling a Dubious Category.* Princeton: Princeton University Press, 1996.

Williams, Michael A. *The Immovable Race: A Gnostic Designation and the Theme of Stability in Late Antiquity.* Leiden: Brill, 1985.

Wucherpfennig, Ansgar. *Heracleon Philologus: Gnostische Johannesexegese im zweiten Jahrhundert.* WUNT 142. Tübingen: Mohr Siebeck, 2002.

Index

CPSIA information can be obtained
at www.ICGtesting.com
Printed in the USA
LVHW081331260422
717279LV00017B/234